I0483488

THE LANGUAGE OF COMPLIANCE

A GLOSSARY OF ACRONYMS, TERMS, AND EXTENDED DEFINITIONS

Dorian J. Cougias · Marcelo Halpern, esq

Erikka Innes (research analyst) · E.L. Heiberger, CISA (ed.)

Copyright information

© 2006 – 2007 Network Frontiers, LLC, and Latham Watkins LLP. All rights reserved. No part of this publication may be used, reproduced, photocopied, transmitted, or stored in any retrieval system of any nature, without the written permission of the copyright owner (info@netfrontiers.com). This publication includes statements of a general nature which may not be applicable to specific situations. The authors attempt to ensure that all information and commentary contained in this publication is accurate, but assumes no liability for its interpretation or use.

All regulatory guideline material covered in this book is presumed copyright © to the publication listed, and is used with permission of the author group as a derivative work.

Portions of this material relating to the UCP are © The IT Compliance Institute and used by permission.

The information contained in this publication should not be construed as legal advice. We encourage you to consult with an attorney experienced in these areas, if you need further analysis or explanation of the laws or regulations discussed herein.

Schaser-Vartan Books

US Offices:
5620 West Dayflower Path
Lecanto, FL 34461

Feedback: info@netfrontiers.com

For bulk orders: (510) 835-2415, XT 111

SAN # 255-2582

http://www.glossarybook.com

Print Book:
ISBN: 0-9729039-3-3
ISBN 13: 978-0-9729039-3-6

eBook:
ISBN: 0-9729039-5-X
ISBN 13: 978-0-9729039-5-0

Library of Congress Catalog Card Number: 2006906907
Printed in the United States of America
10 9 8 7 6 5 4 3 2 1

Table of contents

Dedication

This is dedicated to two great field editors – Dr. Larry Dietz and Michael Swan.

Dr. Dietz, has become a friend of both of ours through our interaction at the NetFocus working groups and meetings. He routinely teaches us not to use words that the common man doesn't understand, and pushes us to make our definitions more clear.

Michael challenges us to ensure that we are clarifying our terms and their usage. He inspired us to create the Spotlight Definitions section of the book.

Our collective hats are off to both of them.

Special Thanks

We also want to thank the myriad field editors who have made significant contributions to this book. Especially Russell Kohn of Chaparral Software who created EZxslt that we use to export the acronyms and glossary entries from our database to our book.

We would like to thank the Sedona Conference, ISACA, ARMA, AIIM, and other such groups for allowing us to create a derivative work from their glossaries.

And the highest thanks and most endearing gratitude to the rest of our field editors who have given us feedback and provided materials: Allen Bernard, Anne Rogers, Chuck Hibnick, Daniel Epstein, David Barnett, David Rotman, David Salav, Harry L. Bouris, Janice Schuck, Jason Taule, Lyndon Bird, Mark Handelman, Mark Heinrich, Melissa Brown, Sam Thomas, Steve Knight, Tom Barclay, Vinny DiSpigno, and Walter Kobus.

Register on line

By the time you are reading this, there will be material posted online that isn't in the glossary. Ensure that you register as a book owner so that you can receive the updates and stay informed! Register at http://www.glossarybook.com.

Why a glossary in book form?

If the United Kingdom and the United States are two countries separated by a common language, think of the complexity and misunderstanding that the couple hundred regulators, standards, guidelines, and best practice creators have brought to the compliance world. We put forward this glossary in hopes that we can bring to light both the sameness as well as the differences in the usage of compliance language and meaning.

Our work is divided into three parts:

1. A listing of acronyms that point to the terms they represent.

2. A listing of all of the terms that have been *harmonized* between the different compliance documents.

3. A series of spotlight definitions suggested by our field editors for further clarification.

Each acronym and term is presented with the title, the definition (in the case of the acronyms, the reference to the term), and then the compliance documents that use the definition we've presented.

With regard to the spotlight definitions, we list each term and then note either the problems we found within the usage in the compliance documents, or we've given a clarifying explanation where none was provided in any of the compliance documents.

Our method

Our method is simple. Every time we run across a glossary in any of the compliance documents, we pass the contents of the glossary through our current listing of acronyms and terms. Any new terms are simply added as-is. Any existing terms are checked against the prevailing definition we've listed, and then the differences are either added as minor points, or major differences in usage are pointed out and clarified.

The glossary is then added to our working index, and each time we write about a new control within the Unified Compliance Framework, we check the control documents against our glossary-index. Any new terms are then researched and checked for consistency.

Salting to taste...

If, in your compliance readings, we've missed a definition, missed an entire compliance document, or mangled a definition, then contact us through the forms strewn throughout this book. We'll be glad to add to our collective work and ensure that we update the material. We know that this book is subject to change about the same time that we hit the print button. Therefore, for registered owners of this book we are providing regular updates and other online capabilities.

Therefore, please register your book at http://www.glossarybook.com.

We hope you enjoy...

Dorian J. Cougias & Marcelo Halpern

THE TERMS AND ACRONYMS OF COMPLIANCE

# #

Fourth Generation Language (4GL)

English-like, user friendly, nonproce-
dural computer languages used to program and/or read and process computer
files.

ISACA

Triple DES (3DES)

A triple strength version of the DES
cryptographic standard, usually using a
168-bit key. Triple DES provides much
stronger encryption than ordinary DES
but it is less secure than AES. See also
Data Encryption Standard.

*Workgroup for Electronic Data Interchange,
US National Information Assurance (IA)
Glossary, PCI-DSS, NIST 800 Series*

A

Abend

An abnormal end to a computer job; termination of a task prior to its completion because of an error condition that cannot be resolved by recovery facilities while the task is executing.

ISACA

Ablate

Describes the process by which laser-readable "pits" are burned into the recorded layer of optical discs, DVD-ROMs and CD-ROMs.

Sedona Conference

Ablative

Unalterable data. See also Ablate

Sedona Conference

Absorbed overhead

A part of financial management, it is the indirect cost of providing a service, which can be fairly allocated to specific customers. This can be based on usage or some other fair measurement. For example, cost of providing network bandwidth or shared servers. See also direct cost, indirect cost, unabsorbed overhead.

ITIL

Acceptable level of risk

The tolerable level of risk that is determined from: an analysis of threats and vulnerabilities, the sensitivity of data and applications, a cost/benefit analysis, and a study of the technical and operational feasibility of available controls.

Centers for Medicare & Medicaid Services (CMS)

Acceptance

See assurance.

ITIL

Access

A property of threat that defines how a threat actor accesses an asset (network access, physical access). This only applies to human actors. In terms of information management it means the right, opportunity, means of finding, using, or retrieving information. This results in the flow of information between one source and another.

CERT OCTAVE, ISO 15489, DIRKS, Centers for Medicare & Medicaid Services (CMS), ISO/IEC 27001:2005, US National Information Assurance (IA) Glossary, NIST 800 series

Access Authority

An entity responsible for monitoring and granting access privileges for other authorized entities.

NIST 800 series

Access control

Measures that limit access to information or information processing resources to those authorized persons or applications according to the system or data classification. HIPAA defines this as the ability to implement a mechanism to encrypt and decrypt regulated data. However, NIST defines this as the ability to enable authorized use of a resource while preventing unauthorized use or use in an unauthorized manner. Both share the same underlying principle of ensuring confidentiality and integrity. Access control can be defined by the system (mandatory access control, or MAC) or defined by the user who owns the object (discretionary access control, or DAC).

HIPAA, NIST 800 series, ISACA, FISCAM, Centers for Medicare & Medicaid Services (CMS), CobiT, ISO/IEC 27001:2005, PCI-DSS, Workgroup for Electronic Data Interchange, US National Information Assurance (IA) Glossary, FIPS Pubs

Access Control Facility (ACF2)

FISCAM

Access Control Lists (ACL)

A register of 1) users (including groups, machines, processes) who have been given permission to use a particular system resource, and 2) the types of access they have been permitted.

NIST 800 series, Centers for Medicare & Medicaid Services (CMS), Sedona Conference, US National Information Assurance (IA) Glossary

Access control mechanism

Security safeguard designed to detect and deny unauthorized access and permit authorized access in an IS.

US National Information Assurance (IA) Glossary

Access control software

Mechanisms that restrict access to computer resources. This type of software, which is external to the operating system, provides a means of specifying who has access to a system, who has access to specific resources, and what capabilities authorized users are granted. Access control software can generally be implemented in different modes that provide varying degrees of protection such as denying access for which the user is not expressly authorized, allowing access which is not expressly authorized but providing a warning, or allowing access to all resources without warning regardless of authority.

Centers for Medicare & Medicaid Services (CMS), FISCAM

Access control table

An internal computerized table of access rules regarding the levels of computer access permitted to logon IDs and computer terminals.

ISACA

Access level

Hierarchical portion of the security level used to identify the sensitivity of IS data and the clearance or authorization of users. Access level, in conjunction with the nonhierarchical categories, forms the sensitivity label of an object. See also category.

US National Information Assurance (IA) Glossary

Access list

Compilation of users, programs, or processes and the access levels and types to which each is authorized. Also, a roster of individuals who have admittance to a controlled area.

US National Information Assurance (IA) Glossary

Access method

The technique used for selecting records in a file for processing, retrieval, or storage. The access method is related to, but distinct from, the file organization that determines how the records are stored.

FISCAM, ISACA, Centers for Medicare & Medicaid Services (CMS)

Access path

Ways in which information or services can be accessed via an organization's network. Any component capable of enforcing access restrictions or any component that could be used to bypass an access restriction should be considered part of the access path. The access path can also be defined as the path through which user requests travel, including the telecommunications software, transaction processing software, application programs, etc. See also data flow.

CERT OCTAVE, FISCAM, ISACA, Centers for Medicare & Medicaid Services (CMS)

Access point

In a wireless local area network (WLAN), an access point transmits and receives data. It connects users to other users within the network and can serve multiple users within a certain area.

Network Frontiers

Access privileges

See access rights.

FISCAM

Access profile

Associates each user with a list of protected objects the user may access.

US National Information Assurance (IA) Glossary

Access rights

Precise statements that define the extent to which an individual can access computer systems and use or modify the programs and data on the system, and under what circumstances this access

will be allowed. Access rights determine the actions users can perform (e.g., read, write, execute, create, and delete) on files in shared volumes or file shares on the server.

ISACA, ISO/IEC 27001:2005

Access script

A program or a series of encoded commands that enable a user to log onto a system.

Centers for Medicare & Medicaid Services (CMS)

Access type

Privilege to perform action on an object. Read, write, execute, append, modify, delete, and create are examples of access types.

US National Information Assurance (IA) Glossary

Accession log

A serial list of numbers assigned to records in a numeric storage system, also called an accession file or a numeric file list.

ARMA

Account harvesting

A method to determine existing user accounts based on trial and error. For example, giving too much information in an error message can disclose information that makes it easier for an attacker to penetrate or compromise the system.

PCI-DSS

Account management

In network and systems management, a set of functions that 1) enables network or system service use to be measured and the costs of such use to be determined; and 2) includes all the resources consumed, the facilities used to collect accounting data, the facilities used to set billing parameters for the services used by customers, maintenance of the databases used for billing purposes, and the preparation of resource usage and billing reports.

Centers for Medicare & Medicaid Services (CMS)

Account Manager

In business relationship management, a role that is very similar to business relationship manager, but includes more commercial aspects. Most commonly used when dealing with external customers.

ITIL

Account number

The payment card number (credit or debit) that identifies the issuer and the particular cardholder account. The 16-digit account number that appears in print on the front of all valid Visa cards.

The number is one of the card security features that should be checked by merchants to ensure that a card-present transaction is valid

PCI-DSS, VISA Glossary of Terms

Account Risk Analysis (ARA)

GAO/PCIE Financial Audit Manual

Accountability

Accountability is the ability to hold responsible the owners, providers, and users of information systems and other parties. Hence it is the repercussions of actions taken by individuals. It is the principle that individuals, organizations, and the community are responsible for their actions and may be required to explain them to others. NIST 800-33 would say that accountability is the security objective that generates the requirement for actions of an organization to be traced uniquely to that organization. This supports non-repudiation, deterrence, fault isolation, intrusion detection and prevention, after-action recovery, and legal action. This accountability needs to be made explicit in terms of sanctions for not being accountable. In terms of HIPAA and FISCAM, accountability is accomplished through maintaining a record of the movements of hardware and electronic media and any person responsible for that movement. All requests for and access granted to stored information must be logged for review and possible investigation. Logging should include such items as a date/time stamp, the identification of the user, the type of access, e.g., create, read, modify, delete, the success or failure of the request, and identification of the data acted upon.

HIPAA, NIST 800 series, ISO 15489, DIRKS, FISCAM, ISACA, Centers for Medicare & Medicaid Services (CMS), ISO/IEC 27001:2005, US National Information Assurance (IA) Glossary

Accountability report

An agency's accountability report integrates the 1) Federal Managers' Financial Integrity Act (FMFIA) Report; 2) Chief Financial Officers' (CFO) Act Annual Report, including audited financial statements; 3) Management's Report on Final Action as required by the Inspector General Act; 4) the Debt Collection Improvement Act, Civil Monetary Penalty Act and Prompt Payment Act reports; and 5) available information on organizational performance compared with the agency's stated goal and objectives.

GAO/PCIE Financial Audit Manual

Accountable

See accountability.

CobiT

Accounting

In the context of IT service management, this is a synonym for IT accounting, which is the tracking of user's network resources.

ITIL, PCI-DSS

Accounting Legend Code (ALC)

Numeric code used to indicate the minimum accounting controls required for items of accountable COMSEC material within the COMSEC Material Control System.

US National Information Assurance (IA) Glossary

Accounting and Auditing Policy Committee (AAPC)

GAO/PCIE Financial Audit Manual

Accounting applications

The procedures and records used to identify, record, process, summarize, and report a class of transactions. Common accounting applications are 1) billings, 2) accounts receivable, 3) cash receipts, 4) purchasing and receiving, 5) accounts payable, 6) cash disbursements, 7) payroll, 8) inventory control, and 9) property and equipment.

GAO/PCIE Financial Audit Manual

Accounting number

The number assigned to an item of COMSEC material to facilitate its control.

US National Information Assurance (IA) Glossary

Accounting period

Within financial management, a period of time for which budgets, charges, depreciation and other financial calculations are made. Usually one year. See also financial year.

AICPA

Accounting Standards Executive Committee of the AICPA (AsSEC)

GAO/PCIE Financial Audit Manual

Accounting system

The methods and records established to identify, assemble, analyze, classify, record, and report an entity's transactions and to maintain accountability for the related assets and liabilities.

GAO/PCIE Financial Audit Manual

Accreditation

The official management authorization for the operation of an application and is based on the certification process as well as other management considerations. A formal declaration that the system is approved to operate in a particular security mode using a prescribed set of safeguards. Accreditation is the official management authorization for operation of the system and is based on the certification process as well as other management considerations. The accreditation statement affixes security responsibility and shows that due care has been taken for security.

Centers for Medicare & Medicaid Services (CMS), FIPS Pubs, US National Information Assurance (IA) Glossary, NIST 800 series

Accreditation Authority

See Authorizing Official

NIST 800 series

Accreditation boundary

Identifies the information resources covered by an accreditation decision, as distinguished from separately accredited information resources that are interconnected or with which information is exchanged via messaging. For the purposes of identifying the Protection Level for confidentiality of a system to be accredited, the system has a conceptual boundary that extends to all intended users of the system, both directly and indirectly connected, who receive output from the system.

US National Information Assurance (IA) Glossary, NIST 800 series

Accreditation package

Product comprised of a System Security Plan (SSP) and a report documenting the basis for the accreditation decision. The combination of which provides the evidence provided to the authorizing official to be used in the security accreditation decision process. Evidence includes, but is not limited to: 1) the system security plan; 2) the assessment results from the security certification; and 3) the plan of action and milestones.

US National Information Assurance (IA) Glossary, NIST 800 series

Accredited

Officially authorized to carry out a role. For example, an accredited body may be authorized to provide training or to conduct audits. Within security management, official authorization for a certified configuration to be used for a specific purpose. See also Registered Certification Body (RCB).

ITIL

Accrediting authority

Official with the authority to formally assume responsibility for operating an information system at an acceptable level of risk to agency operations (including mission, functions, image, or reputation), agency assets, or individuals. See also Designated Accrediting Authority (DAA), Principal Accrediting Authority,

US National Information Assurance (IA) Glossary, NIST 800 series

Accrediting official or committee

The accrediting official is the person within the organization who has the authority to accept a systems continuity plan's safeguards and approve the plan for operation. Therefore, this person or committee must be authorized to allocate resources to achieve continuity and remedy any deficiencies found in the auditing process. This is also the person or committee held liable for continuity inadequacies.

NIST 800 series

Accuracy ratio

A measure of a record filer's ability to find requested records.

ARMA

Acetate-base film

A safety film (ANSI Standard) substrate used to produce microfilm.

Sedona Conference

Acknowledgement (ACK)

A flag set in a packet to indicate to the sender that the previous packet sent was accepted correctly by the receiver without errors, or that the receiver is now ready to accept a transmission.

de facto

Acquirer

A bankcard association member that initiates and maintains relationships with merchants that accept Visa or Master-Card cards.

PCI-DSS, VISA Glossary of Terms

Acquisition and Implementation

A high-level control objective that defines how IT solutions need to be identified, developed or acquired, as well as implemented and integrated into the business process. In addition, changes in and maintenance of existing systems are covered by this domain to make sure that the life cycle is continued for these systems.

CobiT

Action list

Defines actions that people in an organization can take in the near term without the need for specialized training, policy or system changes, etc. It is essentially a list of near-term action items.

CERT OCTAVE

Action tracking

A process in which time limits for actions are monitored and imposed upon those conducting the business.

ISO 15489

Activation Data

Private data, other than keys, that are required to access cryptographic modules.

NIST 800 series

Active Content

Active content refers to electronic documents that are able to automatically carry out or trigger actions on a computer platform without the intervention of a user.

NIST 800 series

Active data

Active Data is information residing on the direct access storage media (disk drives or servers) of computer systems, which is readily visible to the operating system and/or application software with which it was created and immediately accessible to users without restoration or reconstruction.

Sedona Conference

Active record

A record needed to perform current operations. It is subject to frequent use (at least 3 or more times a month). An active record resides in native application format and is accessible for purposes of business processing with no restrictions on alteration beyond normal business rules. See also Inactive records.

ARMA, Sedona Conference

Active recovery site

Recovery strategy that involves two active sites, each capable of taking over the other's workload in the event of a disaster. Each site will have enough idle processing power to restore data from the other site and to accommodate the excess workload in the event of a disaster. See also dedicated work area, immediate recovery.

ISACA

Active response

A response, in which the system (automatically or in concert with the user) blocks or otherwise affects the progress of a detected attack. The response takes one of three forms -- amending the environment, collecting more information or striking back against the perpetrator.

ISACA

Activity

Activities are the major tasks performed by the organization to accomplish each of its functions. Activities are usually defined as part of processes or plans, and are documented in procedures. Several activities may be associated with each function. An activity is identified by the name it is given and its scope (or definition). The scope of the activity encompasses all of the transactions that take place in relation to it. Depending on the nature of the transactions involved, an activity may be performed in relation to one function, or it may be performed in relation to many functions. In cost accounting, an activity is the actual work task or step performed in producing and delivering products and services. An aggregation of activities performed within an organization that is useful for purposes of activity-based costing. CobiT lists this as the main actions taken to operate the CobiT process.

DIRKS, GAO/PCIE Financial Audit Manual, CobiT, ISO/IEC 27001:2005, ITIL, BS 25999

Activity ratio

A measure of frequency of records use.

ARMA

Actor

A property of threat that defines who or what may violate the security requirements (confidentiality, integrity, availability) of an asset.

CERT OCTAVE

Add-on security

Incorporation of new hardware, software, or firmware safeguards in an operational IS.

US National Information Assurance (IA) Glossary

Address

The code used to designate the location of a specific piece of data within computer storage. Also, addresses using a number of different protocols are commonly used on the Internet. These addresses include e-mail addresses (Simple Mail Transfer Protocol or SMTP), IP (Internet Protocol) addresses and URLs (Uniform Resource Locators), commonly known as Web addresses.

ISACA, ISO/IEC 27001:2005, Sedona Conference

Address Resolution Protocol (ARP)

A protocol used to obtain a node's physical address. A client station broadcasts an ARP request onto the network with the Internet Protocol (IP) address of the target note it wishes to communicate with, and the node with the address response by sending back its physical address so that packets can be transmitted.

Workgroup for Electronic Data Interchange

Address space

The number of distinct locations that may be referred to with a machine address. For most binary machines, it is equal to 2 to the power of n, where n is the number of bits in the machine address.

ISACA

Address Verification Service (AVS)

AVS allows merchants that accept card-not-present transactions to compare the billing address (the address to which the card issuer sends its monthly statement for that account) given by a customer with the billing address on the card issuer's master file before shipping an order. AVS helps merchants minimize the risk of accepting fraudulent transactions in a card-not-present environment by indicating the result of the address comparison.

VISA Glossary of Terms

Addressing

The method used to identify the location of a participant in a network. Ideally, addressing specifies where the participant is located rather than who they are (name) or how to get there (routing).

ISACA, ISO/IEC 27001:2005

Adequate

Records should be adequate for the purposes for which they are kept. Thus, a major initiative will be extensively documented, while a routine administrative action can be documented with an identifiable minimum of information. There should be adequate evidence of the conduct of business activity to be able to account for that conduct. See also full and accurate records.

DIRKS, ISO/IEC 27001:2005

Adequate security

Security commensurate with the risk and magnitude of harm resulting from the loss, misuse, or unauthorized access to or modification of information. This includes assuring that information systems operate effectively and provide appropriate confidentiality, integrity, and availability, through the use of cost-effective management, personnel, operational, and technical controls according to the level of concern as identified by the organization. See also level of concern.

OMB Circular A-130, US National Information Assurance (IA) Glossary, FIPS Pubs, Clinger-Cohen Act, NIST 800 series

Adjusting period

The calendar can contain "real" accounting periods and/or adjusting accounting periods. The "real" accounting periods must not overlap, and cannot have any gaps between "real" accounting periods. Adjusting accounting periods can overlap with other accounting periods. For example, a period called DEC-93 can be defined that includes 01-DEC-1993 through 31-DEC-1993. An adjusting period called DEC31-93 can also be defined that includes only one day: 31-DEC-1993 through 31-DEC-1993.

ISACA

Administrative controls

The actions/controls encompassing operational effectiveness, efficiency, and adherence to regulations and management policies.

ISACA

Administrative Functions Disposal Authority (AFDA)

The Administrative Functions Disposal Authority was released in March 2000 by the National Archives and relates to common administrative functions performed by most Commonwealth agencies. The structure of the Authority is based on the business classification scheme of the Keyword AAA: Thesaurus of General Terms Commonwealth Version. See also disposal authorities.

DIRKS

Administrative Safeguards

Administrative actions, policies, and procedures to manage the selection, development, implementation, and maintenance of security measures to protect electronic health information and to manage the conduct of the covered entity's workforce in relation to protecting that information.

NIST 800 series

Advanced Encryption Standard (AES)

Advanced Encryption Standard (AES) is the Rijndael cryptographic algorithm adopted by the National Institute of Standards and Technology (NIST) as the new Federal Information Processing Standard (FIPS). AES replaces DES and 3DES, and is one of the recommended encryption standards meeting HIPAA requirements. See also data encryption standard.

FIPS Pubs

Advisory

Notification of significant new trends or developments regarding the threat to the IS of an organization. This notification may include analytical insights into trends, intentions, technologies, or tactics of an adversary targeting information systems.

US National Information Assurance (IA) Glossary

Agency

Agency means any executive department, military department, government corporation, government controlled corporation, or other establishment in the executive branch of the government, or any independent regulatory agency. Within the Executive Office of the President, the term includes only the Office of Management and Budget and Office of Administration. The term agency does not include: 1) the Government Accountability Office; 2) the Federal Election Commission; 3) the governments of the District of Columbia and of the territories and possessions of the United States, and their various subdivisions; or 4) government-owned contractor-operated facilities, including laboratories engaged in national defense research and production activities. See also organization, or entity. See also Executive Agency.

Network Frontiers, Centers for Medicare & Medicaid Services (CMS), OMB Circular A-130, FIPS Pubs, NIST 800 series

Agency Certification Authority (CA)

A CA that acts on behalf of an Agency, and is under the operational control of an Agency.

NIST 800 series

Agency Locator Code

GAO/PCIE Financial Audit Manual

Agent

A program used in distributed denial of service (DDoS) attacks that sends malicious traffic to hosts based on the instructions of a handler.

NIST 800 series

Aggregation

The process of combining data inputs from different creation and authoring tools and other systems.

AIIM

Agreed service time

Within availability management, a synonym for service hours, commonly used in formal calculations of availability. See also downtime.

ITIL

Agreed Upon Procedures (AUP)

GAO/PCIE Financial Audit Manual

Agreement

A document that describes a formal understanding between two or more parties. An agreement is not legally binding, unless it forms part of a contract. See also service level agreement, operational level agreement.

ITIL

AIIM: the ECM Association (AIIM)

AIIM formerly stood for Association for Information and Image Management. It has since changed its name to the Enterprise Content Management (ECM) Association. For more information, see http://www.aiim.org.

AIIM, Sedona Conference

Alert

A warning that a threshold has been reached, something has changed, or a failure has occurred. Alerts are often created and managed by system management tools and are managed by the event management process.

ITIL, US National Information Assurance (IA) Glossary

Algorithm

A detailed formula or set of steps for solving a particular problem. To be an algorithm, a set of rules must be unambiguous and have a clear stopping point

Sedona Conference

Aliasing

When computer graphics output has jagged edges or a stair-stepped, rather than a smooth, appearance when magnified. The graphics output can be smoothed using anti-aliasing algorithms.

Sedona Conference

Allocation entry

A recurring journal entry used to allocate revenues or costs. For example, an allocation entry could be defined to allocate costs to each department based on headcount.

ISACA

Alpha

The use of alphabetic characters or an alphabetic character string.

ISACA

Alphanumeric

Characters composed of letters, numbers (and sometimes punctuation marks). Excludes control characters.

Sedona Conference

Alternate COMSEC custodian

Individual designated by proper authority to perform the duties of the COMSEC custodian during the temporary absence of the COMSEC custodian.

US National Information Assurance (IA) Glossary

Alternate emergency coordinator

A person who is trained to perform the duties of an emergency coordinator in the absence of the primary coordinator, or in case he/she needs assistance.

Centers for Medicare & Medicaid Services (CMS)

Alternate site

An operating location other than the one at which an activity is usually performed for use by business functions

when the primary facilities are unavailable.

Centers for Medicare & Medicaid Services (CMS)

Alternative work site

Allowing employees to work at home or at geographically convenient satellite offices for part of the work week (e.g., telecommuting).

US National Information Assurance (IA) Glossary

Ambient data

See Residual data.

Sedona Conference

Ambient functions

High-level functions that define and provide context and meaning to the activities of records creators in any domain other than the native organization or recordkeeping system of the records creator.

DIRKS

American Bar Association (ABA)

GAO/PCIE Financial Audit Manual

American Institute of Certified Public Accountants (AICPA)

Committed to member service and the public interest, the American Institute of Certified Public Accountants and its predecessors have been serving the accounting profession since 1887. See also http://www.aicpa.org/index.htm for more information.

GAO/PCIE Financial Audit Manual

American National Standards Institute (ANSI)

The American National Standards Institute (ANSI) coordinates the development and use of voluntary consensus standards in the United States and represents the needs and views of US stakeholders in standardization forums around the globe. The Institute oversees the creation, promulgation and use of thousands of norms and guidelines that directly impact businesses in nearly every sector: from acoustical devices to construction equipment, from dairy and livestock production to energy distribution, and many more. ANSI is also actively engaged in accrediting programs that assess conformance to standards – including globally-recognized cross-sector programs such as the ISO 9000 (quality) and ISO 14000 (environmental) management systems. See also http://www.ansi.org for more information.

de facto, PCI-DSS, Sedona Conference

American Standard Code for Information Interchange (ASCII)

Pronounced "ask-ee," ASCII is a non-proprietary text format, standard seven-bit code for representing (or 255 for extended ASCII) alphanumeric and control characters that was adopted by the American Standards Association to achieve compatibility between data devices. Documents in ASCII format consist of only text with no formatting and can be read by most computer systems.

Sedona Conference

Analog

A transmission signal that varies continuously in amplitude and time and is generated in wave formation. Analog signals are used in telecommunications. Analog is the opposite of digital.

ISACA, Sedona Conference

Analog to Digital Converter (ADC)

Converts analog data to a digital format.

Sedona Conference

Analysis

The examination of acquired data for its significance and probative value to the case.

NIST 800 series

Analysis team

An interdisciplinary team comprising representatives of both the mission-related and information technology areas of the organization. The analysis team conducts the evaluation and analyzes the information. An analysis team consists of about three to five people, depending on the size of the overall organization and the scope of the evaluation.

CERT OCTAVE

Analytical Modeling

A technique that uses mathematical models to predict the behavior of a configuration item or IT service. Analytical models are commonly used in capacity management and availability management. See also modeling.

ITIL

Analytical procedures

The comparison of recorded account balances with expectations developed by the auditor, based on an analysis and understanding of the relationships between the recorded amounts and other data, to form a conclusion on the recorded amount. A basic premise underlying the application of analytical procedures is that plausible relationships among data may reasonably be expected to continue unless there are known conditions that would change the relationships.

GAO/PCIE Financial Audit Manual

Annotations

The changes, additions, or editorial comments made or applicable to a document - usually an electronic image file - using electronic sticky notes, highlighter, or other electronic tools. Annotations should be overlaid and not change the original document.

Sedona Conference

Annual financial statement

As defined by OMB, the annual financial statement comprises an overview of the reporting organization (or Management's discussion and Analysis, MD&A), the financial statements and related notes, required supplementary stewardship information, required supplementary information, and other accompanying information.

GAO/PCIE Financial Audit Manual

Annualized Loss Expectancy (ALE)

The total expected monetary loss of an information asset over one year; calculated as the SLE times the EAF.

Network Frontiers

Anomaly

Unusual or statistically rare.

ISACA

Anomaly detection

Detection on the basis of whether the system activity matched that defined as abnormal.

ISACA

Anonymity

The quality or state of not being named or identified.

ISACA

Anonymous File Transfer Protocol

A method for downloading public files using the File Transfer Protocol (FTP). Anonymous FTP is called anonymous because users do not need to identify themselves before accessing files from a particular server. In general, users enter the word anonymous when the host prompts for a username; anything can be entered for the password, such as the user's e-mail address or simply the word guest. In many cases, an anonymous FTP site will not even prompt users for a name and password.

ISACA

Anti-jam

Measures ensuring that transmitted information can be received despite deliberate jamming attempts.

US National Information Assurance (IA) Glossary

Anti-spoof

Measures taken to prevent the unauthorized use of legitimate Identification & Authentication (I&A) data, however it was obtained, to mimic a subject different from the attacker.

US National Information Assurance (IA) Glossary

Anti-virus software

Applications that detect, prevent and possibly remove all known viruses from files.

ISACA, Centers for Medicare & Medicaid Services (CMS), PCI-DSS

Anti-virus/Anti-Spam server

A computer that houses applications that manage virus and spam detection and elimination.

Network Frontiers

Antivirus software

A program that monitors a computer or network to identify all major types of malware and prevent or contain malware incidents.

NIST 800 series

Aperture card

An IBM punch card with a window which holds a 35mm frame of microfilm. Indexing information is punched in the card.

Sedona Conference

Appearance

The act of giving the idea or impression of being or doing something.

ISACA

Appearance of independence

Behavior adequate to meet the situations occurring during audit work (interviews, meetings, reporting, etc.). The IS auditor should be aware that appearance of independence depends upon the perceptions of others and can be influenced by improper actions or associations.

ISACA

Applet

A program written in a portable, platform independent computer language, such as Java. It is usually embedded in an HTML page and then executed by a browser. Applets can only perform a restricted set of operations, thus preventing, or at least minimizing, the possible security compromise of the host computers.

ISACA

Applicant

The subscriber is sometimes called an "applicant" after applying to a certification authority for a certificate, but before the certificate issuance procedure is completed.

NIST 800 series

Application

In the boradest sense, the use of information resources (information and information technology) to satisfy a specific set of user requirements. When speaking about software, any program designed to perform a specific function directly for the user or, in some cases, for another application. A computer program designed to help people perform a certain type of work, including specific functions, such as payroll, inventory control, accounting, and mission support. Depending on the work for which it was designed, an application can manipulate text, numbers, graphics, or a combination of these elements. An application contrasts with systems program, such as an operating system or network control program, and with utility programs, such as copy or sort. See also program, application management, application portfolio.

FISCAM, ISACA, Centers for Medicare & Medicaid Services (CMS), ISO/IEC 27001:2005, ITIL, US National Information Assurance (IA) Glossary, Clinger-Cohen Act, PCI-DSS, Sedona Conference, NIST 800 series

Application acquisition review

An evaluation of an application system being acquired or evaluated, which considers such matters as: appropriate controls are designed into the system; the application will process information in a complete, accurate and reliable manner; the application will function as intended; the application will function in compliance with any applicable statutory provisions; the system is acquired in compliance with the established system acquisition process.

ISACA

Application Content Filtering

Application content filtering is performed by a software proxy agent to remove or quarantine viruses that may be contained in email attachments, to block specific Multipurpose Internet Mail Extensions (MIME) types, or to filter other active content such as Java, JavaScript, and ActiveX® Controls.

NIST 800 series

Application controls

Application controls are directly related to individual applications. They ensure that transactions are valid, properly authorized, and completely and accurately processed and reported. They are management's control activities (procedures) that are incorporated directly into individual computer applications to provide reasonable assurance of accurate and reliable procession. Application controls address 1) data input, 2) data processing, and 3) data output. FISCAM categories of application controls that more closely tie into the FAM methodology are 1) authorization control, 2) completeness control, 3) accuracy control, and 4) control over integrity of processing and data files. Examples of application controls include data input validation, agreement of batch totals, and encryption of data transmitted.

FISCAM, GAO/PCIE Financial Audit Manual, ISACA, Centers for Medicare & Medicaid Services (CMS), CobiT, ISO/IEC 27001:2005

Application development review

An evaluation of an application system under development which considers matters such as: appropriate controls are designed into the system; the application will process information in a complete, accurate and reliable manner; the application will function as intended; the application will function in compliance with any applicable statutory provisions; the system is developed in compliance with the established systems development life cycle process.

ISACA

Application implementation review

An evaluation of any part of an implementation project (e.g., project management, test plans, user acceptance testing procedures).

ISACA

Application layer

A layer within the International Organization for Standardization (ISO)/Open Systems Interconnection (OSI) model. It is used in information transfers between users through application programs and other devices. In this layer various protocols are needed. Some of them are specific to certain applications and others are more general for network services.

ISACA

Application maintenance review

An evaluation of any part of a project to perform maintenance on an application system (e.g., project management, test plans, user acceptance testing procedures).

ISACA

Application management

The process responsible for managing applications throughout their lifecycle. See also application portfolio.

ITIL

Application portfolio

A database used to manage Applications throughout their lifecycle. An application portfolio contains key attributes of all applications deployed in the business. See also portfolio of services.

ITIL

Application program

See application.

ISACA

Application Program [or programming] Interface (API)

AIIM

Application programmer

A person who develops and maintains application programs, as opposed to system programmers who develop and maintain the operating system and system utilities. See application programming.

FISCAM, Centers for Medicare & Medicaid Services (CMS)

Application Programming Interface

A set of routines, protocols, and tools referred to as "building blocks" used in business application software development. A good API makes it easier to develop a program by providing all the building blocks related to the functional characteristics of an operating system because the applications need to specify different methods for interfacing with different operating systems (e.g., MS-Windows, different versions of UNIX). A programmer would utilize these APIs in developing applications that can operate effectively and efficiently on the platform chosen.

ISACA

31

Application programs

See applications.

Centers for Medicare & Medicaid Services (CMS)

Application proxy firewall

A proxy service that connects programs running on internal networks to services on exterior networks by creating two connections, one from the requesting client and another to the destination service. Software implemented on a server that acts as an intermediary between two computer systems engaged in communication. The application proxy firewall accepts service requests to and from client computers (computers placed behind and protected by the firewall) and makes the connection to a desired destination on behalf of the requesting party. As application proxy firewalls act on behalf of client computers and internal systems, network structures are protected and hidden from public view. Application proxy firewalls differ from simple packet screening firewalls because they have the capability to view application layer data (web content, e-mail) and make informed decisions based on packet content rather than simply packet headers.

ISACA, Centers for Medicare & Medicaid Services (CMS)

Application security

See application security controls.

ISACA

Application security controls

Refers to the security aspects supported by any application, primarily with regard to the roles or responsibilities and audit trails within the applications.

Network Frontiers

Application Service Provider (ASP)

A third party that delivers and manages applications and computer services, including security services to multiple users via the Internet or a private network.

ISACA, AIIM

Application sizing

A part of capacity management, the activity responsible for understanding the resource requirements needed to support a new application, or a major change to an existing application. Application sizing helps to ensure that the IT service can meet its agreed service level targets for capacity and performance.

ITIL

Application software

See application.

Centers for Medicare & Medicaid Services (CMS)

Application software tracing and mapping

Specialized tools that can be used to analyze the flow of data through the processing logic of the application software and document the logic, paths, control conditions, and processing sequences. Both the command language or job control statements and programming language can be analyzed. This technique includes program/system mapping, tracing, snapshots, parallel simulations, and code comparisons.

ISACA

Application system

These are understood to be the sum of manual and programmed procedures and applications. An integrated set of computer programs designed to serve a particular function that has specific input, processing, and output activities (e.g., general ledger, manufacturing resource planning, human resource management).

CobiT, ISACA, Centers for Medicare & Medicaid Services (CMS), ISO/IEC 27001:2005

Appraisal

The process of evaluating business activities to determine which records need to be captured and how long the records need to be kept to meet business needs, the requirements of organizational ac-countability, and community expectations.

DIRKS

Appropriation

The most common form of budget authority; an authorization by an act of Congress that permits federal agencies to incur obligations and to make payments out of the Treasury for specified purposes. Appropriations do not represent cash actually set aside in the Treasury for purposes specified in the appropriation acts. They represent limitations of amounts that agencies may obligate during the period specified in the appropriation acts.

GAO/PCIE Financial Audit Manual

Approved

Federal Information Processing Standard (FIPS) approved or National Institute of Standards and Technology (NIST) recommended. An algorithm or technique that is either 1) specified in a FIPS or NIST Recommendation, or 2) adopted in a FIPS or NIST Recommendation.

NIST 800 series, FIPS Pubs, FIPS Pubs

Approved Mode of Operation

A mode of the cryptographic module that employs only Approved security functions (not to be confused with a specific mode of an Approved security function, e.g., Data Encryption Standard (DES) Cipher Block Chaining (CBC) mode).

NIST 800 series, FIPS Pubs

Approved Security Function

A security function (e.g., cryptographic algorithm, cryptographic key management technique, or authentication technique) that is either 1) specified in an Approved standard, 2) adopted in an Approved standard and specified either in an appendix of the Approved standard or in a document referenced by the Approved standard, or 3) specified in the list of Approved security functions.

NIST 800 series, FIPS Pubs

Approved standards

Approved standards are standardized algorithms (like in ISO and ANSI) and well-known commercially available standards (like Blowfish) that meet the intent of strong cryptography. Examples of approved standards are AES (128 bits and higher), TDES (two or three independent keys), RSA (1024 bits) and ElGamal (1024 bits).

PCI-DSS

Architecture

The term architecture refers to the hardware, software or combination of hardware and software comprising a computer system or network. The ar-

chitecture of a system always defines its broad outlines, and may define precise mechanisms as well. For example, it may describe functional requirements of the system and the information interaction between entities of the system. The term "open architecture" is used to describe computer and network components that are more readily interconnected and interoperable. Conversely, the term "closed architecture" describes components that are less readily interconnected and interoperable.

Centers for Medicare & Medicaid Services (CMS), Sedona Conference

Archival authority

Also known as the archival organization, archival institution, archival program. This is the organization or program responsible for selecting, acquiring and preserving archives, making them available, and approving destruction of other records.

ISO 15489

Archival data

Archival Data is information an organization maintains for long-term storage and record keeping purposes, but which is not immediately accessible to the user of a computer system. Archival data may be written to removable media such as a CD, magneto-optical media, tape or other electronic storage device, or may be maintained on system hard drives. Some systems allow users to retrieve archival data directly while other systems require the intervention of an IT professional.

Sedona Conference

Archive

Information and records formatted for long-term storage for disaster recovery or other purposes. Items commonly archived include but are not limited to, magnetic media copies of operating system software, application software, and data and hardcopies of system records such as console logs, data listings, and software and firmware listings. Electronic archives preserve the content, prevent or track alterations, and control access to electronic records.

Centers for Medicare & Medicaid Services (CMS), ARMA, Sedona Conference

Archive record

A record that has continuing or historical value and is preserved permanently by an organization.

ARMA

Area of concern

A situation or scenario where someone is concerned about a threat to important assets. Typically, areas of concern have a source and an outcome - a causal action that has an effect on the organization.

CERT OCTAVE

Arithmetic Logic Unit (ALU)

The area of the central processing unit that performs mathematical and analytical operations.

ISACA

ARMA: the Association for Information Management Professionals (ARMA)

ARMA International is a not-for-profit professional association and the authority on managing records and information – paper and electronic. For more information, see http://www.arma.org/about/index.cfm .

ARMA, Sedona Conference

Arson

Any willful or malicious burning or attempt to burn, with or without intent to defraud, a dwelling house, public building, motor vehicle, personal property of another, etc.

Centers for Medicare & Medicaid Services (CMS)

Artificial Intelligence (AI)

The subfield of computer science concerned with the concepts and methods of symbolic inference by computer and symbolic knowledge representation for use in making inferences - an attempt to model aspects of human thought on computers. It is also sometimes defined as trying to solve by computer any problem once believed to be solvable only by humans. AI is the capability of a device to perform functions that are normally associated with human intelligence, such as reasoning and optimization through experience. It attempts to approximate the results of human reasoning by organizing and manipulating factual and heuristic knowledge. Areas of AI activity include expert systems, natural language understanding, speech recognition, vision, and robotics.

ISACA, Sedona Conference

Aspect ratio

The relationship of the height and width of any image. The aspect ratio of an image must be maintained to prevent distortion.

Sedona Conference

Assembler

A program that takes as input a program written in assembly language and translates it into machine code or relocatable code.

ISACA

Assembly CI

A part of configuration management, a configuration item (CI), that is made up from a number of other CIs. For example, a server CI may contain CIs for CPUs, discs, memory etc. An IT service CI may contain many hardware, software and other CIs. See also component CI, build.

ITIL

Assembly language

A low-level procedural programming language in which each program statement corresponds directly to a single machine instruction. Assembly languages are thus specific to a given processor.

FISCAM, ISACA

Assertion

Financial statement assertions are management representations that are embodied in financial statement components. The assertions can be either explicit or implicit and can be classified into the following broad categories: existence or occurrence (an entity's assets or liabilities exist at a given date and recorded transactions have occurred during a given period), completeness (all transactions and accounts that should be presented in the financial statements are so included), rights and obligations (assets are the rights of the organization, and liabilities are the obligations of the organization at a given date), valuation or allocation (asset, liability, revenue, and expense components have been included in the financial statements at appropriate amounts), and presentation and disclosure (the particular components of the financial statements are properly classified, described, and disclosed).

FISCAM, GAO/PCIE Financial Audit Manual

Assessing control risk

The process of evaluating the effectiveness of an entity's internal control in preventing or detecting misstatements in financial statement assertions.

GAO/PCIE Financial Audit Manual

Assessment Method

A focused activity or action employed by an assessor for evaluating a particular attribute of a security control.

NIST 800 series

Assessment Procedure

A set of activities or actions employed by an assessor to determine the extent to which a security control is implemented correctly, operating as intended, and producing the desired outcome with respect to meeting the security requirements for the system.

NIST 800 series

Asset

Something of value to the organization. Information technology assets are the combination of logical and physical assets and are grouped into the specific classes (information, systems, software, hardware, people). Assets that need to be individually managed are also configuration items. For example, the door lock on a computer room or a consumable item would not be a configuration item. In the context of financial management, items below a specific value are not considered to be assets as it would not be cost effective to track and manage them. See also asset management, depreciation, risk assessment, critical assets, components.

CERT OCTAVE, Centers for Medicare & Medicaid Services (CMS), ISO/IEC 13335-1:2004, ISO/IEC 27001:2005, PCI-DSS, ITIL, NIST 800 series

Asset evaluation

A quantitative and/or qualitative assessment to determine the importance of the physical resources of the facilities, information, sensitivity of information, the operational impact of loss and/or denial of support, and the automated information systems resources providing that support.

Centers for Medicare & Medicaid Services (CMS)

Asset management

A part of financial management, asset management is the business process responsible for tracking and reporting the value and ownership of financial assets throughout their lifecycle. See also asset register.

ITIL

Asset register

A part of financial management, a list of assets, which includes their ownership and value. The asset register is maintained by asset management.

ITIL

Assurance

Grounds for confidence that the other four security objectives (integrity, availability, confidentiality, and accountability) have been adequately met by a specific implementation. "Adequately met" includes 1) functionality that performs correctly, 2) sufficient protection against unintentional errors (by users or software), and 3) sufficient resistance to intentional penetration or by-pass. Assurance is the complement of audit risk, which is an auditor judgment. This is not the same as confidence level, which relates to an individual sample.

NIST 800 series, GAO/PCIE Financial Audit Manual, Centers for Medicare & Medicaid Services (CMS), ITIL, PAS 56,

US National Information Assurance (IA) Glossary

Assured software

Software that has been designed, developed, analyzed and tested using processes, tools, and techniques that establish a level of confidence in its trustworthiness appropriate for its intended use.

US National Information Assurance (IA) Glossary

Asymmetric key

A cipher technique whereby different cryptographic keys are used to encrypt and decrypt a message. See also public key. Two related keys, a public key and a private key that are used to perform complementary operations, such as encryption and decryption or signature generation and signature verification.

ISACA, NIST 800 series, FIPS Pubs

Asynchronous Transfer Mode (ATM)

ATM is a high-bandwidth low-delay switching and multiplexing technology. It is a data link layer protocol. This means that it is a protocol-independent transport mechanism. ATM allows integration of real-time voice and video as well as data. ATM allows very high speed data transfer rates at up to 155 Mbit/s.

ISACA

Asynchronous transmission

Transmission of data in which time intervals between transmitted characters may be of unequal length. Transmission is controlled by start and stop bits at the beginning and end of each character. In modem communication, a form of data transmission in which data is sent intermittently, one character at a time, rather than in a steady stream with characters separated by fixed time intervals. Asynchronous transmission relies on the use of a start bit and stop bit(s), in addition to the bits representing the character (and an optional parity bit), to distinguish separate characters. In data transmission, each character is individually synchronized, usually by start bits and stop bits. Timing information is usually included in the transmitted character.

ISACA

Attachment

An attachment is a record or file associated with another record for the purpose of retention or transfer. There may be multiple attachments associated with a single "parent" or "master" record. In many records and information management programs the attachments and associated record are managed and processed as a single unit. In common use, this term refers to a file (or files) associated with an e-mail for retention and storage as a single message unit.

Sedona Conference

Attack

The act of trying to bypass security controls on a system. An attack may be active, resulting in the alteration of data; or passive, resulting in the release of data. Note: The fact that an attack is made does not necessarily mean that it will succeed. The degree of success depends on the vulnerability of the system or activity and the effectiveness of existing countermeasures.

Centers for Medicare & Medicaid Services (CMS), US National Information Assurance (IA) Glossary

Attack Sensing and Warning (AS&W)

Detection, correlation, identification, (AS&W) and characterization of intentional unauthorized activity with notification to decision makers so that an appropriate response can be developed.

US National Information Assurance (IA) Glossary

Attack signature

A specific sequence of events indicative of an unauthorized access attempt.

NIST 800 series

Attest reporting engagement

An engagement where an IS auditor either examines management's assertion regarding a particular subject matter or examines the subject matter directly.

The IS auditor's report consists of an opinion on one of the following: The subject matter. These reports relate directly to the subject matter itself rather than an assertion. In certain situations, management will not be able to make an assertion over the subject of the engagement. An example of this situation is when IT services are out-sourced to third party. Management will not ordinarily be able to make an assertion over the controls that the third-party is responsible for. Hence, an IS auditor would have to report directly on the subject matter rather than an assertion. Management's assertion about the effectiveness of the control procedures. Examination reporting engagement where the IS auditor is engaged to issue an opinion on particular subject matter. These engagements can include reports on controls implemented by management and on their operating effectiveness.

ISACA

Attestation Reference (AT)

Reference to statements on standards for attestation engagements in the sections of the Codification of Statements on Auditing Standards.

GAO/PCIE Financial Audit Manual

Attitude

Way of thinking, behaving, feeling, etc.
ISACA

Attribute

An attribute is a characteristic of data that sets it apart from other data, such as location, length, or type. The term attribute is sometimes used synonymously with "data element" or "property."

Sedona Conference

Attribute Authority

An entity, recognized by the Federal Public Key Infrastructure (PKI) Policy Authority or comparable Agency body as having the authority to verify the association of attributes to an identity.

NIST 800 series

Attribute sampling

Statistical sampling that reaches a conclusion about the population in terms of a rate of occurrence. An audit technique used to select items from a population for audit testing purposes based on selecting all those items that have certain attributes or characteristics (such as all items over a certain size).

GAO/PCIE Financial Audit Manual, ISACA

Audio-Video Interleave (AVI)

A Microsoft standard for Windows animation files that interleaves audio and video to provide medium quality multimedia.

Sedona Conference

Audit

The formal process of generating, recording and reviewing a chronological record of system events to ascertain their accuracy, effectiveness, and efficiency (or all three) according to a formal set of guidelines. Auditing is an activity to determine the adequacy of and adherence (compliance) to established procedures, instructions, specifications, codes and standards, or other applicable contractual and licensing requirements, and effectiveness of implementation. In addition, audits recommend necessary changes in controls, policies, or procedures. Most common forms of audits are compliance, operational, or vulnerability. An audit may be carried out by internal or external groups. See also certification, assurance.

ISACA, Centers for Medicare & Medicaid Services (CMS), ISO/IEC 27001:2005, ITIL, US National Information Assurance (IA) Glossary, NIST 800 series

Audit accountability

Performance measurement of service delivery including cost, timeliness, and quality against agreed service levels.

ISACA

Audit authority

A statement of the position within the organization, including lines of reporting and the rights of access.

ISACA

Audit charter

A document which defines the IS audit function's responsibility, authority and accountability, and approved by the board.

ISACA, CobiT

Audit data

Chronological record of system activities to enable the reconstruction and examination of the sequence of events and changes in an event.

NIST 800 series

Audit evidence

The information systems auditor (IS auditor) gathers information in the course of performing an IS audit. The information used by the IS auditor to meet audit objectives is referred to as audit evidence (evidence). Also used to describe the level of risk that an auditor is prepared to accept during an audit engagement.

ISACA

Audit expert systems

Expert or decision support systems that can be used to assist IS auditors in the decision-making process by automating the knowledge of experts in the field. This technique includes automated risk analysis, systems software, and control objectives software packages.

ISACA

Audit log

A chronological record of system activities that is sufficient for the reconstruction, reviewing, and examination of the sequence of environments and activities surrounding or leading to an operation, a procedure, or an event in a transaction from its inception to final results. Sometimes specifically referred to as a security audit trail.

PCI-DSS

Audit objective

The specific goal(s) of an audit. These often center on substantiating the existence of internal controls to minimize business risk.

ISACA

Audit plan

A high level description of the audit work to be performed in a certain period of time (ordinarily a year). It includes the areas to be audited, the type of work planned, the high level objectives and scope of the work, and topics such as budget, resource allocation, schedule dates, type of report, and its in-

tended audience and other general aspects of the work.

ISACA

Audit program

A series of steps to complete an audit objective.

ISACA

Audit Reduction Tools

Preprocessors designed to reduce the volume of audit records to facilitate manual review. Before a security review, these tools can remove many audit records known to have little security significance. These tools generally remove records generated by specified classes of events, such as records generated by nightly backups.

NIST 800 series

Audit Reference (AU)

Reference to Statements on Auditing Standards in the sections of the Codification of Statements on Auditing Standards.

GAO/PCIE Financial Audit Manual

Audit responsibility

The roles, scope, and objectives documented in the service level agreement between management and audit.

ISACA

Audit risk

The risk that information or financial reports will contain material errors that the auditor may not detect. The overall risk that the auditor may unknowingly fail to appropriately modify his or her opinion on financial statements that are materially misstated. This is an auditor judgment.

FISCAM, GAO/PCIE Financial Audit Manual, ISACA

Audit sampling

See sampling.

ISACA

Audit software

Generic audit software consists of a special program or set of programs designed to audit data stored on computer media. Audit software performs functions such as data extraction and reformatting, file creation, sorting, and downloading. This type of audit software may also be used to perform computations, data analysis, sample selection, summarization, file stratification, field comparison, file matching, or statistical analysis. The term audit software may also refer to programs that audit specific functions, features, and controls associated with specific types of computer systems to evaluate integrity and identify security exposures. See also audit expert systems.

FISCAM

Audit trail

A visible trail of evidence enabling one to trace information contained in statements or reports back to the original input source. The log of who changed what and when for accountability. These recordings must enable the re-creation, review, and examination of all events surrounding counter-policy activities within the system. In an accounting package, any program feature that automatically keeps a record of transactions so you can backtrack to find the origin of specific figures that appear on reports. In computer systems, a step-by-step (chronological) history of a transaction, especially a transaction with security sensitivity. Includes source documents, electronic logs, and records of accesses to restricted files.

AIIM, FISCAM, ISACA, Centers for Medicare & Medicaid Services (CMS), US National Information Assurance (IA) Glossary, Sedona Conference, NIST 800 series

Auditability

The level to which transactions can be traced and audited through a system.

ISACA

Auditing

The process of conducting an audit, or being audited. If you are being audited, this feels very much like a proctologic exam. See also audit.

de facto

Auditor

The auditor's intent is to discover unrecognized risks and to help the organization mitigate them. The IS auditor's job is to "drill down" into the technical specifications, question vendor claims, and identify potential technical or security problems, and business risks. Auditors can either inside or outside of the organization. See also information systems auditor.

NIST 800 series, 17 CFR 240.17a-3 & 4

Authenticate

To verify the identity of a user, user device, or other entity, or the integrity of data stored, transmitted, or otherwise exposed to unauthorized modification in an IS, or to establish the validity of a transmission.

US National Information Assurance (IA) Glossary, NIST 800 series

Authentication

The act of verifying the identity of a user and the user's eligibility to access computerized information. Designed to protect against fraudulent activity. NIST 800-33 would say that verifying the identity of a user, process, or device, often as a prerequisite to allowing access to resources in a system is the definition of authentication. All systems that store, process or protect regulated data need to implement access controls in order to manage where this information is allowed to flow and who is allowed to create, view or change it. If the authentication attempt fails then access has to be blocked. For HIPAA, all attempts to gain access to a system containing ePHI have to be logged for later investigation. Authentication can also refer to the verification of the correctness of a piece of data. See also identification, key management, system access control.

HIPAA, NIST 800 series, FISCAM, ISACA, Centers for Medicare & Medicaid Services (CMS), CobiT, ISO/IEC

27001:2005, PCI-DSS, FIPS Pubs, US National Information Assurance (IA) Glossary, FIPS Pubs, FIPS Pubs

Authentication code

A cryptographic checksum based on an Approved security function (also known as a Message Authentication Code (MAC)).

NIST 800 series

Authentication Header (AH)

A security protocol that authenticates packets from servers and ensures messages are not tampered with while en route.

Network Frontiers

Authentication mechanism

Hardware or software-based mechanisms that force users to prove their identity before accessing data on a device.

NIST 800 series

Authentication mode

A block cipher mode of operation that can provide assurance of the authenticity and, therefore, the integrity of data.

NIST 800 series

Authentication protocol

A well specified message exchange process that verifies possession of a token to remotely authenticate a claimant. Some authentication protocols also generate cryptographic keys that are used to protect an entire session, so that the data transferred in the session is cryptographically protected.

NIST 800 series

Authentication system

A computer that houses software that authenticates users and data attempting to access the network. Restriction of access to computer systems is the first defense against system compromise.

US National Information Assurance (IA) Glossary

Authentication tag

A pair of bit strings associated to data to provide assurance of its authenticity.

NIST 800 series

Authentication token

Authentication information conveyed during an authentication exchange.

NIST 800 series, FIPS Pubs

Authentication, Authorization and Accounting protocol (AAA)

Authentication refers to the confirmation that a user who is requesting services is a valid user of the network services requested. Authentication is accomplished via the presentation of an identity and credentials. Examples of types of credentials are passwords, one-time tokens, digital certificates, and phone numbers (calling/called). Authorization refers to the granting of specific types of service (including "no service") to a user, based on their authentication, what services they are requesting, and the current system state. Authorization may be based on restrictions, for example time-of-day restrictions, or physical location restrictions, or restrictions against multiple logins by the same user. Authorization determines the nature of the service which is granted to a user. Examples of types of service include, but are not limited to: IP address filtering, address assignment, route assignment, QoS/differential services, bandwidth control/traffic management, compulsory tunneling to a specific endpoint, and encryption. Accounting refers to the tracking of the consumption of network resources by users. This information may be used for management, planning, billing, or other purposes. Real-time accounting refers to accounting information that is delivered concurrently with the consumption of the resources. Batch accounting refers to accounting information that is saved until it is delivered at a later time. Typical information that is gathered in accounting is the identity of the user, the nature of the service delivered, when the service began, and when it ended.

PCI-DSS, Wikipedia

Authenticator

Means used to confirm the identity of a station, originator, or individual.

US National Information Assurance (IA) Glossary

Authenticity

(for records) An authentic record is one that can be proven: 1) to be what it purports to be, 2) to have been created or sent by the person purported to have created or sent it, and 3) to have been created or sent at the time purported. To ensure the authenticity of records, organizations should implement and document policies and procedures which control the creation, receipt, transmission, maintenance, and disposition of records to ensure that records creators are authorized and identified and that records are protected against unauthorized addition, deletion, alteration, use, and concealment. See also nonrepudiation.

ISO 15489, NIST 800 series

Author

The author of a document is the person, office or designated position responsible for its creation or issuance. In the case of a document in the form of a letter, the author or originator is usually indicated on the letterhead or by signature. In some cases, the software application producing the document may capture the author's identity and associate it with the document. For records management purposes, the author or originator may be designated as a person, official title, office symbol, or code.

Sedona Conference

Authority

An authority is the source by which rules are drawn, they are the convincing force behind an argument to do something. Two common forms of authority are governmental agencies and institutional authorities. Within the world of compliance, local and national governments create laws and regulations that provide the authority necessary to enforce compliance. However, institutions such as VISA and MasterCard have banded together to form the Payment Card Industry standards act as institutional authorities behind their compliance standard, the PCI-DSS.

de facto

Authorization

This term has two uses, one for information assurance, and another for the Payment Card Industry. 1) In terms of Information Technology security, authorization is the process of determining what types of activities are permitted and the granting of access for those activities. After the authentication process has identified the person, program, or process accessing the system and authen-

ticated the claimed identity, an authorization mechanism needs to determine what data the user is allowed to access and what functions may be performed. The mechanism can be based on a role a person fulfills in the organization and use technologies such as LDAP. Authorization has to be implemented at the lowest level possible to ensure that all access to all regulated data is correctly managed. It must be non-bypassable to ensure that all access attempts are controlled and that no one can circumvent it. At the same time, in the case of a documented crisis, a procedure for emergency override access has to be provided. 2) For the payment card industry, this is the process by which a card issuer approves or declines a Visa card purchase. Authorization occurs automatically when you swipe the magnetic stripe of a payment card through a card reader. See also Voice Authorization Center.

HIPAA, NIST 800 series, ISACA, Centers for Medicare & Medicaid Services (CMS), ISO/IEC 27001:2005, PCI-DSS, US National Information Assurance (IA) Glossary, VISA Glossary of Terms

Authorize processing

The official management decision given by a senior agency official to authorize operation of an information system and to explicitly accept the risk to agency operations (including mission, functions, image, or reputation), agency assets, or individuals, based on the implementation of an agreed-upon set of security controls.

NIST 800 series

Authorized examination center

A body authorized by an examination board to host examinations. The authorized examination center provides a place where examinations may be taken and may also provide exam supervision and automated marking.

ITIL

Authorized program facility (APF)

An operating system facility that controls which programs are allowed to use restricted system functions.

FISCAM

Authorized vendor

Manufacturer of INFOSEC equipment authorized to produce quantities in excess of contractual requirements for direct sale to eligible buyers. Eligible buyers are typically U.S. Government organizations or U.S. Government contractors.

US National Information Assurance (IA) Glossary

Authorized Vendor Program (AVP)

Program in which a vendor, producing an (AVP) INFOSEC product under con-

tract to NSA, is authorized to produce that product in numbers exceeding the contracted requirements for direct marketing and sale to eligible buyers. Eligible buyers are typically U.S. Government organizations or U.S. Government contractors. Products approved for marketing and sale through the AVP are placed on the Endorsed Cryptographic Products List (ECPL).

US National Information Assurance (IA) Glossary

Authorizing official

Official with the authority to formally assume responsibility for operating an information system at an acceptable level of risk to agency operations (including mission, functions, image, or reputation), agency assets, or individuals. See also accreditation authority.

FIPS Pubs, NIST 800 Series

Automated controls

Electronic mechanisms to automate the protection of digital assets, such as log readers, intrusion prevention and detection systems, etc.

Network Frontiers

Automated information

Automated information is information that is held in any electronic state, locally, centrally, or in transit. See also Automated Information System.

Workgroup for Electronic Data Interchange

Automated information security

See automated controls.

Centers for Medicare & Medicaid Services (CMS)

Automated Information System (AIS)

An assembly of computer hardware, software, and/or firmware that is configured to collect, create, communicate, compute, disseminate, process, store, and/or control data or information.

Centers for Medicare & Medicaid Services (CMS)

Automated key transport

The transport of cryptographic keys, usually in encrypted form, using electronic means such as a computer network (e.g., key transport/agreement protocols).

NIST 800 series, FIPS Pubs

Automated password generator

An algorithm which creates random passwords that have no association with a particular user.

NIST 800 series, FIPS Pubs

Automated security monitoring

Use of automated procedures to ensure security controls are not circumvented or the use of these tools to track actions taken by subjects suspected of misusing the IS.

US National Information Assurance (IA) Glossary

Automated Teller Machine (ATM)

A 24-hour, stand-alone mini-bank, located outside branch bank offices or in public places such as shopping malls. Through ATMs, clients can make deposits, withdrawals, account inquiries, and transfers. Typically, the ATM network is comprised of two spheres; a proprietary sphere, in which the bank manages the transactions of its clients, and the public or shared domain, in which a client of one financial institution can use another's ATMs.

ISACA

Automatic Call Distribution (ACD)

Part of the service desk, this is the use of information technology to direct an incoming telephone call to the most appropriate person in the shortest possible time. ACD is sometimes called automated call distribution.

ITIL

Automatic Document Feeder (ADF)

Automatic Document Feeder. This is the means by which a scanner feeds the paper document.

Sedona Conference

Automatic remote rekeying

Procedure to rekey a distant crypto-equipment electronically without specific actions by the receiving terminal operator. See also manual remote rekeying.

US National Information Assurance (IA) Glossary

Availability

Availability relates to information being available when required by the business process now and in the future. It also concerns the safeguarding of necessary resources and associated capabilities. This requirement is intended to assure that systems work promptly and service is not denied to authorized users. Therefore this is the security objective that generates the requirement for protection against intentional or accidental attempts to perform unauthorized deletion of data or otherwise cause a denial of service or data. You could also think of this as when or how often an asset must be present or ready for use, thus, it also concerns the safeguarding of necessary resources and associated capabilities. Availability is determined by reliability, maintainability, serviceability, performance, and security. Availability is usually calculated as a percentage. This calculation is often based on agreed service time and downtime. It is best practice to calculate availability using measurements of the business output of the IT service. See also security principle.

NIST 800 series, CERT OCTAVE, CobiT, ISACA, Centers for Medicare & Medicaid Services (CMS), ISO/IEC 27001:2005, ISO/IEC 13335-1:2004, FIPS Pubs, ITIL, US National Information Assurance (IA) Glossary

Availability management

The process responsible for defining, analyzing, planning, measuring and improving all aspects of the availability of IT services. Availability management is responsible for ensuring that all IT infrastructure, processes, tools, roles etc. are appropriate for the agreed service level targets for availability.

ITIL

Availability Management Database (AMDB)

A database containing all data needed to support availability management. The AMDB may be part of the configuration management database.

ITIL

Availability plan

A plan to ensure that existing and future availability requirements for IT services can be provided cost effectively.

ITIL

Awareness

Owners, providers, and users of information systems should readily be able (consistent with maintaining security) to gain appropriate knowledge of and be informed about the existence and general extent of measures for the continuity of information systems.

NIST 800 series, ISO/IEC 27001:2005

Awareness principle

Participants should be aware of the need for security of information systems and networks and what they can do to enhance security.

OECD Guidelines for the Security of Information Systems and Networks

B

Back door

A malicious software program that allows an attacker to issue commands to or access a compromised system. An undocumented way to gain access to a program, data, or an entire computer system, often known only to the programmer who created it. Backdoors can be handy when the standard way of getting information is unavailable, but they usually constitute a security risk.

US National Information Assurance (IA) Glossary, FISCAM

Back door authority

Any type of budget authority that is provided by legislation or organizational power structures outside the normal appropriations process. See also contract authority.

GAO/PCIE Financial Audit Manual

Back office function

An office, building, or function that is used by an organization to conduct support activities.

Centers for Medicare & Medicaid Services (CMS)

Back out plan

A part of change management and release management. A plan that documents the steps required to recover to a known working state if a change or release fails.

ITIL

Backbone

The top level of a hierarchical network. It is the main channel along which data is transferred.

Sedona Conference

Backfiles

Existing paper or microfilm files.

Sedona Conference

Backlog processing

The processing of work that has built up due to a disruption in a mission critical activity (MCA).

PAS 56

Backup

A part of availability and IT service continuity management, a secondary copy of data that is generally used for restoration in the event of damage or loss to the primary copy of data. Any duplicate of a primary resource function or component (as opposed to a duplicate of the information or application only, such as a copy of a computer program or data file). This standby is used in case of loss or failure of the primary resource. See also Backup data.

NIST 800 series, FISCAM, ISACA, Centers for Medicare & Medicaid Services

(CMS), ISO/IEC 27001:2005, PCI-DSS, ITIL, US National Information Assurance (IA) Glossary, Sedona Conference

Backup and recovery test

A test to verify that a system can be re-established after a failure. This is accomplished by returning to a point in the processing cycle before any errors or loss occurred and reprocessing subsequent transactions.

Centers for Medicare & Medicaid Services (CMS)

Backup data

An exact copy of system data which serves as a source for recovery in the event of a system problem or disaster. Backup Data is generally stored separately from Active Data on portable media. Backup Data is distinct from Archival Data in that Backup Data may be a copy of Active Data, but the more meaningful difference is the method and structure of storage which impact its suitability for certain purposes.

Sedona Conference

Backup operation or procedures

The process of preparing and copying selected data (usually new or altered files) from a primary source to a secondary destination.

The Backup Book, FISCAM

Backup plan

Establish and implement procedures to create and maintain retrievable exact copies of regulated data, when needed, before movement of equipment. See also contingency plan.

HIPAA, Centers for Medicare & Medicaid Services (CMS)

Backup tape recycling

Backup Tape Recycling describes the process whereby an organization's backup tapes are overwritten with new data, usually on a fixed schedule determined jointly by records management, legal, and IT sources. For example, the use of nightly backup tapes for each day of the week with the daily backup tape for a particular day being overwritten on the same day the following week; weekly and monthly backups being stored offsite for a specific period of time before being placed back in the rotation.

Sedona Conference

Backup tapes

Magnetic tapes used to store copies of data, for use when restoration or recovery of data is required. Data on backup tapes are generally recorded and stored sequentially, rather than randomly, meaning in order to locate and access a specific file or data set, all data on the tape preceding the target must first be read, a time-consuming and inefficient process. Backup tapes typically use data compression, which increases restoration time and expense, given the lack of uniform standards governing data compression.

Sedona Conference

Balance check

A part of financial management, a calculation to verify that the sum of all individual costs or charges equals the total cost or charge. Used to check that all amounts have been fully accounted for.

ITIL

Balanced scorecard

A method for measuring an enterprise's activities in terms of its vision and strategies by giving managers a fast, comprehensive view of the performance of a business. It is a management tool that seeks to measure a business from the following perspectives: financial, customer, business, and learning.

CobiT, ITIL

Bandwidth

Strictly speaking in technology terms, this means the range between the highest and lowest transmittable frequencies. It equates to the transmission capacity of an electronic line and is expressed in bytes per second or Hertz (cycles per second). However, it has come to mean the amount of data that can be transmitted via a given communications channel (such as a computer network) in a given unit of time (generally one second). Bandwidth is usually stated in kilobits per second (kbps) or megabits per second (mps).

FISCAM, ISACA, Sedona Conference

Banner

Display on an IS that sets parameters for system or data use.

US National Information Assurance (IA) Glossary

Bar case

A standardized body of data created for testing purposes. Users normally establish the data. Base case validates production application systems and tests the ongoing accurate operation of the system.

ISACA

Bar code

A printed, machine-readable code that consists of parallel bars of varied width and spacing that can be read by a laser or an optical scanner. In records management and electronic discovery, bar codes are often affixed to specific records for indexing, tracking and retrieval purposes.

ISACA, Sedona Conference

Base case

See bar case.

ISACA

Base Case System Evaluations (BCSE)

Base case system evaluation is a special case of test data that requires an all-inclusive set of test data in order to test every possible data and processing condition. This method is time-consuming and expensive and best developed by an internal audit staff. The external auditor should refer to professional standards in deciding whether to rely upon the work of an internal audit department.

SAS 65

Base data

Data used to develop the expectation in an analytical procedure.

GAO/PCIE Financial Audit Manual

Baseband

A form of modulation in which data signals are pulsed directly on the transmission medium without frequency division and usually utilize a transceiver. In baseband the entire bandwidth of the transmission medium (e.g., coaxial cable) is utilized for a single channel.

ISACA

Basel Committee on Banking Supervision (BCBS)

See Basel II.

de facto

Basel II

The Basel Committee on Banking Supervision (BCBS) in Basel, Switzerland, conducted a round of deliberations aimed at producing uniformity in the way banks and banking regulators approach risk management across national borders.

de facto

Baseline

An agreed upon specification or standard against which changes can be made. A baseline should be changed only through formal change control procedures. The recorded state of something at a specific point in time. A baseline can be created for a configuration, a process, or any other set of data. For example, a baseline can be used in 1) Continuous service improvement, to establish a starting point for planning improvements. 2) Capacity management, to document performance characteristics during normal operations. 3) Configuration management, to enable the IT infrastructure to be restored to a known configuration if a change fails. Also used to specify a standard configuration for data capture, release or audit purposes.

Centers for Medicare & Medicaid Services (CMS), ITIL

Baseline security

A part of security management. The minimum security controls required for safeguarding an IT system based on its identified needs for confidentiality, integrity and/or availability protection.

ITIL, NIST 800 Series

Baselining

Monitoring resources to determine typical utilization patterns so that significant deviations can be detected.

NIST 800 series

Basic Input Output System (BIOS)

The program that starts up your computer and communicates between the devices in your computer (such as your hard drive and graphics card) and the system. The set of user-independent computer instructions stored in a computer's ROM, immediately available to the computer when the computer is turned on. BIOS information provides the code necessary to control the keyboard, display screen, disk drives and communication ports in addition to handling certain miscellaneous functions.

Centers for Medicare & Medicaid Services (CMS), Sedona Conference

Bastion host

A bastion host is typically a firewall implemented on top of an operating system that has been specially configured and hardened to be resistant to attack.

NIST 800 series

Batch control

Correctness checks built into data processing systems and applied to batches of input data, particularly in the data preparation stage. There are two main forms of batch controls: 1) sequence control, which involves numbering the records in a batch consecutively so that the presence of each record can be confirmed, and 2) control total, which is a total of the values in selected fields within the transactions.

ISACA

Batch processing

A mode of operation in which transactions are accumulated over a period of time, such as a day, week, or month, and then processed in a single run. In batch processing, users do not interact with the system while their programs and data are processing as they do during interactive processing.

FISCAM, ISACA, Centers for Medicare & Medicaid Services (CMS), Sedona Conference

Bates number

Sequential numbering used to track documents and images in production data sets, where each page is identified by a unique production number. Often used in conjunction with a suffix or prefix to identify the producing party, the litigation, or other relevant information. See also Production number.

Sedona Conference

Baud rate

The rate of transmission for telecommunication data. It is expressed in bits per second (bps). A 2400-baud modem changes the signal 2400 times a second.

ISACA, Sedona Conference

Beginners all-purpose symbolic instruction code (BASIC)

A very rudimentary programming language used mainly for creating in-house organizational applications.

AIIM

Beginning Document Number or BegDoc#

The Bates Number identifying the first page of a document or record.

Sedona Conference

Behavioral outcome

What an individual who has completed the specific training module is expected to be able to accomplish in terms of IT security-related job performance.

NIST 800 series

Benchmark

A test that has been designed to evaluate the performance of a system. In a benchmark test, a system is subjected to a known workload, and the performance of the system against this workload is measured. Typically, the purpose is to compare the measured performance with that of other systems that have been subject to the same benchmark test. It is also a process used in management, and particularly strategic management, in which companies evaluate various aspects of their business processes in relation to best practice, usually within their own industry.

ISACA, CobiT, ITIL, BS 25999

Benign

Condition of cryptographic data that cannot be compromised by human access.

US National Information Assurance (IA) Glossary

Benign environment

Nonhostile environment that may be protected from external hostile elements by physical, personnel, and procedural security countermeasures.

US National Information Assurance (IA) Glossary

Best practices

Best practices are leading edge, proven models of methods or actions for others to follow. These are combinations of activities, processes, policies, or procedures that document the best possible way of doing something. ITIL is an example of best practices.

de facto

Bi-Tonal

A bi-tonal image uses only black and white.

Sedona Conference

Bibliographical/Objective coding

Extracting objective information from electronic documents such as date created, author/recipient/copies, and associating the information with a specific electronic document.

Sedona Conference

Billing

A part of financial management. Part of the charging process. Billing is the activity responsible for producing an invoice or a bill and recovering the money from customers. See also pricing.

ITIL

Binary

The Base 2 numbering system used in digital computing which represents all numbers using combinations of zero and one.

Sedona Conference

Binary code

A code whose representation is limited to 0 and 1. See also Binary.

ISACA

Binary Large Object (BLOB)

A term for a binary file stored as part of a database record. A smart large object data type that stores any kind of binary data, including images. BLOB's are handy for storing digitized information (eg, images, audio, video).

AIIM

Binary Term (Byte)

A Byte is the basic measurement of most computer data and consists of 8 bits. Computer storage capacity is generally measured in bytes. Although characters are stored in bytes, a few bytes are of little use for storing a large amount of data. Therefore, storage is measured in larger increments of bytes. See also Kilobyte, Megabyte, Gigabyte, Terabyte, Petabyte and Exabyte.

Sedona Conference

Binding

Process of associating a specific communications terminal with a specific cryptographic key or associating two related elements of information. An acknowledgment by a trusted third party that associates an entity's identity with its public key. This may take place through (1) a certification authority's generation of a public key certificate, (2) a security officer's verification of an entity's credentials and placement of the entity's public key and identifier in a secure database, or (3) an analogous method.

US National Information Assurance (IA) Glossary, NIST 800 Series

Biometric

Personal physical characteristics, such as a fingerprint, voice, retina, or writing pattern. A measurable, physical characteristic or personal behavioral trait used to recognize the identity, or verify the claimed identity, of an applicant. Facial images, fingerprints, and handwriting samples are all examples of biometrics.

US National Information Assurance (IA) Glossary, ISACA, NIST 800 Series

Biometric authentication

The process of verifying or recognizing the identity of a person based on physiological or behavioral characteristics. Biometric devices include fingerprints, retina patterns, hand geometry, speech patterns, and keystroke dynamics.

FISCAM, Centers for Medicare & Medicaid Services (CMS)

Biometric information

The stored electronic information pertaining to a biometric. This information can be in terms of raw or compressed pixels or in terms of some characteristic (e.g. patterns.).

NIST 800 series, FIPS Pubs

Biometric locks

Door and entry locks that are activated by such biometric features as voice, eye retina, fingerprint, or signature.

ISACA

Biometric system

An automated system capable of: 1) capturing a biometric sample from an end user; 2) extracting biometric data from that sample; 3) comparing the biometric data with that contained in one or more reference templates; 4) deciding how well they match; and 5) indicating whether or not an identification or verification of identity has been achieved.

NIST 800 series, FIPS Pubs

Biometric template

A characteristic of biometric information (e.g. minutiae or patterns.).

NIST 800 series, FIPS Pubs

Bit

A bit (binary digit) is the smallest unit of computer data. A bit consists of either 0 or 1. There are eight bits in a byte.

Sedona Conference

Bit error rate

Ratio between the number of bits incorrectly received and the total number of bits transmitted in a telecommunications system.

US National Information Assurance (IA) Glossary

Bit Map

A Bit Map provides information on the placement and color of individual bits and allows the creation of characters or images by creating a picture composed of individual bits (pixels).

Sedona Conference

Bit stream back up

A bit stream back up is a sector-by-sector/bit-by-bit copy of a hard drive, preserving all latent data in addition to the files and directory structures. Bit stream back up may be created using applications such as Encase, SnapBack and Ghost. See also Forensic Copy.

Sedona Conference

Bitmap graphical image format (BMP)

A proprietary Microsoft Windows image format. A resolution-dependent file format for images created by Windows Paint, PaintBrush, and other applications.

AIIM, Microsoft

Bits Per Inch (BPI)

BPI measures data densities in disk and magnetic tape systems.

Sedona Conference

Bits Per Second (BPS)

Sedona Conference

BLACK

Designation applied to information systems, and to associated areas, circuits, components, and equipment, in which national security information is encrypted or is not processed.

US National Information Assurance (IA) Glossary

Black box testing

A testing approach which focuses on the functionality of the application or product and does not require knowledge of the code intervals.

ISACA

Blended attack

Malicious code that uses multiple methods to spread.

NIST 800 series

Blended threat

A multifaceted threat that may include two or more traditional threats, such as viruses, worms, backdoors, keystroke recording, denial of service attacks, and configuration manipulation.

Network Frontiers

Block

Sequence of binary bits that comprise the input, output, State, and Round Key. The length of a sequence is the number of bits it contains. Blocks are also interpreted as arrays of bytes.

FIPS Pubs, NIST 800 Series

Block allocation

Block allocation is a method of allocating blocks where the file system allocates one block at a time. In this method, a pointer to every block in a file is maintained and recorded.

The Backup Book

Block cipher

A symmetric key cryptographic algorithm that transforms a block of information at a time using a cryptographic key. For a block cipher algorithm, the length of the input block is the same as the length of the output block.

NIST 800 series

Block cipher algorithm

A family of functions and their inverses that is parameterized by a cryptographic key; the function maps bit strings of a fixed length to bit strings of the same length.

NIST 800 series

Board

See board of directors.

de facto

Board of directors (BOD)

A board of directors, also called a board of trustees, a board of governors, a board of managers, or a board of curators, is a group of people who oversee the affairs of a corporation. One member of the group may be designated or elected to serve as chairperson and is referred to as the chairman of the board.

de facto, Wikipedia

Bookmark

A link to a Web site or page previously visited.

Sedona Conference

Boolean Search

Boolean Searches use the logical operators "and," "or" and "not" to include or exclude terms from a search.

Sedona Conference

Boot

To start up or reset a computer.

Sedona Conference

Boot sector

The very first sector on a hard drive which contains the computer code (boot strap loader) necessary for the computer to start up and the partition table describing the organization of the hard drive.

Sedona Conference

Boot sector virus

A virus that plants itself in a system's boot sector and infects the master boot record.

NIST 800 series

Border router

See external router.

ISACA

Borrowing authority

Statutory authority that permits obligations to be incurred but requires that funds be borrowed to liquidate the obligations (see title 7 of the GAO Policies and Procedures Manual for Guidance of Federal Agencies). Usually, the amount that may be borrowed and the purposes for which the borrowed funds must be used are stipulated by the authorizing statute. Borrowing authority sometimes is referred to as back door authority.

GAO/PCIE Financial Audit Manual

Boston Computer Society (BCS)

Boston Computer Society, one of the first associations of PC/Apple users and one of the largest and most active.

Sedona Conference

Boundary

A definition that indicates or fixes a limit or extent. See also system boundaries. The software, hardware, or physical barrier that limits access to a system or part of a system.

de facto, US National Information Assurance (IA) Glossary

Boundary protection

Monitoring and control of communications at the external boundary between information systems completely under the management and control of the organization and information systems not completely under the management and control of the organization, and at key internal boundaries between information systems completely under the management and control of the organization, to prevent and detect malicious and other unauthorized communication, employing controlled interfaces (e.g., proxies, gateways, routers, firewalls, encrypted tunnels).

NIST 800 series

Boundary router

A boundary router is located at the organizations boundary to an external network.

NIST 800 series

Brainstorming

A technique that helps a team to generate ideas. Ideas are not reviewed during the brainstorming session, but at a later stage. Brainstorming is often used by problem management to identify possible causes.

ITIL

Breach

The circumvention of some element of computer security, with or without detection, which could result in a penetration of the affected computer's software or databases, another device or the network to which the affected computer may be connected.

Centers for Medicare & Medicaid Services (CMS), ISO/IEC 27001:2005

Brevity list

List containing words and phrases used to shorten messages.

US National Information Assurance (IA) Glossary

Bridge

A device that allows two networks, even ones dissimilar in topology, wiring, or communications protocols, to exchange data. In modern network design, bridges have been replaced with hubs and switches.

FISCAM, ISACA

British Standards Institute or Bundesamt für Sicherheit in der Informationstechnik (BSI)

See British Standards Institute, Bundesamt für Sicherheit in der Informationstechnik

de facto

British Standards Institution

The UK national standards body, responsible for creating and maintaining British standards. See also ISO, and http://www.bsi-global.com for more information.

ITIL

Broadband

Communications of high capacity and usually of multimedia content. In broadband, multiple channels are formed by dividing the transmission medium into discrete frequency segments. It generally requires the use of a modem.

ISACA, Sedona Conference

Broker-Dealer

A broker/dealer is any individual or firm in the business of buying or selling securities for itself and others.

17 CFR 240.17a-3 & 4

Brouters

Devices that perform the functions of both bridges and routers, are called brouters. Naturally, they operate at both the data link and the network layers. A brouter connects same data link type LAN segments as well as different data link ones, which is a significant advantage. Like a bridge it forwards packets based on the data link layer address to a different network of the same type.

Also, whenever required, it processes and forwards messages to a different data link type network based on the network protocol address. When connecting same data link type networks, they are as fast as bridges besides being able to connect different data link type networks.

ISACA

Browser

A computer program that enables the user to retrieve information that has been made publicly available on the Internet; also, that permits multimedia (graphics) applications on the World Wide Web. Not to be confused with browsing.

ISACA, Sedona Conference

Browsing

The act of electronically perusing files and records without authorization. The act of searching through storage to locate or acquire information without necessarily knowing of the existence or the format of the information being sought.

FISCAM, Centers for Medicare & Medicaid Services (CMS), US National Information Assurance (IA) Glossary

Brute force

The name given to a class of algorithms that repeatedly try all possible combinations until a solution is found.

ISACA

Brute force password attack

A method of accessing an obstructed device through attempting multiple combinations of numeric and/or alphanumeric passwords.

NIST 800 series

BS 15000

British Standards Institution specification and code of practice for IT service management. BS 15000 is based on ITIL best practice and has been superseded by ISO/IEC 20000.

ITIL

BS 7799

British Standards Institution specification and code of practice for information security management. BS 7799 has been superseded by ISO/IEC 17799 and ISO/IEC 27001.

ITIL

Budget

Estimated cost and revenue amounts for a given range of periods and set of books. Within the realm of financial management, a list of all the money an organization or business unit plans to receive, and plans to pay out, over a specified period of time. There can be multiple budget versions for the same set of books. See also budgeting, planning.

ISACA, ITIL

Budget authority

Authority provided by law 1) to enter into obligations that will result in immediate or future outlays involving government funds or 2) to collect offsetting receipts (2 U.S.C. 622(2)). The Congress provides an organization with budget authority and may place restrictions on the amount, purpose, and timing of the obligation or expenditure of such authority. The three forms of budget authority are appropriations, borrowing authority, contract authority.

GAO/PCIE Financial Audit Manual

Budget controls

Management's policies and procedures to manage and control the use of appropriated funds and other forms of budget authority. These are considered part of financial reporting and compliance controls.

GAO/PCIE Financial Audit Manual

Budget formula

A mathematical expression used to calculate budget amounts based on actual results, other budget amounts, and statistics. With budget formulas, budgets using complex equations, calculations, and allocations can be automatically created.

ISACA

Budget functional classification

A way of grouping budgetary resources so that all budget authority and outlays of on-budget and off-budget federal organizations and tax expenditures can be presented according to national needs being addressed. To the extent feasible, functional classifications are made without regard to organization or organizational distinctions.

GAO/PCIE Financial Audit Manual

Budget hierarchy

A group of budgets linked together at different levels such that the budgeting authority of a lower-level budget is controlled by an upper-level budget.

ISACA

Budget organization

An entity (department, cost center, division, or other group) responsible for entering and maintaining budget data.

ISACA

Budgeting

Within financial management, the activity of predicting and controlling the spending of money. Consists of a periodic negotiation cycle to set future budgets (usually annual) and the day-to-day monitoring and adjusting of current budgets. See also accounting period.

ITIL

Buffer

Memory reserved to temporarily hold data. Buffers are used to offset differences between the operating speeds of different devices, such as a printer and a computer. In a program, buffers are reserved areas of RAM that hold data while they are being processed.

ISACA

Buffer overflow

A condition at an interface under which more input can be placed into a buffer or data holding area than the capacity allocated, overwriting other information. Attackers exploit such a condition to crash a system or to insert specially crafted code that allows them to gain control of the system.

NIST 800 series

Buffer overflow attack

A method of overloading a predefined amount of space in a buffer, which can potentially overwrite and corrupt data in memory.

NIST 800 series

Bug

A flaw in a computer program that causes it to produce incorrect or inappropriate results.

FISCAM, Sedona Conference

Build

A part of release management, the activity of assembling a number of configuration items to create part of an IT service. The term build is also used to refer to a release that is authorized for distribution. For example, server build or laptop build. See also assembly CI.

ITIL

Build environment

A part of release management, a controlled environment where applications, IT services and other builds are assembled prior to being moved into a test or live environment.

ITIL

Bulk data transfer

A data recovery strategy that includes a recovery from complete backups that are physically shipped off site once a week. Specifically, logs are batched electronically several times daily, and then loaded into a tape library located at the same facility as the planned recovery.

ISACA

Bulk encryption

Simultaneous encryption of all channels of a multichannel telecommunications link.

US National Information Assurance (IA) Glossary

Bulletin Board System (BBS)

A computer system or service that users access to participate in electronic discussion groups, post messages and/or download files.

Sedona Conference

Bundesamt für Sicherheit in der Informationstechnik

The central IT security service provider for the German government. The BSI's services and products are aimed at the users and manufacturers of information technology products. Those are primarily the public administration at federal, state and municipal level, in addition companies and private users. As Germany's National Security Agency, it is their goal to promote IT security in Germany so that everyone can make the most of the opportunities opened up by the information society. See also http://www.bsi.de for more information.

de facto

Burn

The process of a creating a copy of information onto a CD or DVD. Bus:A parallel circuit that connects the major components of a computer, allowing the transfer of electric impulses from one connected component to any other.

Sedona Conference

Bus

Common path or channel between hardware devices. It can be between components internal to a computer or between external computers in a communications network.

ISACA, ISO/IEC 27001:2005

Bus topology

A type of local area network (LAN) architecture in which each station is directly attached to a common communication channel. Signals transmitted over the channel take the form of messages. As each message passes along the channel, each station receives it. Each station then determines, based on an address contained in the message, whether to accept and process the message or simply to ignore it.

ISACA

Business

An overall corporate entity or organization formed of a number of business units. In the context of IT Service Management, the term business includes public sector and not-for-profit organizations, as well as companies. An IT service provider provides IT services to a customer within a business. The IT service provider may be part of the same business as their customer (internal service provider), or part of another business (external service provider).

ITIL

Business activity

An umbrella term covering all the functions, processes, activities, and transactions of an organization and its employees. It includes public administration as well as commercial business. Note: This term is distinguished from "Activity" which is used to denote a specific activity carried out within the scope of each of the functions carried out by one organization.

DIRKS

Business associate

A person or organization that performs a function or activity on behalf of a CE but is not part of the CE's workforce. See also third party.

HIPAA

Business Case Analysis (BCA)

The analysis establishes sound business reasons for proceeding with a project by providing insight into how the project supports business needs and the strategic goals of CMS. The BCA describes how the project aligns with CMS's information technology architecture and identifies the project's assumptions and constraints. The BCA identifies the gap between current capability and new business needs, discusses alternatives for accomplishing the project, contains a cost/benefit analysis that is consistent with the preferred alternative, and presents a high-level logical design. The design verifies that the proposed solution will be compatible with the CMS architecture and begins to establish the impact of the project on the infrastructure. The BCA next provides an assessment of business risks, describes the acquisition strategy, and outlines the project plan. Finally, an appendix containing the documented and validated user and system requirements shall be included. Additional details of the alternatives analysis may also be included as an appendix, if necessary.

Centers for Medicare & Medicaid Services (CMS)

Business classification scheme

An articulation of the functions and activities of the organization derived from the analysis of business activity. The business classification scheme contains terms and scope notes that represent and describe functions, activities, transactions, or other elements, and shows their relationships. The number of levels within the scheme can vary depending on the level of refinement required and how the scheme will be used. The structure of the scheme is hierarchical, moving from the general to the specific. Each function has activities that are identified in relation to it, and each activity (linked to the function) has categories of transactions that are encountered.

DIRKS

Business continuity

The strategic and tactical capability, pre-approved by management, of an organization to plan for and respond to incidents and business interruptions in order to continue business operations at an acceptable predefined level.

BS 25999

Business Continuity & Contingency Planning (BCCP)

The act of creating a business continuity or contingency plan. See also business continuity management, business continuity planning.

Centers for Medicare & Medicaid Services (CMS)

Business Continuity Institute (BCI)

The Business Continuity Institute (BCI) was established in 1994 to enable members to obtain guidance and support from fellow business continuity practitioners. The role of the BCI is to promote the highest standards of professional competence and commercial ethics in the provision and maintenance of business continuity planning and services. See also http://www.thebci.org for more information.

de facto

Business Continuity Management (BCM)

A part of IT service continuity management, business continuity management is the business process which sets the objectives, scope and requirements for IT service continuity management. BCM is responsible for managing risks that could seriously impact the business. BCM ensures that the business can always operate to a minimum agreed level, by reducing the risk to an acceptable level and planning to restore business processes.

ITIL, PAS 56, BS 25999

Business continuity management lifecycle

The series of business continuity activities which collectively cover all aspects and phases of the business continuity management program.

BS 25999

Business continuity management program

See business continuity management.

BS 25999

Business Continuity Plan (BCP)

A plan for emergency response, backup operations, and post disaster recovery maintained by an activity as a part of its security program that will ensure the availability of critical resources and facilitate continuity of operations in emergency situations. The plan will also identify the triggers for invocation, people to be involved, communications etc. IT service continuity plans form a significant part of business continuity plans. See also business continuity management.

Centers for Medicare & Medicaid Services (CMS), ITIL, BS 25999, NIST 800 Series

Business continuity planning

Advance planning and preparation which is necessary to identify the impact of potential losses, to formulate and implement viable continuity strategies, and to develop continuity plan(s) which ensure continuity of organizational services in the event of an incident. The deliverable from business continuity planning is a business continuity plan (BCP) which is a documented collection of procedures and information that is developed, compiled and maintained in readiness for use in an incident.

PAS 56

Business continuity strategy

An approach by an organization that will ensure its recovery and continuity in the face of a disaster or other major incident or business interruption.

BS 25999

Business continuity team

A part of IT service continuity management. The team of people responsible for carrying out activities defined in a business continuity plan.

ITIL

Business customer

See customer.

de facto, ITIL

Business driver

Something that influences the definition of business objectives and strategy. For example, new legislation or the actions of competitors. The term business driver is sometimes used as a synonym for business objective or strategy.

ITIL

Business Impact Analysis (BIA)

An exercise that determines the impact of losing the support of any resource to an organization and establishes the escalation of that loss over time, identifying the minimum resources needed to recover and prioritizes the recovery of processes and supporting systems. The process involves identifying vital business functions and their dependencies. These dependencies may include suppliers, people, other business processes, IT services, etc. The BIA also defines the recovery requirements for IT services. These requirements include recovery time objectives, recovery point objectives, and minimum service level targets for each IT service.

NIST 800 Series

Business interruption

An event, whether anticipated (e.g., a public service strike or hurricane) or unanticipated (e.g. a blackout or earthquake), which disrupts the normal course of business operations.

BS 25999

Business IT Alignment (BITA)

Understanding how the IT service provider provides value to the business, and ensuring that IT strategy, plans, and services support the business objectives, and vision. See also service culture.

ITIL

Business objectives

The objective of a business process, or of the business as a whole. Business objectives support the business vision, provide guidance for the IT strategy, and are often supported by IT services.

ITIL

Business operations

The day-to-day execution, monitoring and management of business processes. See also operate.

ITIL

Business owner or partner

The entity or entities responsible for defining, promoting, endorsing and upholding the business needs and user requirements for the system, and for performing user acceptance testing of the final product(s) based on those business needs and user requirements. The business owner/partner defines and validates system functionality, access rights, business rules, and the privacy classification, timeliness, completeness, and accuracy of data.

Centers for Medicare & Medicaid Services (CMS)

Business perspective

An understanding of the service provider and IT services from the point of view of the business, and an understanding of the business from the point of view of the service provider. See also business IT alignment.

ITIL

Business process

See process.

CobiT, ISO/IEC 27001:2005, ITIL

Business Process Analysis (BPA)

A means of analyzing current and future business processes and document the activities, offices, and documents which are part of the process.

de facto

Business Process Automation (BPA)

The process of integrating enterprise applications, reducing human intervention wherever possible, and assembling software services into end-to-end process flows. As a significant part of business process reengineering, BPA improves operational efficiencies and reduces risks. BPA is made possible through enterprise application integration and service-oriented architecture solutions.

AIIM, Wikipedia

Business Process Integration (BPI)

AIIM

Business process integrity

Controls over the business processes that are supported by the ERP.

ISACA

Business Process Management (BPM)

AIIM

Business Process Modeling Language (BPML)

AIIM

Business Process Outsourcing (BPO)

Business process outsourcing occurs when an organization turns over the management of a business function, such as accounts payable, purchasing, payroll or information technology to a third party.

AIIM, Sedona Conference

Business Process Reengineering (BPR)

Modern expression for organizational development stemming from IS/IT impacts. The ultimate goal of BPR is to yield a better performing structure, more responsive to the customer base and market conditions, while yielding material cost savings. To reengineer means to redesign a structure and procedures with intelligence and skills, while being well informed about all of the attendant factors of a given situation, so as to obtain the maximum benefits from mechanization as basic rationale.

ISACA, AIIM

Business Recovery-Resumption Plan (BRP)

The documentation of a predetermined set of instructions or procedures that describe how business processes will be restored after a significant disruption has occurred.

NIST 800 series

Business Relationship Management (BRM)

The process responsible for maintaining a relationship with the business. This process usually includes: 1) Managing personal relationships with business managers. 2) Portfolio management. 3) Ensuring that the IT service provider is satisfying the business needs of the customers. This process has strong links with service level management. See also account manager.

ITIL

Business relationship manager

A part of business relationship management, a role responsible for maintaining the relationship with one or more customers. This role is often combined with the service level manager role. See also account manager.

ITIL

Business response work area

Work space shared by a limited number of organizations that require facilities to be obtained and installed for recovery.

PAS 56

Business risk

Risks that could impact the organization's ability to perform business or provide a service. They can be financial, regulatory, or control oriented.

ISACA, ISO/IEC 27001:2005, PAS 56

Business Roundtable (BR)

Business Roundtable is an association of chief executive officers of leading US companies with over $4.5 trillion in annual revenues and more than 10 million employees. Member companies comprise nearly a third of the total value of the US stock market and represent nearly a third of all corporate income taxes paid to the federal government. See also http://www.businessroundtable.org for more information.

de facto

Business service

A service that is delivered to business customers by business units. For example, delivery of financial services to customers of a bank, or goods to the customers of a retail store. Successful delivery of business services often depends on one or more IT services.

ITIL

Business Service Provider (BSP)

An ASP that also provides outsourcing of business processes such as payment processing, sales order processing, and application development.

ISACA, AIIM

Business Software Alliance (BSA)

BSA is the foremost organization dedicated to promoting a globally robust, competitive and innovative computer industry. BSA policy issues include strengthening intellectual property protections, patent reform, fostering trust in the Internet and e-commerce, and assuring open international marketplaces through pro-growth business policies. See also http://www.bsa.org/globalhome.cfm for more information.

de facto

Business system

A system designed to enable the realization of desired business outcomes and outputs through the efficient management and facilitation of interrelated business processes.

DIRKS

Business to business (B2B)

The exchange of products, services, or information between businesses rather than between businesses and consumers. See also business to consumer.

de facto, AIIM

Business to consumer (B2C)

Business-to-consumer electronic commerce. This is used when referring a business which sells its products or services to a consumer. See also business to business.

ISACA, US National Information Assurance (IA) Glossary, AIIM

Business to consumer e-commerce

Refers to the processes by which organizations conduct business electronically with their customers and or public at large using the Internet as the enabling technology.

ISACA

Business to employee (B2E)

Business-to-employee information sharing.

AIIM

Business unit

A segment of the business which has its own plans, metrics, income, and costs.

ITIL

Bypass label processing (BLP)

A technique of reading a computer file while bypassing the internal file/data set label. This process could result in bypassing security access controls.

ISACA, FISCAM

C

Cache

A dedicated, high speed storage location which can be used for the temporary storage of frequently used data. As data may be retrieved more quickly from cache than the original storage location, cache allows applications to run more quickly. Web site contents often reside in cached storage locations on a hard drive.

Sedona Conference

Caching

The temporary storage of frequently used data to speed access. See also Cache.

Sedona Conference

Cadbury

The Committee on the Financial Aspects of Corporate Governance, set up in May 1991 by the UK Financial Reporting Council, the London Stock Exchange and the UK accountancy profession, was chaired by Sir Adrian Cadbury and produced a report on the subject commonly known, in the UK, as the Cadbury Report.

ISACA

Call

A part of the service desk and incident management, a telephone call to the service desk from a user. A call could result in an incident or a service request being logged.

ITIL

Call back

Procedure for identifying and authenticating a remote IS terminal, whereby the host system disconnects the terminal and reestablishes contact. Also known as dial back

US National Information Assurance (IA) Glossary

Call center

A part of the service desk, the organization or business unit which handles large numbers of incoming and outgoing telephone calls. See also service desk.

ITIL

Call or Call Center response

A response to a merchant's authorization request indicating that the card issuer needs more information about the card or cardholder before a transaction can be approved; also called a referral response.

VISA Glossary of Terms

Call type

A part of the service desk, a category that is used to distinguish incoming requests to a service desk. Common call types are incident, service request, and complaint.

ITIL

Canadian Institute of Chartered Accountants (CICA)

The CICA, together with the CA institutes/ordre, represents approximately 70,000 CAs and 8,500 students in Canada and Bermuda. The CICA conducts research into current business issues and supports the setting of accounting, auditing and assurance standards for business, not-for-profit organizations and government. It issues guidance on control and governance, publishes professional literature, develops continuing education programs and represents the CA profession nationally and internationally. See also http://www.cica.ca for more information.

de facto

Canister

Type of protective package used to contain and dispense keying material in punched or printed tape form.

US National Information Assurance (IA) Glossary

Capability

Having the needed attributes to perform or accomplish.

CobiT, ISO/IEC 27001:2005

Capability Maturity Model (CMM)

The Capability Maturity Model for Software (CMM), from the Software Engineering Institute (SEI) at Carnegie Melon University, is a model used by many organizations to identify best practices useful in helping them assess and increase the maturity of their software development processes. In 2000, the SW-CMM was upgraded to CMMI (Capability Maturity Model Integration). The SEI no longer maintains the SW-CMM model, its associated appraisal methods, or training materials. See also capability maturity model integration.

CobiT, ITIL

Capability Maturity Model Integration (CMMI)

A process improvement approach developed by the Software Engineering Institute (SEI) of Carnegie Mellon university. CMMI provides organizations with the essential elements of effective processes. It can be used to guide process improvement across a project, a division, or an entire organization. CMMI helps integrate traditionally separate organizational functions, set process improvement goals and priorities, provide guidance for quality processes, and provide a point of reference for appraising current processes. See also CMM, continuous improvement, process maturity, and http://www.sei.cmu.edu/cmmi/ for more information.

ITIL

Capacity

The maximum throughput that a configuration item or IT service can deliver whilst meeting agreed service level targets. For some types of CI, capacity may be the size or volume, for example, a disk drive.

ITIL

Capacity management

The process responsible for ensuring that the capacity of IT services and the IT infrastructure is able to deliver agreed service level targets in a cost effective and timely manner. Capacity management considers all resources required to deliver the IT service, and plans for short, medium and long term business requirements.

ITIL

Capacity Management Database (CDB)

A database containing all data needed to support capacity management. The capacity management database is usually separate from the configuration management database (CMDB) because it contains large amounts of rapidly changing data.

ITIL

Capacity plan

A capacity plan is used to manage the resources required to deliver IT services. The plan contains scenarios for different predictions of business demand, and costed options to deliver the agreed service level targets. See also capacity planning.

ITIL

Capacity planning

A part of capacity management, the activity within capacity management responsible for creating a capacity plan.

ITIL

Capacity stress testing

Testing an application with large quantities of data to evaluate its performance during peak periods. It also is called volume testing.

ISACA

Capacity to download indexes and records

The source of confusion with this requirement is the definition of an "index". This is because the business indices (Social Security Number), the ones easiest for the examiners to use and understand, are used by many applications and are, by necessity, stored in a format that allows changes. Thus, high-level indices and record retention have mutually exclusive requirements. Compliance with the index rule can be demonstrated by printing the record and highest level system index stored on the compliant medium, specifically, the pathname on Windows and Unix systems, and the dataset name and volume ID on mainframe and database systems.

17 CFR 240.17a-4

Capital costs

A part of financial management, the cost of purchasing something that will become a financial asset, for example, computer equipment and buildings. The value of the asset is depreciated over multiple accounting periods. See also operational cost.

ITIL

Capital Expenditure (CAPEX)

See capital cost.

ITIL

Capital item

A part of financial management) synonym for an asset that is of interest to financial management because it is above an agreed financial value.

ITIL

Capitalization

A part of financial management, identifying major cost as capital, even though no asset is purchased. This is done to spread the impact of the cost over multiple accounting periods. The most common example of this is software development or purchase of a software license.

ITIL

Capture

A deliberate action which results in the registration of a record into a recordkeeping system. For certain business activities, this action may be designed into electronic systems so that the capture of records is concurrent with the creation of records. It can also denote the method of taking a biometric sample from an end user.

DIRKS, NIST 800 Series

Card expiration date

See Good Thru date.

VISA Glossary of Terms

Card issuer

A financial institution that issues credit cards.

VISA Glossary of Terms

Card security features

The alphanumeric, pictorial, and other design elements that appear on the front and back of all valid Visa credit and debit cards. Card-present merchants must check these features when processing a transaction at the point of sale to ensure that a card is valid.

VISA Glossary of Terms

Card swipes

A physical control technique that uses a secured card or ID to gain access to a highly sensitive location. Card swipes, if built correctly, act as a preventative control over physical access to those sensitive locations. After a card has been swiped, the application attached to the physical card swipe device logs all card users that try to access the secured location. The card swipe device prevents unauthorized access and logs all attempts to enter the secured location.

ISACA

Card validation code (CVC)

The three-digit value printed on the signature panel of a payment card used to verify card-not-present transactions. On a MasterCard payment card this is called CVC2. On a Visa payment card this is called CVV2. See also Card Verification Value 2.

PCI-DSS

Card Verification Value 2 (CVV2)

A credit card fraud prevention system used in card-not-present transactions to ensure that the card is valid. The CVV2 is the three-digit value that is printed on the back of all Visa cards. Card-not-present merchants ask the customer for the CVV2 and submit it as part of their authorization request. For information security purposes, merchants are prohibited from storing CVV2 data.

Card-not-present

A merchant, market, or sales environment in which transactions are completed without a valid credit card or cardholder being present. Card-not-present is used to refer to mail order, telephone order, and Internet merchants and sales environments.

VISA Glossary of Terms

Card-present

A merchant, market or sales environment in which transactions can be completed only if both a valid credit card and cardholder are present. Card-present transactions include traditional retail-department and grocery stores, electronics stores, boutiques, etc.-cash disbursements, and self-service situations, such as gas stations and grocery stores, where cardholders use unattended payment devices.

VISA Glossary of Terms

Cardholder

The customer to whom a card has been issued or the individual authorized to use the card. See also customer. An individual possessing an issued Personal Identity Verification (PIV) card.

PCI-DSS, VISA Glossary of Terms, FIPS Pubs, NIST 800 Series

Cardholder data

All personally identifiable data about the cardholder and relationship to the member (i.e., account number, expiration date, data provided by the member, other electronic data gathered by the merchant/agent, and so on). This term also accounts for other personal insights gathered about the cardholder (i.e., addresses, telephone numbers, and so on). See also confidential information.

PCI-DSS

Cardholder data environment

Area of computer system network that possesses cardholder data or sensitive authentication data and those systems and segments that directly attach or support cardholder processing, storage, or transmission. Adequate network segmentation, which isolates systems that store, process, or transmit cardholder data from those that do not, may reduce the scope of the cardholder data environment and thus the scope of the PCI assessment.

PCI-DSS

Cardholder Information Security Program (CISP)

A Visa program that establishes data security standards, procedures, and tools for all entities-merchants, service providers, issuers, and merchant banks-that store Visa cardholder account information. CISP compliance is mandatory.

Visa CISP, VISA Glossary of Terms

Carnegie Mellon University (CMU)

Some of the Software Engineering Institute (SEI). See also http://www.cmu.edu for more information.

de facto

Carrier sense multiple access/collision detection (CSMA/CD)

de facto

Cascading

Downward flow of information through a range of security levels greater than the accreditation range of a system network or component.

US National Information Assurance (IA) Glossary

Case deduplication

Eliminates duplicates to retain only one copy of each document per case. For example, if an identical document resides with three custodians, only the first custodian's copy will be saved. See also Deduplication.

Sedona Conference

Case study

See nonsampling selection.

GAO/PCIE Financial Audit Manual

Cash disbursement

A bankcard transaction involving the payment of cash or travelers cheques to a cardholder. In general, only financial institution branches are allowed to make cash disbursements.

VISA Glossary of Terms

Catalog

See Index.

Sedona Conference

Catalog of practices

A collection of good strategic and operational security practices that an organization can use to manage its security.

CERT OCTAVE

Catalog of vulnerabilities

A collection of vulnerabilities based on platform and application. It is used to evaluate an organization's computing infrastructure for technology vulnerabilities.

CERT OCTAVE

Categorization

Organizing documents, Web pages, and other content into logical groupings based on their contents.

AIIM

Category

A named group of things that have something in common. Categories are used to group similar things together. For example, cost types are used to group similar types of cost. Incident categories are used to group similar types of incident, CI types are used to group similar types of configuration items. Alternately, a restrictive label applied to classified or unclassified information to limit access.

ITIL, US National Information Assurance (IA) Glossary

Cathode Ray Tube (CRT)

A vacuum tube that displays data by means of an electron beam striking the screen which is coated with suitable phosphor material, or a device similar to a television screen upon which data can be displayed.

ISACA, Sedona Conference

Cause and effect basis

In cost accounting, a way to group costs into cost pools in which an intermediate activity may be a link between the cause and the effect.

GAO/PCIE Financial Audit Manual

Cause and effect diagram

In problem management, a technique that helps a team to identify all the possible causes of an effect, such as a problem. Originally devised by Kaoru Ishikawa and often called an Ishikawa diagram, the output of this technique is a diagram that looks like a fishbone.

ITIL

CCI assembly

Device embodying a cryptographic logic or other COMSEC design that NSA has approved as a Controlled Cryptographic Item (CCI). It performs the entire COMSEC function, but depends upon the host equipment to operate.

US National Information Assurance (IA) Glossary

CCI component

Part of a Controlled Cryptographic Item (CCI) that does not perform the entire COMSEC function but depends upon the host equipment, or assembly, to complete and operate the COMSEC function.

US National Information Assurance (IA) Glossary

CCI equipment

Telecommunications or information handling equipment that embodies a Controlled Cryptographic Item (CCI) component or CCI assembly and performs the entire COMSEC function without dependence on host equipment to operate.

US National Information Assurance (IA) Glossary

CCITT Group 4

A lossless compression technique/format that reduces the size of a file, generally about 5:1 over RLE and 40:1 over bitmap. CCITT Group 4 compression may only be used for bi-tonal images.

Sedona Conference

CCTA Risk Analysis & Management Method (CRAMM)

A methodology and tool for analyzing and managing risks. CRAMM was developed by the UK government, but is now privately owned. Further information is available from http://www.cramm.com/.

ITIL

Cellular Digital Packet Data (CDPD)

A data communication standard utilizing the unused capacity of cellular voice providers to transfer data.

Sedona Conference

Center for Internet Security (CIS)

The Center for Internet Security (CIS) is a non-profit enterprise whose mission is to help organizations reduce the risk of business and e-commerce disruptions resulting from inadequate technical security controls. Click Here to learn more about CIS's mission. See also http://www.cisecurity.org for more information.

de facto, PCI-DSS

Centers for Medicare & Medicaid Services (CMS)

US federal agency which administers Medicare, Medicaid, and the State Children's Health Insurance. See also http://www.cms.hhs.gov for more information.

Centers for Medicare & Medicaid Services (CMS)

Central Communications and Telecommunications Agency (CCTA)

The original author of ITIL. This organization no longer exists and its functions are now carried out by of the Office of Government Commerce (OGC).

ITIL

Central Office (CO)

A telecommunications carrier's facilities in a local area in which service is provided where local service is switched to long distance.

ISACA

Central Office of Record (COR)

Office of a federal department or agency that keeps (COR) records of accountable COMSEC material held by elements subject to its oversight.

US National Information Assurance (IA) Glossary

Central processing unit (CPU)

The computational and control unit of a computer; the device that interprets and executes instructions. The primary silicon chip that runs a computer's operating system and application software. It performs a computer's essential mathematical functions and controls essential operations.

FISCAM, Sedona Conference

Centralized data processing

Identified by one central processor and databases that form a distributed processing configuration.

ISACA

Centronics interface

A parallel interface standard for connecting printers and other devices to computers.

Sedona Conference

CERT Coordination Center (CERT/CC)

The CERT Coordination Center (CERT/CC) is a center of Internet security expertise. It is located at the Software Engineering Institute, a federally funded research and development center operated by Carnegie Mellon University. The CERT/CC studies Internet security vulnerabilities, handles computer security incidents, publishes a variety of security alerts, does research for long-term changes in networked systems, and develops information and training to help improve security. See also http://www.cert.org for more information.

de facto

Certificate

Security information electronically signed by an authority and used as identification. Digitally signed document that binds a public key with an identity. The certificate contains a digital representation of information which at least 1) identifies the certification authority issuing it, 2) names or identifies its subscriber, 3) contains the subscriber's public key, 4) identifies its operational period, and 5) is digitally signed by the certification authority issuing it.

Centers for Medicare & Medicaid Services (CMS), US National Information Assurance (IA) Glossary, Sedona Conference, NIST 800 Series

Certificate authority (CA)

A trusted third party that issues and maintains digital certificates. By digitally signing each certificate issued, the user's identity is certified, and the association of the certified identity with a public key is validated. Also the official responsible for performing the comprehensive evaluation of the security features of an information system and determining the degree to which it meets its security requirements.

ISACA, US National Information Assurance (IA) Glossary

Certificate management

Process whereby certificates (as defined above) are generated, stored, protected, transferred, loaded, used, and destroyed.

US National Information Assurance (IA) Glossary

Certificate Management Authority (CMA)

A Certification Authority (CA) or a Registration Authority (RA).

NIST 800 series

Certificate Policy (CP)

A Certificate Policy is a specialized form of administrative policy tuned to electronic transactions performed during certificate management. A Certificate Policy addresses all aspects associated with the generation, production, distribution, accounting, compromise recovery and administration of digital certificates. Indirectly, a certificate policy can also govern the transactions conducted using a communications system protected by a certificate-based security system. By controlling critical certificate extensions, such policies and associated enforcement technology can support provision of the security services required by particular applications.

NIST 800 series

Certificate repository

A database, such as an LDAP directory, that stores individuals' digital certificates.

Network Frontiers

Certificate Revocation List (CRL)

A list of retracted but un-expired certificates. A list of revoked public key certificates created and digitally signed by a Certification Authority.

ISACA, US National Information Assurance (IA) Glossary, NIST 800 Series

Certificate status authority

A trusted entity that provides on-line verification to a Relying Party of a subject certificate's trustworthiness, and may also provide additional attribute information for the subject certificate.

NIST 800 series

Certificate-related information

Information, such as a subscriber's postal address, that is not included in a certificate. May be used by a Certification Authority (CA) managing certificates.

NIST 800 series

Certification

CMS defines this as a technical evaluation of a sensitive application to see how well it meets security requirements. The general definition is of a formal process by which an agency official verifies, initially or by periodic reassessment, that a system's security features meet a set of specified requirements. The formal process includes a comprehensive assessment of the management, operational, and technical security controls in an information system, made in support of security accreditation, to determine the extent to which the controls are implemented correctly, operating as intended, and producing the desired outcome with respect to meeting the security requirements for the system. The term certification is also used to mean awarding a certificate to verify that a person has achieved a qualification.

Centers for Medicare & Medicaid Services (CMS), FIPS Pubs, ITIL, Workgroup for Electronic Data Interchange, US National Information Assurance (IA) Glossary, NIST 800 Series

Certification agent

The individual, group, or organization responsible for conducting a security certification.

NIST 800 series

Certification and accreditation

A comprehensive assessment of the management, operational, and technical security controls in an information system, made in support of security accreditation, to determine the extent to which the controls are implemented correctly, operating as intended, and producing the desired outcome with respect to meeting the security requirements for the system. Accreditation is the official management decision given by a senior agency official to authorize operation of an information system and to explicitly accept the risk to agency operations (including mission, functions, image, or reputation), agency assets, or individuals, based on the implementation of an agreed-upon set of security controls.

NIST 800 series

Certification authority

A trusted entity that issues and revokes public key certificates. The entity in a public key infrastructure (PKI) that is responsible for issuing certificates and exacting compliance to a PKI policy.

NIST 800 series, FIPS Pubs

Certification authority facility

The collection of equipment, personnel, procedures and structures that are used by a Certification Authority to perform certificate issuance and revocation.

NIST 800 series

Certification Authority Workstation (CAW)

Commercial-off-the-shelf (COTS) workstation with a trusted operating system and special purpose application software that is used to issue certificates.

US National Information Assurance (IA) Glossary

Certification package

Product of the certification effort documenting the detailed results of the certification activities.

US National Information Assurance (IA) Glossary

Certification Practice Statement (CPS)

A statement of the practices that a Certification Authority employs in issuing, suspending, revoking and renewing certificates and providing access to them, in accordance with specific requirements (i.e., requirements specified in this Certificate Policy, or requirements specified in a contract for services).

NIST 800 series

Certification Test and Evaluation (CT&E)

Software and hardware security tests conducted during development of an IS.

US National Information Assurance (IA) Glossary

Certified Document Imaging Architect (CDIA)

AIIM

Certified TEMPEST Technical Authority (CTTA)

An experienced, technically qualified US Government employee who has met established certification requirements in accordance with CNSS (NSTISSC)-approved criteria and has been appointed by a US Government Department or Agency to fulfill CTTA responsibilities.

US National Information Assurance (IA) Glossary

Certifier

Individual responsible for making a technical judgment of the system's compliance with stated requirements, identifying and assessing the risks associated with operating the system, coordinating the certification activities, and consolidating the final certification and accreditation packages.

US National Information Assurance (IA) Glossary

Chaff/winnowing

Advanced encryption technique involving data dispersal and mixing.

Sedona Conference

Chain of custody

Documentation and testimony regarding the possession, movement, handling and location of evidence from the time it is obtained to the time it is presented in court; used to prove that evidence has not been altered or tampered with in any way; necessary both to assure admissibility and probative value.

Sedona Conference, NIST 800 Series

Challenge and reply authentication

Prearranged procedure in which a subject requests authentication of another and the latter establishes validity with a correct reply. See also challenge/response token.

US National Information Assurance (IA) Glossary

Challenge Handshake Authentication Protocol (CHAP)

ISACA

Challenge-response protocol

An authentication protocol where the verifier sends the claimant a challenge (usually a random value or a nonce) that the claimant combines with a shared secret (often by hashing the challenge and secret together) to generate a response that is sent to the verifier. The verifier knows the shared secret and can independently compute the

response and compare it with the response generated by the claimant. If the two are the same, the claimant is considered to have successfully authenticated himself. When the shared secret is a cryptographic key, such protocols are generally secure against eavesdroppers. When the shared secret is a password, an eavesdropper does not directly intercept the password itself, but the eavesdropper may be able to find the password with an off-line password guessing attack.

NIST 800 series

Challenge/Response

An authentication process where the system prompts (the challenge) users to provide a password, code or pass phrase (the response). See also challenge/response token.

Network Frontiers

Challenge/response token

A method of user authentication. Challenge response authentication is carried out through use of the Challenge Handshake Authentication Protocol (CHAP). When a user tries to log into the server, the server sends the user a "challenge," which is a random value. The user enters a password, which is used as an encryption key to encrypt the "challenge" and return it to the server. The server is aware of the password. It, therefore, encrypts the "challenge" value and compares it with the value received from the user. If the values match, the user is authenticated. The challenge/response activity continues throughout the session and this protects the session from password sniffing attacks. In addition, CHAP is not vulnerable to "man in the middle" attacks as the challenge value is a random value that changes on each access attempt.

ISACA

Change

A part of change management, the addition, modification or removal of anything that could have an effect on IT services. The scope should include all configuration items, processes, documentation, etc.

ITIL

Change Advisory Board (CAB)

A group of people that assists the change manager in the assessment, prioritization and scheduling of changes. This board is usually made up of representatives from all areas within the IT service provider, representatives from the business, and third parties such as suppliers.

ITIL

Change Advisory Board Emergency Committee (CAB/EC)

A subset of the Change Advisory Board who make decisions about emergency changes. Membership of the CAB/EC may be decided at the time a meeting is called and depends on the nature of the emergency change.

ITIL

Change history

Information about all changes made to a configuration item during its life. Change history consists of all those change records that apply to the CI.

ITIL

Change management

The process responsible for controlling the lifecycle of all changes. The primary objective of change management is to enable beneficial changes to be made with minimum disruption to IT services.

ITIL

Change model

A repeatable way of dealing with a particular category of change. A change model defines specific pre-defined steps that will be followed for a change of this category. Change models may be very simple, with no requirement for approval (e.g. password reset) or may be very complex with many steps that require approval (e.g. major software release). See also standard change, Change Advisory Board.

ITIL

Change record

A record containing the details of a change. Each change record documents the lifecycle of a single change. A change record is created for every request for change that is received, even those that are subsequently rejected. Change records should reference the configuration items that are affected by the change. Change records are often stored in a configuration management database.

ITIL

Change request

A request to modify any aspect of a system or environment including baseline requirements, hardware, or software. See also request for change.

Centers for Medicare & Medicaid Services (CMS), ITIL

Change schedule

A document that lists all approved changes and their planned implementation dates. A change schedule is sometimes called a forward schedule of change. See also projected service availability (PSA).

ITIL

Change slot

A regular, agreed time when changes may be implemented with minimal impact on services. Change slots are usually documented in SLAs. See also planned downtime.

ITIL

Character treatment

The use of all caps or another standard form of treating letters in a coding project.

Sedona Conference

Characteristic

A characteristic is a definable or measurable feature of a process, an asset, or a system. An example would be the level of impact that a system has on a company, such as a low impact system, medium impact system, or high impact system where the term "low, medium, high" refers to a characteristic of the impact the system has on the organization. Characteristics of controls are used by the authors of the Unified Compliance Framework to define either the uniqueness or commonality of controls when we decide where to place the controls in our harmonized list of all controls.

de facto, Network Frontiers

Characters Per Inch (CPI)

Sedona Conference

Charge Coupled Device (CCD)

A computer chip the output of which correlates with the light or color passed by it. Individual CCDs or arrays of these are used in scanners as a high-resolution, digital camera to read documents.

Sedona Conference

Chargeable item

A deliverable of an IT service that is used in calculating charges to customers. For example, number of transactions, number of desktop PCs.

ITIL

Chargeback

A transaction that is returned as a financial liability to a merchant bank by a card issuer, usually because of a disputed transaction. The merchant bank may then return or "charge back" the transaction to the merchant.

VISA Glossary of Terms

Charging

Requiring payment for IT services. Charging for IT services is optional, and many organizations choose to treat their IT service provider as a cost center. See also charging process, charging policy.

ITIL

Charging policy

A policy specifying the objective of the charging process and the way in which charges will be calculated. See also cost, cost plus, going rate, market rate.

ITIL

Charging process

The process responsible for deciding how much customers should pay (pricing) and recovering money from them (billing).

ITIL

Check digit

A numeric value, which has been calculated mathematically, is added to data to ensure that original data have not been altered or that an incorrect, but valid match has occurred. This control is effective in detecting transposition and transcription errors.

ISACA

Check digit verification

A programmed edit or routine that detects transposition and transcription errors by calculating and checking the check digit.

ISACA

Check word

Cipher text generated by cryptographic logic to detect failures in cryptography.

US National Information Assurance (IA) Glossary

Checklist

A vulnerability evaluation tool that provides the same functionality as automated tools. However, unlike automated tools, checklists are manual, not automated. Checklists require a consistent review of the items being checked and must be routinely updated.

CERT OCTAVE

Checkpoint

The process of saving the current state of a program and its data, including intermediate results to disk or other non-volatile storage, so that if interrupted the program could be restarted at the point at which the last checkpoint occurred.

FISCAM, ISACA, Centers for Medicare & Medicaid Services (CMS)

Checkpoint restart procedures

See checkpoint.

ISACA

Checksum

Value computed on data to detect error or manipulation during transmission. See also hash total.

US National Information Assurance (IA) Glossary

Chief Executive Officer (CEO)

CobiT

Chief Financial Officer (CFO)

GAO/PCIE Financial Audit Manual, CobiT

Chief Information Officer, also, Career Is Over (CIO)

The CIO is responsible for the implementation and administration of the AIS security program within an organization (CMS). FIPS describes the CIO as an agency official responsible for: 1) providing advice and other assistance to the head of the executive agency and other senior management personnel of the agency to ensure that information technology is acquired and information resources are managed in a manner that is consistent with laws, Executive Orders, directives, policies, regulations, and priorities established by the head of the agency; 2) developing, maintaining, and facilitating the implementation of a sound and integrated information technology architecture for the agency; and 3) promoting the effective and efficient design and operation of all major information resources management processes for the agency, including improvements to work processes of the agency.

CobiT, Centers for Medicare & Medicaid Services (CMS), Network Frontiers, FIPS Pubs, NIST 800 Series

Chief Information Security Officer (CISSO)

See Senior Agency Information Security Officer.

FIPS Pubs, NIST 800 Series

Chip

A silicon wafer on which circuit elements have been imprinted. Also referred to as a microchip.

FISCAM

CI type

A category that is used to classify CIs. The CI type identifies the required attributes and relationships for a configuration record. Common CI types include hardware, document, user etc.

ITIL

Cine-Mode

Data recorded on a film strip such that it can be read by a human when held vertically.

Sedona Conference

Cinepak

A compression algorithm; See MPEG

Sedona Conference

Cipher

Also known as a cryptographic algorithm, it is the mathematical function used to scramble and unscramble messages. See also ciphertext, cipher key lock.

Workgroup for Electronic Data Interchange, US National Information Assurance (IA) Glossary, NIST 800 Series, FIPS Pubs

Cipher Block Chaining-Message Authentication Code (CBC-MAC)

A secret-key block-cipher algorithm used to encrypt data and to generate a Message Authentication Code (MAC) to provide assurance that the payload and the associated data are authentic.

NIST 800 series

Cipher key

Secret, cryptographic key that is used by the Key Expansion routine to generate a set of Round Keys; can be pictured as a rectangular array of bytes, having four rows and Nk columns.

NIST 800 series, FIPS Pubs

Cipher key lock

A lock with a key pad-like device that requires the manual entry of a predetermined code for entry.

FISCAM

Cipher suite

Negotiated algorithm identifiers. Cipher suites are identified in human readable form using a pneumonic code.

NIST 800 series

Cipher text

Information generated by an encryption algorithm to protect the plaintext. The cipher text is unintelligible to the unauthorized reader.

ISACA, Workgroup for Electronic Data Interchange, US National Information Assurance (IA) Glossary

Cipher Text Auto Key (CTAK)

Cryptographic logic that uses previous cipher text to generate a key stream.

US National Information Assurance (IA) Glossary

Ciphertext

Data in its encrypted form that is output from the Cipher or input to the Inverse Cipher.

NIST 800 series, FIPS Pubs

Ciphony

Process of enciphering audio information, resulting in encrypted speech.

US National Information Assurance (IA) Glossary

Circuit switched network

A data transmission service requiring the establishment of a circuit-switched connection before data can be transferred from source data terminal equipment (DTE) to a sink DTE. A circuit-switched data transmission service uses a connection network.

ISACA

Circular routing

In open systems architecture, circular routing is the logical path of a message in a communications network based on a series of gates at the physical network layer in the open systems interconnection (OSI) model.

ISACA

Civil Service Retirement System (CSRS)

A federal government retirement system which provides annuities to qualified employees who retire because of age and years of service, involuntary separation not for cause, or disability, to widows or widowers and minor children of employees who die and, in certain circumstances, to the survivors of annuitants.

The Civil Service Retirement System (CSRS) originated in 1920 and has provided retirement, disability and survivor benefits for most civilian employees in the US Federal government, until the creation of a new Federal Employees Retirement System (FERS) in 1987.

GAO/PCIE Financial Audit Manual

Claimant

A party whose identity is to be verified using an authentication protocol. An entity which is or represents a principal for the purposes of authentication, together with the functions involved in an authentication exchange on behalf of that entity. A claimant acting on behalf of a principal must include the functions necessary for engaging in an authentication exchange. (e.g., a smartcard (claimant) can act on behalf of a human user (principal)).

NIST 800 series, FIPS Pubs

Classical probability proportional to size sampling

A sampling approach where the sample is selected proportional to the size (usually dollar amount) of an item and the evaluation is performed using variables methods (not dollar unit sampling).

GAO/PCIE Financial Audit Manual

Classical variables estimation sampling

A sampling approach that measures precision using the variation of the underlying characteristic of interest. This method includes mean per unit sampling, difference estimation, ratio estimation, and regression estimation.

GAO/PCIE Financial Audit Manual

Classification

The systematic identification and arrangement of business activities and/or records into categories according to logically structured conventions, methods, and procedural rules represented in a classification system. The process of devising and applying schemes based on the business activities that generate records, whereby they are categorized in systematic and consistent ways to facilitate their capture, retrieval, maintenance, and disposal. Classification includes determining document or file naming conventions, user permissions, and security restrictions on records. A fundamental component of the intellectual control processes in a recordkeeping system is the use of a scheme for classifying records. The classification of a record is an essential element of the meta data that describes that record. This in turn enables the record to be managed, understood, linked to other related records and retrieved by users. Australian Standard AS 4390–1996, Records Management, requires records classification schemes to be based on a rigorous classification of business activities. This means that records are classified on the basis of why they exist (their function or the activity that caused the record to be brought into existence), rather than on the basis of what they are about (their subject). As such, the focus of classification is the context of a record's creation and use, rather than the content of the record itself. In addition to records, CIs, incidents, problems, changes etc. are usually classified.

ISO 15489, DIRKS, Australian Standard AS 4390–1996, ISO/IEC 27001:2005, ITIL

Classified information

Data or information that requires safeguarding in the interest of national security. Information that has been determined pursuant to Executive Order 12958 or any predecessor Order, or by the Atomic Energy Act of 1954, as amended, to require protection against unauthorized disclosure and is marked to indicate its classified status. Much stronger term than confidential information.

Centers for Medicare & Medicaid Services (CMS), US National Information Assurance (IA) Glossary, NIST 800 Series

Classified information spillage

Security incident that occurs whenever classified data is spilled either onto an unclassified IS or to an IS with a lower level of classification.

US National Information Assurance (IA) Glossary

Clear text

Data that is not encrypted. Also known as plaintext.

ISACA

Clearance

Formal security determination by an authorized adjudicative office that an individual is authorized access, on a need to know basis, to a specific level of collateral classified information (TOP SECRET, SECRET, CONFIDENTIAL).

US National Information Assurance (IA) Glossary

Clearing

Removal of data from an information system, its storage devices, and other peripheral devices with storage capacity, in such a way that the data may not be reconstructed using common system capabilities (i.e., keyboard strokes); however, the data may be reconstructed using laboratory methods. Cleared media may be reused at the same classification level or at a higher level.

Overwriting is one method of clearing. See also degauss.

US National Information Assurance (IA) Glossary

Client

A computer that is used directly by a user, for example, a PC, handheld computer, or workstation. The term client is also used to mean the part of a client-server application that the user directly interfaces with. For example, an e-mail client. The term client is also used to mean customers or the business in a general sense. For example, client manager may be used as a synonym for account manager.

ITIL, Workgroup for Electronic Data Interchange, US National Information Assurance (IA) Glossary, Sedona Conference

Client access license

A software license that permits one client to make use of resources on a server.

ITIL

Client application

A system entity, usually a computer process acting on behalf of a human user, that makes use of a service provided by a server.

NIST 800 series

Client/server model

A design model used on a network where individual workstations (clients) and shared servers work together to process applications. In this model, certain functions are allocated to the client workstations and the server. Typically, the server provides centralized, multi-user services, whereas the client workstations support user interaction. However, processing may take place on either the client or the server but it is transparent to the user.

FISCAM, ISACA, Sedona Conference

Clinger-Cohen Act of 1996

Also known as Information Technology Management Reform Act. A statute that substantially revised the way that IT resources are managed and procured, including a requirement that each agency design and implement a process for maximizing the value and assessing and managing the risks of IT investments.

NIST 800 series

Clipboard

A holding area that temporarily stores information copied or cut from a document.

Sedona Conference

Closed

The final status in the lifecycle of an incident, problem, change, etc. When the status is closed, no further action is taken.

ITIL

Closed account

A budget account for which the expired budget authority has been canceled.

GAO/PCIE Financial Audit Manual

Closed security environment

Environment providing sufficient assurance that applications and equipment are protected against the introduction of malicious logic during an IS life cycle. Closed security is based upon a system's developers, operators, and maintenance personnel having sufficient clearances, authorization, and configuration control.

US National Information Assurance (IA) Glossary

Closed system

An environment in which system access is controlled by person(s) responsible for the content of electronic records on the system.

21 CFR Part 11

Closure

The act of changing the status of an incident, problem, change etc. to closed.

ITIL

Closure code

A category that is assigned to an incident or problem before it is closed. This code identifies the cause and is intended for use in reporting and trend analysis. For example, "customer training required," "documentation error," or "software bug".

ITIL

Cluster (file)

The smallest unit of storage space that can be allocated to store a file on operating systems that use a file allocation table (FAT) architecture. Windows and DOS organize hard discs based on Clusters (also known as allocation units), which consist of one or more contiguous sectors. discs using smaller Cluster sizes waste less space and store information more efficiently.

Sedona Conference

Cluster (system)

A collection of individual computers that appear as a single logical unit. Also referred to as matrix or grid systems.

Sedona Conference

Cluster bitmaps

Used in NTFS to keep track of the status (free or used) of clusters on the hard drive.

Sedona Conference

Cluster controller

A communications terminal control hardware unit that controls a number of computer terminals. All messages are buffered by the controller and then transmitted to the receiver.

ISACA

Coaxial cable

It is composed of an insulated wire that runs through the middle of each cable, a second wire that surrounds the insulation of the inner wire like a sheath, and the outer insulation which wraps the second wire. Coaxial cable has a greater transmission capacity (which does not equate to greater speed) than standard twisted-pair cables but has a limited range of effective distance.

ISACA

Code

Instructions written in a computer programming language. Within the world of COMSEC, code represents a system of communication in which arbitrary groups of letters, numbers, or symbols represent units of plain text of varying length. See also object code and source code.

FISCAM, Centers for Medicare & Medicaid Services (CMS), ISO/IEC 27001:2005, US National Information Assurance (IA) Glossary

Code 10 call

A call made by a sales associate to the merchant's voice authorization center when the appearance of a card or the actions of a cardholder suggest the possibility of fraud. The term "Code 10" is used so calls can be made without arousing suspicion while the cardholder is present. Specially trained operators then provide assistance to point-of-sale staff on how to handle the transaction.

VISA Glossary of Terms

Code book

Document containing plain text and code equivalents in a systematic arrangement, or a technique of machine encryption using a word substitution technique.

US National Information Assurance (IA) Glossary

Code group

Group of letters, numbers, or both in a code system used to represent a plain text word, phrase, or sentence.

US National Information Assurance (IA) Glossary

Code of Practice (COP)

A guideline published by a public body or a standards organization, such as ISO or BSI. Many standards consist of a code of practice and a specification. The code of practice describes recommended best practice. See also standards.

ITIL

Code vocabulary

Set of plain text words, numerals, phrases, or sentences for which code equivalents are assigned in a code system.

US National Information Assurance (IA) Glossary

Coding

Automated or human process through which documents are examined and evaluated using predetermined codes, and the results of those comparisons are logged. Coding usually identifies names, dates, and relevant terms or phrases. Coding may be structured (limited to the selection of one of a finite number of choices), or unstructured (a narrative comment about a document). Coding may be objective, i.e., the name of the sender or the date, or subjective, i.e., evaluation as to the relevancy or probative value of documents.

Sedona Conference

Cohesion

The extent to which a system unit (e.g., subroutine, program, module, component, subsystem) performs a single dedicated function. Generally, the more cohesive the units are, the easier it is to maintain and enhance a system since it is easier to determine where and how to apply a change.

ISACA

Cold site

An organizational backup facility that has the necessary electrical and physical components of a computer facility, but does not have the computer equipment in place. The site is ready to receive the necessary replacement computer equipment in the event that the user has to move from their main computing location to an alternative computing location. See also cold standby.

FISCAM, ISACA, Centers for Medicare & Medicaid Services (CMS), NIST 800 Series

Cold standby

See gradual recovery.

ITIL

Cold start

Procedure for initially keying crypto-equipment.

US National Information Assurance (IA) Glossary

Collaboration tools

Tools (collaborative authoring, video conferencing, shared whiteboards, etc.) that allow multiple users to work on the same content in a common environment.

AIIM

Collaborative computing

Applications and technology (e.g. , whiteboarding, group conferencing) that allow two or more individuals to share information real time in an inter- or intra-enterprise environment.

US National Information Assurance (IA) Glossary

Collaborative Product Definition Management (CPDM)

AIIM

Collision

Two or more distinct inputs produce the same output.

NIST 800 series

Color Graphics Adapter (CGA)

See Video Graphics Adapter.

Sedona Conference

Comb

A series of boxes with their top missing. Tick marks guide text entry. Used in forms processing rather than boxes.

Sedona Conference

Combined Code on Corporate Governance

The consolidation in 1998 of the "Cadbury," "Greenbury" and "Hampel" Reports. Named after the Committee Chairs, these reports were sponsored by the UK Financial Reporting Council, the London Stock Exchange, the Confederation of British Industry, the Institute of Directors, the Consultative Committee of Accountancy Bodies, the National Association of Pension Funds and the Association of British Insurers to address the Financial Aspects of Corporate Governance, Directors' Remuneration and the implementation of the Cadbury and Greenbury recommendations.

ISACA

Combined precision

A judgment of precision for all tests in the audit. Used at the end of the audit to evaluate the results of all tests.

GAO/PCIE Financial Audit Manual

Combined risk

The auditor's judgment of the combined inherent and control risk (high, moderate, or low); the risk that the financial statements contain material misstatements before audit.

GAO/PCIE Financial Audit Manual

Comic Mode

Human-readable data, recorded on a strip of film which can be read when the film is moved horizontally to the reader.

Sedona Conference

Comma Separated Value (CSV)

A record layout that separates data fields/values with a comma and typically encloses data in quotation marks.

Sedona Conference

Command

A job control statement or a message, sent to the computer system, that initiates a processing task.

FISCAM, Centers for Medicare & Medicaid Services (CMS)

Command authority

Individual responsible for the appointment of user representatives for a department, agency, or organization and their key ordering privileges.

US National Information Assurance (IA) Glossary

Command List (CLIST)

In TSO/E, CLISTS are programs that perform given tasks or groups of tasks. The most basic CLIST is a list of TSO/E commands. However, two command languages available in TSO/E (CLIST and REXX) provide the programming tools needed to create structured applications or manage programs written in other languages.

FISCAM

Command, control, and communications

The processes and infrastructure that enable an organization to effectively pass instructions and information. This enables management control of resources. This term is typically used in the management of major incidents, business continuity, and IT service continuity.

ITIL

Commercial off-the-shelf software (COTS)

Hardware or software products that are commercially manufactured, ready-made and available for use by the general public without the need for customization. See also off-the-shelf software.

Centers for Medicare & Medicaid Services (CMS), Network Frontiers, Sedona Conference

Commission International de l'Eclairage (CIE)

The international commission on color matching and illumination systems.

Sedona Conference

Committee

A committee is a group that has been specifically delegated to consider any type of matter or investigate a particular issue or area of concern. Many people think that committees are time wasting events and follow the comedian Milton Berle's definition as a "group that keeps minutes and loses hours".

de facto

Committee for National Security Systems (CNSS)

Under Executive Order (E.O.) 13231 of October 16, 2001, Critical Infrastructure Protection in the Information Age, the President redesignated the National Security Telecommunications and Information Systems Security Committee (NSTISSC) as the Committee on National Security Systems (CNSS). The Department of Defense continues to chair the Committee under the authorities established by NSD-42. This was reaffirmed by Executive Order 13284, dated January 23, 2003, Executive Order Amendment of Executive Orders and Other Actions, in Connection with the Transfer of Certain Functions to the Secretary of Homeland Security. The CNSS provides a forum for the discussion of policy issues, sets national policy, and promulgates direction, operational procedures, and guidance for the security of national security systems. See

also http://www.cnss.gov for more information.

FIPS Pubs

Committee of Sponsoring Organizations for the Commission on Fraudulent Financial Reporting [Treadway Commission] (COSO)

COSO was originally formed in 1985 to sponsor the National Commission on Fraudulent Financial Reporting, an independent private sector initiative which studied the causal factors that can lead to fraudulent financial reporting and developed recommendations for public companies and their independent auditors, for the SEC and other regulators, and for educational institutions. The National Commission was jointly sponsored by five major professional associations in the United States, the American Accounting Association, the American Institute of Certified Public Accountants, Financial Executives International, The Institute of Internal Auditors, and the National Association of Accountants (now the Institute of Management Accountants). The Commission was wholly independent of each of the sponsoring organizations, and contained representatives from industry, public accounting, investment firms, and the New York Stock Exchange. See also http://www.coso.org/ for more information.

CobiT, GAO/PCIE Financial Audit Manual

Common business-oriented language (COBOL)

A high-level programming language specially designed for business applications.

FISCAM

Common Criteria

Provides a comprehensive, rigorous method for specifying security function and assurance requirements for products and systems. (International Standard ISO/IEC 5408, Common Criteria for Information Technology Security Evaluation [ITSEC])

US National Information Assurance (IA) Glossary

Common data source

In cost accounting, this includes all financial and nonfinancial data, such as environmental data, that are necessary for budgeting and financial reporting, as well as evaluation and decision information developed as a result of prior reporting and feedback.

GAO/PCIE Financial Audit Manual

Common fill device

One of a family of devices developed to read-in, transfer, or store key.

US National Information Assurance (IA) Glossary

Common Object Request Broker Architecture (CORBA)

ISACA

Common security control

Security control that can be applied to one or more agency information systems and has the following properties: 1) the development, implementation, and assessment of the control can be assigned to a responsible official or organizational element (other than the information system owner); and 2) the results from the assessment of the control can be used to support the security certification and accreditation processes of an agency information system where that control has been applied.

NIST 800 series, FIPS Pubs

Common threat sources

Natural threats: floods, earthquakes, tornadoes, landslides, avalanches, electrical storms, and other such events. Human threats: events that are either enabled by or caused by human beings, such as unintentional acts (inadvertent data entry) or deliberate actions (network based attacks, malicious software upload, unauthorized access to confidential information). Environmental threats: long-term power failure, pollution, chemicals, liquid leakage.

NIST 800 series

Common Vulnerabilities and Exposures (CVE)

A dictionary of common names for publicly known IT system vulnerabilities.

NIST 800 series

Communications controller

Small computers used to connect and coordinate communication links between distributed or remote devices and the main computer, thus freeing the main computer from this overhead function.

ISACA

Communications cover

Concealing or altering of characteristic communications patterns to hide information that could be of value to an adversary.

US National Information Assurance (IA) Glossary

Communications deception

Deliberate transmission, retransmission, or alteration of communications to mislead an adversary's interpretation of the communications. See also imitative communications deception and manipulative communications deception.

US National Information Assurance (IA) Glossary

Communications profile

Analytic model of communications associated with an organization or activity. The model is prepared from a systematic examination of communications content and patterns, the functions they reflect, and the communications security measures applied.

US National Information Assurance (IA) Glossary

Communications program

A program that enables a computer to connect with another computer and exchange information by transmitting or receiving data over telecommunications networks.

FISCAM

Communications protocol

The standards that govern the transfer of information among computers on a network.

FISCAM

Communications security (COMSEC)

These are security controls in place to ensure that data transmission is protected from eavesdropping and message tampering. The information transmitted can be authenticated via strong cryptography and the exchange of strong encryption key information to protect all information from unauthorized users.

Centers for Medicare & Medicaid Services (CMS), US National Information Assurance (IA) Glossary

Community risk

Probability that a particular vulnerability will be exploited within an interacting population and adversely impact some members of that population.

US National Information Assurance (IA) Glossary

Compact Disc (CD)

A type of optical disk storage media, compact discs come in a variety of formats. These formats include CD-ROMs (CD Read-Only Memory) that are read-only; CD-Rs (CD Recordable) that are write to once and are then read-only; and CD-RWs (CD Re-Writable) that can be written to multiple times.

FISCAM, Sedona Conference

Compact Disc - Read Only Memory (CD-ROM)

See Compact disk.

AIIM, Sedona Conference

Compact Disc - Recordable (CD-R)

A CD-ROM on which a user may permanently record data once using a CD Burner.

AIIM, Sedona Conference

Compact Disc - ReWriteable (CD-RW)

A CD-ROM on which a user may record data multiple times.

AIIM, Sedona Conference

Compact Disk-Read Only Memory

A form of optical rather than magnetic storage. CD-ROM devices are generally read-only.

FISCAM, Centers for Medicare & Medicaid Services (CMS)

Comparison

The process of comparing a biometric with a previously stored reference template or templates.

NIST 800 series, FIPS Pubs

Comparison program

A program for the examination of data, using logical or conditional tests to determine or to identify similarities or differences.

ISACA

Compartmentalization

A nonhierarchical grouping of sensitive information used to control access to data more finely than with hierarchical security classification alone.

US National Information Assurance (IA) Glossary

Compartmented mode

Mode of operation wherein each user with direct or indirect access to a system, its peripherals, remote terminals, or remote hosts has all of the following: (a) valid security clearance for the most restricted information processed in the system; (b) formal access approval and signed nondisclosure agreements for that information which a user is to have access; and (c) valid need-to-know for information which a user is to have access.

US National Information Assurance (IA) Glossary

Compatibility

The ability of two or more systems or components to seamlessly perform required services. The capability of a computer, device, or program to function with or substitute for another make and model of computer, device, or program. Also, the capability of one computer to run the software written to run on another computer. Standard interfaces, languages, protocols, and data formats are key to achieving compatibility.

FISCAM, Centers for Medicare & Medicaid Services (CMS), ISO/IEC 27001:2005

Compensating control

An internal control that reduces the risk of an existing or potential control weakness that could result in errors or omissions. Compensating controls may be considered when an organization does not wish to meet a requirement explicitly as stated, due to legitimate technical or documented business constraints but has sufficiently mitigated the risk associated with the requirement through implementation of other controls. Compensating controls must 1) meet the intent and rigor of the original stated requirement; 2) repel a compromise attempt with similar force; 3) be "above and beyond" other requirements (not simply in compliance with other requirements); and 4) be commensurate with the additional risk imposed by not adhering to the originally stated requirement

FISCAM, ISACA, Centers for Medicare & Medicaid Services (CMS), PCI-DSS

Compensating controls

The management, operational, and technical controls (i.e., safeguards or countermeasures) employed by an organization in lieu of the recommended controls in the low, moderate, or high security control baselines, that provide equivalent or comparable protection for an information system.

NIST 800 series, FIPS Pubs

Compensating security controls

The management, operational, and technical controls (i.e., safeguards or countermeasures) employed by an organization in lieu of the recommended controls in the low, moderate, or high baselines described in NIST Special Publication 800-53, that provide equivalent or comparable protection for an information system.

NIST 800 series

Compiler

A program that reads the statements in a human-readable programming language and translates them into a machine-readable executable program.

FISCAM, ISACA

Completeness check

A procedure designed to ensure that no fields are missing from a record.

ISACA

Complexity

The degree of intricacy of a system or system component, determined by such factors as the number of conditional branches, the degree of nesting and the length and types of data structures.

Centers for Medicare & Medicaid Services (CMS), ISO/IEC 27001:2005

Compliance

Ensuring that the requirements of laws, regulations, industry codes and organizational standards are met. This also applies to contractual arrangements to which the business process is subject, i.e., externally imposed business criteria. See also audit.

DIRKS, CobiT, ISO/IEC 27001:2005, ITIL

Compliance control

A process, effected by management and other personnel, designed to provide reasonable assurance that transactions are executed in accordance with 1) laws governing the use of budget authority and other laws and regulations that could have a direct and material effect on the financial statements or required supplementary stewardship information and 2) any other laws, regulations, and government wide policies identified in OMB audit guidance.

GAO/PCIE Financial Audit Manual

Compliance program

Compliance programs aim to prevent, and where necessary, identify and respond to, breaches of laws, regulations, codes or organizational standards occurring in the organization. They should promote a culture of compliance within the organization.

DIRKS

Compliance search

The identification of relevant terms and/or parties in response to a discovery request.

Sedona Conference

Compliance tests/testing

Tests to obtain evidence on the entity's compliance with significant laws and regulations. Tests of control designed to obtain audit evidence on both the effectiveness of the controls and their operation during the audit period.

GAO/PCIE Financial Audit Manual, ISACA

Compliant

See compliance.

de facto

Comply

See compliance, audit.

de facto

Component

A general term that is used to mean one part of something more complex. A single resource with defined characteristics. These components are defined by their relationship to other components. For example, a computer system may be a component of an IT service, an application may be a component of a release unit. Components that need to be man-

aged should be Configuration Items. See also IT asset.

FISCAM, Centers for Medicare & Medicaid Services (CMS), ITIL

Component CI

A configuration item that is part of an assembly CI. For example, a CPU or memory CI may be part of a server CI.

ITIL

Component Failure Impact Analysis (CFIA)

A part of problem management and availability management, a technique that helps to identify the impact of CI failure on IT services. A matrix is created with IT services on one edge and CIs on the other. This enables the identification of critical CIs (that could cause the failure of multiple IT services) and of fragile IT services (that have multiple single points of failure).

ITIL

Components as a part of component based development

Cooperating packages of executable software that make their services available through defined interfaces. Components used in developing systems may be commercial off-the-shelf software (COTS) or may be purposely built. However, the goal of component-based development is to ultimately use as much predeveloped, pretested components as possible.

ISACA

Composite Video

Combines red, green, blue and synchronization signals into one video signal so that only one connector is required; used by most TVs and VCRs.

Sedona Conference

Compound Annual Growth Rate (CAGR)

AIIM

Comprehensive audit

An audit designed to determine the accuracy of financial records as well as evaluate the internal controls of a function or department.

ISACA

Compression

Compression algorithms such as Zip and RLE reduce the size of files saving both storage space and reducing bandwidth required for access and transmission. Data compression is widely used in backup utilities, spreadsheet applications and database management systems. Compression generally eliminates redundant information and/or predicts where changes will occur. "Lossless" compression techniques such as Zip and RLE preserve the integrity of the input.

Coding standards such as JPEG and MPEG employ "lossy" methods which do not preserve all of the original information, and are most commonly used for photographs, audio, and video.

Sedona Conference

Compression Ratio

The ratio of the size of an uncompressed file to a compressed file, e.g., with a 10:1 compression ratio, a 1 MB file can be compressed to 100 KB.

Sedona Conference

Compromise

An unauthorized disclosure or loss of sensitive data. An intrusion into a computer system where unauthorized disclosure, modification, or destruction of confidential data may have occurred.

Centers for Medicare & Medicaid Services (CMS), FIPS Pubs, PCI-DSS, Workgroup for Electronic Data Interchange, US National Information Assurance (IA) Glossary, NIST 800 Series

Compromising emanations

Unintentional signals that, if intercepted and analyzed, would disclose the information transmitted, received, handled, or otherwise processed by information systems equipment. See also TEMPEST.

US National Information Assurance (IA) Glossary

Computationally greedy

Requiring a great deal of computing power; processor intensive.

ISACA

Computer

Includes but is not limited to network servers, desktops, laptops, notebook computers, mainframes and PDAs (personal digital assistants). See also computer system.

Centers for Medicare & Medicaid Services (CMS), ISO/IEC 27001:2005, Sedona Conference

Computer abuse

Intentional or reckless misuse, alteration, disruption, or destruction of information processing resources.

US National Information Assurance (IA) Glossary

Computer Aided Design (CAD)

AIIM

Computer Aided Drafting and Design (CADD)

AIIM

Computer Aided Software Engineering (CASE)

The use of software packages that aid in the development of all phases of an information system. System analysis, design, programming, and documentation are provided. Changes introduced in one CASE chart will update all other related charts automatically. CASE can be installed on a microcomputer for easy access.

ISACA

Computer architecture

A general term referring to the structure of all or part of a computer system. The term also covers the design of system software, such as the operating system, as well as refers to the combination of hardware and basic software that links the machines on a computer network. Computer architecture refers to an entire structure and to the details needed to make it functional. Thus, computer architecture covers computer systems, circuits, and system programs, but typically does not cover applications, which are required to perform a task but not to make the system run.

FISCAM

Computer assisted audit technique

Any automated audit technique, such as generalized audit software, test data generators, computerized audit programs, and specialized audit utilities.

ISACA

Computer cryptography

Use of a crypto-algorithm program by a computer to authenticate or encrypt/decrypt information.

US National Information Assurance (IA) Glossary

Computer facility

A site or location with computer hardware where information processing is performed or where data from such sites are stored. See also computer processing location, facility.

FISCAM, Centers for Medicare & Medicaid Services (CMS)

Computer Forensics

Computer Forensics (in the context of this document, "forensic analysis") is the use of specialized techniques for recovery, authentication and analysis of electronic data when an investigation or litigation involves issues relating to reconstruction of computer usage, examination of residual data, authentication of data by technical analysis or explanation of technical features of data and computer usage. Computer forensics requires specialized expertise that goes beyond normal data collection and preservation techniques available to end-users or system support personnel, and generally requires strict adherence to chain-of-custody protocols. See also Forensics and Forensic Copy.

Sedona Conference, NIST 800 Series

Computer network

See network.

Centers for Medicare & Medicaid Services (CMS)

Computer operations

The function responsible for operating the computer and peripheral equipment, including providing the tape, disk, or paper resources as requested by the application systems.

FISCAM, Centers for Medicare & Medicaid Services (CMS)

Computer Output to Laser Disk/Enterprise Report Management (COLD/ERM)

Stores and indexes computer output (reports primarily) on magnetic discs, optical discs, and magnetic tape. Once stored the reports can be retrieved, viewed, printed, faxed, or distributed to the Internet. Often used for internet billing applications.

AIIM, Sedona Conference

Computer Output to Microfilm (COM)

A process that outputs electronic records and computer generated reports to microfilm.

Sedona Conference

Computer prioritization listings

A listing of the computer inventory owned by an organization. This listing typically depicts a prioritized ordering of systems or networking components based on their importance to the organization (e.g., mission critical systems, high/medium/low priority systems, administrative systems, support systems).

CERT OCTAVE

Computer processing location

See computer facility.

FISCAM

Computer related controls

Computer-related controls help ensure the reliability, confidentiality, and availability of automated information. They include both general controls which apply to all or a large segment of an entity's information systems, and application controls which apply to individual applications.

FISCAM

Computer resource

See resource.

FISCAM, Centers for Medicare & Medicaid Services (CMS)

Computer room

Room within a facility that houses computers and/or telecommunication devices. This isn't necessarily the data center, as it could easily be a converted closet.

FISCAM, Centers for Medicare & Medicaid Services (CMS)

Computer security

The protection afforded to an automated information system in order to attain the applicable objectives of preserving the integrity, availability, and confidentiality of information system and resources including hardware, software, firmware, information, and telecommunications. See also information systems security and systems security.

NIST 800 series, Centers for Medicare & Medicaid Services (CMS), Workgroup for Electronic Data Interchange, US National Information Assurance (IA) Glossary

Computer Security Act (CSA)

NIST 800 series

Computer security incident

A violation or imminent threat of violation of computer security policies, acceptable use policies, or standard computer security practices. See also incident.

US National Information Assurance (IA) Glossary, NIST 800 Series

Computer Security Incident Response Capability (CSIRC)

That part of the computer security effort that provides the capability to respond to computer security threats rapidly and effectively. A CSIRC provides a way for users to report incidents, and it provides personnel and tools for investigating and resolving incidents, and mechanisms for disseminating incident-related information to management and users. Analysis of incidents also reveals vulnerabilities, which can be eliminated to prevent future incidents.

Centers for Medicare & Medicaid Services (CMS)

Computer Security Incident Response Team (CSIRT)

A capability set up for the purpose of assisting in responding to computer security-related incidents; also called a Computer Incident Response Team (CIRT) or a CIRC (Computer Incident Response Center, Computer Incident Response Capability).

NIST 800 series

Computer Security Institute (CSI)

The Computer Security Institute (CSI) reports that it is the world's leading membership organization specifically dedicated to serving and training the information, computer, and network security professional. Since 1974, CSI has been providing education and aggressively advocating the critical importance of protecting information assets. This has nothing to do with the over-rated television shows. See also http://www.gocsi.com for more information.

de facto

Computer security object

A resource, tool, or mechanism used to maintain a condition of security in a computerized environment. These objects are defined in terms of attributes they possess, operations they perform or are performed on them, and their relationship with other objects.

NIST 800 series

Computer security objects register

A collection of Computer Security Object names and definitions kept by a registration authority.

NIST 800 series

Computer security subsystem

Hardware/software designed to provide computer security features in a larger system environment.

US National Information Assurance (IA) Glossary

Computer sequence checking

Verifies that the control number follows sequentially and any control numbers out of sequence are rejected or noted on an exception report for further research.

ISACA

Computer server

See server.

ISACA

Computer system

A complete computer installation, including peripherals, in which all the components are designed to work with each other. This refers to the entire spectrum of information technology, including application and support systems in which all the components are designed to work with each other. Any equipment or interconnected system or subsystems of equipment used in the automatic acquisition, storage, manipulation, management, movement, control, display, switching, interchange, transmission, or reception of data or information; including computers; ancillary equipment; software, firmware, and similar procedures; services, including support services; and related resources as defined by regulations issued by the Administrator for General Services pursuant to section 111 of the Federal Property and Administrative Services Act of 1949.

NIST 800 series, Centers for Medicare & Medicaid Services (CMS), FISCAM, Federal Property and Administrative Services Act of 1949

Computer Telephony Integration (CTI)

A general term covering any kind of integration between computers and telephone systems. It is most commonly used to refer to systems where an application displays detailed screens relating to incoming or outgoing telephone calls. See also automatic call distribution, interactive voice response.

ITIL

Computer-assisted audit technique (CAAT)

Any automated audit technique such as generalized audit software, test data generators, computerized audit programs, and special audit utilities.

FISCAM, ISACA

Computing environment

Workstation or server (host) and its operating system, peripherals, and applications.

US National Information Assurance (IA) Glossary

Computing security methods

Computing security methods are security safeguards implemented within IT, using the networking, hardware, software, and firmware of IT. This includes 1) the hardware, firmware, and software that implements security functionality and 2) the design, implementation, and verification techniques used to ensure that system assurance requirements are satisfied.

NIST 800 series

COMSEC account

Administrative entity, identified by an account number, used to maintain accountability, custody, and control of COMSEC material.

US National Information Assurance (IA) Glossary

COMSEC account audit

Examination of the holdings, records, and procedures of a COMSEC account ensuring all accountable COMSEC material is properly handled and safeguarded.

US National Information Assurance (IA) Glossary

COMSEC aid

COMSEC material that assists in securing telecommunications and is required in the production, operation, or maintenance of COMSEC systems and their components. COMSEC keying material, callsign/frequency systems, and supporting documentation, such as operating and maintenance manuals, are examples of COMSEC aids.

US National Information Assurance (IA) Glossary

COMSEC assembly

Group of parts, elements, subassemblies, or circuits that are removable items of COMSEC equipment.

US National Information Assurance (IA) Glossary

COMSEC boundary

Definable perimeter encompassing all hardware, firmware, and software components performing critical COMSEC functions, such as key generation, handling, and storage.

US National Information Assurance (IA) Glossary

COMSEC chip set

Collection of NSA approved microchips.

US National Information Assurance (IA) Glossary

COMSEC control program

Computer instructions or routines controlling or affecting the externally performed functions of key generation, key distribution, message encryption/decryption, or authentication.

US National Information Assurance (IA) Glossary

COMSEC custodian

Individual designated by proper authority to be responsible for the receipt, transfer, accounting, safeguarding, and destruction of COMSEC material assigned to a COMSEC account.

US National Information Assurance (IA) Glossary

COMSEC demilitarization

Process of preparing COMSEC equipment for disposal by extracting all CCI, classified, or CRYPTO marked components for their secure destruction, as well as defacing and disposing of the remaining equipment hulk.

US National Information Assurance (IA) Glossary

COMSEC element

Removable item of COMSEC equipment, assembly, or subassembly; normally consisting of a single piece or group of replaceable parts.

US National Information Assurance (IA) Glossary

COMSEC end-item

Equipment or combination of components ready for use in a COMSEC application.

US National Information Assurance (IA) Glossary

COMSEC equipment

Equipment designed to provide security to telecommunications by converting information to a form unintelligible to an unauthorized interceptor and, subsequently, by reconverting such information to its original form for authorized recipients; also, equipment designed specifically to aid in, or as an essential element of, the conversion process. COMSEC equipment includes crypto-equipment, crypto-ancillary equipment, cryptoproduction equipment, and authentication equipment.

US National Information Assurance (IA) Glossary

COMSEC facility

Authorized and approved space used for generating, storing, repairing, or using COMSEC material.

US National Information Assurance (IA) Glossary

COMSEC incident

See incident.

US National Information Assurance (IA) Glossary

COMSEC insecurity

COMSEC incident that has been investigated, evaluated, and determined to jeopardize the security of COMSEC material or the secure transmission of information.

US National Information Assurance (IA) Glossary

COMSEC manager

Individual who manages the COMSEC resources of an organization.

US National Information Assurance (IA) Glossary

COMSEC material

Item designed to secure or authenticate telecommunications. COMSEC material includes, but is not limited to key, equipment, devices, documents, firmware, or software that embodies or describes cryptographic logic and other items that perform COMSEC functions.

US National Information Assurance (IA) Glossary

COMSEC Material Control System (CMCS)

Logistics and accounting system through which COMSEC material marked "CRYPTO" is distributed, controlled, and safeguarded. Included are the COMSEC central offices of record, cryptologistic depots, and COMSEC accounts. COMSEC material other than key may be handled through the CMCS.

US National Information Assurance (IA) Glossary

COMSEC modification

See information systems security equipment modification.

US National Information Assurance (IA) Glossary

COMSEC module

Removable component that performs COMSEC functions in a telecommunications equipment or system.

US National Information Assurance (IA) Glossary

COMSEC monitoring

Act of listening to, copying, or recording transmissions of one's own official telecommunications to analyze the degree of security.

US National Information Assurance (IA) Glossary

COMSEC profile

Statement of COMSEC measures and materials used to protect a given operation, system, or organization.

US National Information Assurance (IA) Glossary

COMSEC survey

Organized collection of COMSEC and communications information relative to a given operation, system, or organization.

US National Information Assurance (IA) Glossary

COMSEC system data

Information required by a COMSEC equipment or system to enable it to properly handle and control key.

US National Information Assurance (IA) Glossary

COMSEC training

Teaching of skills relating to COMSEC accounting, use of COMSEC aids, or installation, use, maintenance, and repair of COMSEC equipment.

US National Information Assurance (IA) Glossary

Concept Of Operations (CONOP)

Document detailing the method, act, process, or effect of using an information system.

US National Information Assurance (IA) Glossary

Concept Search

Searching electronic documents to determine relevance by analyzing the words and putting search requests in conceptual groupings so the true meaning of the request is considered. Concept searching considers both the word and the context in which it appears to differentiate between concepts such as diamond (baseball) and diamond (jewelry).

Sedona Conference

Concurrency

A measure of the number of users engaged in the same operation at the same time. Used in capacity management and license management.

ITIL

Concurrent access

A fail-over process in which all nodes run the same resource group (there can be no IP or MAC addresses in a concurrent resource group) and access the external storage concurrently.

ISACA

Confidence interval

The projected misstatement or point estimate plus or minus precision at the desired confidence level.

GAO/PCIE Financial Audit Manual

Confidence level

The probability associated with the precision; the probability that the true misstatement is within the confidence interval. This is not the same as level of assurance.

GAO/PCIE Financial Audit Manual

Confidential information

Organized data (data are facts, they become information when they are seen in context and convey meaning to people) that requires safeguarding in the interest of client, personnel, or organizational security.

Network Frontiers

Confidentiality

Protection from intentional or accidental attempts to perform unauthorized data reads. Confidentiality covers data in storage, during processing, and while in transit. A requirement that private or confidential information not be disclosed to unauthorized individuals. The need to keep proprietary, sensitive, or personal information private and inaccessible to anyone who is not authorized to see it.

NIST 800 series, CERT OCTAVE, FISCAM, ISACA, Centers for Medicare & Medicaid Services (CMS), CobiT, ISO/IEC 13335-1:2004, ISO/IEC 27001:2005, FIPS Pubs, ITIL, Workgroup for Electronic Data Interchange, US National Information Assurance (IA) Glossary

Configuration

The arrangement or setup of a computer system, application, or component based upon system environment and organizational requirements. A generic term used to describe a group of configuration items that work together to deliver an IT service, or a recognizable part of an IT service. Configuration is also used to describe the parameter settings for one or more CIs.

Centers for Medicare & Medicaid Services (CMS), ISO/IEC 27001:2005, ITIL, Microsoft

Configuration and Change Management (C&CM)

An integrated approach to planning, implementing, and operating configuration management, change management, and release management.

ITIL

Configuration attribute

A part of configuration management. A piece of information about a configuration item. Examples are name, location, version number, and cost. Attributes of CIs are recorded in the Configuration Management Database (CMDB). See also relationship.

ITIL, Microsoft

Configuration baseline

A configuration of a product or system established at a specific point in time, which captures both the structure and details of that product or system and enables that product or system to be rebuilt at a later date.

ITIL, Microsoft

Configuration control

The activity responsible for ensuring that adding, modifying or removing a CI is properly managed, for example, by submitting a request for change or service request.

ITIL, US National Information Assurance (IA) Glossary, Microsoft, NIST 800 Series

Configuration identification

The activity responsible for collecting information about configuration items and their relationships, and loading this information into the CMDB. Configuration identification is also responsible for labeling the CIs themselves, so that the corresponding configuration records can be found.

ITIL

Configuration Item (CI)

Component of an infrastructure (or an item, such as a request for change, associated with an infrastructure) which is (or is to be) under the control of configuration management. CIs may vary widely in complexity, size, and type, from an entire system (including all hardware, software and documentation) to a single module or a minor hardware component. Information about each CI is recorded in a configuration record within the CMDB and is maintained throughout its lifecycle by configuration management. CIs are under the control of change management. CIs typically include hardware, software, buildings, people, and formal documentation such as process documentation and SLAs.

CobiT, ITIL, Microsoft

Configuration management

The control and documentation of changes made to a system's hardware, software, and documentation throughout the development and operational life of the system. Configuration management is the process responsible for maintaining information about configuration items required to deliver an IT service, including their relationships. This information is managed throughout the lifecycle of the CI. The primary objective of configuration management is to underpin the delivery of IT services by providing accurate data to all IT service management processes when and where it is needed. See also configuration and change management.

Centers for Medicare & Medicaid Services (CMS), ITIL, US National Information Assurance (IA) Glossary

Configuration Management Database (CMDB)

A database used to manage configuration records throughout their lifecycle. The CMDB records the attributes of each CI, and relationships with other CIs. A CMDB may also contain other information linked to CIs, for example, incident, problem or change records. The CMDB is maintained by configuration management and is used by all IT service management processes.

ITIL, Microsoft

Configuration Manager

He role that is responsible for managing the activities of the configuration management process for the IT organization. The role also selects, assigns responsibilities to, and trains the configuration management staff.

Microsoft

Configuration record

A record containing the details of a configuration item. Each configuration record documents the lifecycle of a single CI. Configuration records are stored in a configuration management database.

ITIL

Configuration status accounting

The activity responsible for recording and reporting the lifecycle of each configuration item.

ITIL

Configuration structure

The hierarchy and other relationships between all the configuration items that comprise a configuration.

ITIL

Configuration verification and audit

The activities responsible for ensuring that information in the CMDB is accurate and that all configuration items have been identified and recorded in the CMDB. Configuration verification includes routine checks that are part of other processes. For example, verifying the serial number of a desktop PC when a user logs an incident. Configuration audit is a periodic, formal check.

ITIL

Configuration vulnerability

A weakness resulting from an error in the configuration and administration of a system or component.

CERT OCTAVE

Confinement channel

See covert channel.

US National Information Assurance (IA) Glossary

Console

Traditionally, a control unit such as a terminal through which a user communicates with a computer. In the mainframe environment, a console is the operator's station or any screen and keyboard which allows access and control of the server/mainframe in a networked environment.

FISCAM, Centers for Medicare & Medicaid Services (CMS), PCI-DSS

Console log

An automated detail report of computer system activity.

ISACA

Consortium

Currently consists of four CMS offices (Northeastern, Southern, Midwestern, and Western) that oversee the operations at the Regional Offices.

Centers for Medicare & Medicaid Services (CMS)

Consortium Contract Management Officer (CCMO)

Part of the Regional Consortiums, the CCMO is responsible for leading and directing contractor management at the consortium level.

Centers for Medicare & Medicaid Services (CMS)

Consultative Committee for International Telephone & Telegraphy (CCITT)

Sets standards for phones, faxes, modems etc. The standard exists primarily for fax documents.

Sedona Conference

Consumer

One who obtains products or services from an organization selling products and services to be used primarily for personal, family, or household purposes.

ISACA, PCI-DSS

Contamination

Type of incident involving the introduction of data of one security classification or security category into data of a lower security classification or different security category.

US National Information Assurance (IA) Glossary

Content Comparison

A method of de-duplication that compares file content or output (to image or paper) and ignores metadata. See also De-Duplication.

Sedona Conference

Content Distribution Service Provider (CDSP)

AIIM

Content filtering

Controlling access to a network by analyzing the contents of the incoming and outgoing packets and either letting them pass or denying them based on a list of rules. Differs from packet filtering in that it is the data in the packet that are analyzed instead of the attributes of the packet itself (e.g., source/target IP address, TCP flags).

ISACA

Content Management or Configuration management (CM)

See Content Management, Configuration management

de facto

Context

Context is the relationship of every-thing (all circumstances and conditions) that surround an event or environment. It denotes the "completeness" in which something is found. Context is some-thing that many inexperienced auditors forget about when they examine organizational controls.

de facto, Network Frontiers

Contextual Search

The process of returning electronic evidence to its true context: when created, by whom, for what purpose, etc.

Sedona Conference

Contingency

An existing condition, situation, or set of circumstances involving uncertainty as to possible gain or loss.

GAO/PCIE Financial Audit Manual

Contingency key

Key held for use under specific operational conditions or in support of specific contingency plans. See also reserve keying material.

US National Information Assurance (IA) Glossary

Contingency management

Establishing actions to be taken before, during and after an interruption in service.

Centers for Medicare & Medicaid Services (CMS)

Contingency plan

See continuity plan.

FISCAM, Centers for Medicare & Medicaid Services (CMS), NIST 800 Series

Contingency planning

See continuity planning.

FISCAM, Centers for Medicare & Medicaid Services (CMS)

Continuity

The acts preventing, mitigating and recovering from disruption. The terms business resumption planning, disaster recovery planning and contingency planning also may be used in this context; they all concentrate on the recovery aspects of continuity.

ISACA, CobiT, ISO/IEC 27001:2005

Continuity Of Operations Plan (COOP)

A predetermined set of instructions or procedures that describe how an organization's essential functions will be sustained for up to 30 days as a result of a disaster event before returning to normal operations.

Centers for Medicare & Medicaid Services (CMS), US National Information Assurance (IA) Glossary, NIST 800 Series

Continuity of support plan

The documentation of a predetermined set of instructions or procedures mandated by Office of Management and Budget (OMB) A-130 that describe how to sustain major applications and general support systems in the event of a significant disruption.

NIST 800 series

Continuity plan

Management policy and procedures designed to maintain or restore business operations, including computer operations, possibly at an alternate location, in the event of emergencies, system failure, or disaster.

Network Frontiers, NIST 800 Series

Continuity planning

The process for ensuring, in advance, that any reasonable and foreseeable disruptions will have a minimal effect.

Network Frontiers

Continuous auditing approach

This approach allows IS auditors to monitor system reliability on a continuous basis and to gather selective audit evidence through the computer.

ISACA

Continuous availability

An approach or design to achieve 100% availability. A continuously available IT service has no planned or unplanned downtime.

ITIL

Continuous improvement

The process responsible for managing improvements to IT service management processes and IT services. Continuous improvement continually measures achievement and modifies processes and the IT infrastructure to improve efficiency, effectiveness, and cost effectiveness. See also CSIP, SIP, Deming cycle, optimize.

ITIL

Continuous operation

An approach or design to eliminate planned downtime of an IT service.

Note that individual configuration items may be down even though the IT service is available.

ITIL

Continuous Service Improvement Program (CSIP)

A formal program to implement and manage a continuous improvement process.

ITIL

Continuous Tone

An image (e.g. a photograph) which has all the values of gray from white to black.

Sedona Conference

Contract

A legally binding agreement between two or more parties.

ITIL

Contract authority

Statutory authority that permits obligations to be incurred before appropriations or in anticipation of receipts to be credited to a revolving fund or other account (offsetting collections). By definition, contract authority is unfunded and must subsequently be funded by an appropriation to liquidate the obligations incurred under the contract authority or by the collection and use of receipts.

GAO/PCIE Financial Audit Manual

Contract Manager

A role responsible for managing contracts with one or more suppliers. Contract managers usually work closely with service level managers to ensure that supplier contracts support agreed service level targets for IT services.

ITIL

Contractor Integrated Technical Information Service (CITIS)

The Department Of Defense now requires contractors to have an integrated electronic document image and management system.

Sedona Conference

Contractors

Non-federal personnel who perform services for the federal government (or any other contracting organization) under the terms and conditions of a contractual agreement. Contractors need security training commensurate with their responsibilities for performing work under the terms and conditions of their contractual agreements.

Centers for Medicare & Medicaid Services (CMS), ISO/IEC 27001:2005

Contractual value

Contractual value is the measure of an asset's worth from a contractual obligation perspective; this may include penalty costs, loss of future payments, and legal proceedings.

Network Frontiers

Control activities

A component of internal control, in addition to the control environment, risk assessment, monitoring, and information and communication. Organizational control activities are the collected policies, procedures, practices, and organizational structures designed to provide reasonable assurance that the business objectives will be achieved and undesired events will be detected and prevented . These control activities help ensure that management directives are carried out by providing a description of what physical, software, procedural or people related conditions must be met or in existence in order to satisfy a core requirement.

GAO/PCIE Financial Audit Manual, Centers for Medicare & Medicaid Services (CMS)

Control environment

The control environment is an important component of an entity's internal control structure. It sets the "tone at the top" and can influence the effectiveness of specific control techniques. A component of internal control, in addition to risk assessment, monitoring, information and communication, and control activities. The control environment sets the tone of an organization, influencing the control consciousness of its people. It is the foundation for all other components of internal control, providing discipline and structure. The control environment represents the collective effect of various factors on establishing, enhancing, or mitigating the effectiveness of specific control activities. Such factors include 1) integrity and ethical values, 2) commitment to competence, 3) management's philosophy and operating style, 4) organizational structure, 5) assignment of authority and responsibility, 6) human resource policies and practices, 7) control methods over budget formulation and execution, 8) control methods over compliance with laws and regulations, and 9) oversight groups.

FISCAM, GAO/PCIE Financial Audit Manual

Control framework

A control framework is a structured way of categorizing controls to ensure the whole spectrum of control is covered adequately. The framework can be informal or formal. A formal approach will more readily satisfy the various regulatory or statutory requirements for organizations subject to them.

CobiT, Institute of Internal Auditors

Control group

Members of the operations area that are responsible for the collection, logging, and submission of input for the various user groups.

ISACA

Control information

Information that is entered into a cryptographic module for the purposes of directing the operation of the module.

NIST 800 series, FIPS Pubs

Control objective

The objectives of management that are used as the framework for developing and implementing controls (control procedures). A statement of the desired result or purpose to be achieved by implementing control procedures in a particular process.

ISACA, CobiT, ISO/IEC 27001:2005

Control Objectives for Enterprise Governance

A discussion document which sets out an "enterprise governance model" focusing strongly on both the enterprise business goals and the information technology enablers which facilitate good enterprise governance, published by the Information Systems Audit and Control Foundation in 1999.

ISACA

Control objectives for information and related technology (CobiT)

A framework, control objectives, and audit guidelines developed as a generally applicable and accepted standard for good practices for controls over information technology.

ISACA, ITIL

Control or controls

The activities surrounding policies, procedures, practices, and organizational structures designed to provide reasonable assurance that the business objectives will be achieved and undesired events will be prevented or detected. Example controls include policies, procedures, roles, software configurations, passwords, fences, door-locks etc. A control is sometimes called a countermeasure or safeguard. For DIRKS, control systems and processes associated with records management include: registration, which provides evidence of the existence of records in a recordkeeping system; classification, which allows for appropriate grouping, naming, security protection, user permissions, and retrieval; indexing, which allocates attributes or codes to particular records to assist in their retrieval; and tracking, which provides evidence of where a record is located, what action is outstanding on a record, who has seen a record, when such access took place and the recordkeeping transactions that have been undertaken on the record. Control is also used as a generic term meaning to manage something. See also procedures.

DIRKS, ITIL, CobiT, ISO/IEC 27001:2005

Control perimeter

The boundary defining the scope of control authority for an entity. For example, if a system is within the control perimeter, the right and ability exists to control it in response to an attack.

ISACA

Control practice

Key control mechanism that supports the achievement of control objectives through responsible use of resources, appropriate management of risk, and alignment of IT with business.

CobiT

Control risk

Risk that a material misstatement that could occur in an assertion will not be prevented, or detected and corrected on a timely basis by the entity's internal control structure. By definition in the regulations and standards, this is an auditor's judgment call.

FISCAM, GAO/PCIE Financial Audit Manual, ISACA

Control risk self assessment

An empowering method/process by which management and staff of all levels collectively identify and evaluate IS related risks and controls under the guidance of a facilitator who could be an IS auditor. The IS auditor can utilize CRSA for gathering relevant information about risks and controls and to forge greater collaboration with management and staff. CRSA provides a framework and tools for management and employees to: identify and prioritize their business objectives, assess and manage high risk areas of business processes, self-evaluate the adequacy of controls, and develop risk treatment recommendations.

ISACA

Control section

The area of the central processing unit (CPU) that executes software, allocates internal memory and transfers operations between the arithmetic-logic, internal storage, and output sections of the computer.

ISACA

Control techniques

See control activities, procedures.

GAO/PCIE Financial Audit Manual, Centers for Medicare & Medicaid Services (CMS)

Control tests

Tests of a specific control activity to assess its effectiveness in achieving control objectives.

GAO/PCIE Financial Audit Manual

Control weakness

A deficiency in the design or operation of a control procedure. Control weaknesses can potentially result in risks relevant to the area of activity not being reduced to an acceptable level (relevant risks are those that threaten achievement of the objectives relevant to the area of activity being examined). Control weaknesses can be material when the design or operation of one or more control procedures does not reduce to a relatively low level the risk that misstatements caused by illegal acts or irregularities may occur and not be detected by the related control procedures.

ISACA

Controlled access area

Physical area (e.g., building, room, etc.) to which only authorized personnel are granted unrestricted access. All other personnel are either escorted by authorized personnel or are under continuous surveillance.

US National Information Assurance (IA) Glossary

Controlled access protection

Minimum set of security functionality that enforces access control on individual users and makes them accountable for their actions through login procedures, auditing of security-relevant events, and resource isolation.

US National Information Assurance (IA) Glossary

Controlled Cryptographic Item (CCI)

US National Information Assurance (IA) Glossary

Controlled interface

Mechanism that facilitates the adjudication of different interconnected system security policies (e.g., controlling the flow of information into or out of an interconnected system).

US National Information Assurance (IA) Glossary, NIST 800 Series, NIST 800 Series, FIPS Pubs

Controlled space

Three-dimensional space surrounding IS equipment, within which unauthorized individuals are denied unrestricted access and are either escorted by authorized individuals or are under continuous physical or electronic surveillance.

US National Information Assurance (IA) Glossary

Controlled vocabulary

An alphabetical list containing terms or headings which are authorized or controlled so that only one heading or form of heading is allowed to represent a particular concept or name. It contrasts with natural language. A controlled vocabulary is also referred to as a thesaurus.

DIRKS

Controlling authority

Official responsible for directing the operation of a cryptonet and for managing the operational use and control of keying material assigned to the cryptonet.

US National Information Assurance (IA) Glossary

Convergence

Integration of computing, communications and broadcasting systems.

Sedona Conference

Conversion

The process of changing records from one medium to another or from one format to another. It is also the process of changing from one existing system to a new one.

ISO 15489, DIRKS

Cookie

A string of data exchanged between a web server and a web browser to maintain a session. The browser stores the message in a text file. The message is then sent back to the server each time the browser requests a page from the server. Cookies may contain user preferences and personal information. The main purpose of cookies is to identify users and possibly prepare customized Web pages for them.

PCI-DSS, Sedona Conference, NIST 800 Series, FIPS Pubs

Cooperative key generation

Electronically exchanging functions of locally generated, random components, from which both terminals of a secure circuit construct traffic encryption key or key encryption key for use on that circuit. See also per-call key.

US National Information Assurance (IA) Glossary

Cooperative processing

A mode of operation in which two or more computers, such as a mainframe and a microcomputer, can carry out portions of the same program or work on the same data. It enables computers to share programs, workloads, and data files.

FISCAM

Cooperative remote rekeying

Synonymous with manual remote rekeying.

US National Information Assurance (IA) Glossary

Copy request

A request by a card issuer to a merchant bank for a copy or facsimile of a sales receipt for a disputed transaction. Depending on where sales receipts are stored, the merchant bank either fulfills the copy request itself or forwards it to he merchant for fulfillment. A copy request is also known as a retrieval request.

VISA Glossary of Terms

Core Financial Management System (CFMS)

As developed by JFMIP, a system that consists of six functional areas: 1) general ledger management, 2) funds management, 3) payment management, 4) receivable management, 5) cost management, and 6) reporting. It affects all financial event transaction processing because it maintains reference tables used for editing and classifying data, controls transactions, and maintains security.

GAO/PCIE Financial Audit Manual

Core switch

Like other switches, a core switch channels data to its intended destination, but generally handles exchanges within a network and not outside of it (i.e. to the Internet).

Network Frontiers

Corporate exchange rate

An exchange rate which can be used optionally to perform foreign currency conversion. The corporate exchange rate is generally a standard market rate determined by senior financial management for use throughout the organization.

ISACA

Corporate governance

The structure through which the objectives of an organization are set, the means of attaining those objectives, and determining monitoring performance guidelines. Good corporate governance should provide proper incentives for board and management to pursue objectives that are in the interests of the company and stakeholders and should facilitate effective monitoring, thereby encouraging firms to use resources more efficiently.

ISACA, OECD Principles of Corporate Governance, PAS 56

Corrective controls

These controls are designed to correct errors, omissions, and unauthorized uses and intrusions once they are detected.

ISACA

Correctness proof

A mathematical proof of consistency between a specification and its implementation.

US National Information Assurance (IA) Glossary

Corrupted file

A file damaged in some way, such as by a virus, or by software or hardware failure, so that it cannot be read by a computer.

Sedona Conference

Cost

The monetary value of resources used or sacrificed or liabilities incurred to achieve an objective such as to acquire or produce a good or to perform an activity or service.

GAO/PCIE Financial Audit Manual

Cost benefit analysis

An activity that analyses and compares the costs and the benefits involved in one or more alternative courses of action. See also business case, cost effectiveness, cost determination, and investment appraisal.

ITIL, BS 25999

Cost center

A business unit or project to which costs are assigned. A cost center does not charge for services provided. An IT service provider can be run as a cost center or a profit center.

ITIL

Cost determination

The value of efforts determined necessary to moderate identified risks. Cost factors may include labor, time, system response, and financial considerations. See also cost benefit analysis.

Centers for Medicare & Medicaid Services (CMS)

Cost effectiveness

A measure of the balance between the effectiveness and cost of a service, process or activity. A cost effective process is one which achieves its objectives at minimum cost. See also KPI, return on investment, value for money.

ITIL

Cost element

The middle level of category to which costs are assigned in budgeting and accounting. The highest level category is cost type. For example, a cost type of "people" could have cost elements of payroll, staff benefits, expenses, training, overtime, etc. Cost elements can be further broken down to give cost units. For example, the cost element "expenses" could include cost units of hotels, transport, meals, etc.

ITIL

Cost management

A general term that is used to refer to budgeting and accounting, sometimes used as a synonym for financial management for IT services.

ITIL

Cost model

A framework used in budgeting and accounting in which all known costs can be recorded, categorized, and allocated to specific customers, business units or projects. Cost-by-customer and cost-by-service are common types of cost model. See also cost type, cost element, cost unit.

ITIL

Cost plus

A charging policy in which charges are calculated by adding a percentage to the cost of providing the IT service. The additional money is often used for future investment.

ITIL

Cost type

The highest level of category to which costs are assigned in budgeting and accounting. For example, hardware, software, people, accommodation, external and transfer. See also cost element, cost unit, cost model.

ITIL

Cost unit

The lowest level of category to which costs are assigned. Cost units are usually things that can be easily counted (e.g. Staff numbers, software licenses) or things easily measured (e.g. CPU usage, electricity consumed). Cost units are included within cost elements. For example, a cost element of "expenses" could include cost units of hotels, transport, meals, etc.

ITIL

Cost-by-customer cost model

A type of cost model in which costs are identified and allocated to customers.

ITIL

Cost-by-service cost model

A type of cost model in which costs are identified and allocated to IT services.

ITIL

Costing methodology

Methodology for accumulating the costs of resources that directly or indirectly contribute to the production of outputs and assigning those costs to outputs.

GAO/PCIE Financial Audit Manual

Counter with Cipher Block Chaining-Message Authentication Code (CCM)

A mode of operation for a symmetric key block cipher algorithm. It combines the techniques of the Counter (CTR) mode and the Cipher Block Chaining-Message Authentication Code (CBC-MAC) algorithm to provide assurance of the confidentiality and the authenticity of computer data.

NIST 800 series

Countermeasure

Action, device, procedure, technique, or other measure that reduces the vulnerability of an information system.

US National Information Assurance (IA) Glossary

Countermeasures

Actions and system controls present or undertaken to reduce or moderate the effect of specific vulnerabilities. A synonym for control. The term countermeasure can be used to refer to any type of control, but it is most often used when referring to measures that increase resilience, fault tolerance, or reliability of an IT service.

Centers for Medicare & Medicaid Services (CMS), ITIL, NIST 800 Series, FIPS Pubs

Coupling

Measure of interconnectivity among software program modules' structure. Coupling depends on the interface complexity between modules. This can be defined as the point at which entry or reference is made to a module and what data passes across the interface. In application software design, it is preferable to strive for the lowest possible coupling between modules. Simple connectivity among modules results in software that is easier to understand, maintain, and less prone to a ripple or domino effect caused when errors occur at one location and propagate through the system.

ISACA

Coverage

The proportion of known attacks detected by an intrusion detection system.

ISACA

Covered Entity (CE)

A health plan, a healthcare clearing house, or health care provider that electronically exchanges information to carry out financial or administrative activities related to health care.

HIPAA

Covert channel

Unintended and/or unauthorized communications path that can be used to transfer information in a manner that violates an information system security policy. See also overt channel and exploitable channel.

US National Information Assurance (IA) Glossary

Covert channel analysis

Determination of the extent to which the security policy model and subsequent lower-level program descriptions may allow unauthorized access to information.

US National Information Assurance (IA) Glossary

Covert storage channel

Covert channel involving the direct or indirect writing to a storage location by one process and the direct or indirect reading of the storage location by another process. Covert storage channels typically involve a finite resource (e.g.,

sectors on a disk) that is shared by two subjects at different security levels.

US National Information Assurance (IA) Glossary

Covert timing channel

Covert channel in which one process signals information to another process by modulating its own use of system resources (e.g., central processing unit time) in such a way that this manipulation affects the real response time observed by the second process.

US National Information Assurance (IA) Glossary

Create

The act of making a record of a document or information originating in or received by an organization.

DIRKS

Credential analysis

In vulnerability analysis, passive monitoring approaches in which passwords or other access credentials are required. This sort of check usually involves accessing a system data object.

ISACA

Credentials

Information passed from one entity to another that is used to establish the sending entity's access rights. An object that authoritatively binds an identity (and optionally, additional attributes) to a token possessed and controlled by a person.

Workgroup for Electronic Data Interchange, US National Information Assurance (IA) Glossary, NIST 800 Series, FIPS Pubs

Credentials Service Provider (CSP)

A trusted entity that issues or registers subscriber tokens and issues electronic credentials to subscribers. The CSP may encompass Registration Authorities and verifiers that it operates. A CSP may be an independent third party, or may issue credentials for its own use.

NIST 800 series

Credit risk

The risk to earnings or capital arising from an obligor's failure to meet the terms of any contract with the bank or otherwise to perform as agreed. Internet banking provides the opportunity for banks to expand their geographic range. Customers can reach a given bank from literally anywhere in the world. In dealing with customers over the Internet, absent any personal contact, it is challenging for banks to verify the good faith of their customers, which is an important element in making sound credit decisions.

ISACA

Crisis

A critical event that has the ability to dramatically impact an organization's profitability, reputation, or ability to operate.

Centers for Medicare & Medicaid Services (CMS), ISO/IEC 27001:2005

Crisis management

The overall coordination of an organization's response to a crisis in an effective, timely manner with the goal of avoiding or minimizing damage to the organization's profitability, reputation, or ability to operate. See also crisis management team.

Centers for Medicare & Medicaid Services (CMS), ITIL, PAS 56

Crisis management team

A crisis management team is responsible for strategic issues such as managing media relations and shareholder confidence, and decides when to invoke business continuity plans.

Centers for Medicare & Medicaid Services (CMS), ITIL

Criteria

The standards and benchmarks used to measure and present the subject matter and against which the IS auditor evaluates the subject matter. Criteria should be: Objective—free from bias, Measurable—provide for consistent measurement, Complete—include all relevant factors to reach a conclusion, and Relevant—relate to the subject matter.

ISACA

Criteria of Control (COCO)

Published by the Canadian Institute of Chartered Accountants in 1995.

ISACA

Critical assets

The most important assets to an organization. The organization will suffer a large adverse impact if something happens to critical assets.

CERT OCTAVE

Critical Infrastructure Assurance Office (CIAO)

CIAO focuses on developing a national plan for protecting the government's critical infrastructure, as well as education initiatives regarding that infrastructure. CIAO's responsibilities for developing and coordinating national critical infrastructure policy focus on three key areas: 1) promoting national outreach and awareness campaigns both in the private sector and at the state and local government level; 2) assisting Federal agencies to analyze their own risk exposure and critical infrastructure dependencies; and 3) coordinating the preparation of an integrated national strategy for critical infrastructure assur-

ance. See also http://www.bis.doc.gov for more information.

de facto

Critical infrastructures

System and assets, whether physical or virtual, so vital to the U.S. that the incapacity or destruction of such systems and assets would have a debilitating impact on security, national economic security, national public health or safety, or any combination of those matters. [Critical Infrastructures Protection Act of 2001, 42 U.S.C. 5195c(e)]

US National Information Assurance (IA) Glossary

Critical security parameter

Security-related information (e.g., secret and private cryptographic keys, and authentication data such as passwords and Personal Identification Numbers (PINs)) whose disclosure or modification can compromise the security of a cryptographic module.

NIST 800 series, FIPS Pubs

Critical Success Factor (CSF)

Something that must happen if a process, project, plan, change, or IT service is to succeed. KPIs are used to measure the achievement of each CSF. For example, a CSF of "protect IT services when making changes" could be measured by KPIs such as "percentage reduction of unsuccessful changes," "percentage reduction in changes causing incidents," etc.

CobiT, ITIL

Criticality

The level of impact an interruption in service or exposure will have on an organization.

Centers for Medicare & Medicaid Services (CMS), ISO/IEC 27001:2005

Criticality level

Refers to the (consequences of) incorrect behavior of a system. The more serious the expected direct and indirect effects of incorrect behavior, the higher the criticality level.

NIST 800 series

Cross certification

A certificate issued by one certification authority to a second certification authority so that users of the first certification authority are able to obtain the public key of the second certification authority and verify the certificates it has created. Often cross certification refers specifically to certificates issued to each other by two CAs at the same level in a hierarchy.

ISACA

Cross domain solution

Information assurance solution that provides the ability to access or transfer information between two or more security domains. See also multi level security.

US National Information Assurance (IA) Glossary

Cross referencing

See unification.

de facto

Cross-certificate

A certificate used to establish a trust relationship between two Certification Authorities.

NIST 800 series

Cross-custodian de-duplication

Culls a document to the extent multiple copies of that document reside within different custodians' data sets. See also De-Duplication.

Sedona Conference

Cross-site scripting (XSS)

Type of security vulnerability typically found in web applications. Can be used by an attacker to gain elevated privilege to sensitive page content, session cookies, and variety of other objects.

PCI-DSS

Crosswalking

See unification.

Centers for Medicare & Medicaid Services (CMS)

Cryptanalysis

1) Operations performed in converting encrypted messages to plain text without initial knowledge of the crypto-algorithm and/or key employed in the encryption. 2) The study of mathematical techniques for attempting to defeat cryptographic techniques and information system security. This includes the process of looking for errors or weaknesses in the implementation of an algorithm or of the algorithm itself.

US National Information Assurance (IA) Glossary, NIST 800 Series

CRYPTO

Marking or designator identifying COMSEC keying material used to secure or authenticate telecommunications carrying classified or sensitive U.S. Government or U.S. Government-derived information.

US National Information Assurance (IA) Glossary

Crypto officer

An operator or process (subject), acting on behalf of the operator, performing cryptographic initialization or management functions.

NIST 800 series, FIPS Pubs

Crypto-alarm

Circuit or device that detects failures or aberrations in the logic or operation of crypto-equipment. Crypto-alarm may inhibit transmission or may provide a visible and/or audible alarm.

US National Information Assurance (IA) Glossary

Crypto-algorithm

Well-defined procedure or sequence of rules or steps, or a series of mathematical equations used to describe cryptographic processes such as encryption/decryption, key generation, authentication, signatures, etc.

US National Information Assurance (IA) Glossary

Crypto-ancillary equipment

Equipment designed specifically to facilitate efficient or reliable operation of crypto-equipment, without performing cryptographic functions itself.

US National Information Assurance (IA) Glossary

Crypto-equipment

Equipment that embodies a cryptographic logic.

US National Information Assurance (IA) Glossary

Crypto-Ignition Key (CIK)

Device or electronic key used to unlock the secure mode of crypto-equipment.

US National Information Assurance (IA) Glossary

Cryptographic

Pertaining to, or concerned with, cryptography.

US National Information Assurance (IA) Glossary

Cryptographic algorithm

A mathematical procedure used for such purposes as encrypting and decrypting messages and signing documents digitally.

FISCAM, NIST 800 Series

Cryptographic boundary

An explicitly defined continuous perimeter that establishes the physical bounds of a cryptographic module and contains all the hardware, software, and/or firmware components of a cryptographic module.

NIST 800 series, FIPS Pubs

Cryptographic component

Hardware or firmware embodiment of the cryptographic logic. A cryptographic component may be a modular assembly, a printed wiring assembly, a microcircuit, or a combination of these items.

US National Information Assurance (IA) Glossary

Cryptographic hash function

A function that maps a bit string of arbitrary length to a fixed length bit string. Approved hash functions satisfy the following properties: 1) (One-way) It is computationally infeasible to find any input which maps to any pre-specified output, and 2) (Collision resistant) It is computationally infeasible to find any two distinct inputs that map to the same output.

NIST 800 series

Cryptographic initialization

Function used to set the state of a cryptographic logic prior to key generation, encryption, or other operating mode.

US National Information Assurance (IA) Glossary

Cryptographic key

1) A value used to control cryptographic operations, such as decryption, encryption, signature generation or signature verification. 2) A parameter used in con-

junction with a cryptographic algorithm that determines 1) the transformation of plaintext data into ciphertext data, 2) the transformation of ciphertext data into plaintext data, 3) a digital signature computed from data, 4) the verification of a digital signature computed from data, 5) an authentication code computed from data, or 6) an exchange agreement of a shared secret.

NIST 800 series, FIPS Pubs

Cryptographic logic

The embodiment of one (or more) crypto-algorithm(s) along with alarms, checks, and other processes essential to effective and secure performance of the cryptographic process(es).

US National Information Assurance (IA) Glossary

Cryptographic module

The set of hardware, software, firmware, or some combination thereof that implements cryptographic logic or processes, including cryptographic algorithms, and is contained within the cryptographic boundary of the module.

NIST 800 series, FIPS Pubs

Cryptographic module security policy

A precise specification of the security rules under which a cryptographic module will operate, including the rules

derived from the requirements of this standard (FIPS 140-2) and additional rules imposed by the vendor.

NIST 800 series, FIPS Pubs

Cryptographic Module Validation Program (CMVP)

Validates cryptographic modules to Federal Information Processing Standard (FIPS) 140-2 and other cryptography based standards. The CMVP is a joint effort between National Institute of Standards and Technology (NIST) and the Communications Security Establishment (CSE) of the Government of Canada. Products validated as conforming to FIPS 140-2 are accepted by the Federal agencies of both countries for the protection of sensitive information (United States) or Designated Information (Canada). The goal of the CMVP is to promote the use of validated cryptographic modules and provide Federal agencies with a security metric to use in procuring equipment containing validated cryptographic modules.

NIST 800 series, FIPS Pubs

Cryptographic randomization

Function that randomly determines the transmit state of a cryptographic logic.

US National Information Assurance (IA) Glossary

Cryptographic strength

A measure of the expected number of operations required to defeat a cryptographic mechanism.

NIST 800 series

Cryptographic system

The hardware, software, documents, and associated techniques and processes that together provide a means of encryption.

FISCAM

Cryptographic token

A token where the secret is a cryptographic key.

NIST 800 series

Cryptography

1) The conversion of data into a secret code for transmission over a public network. The science of coding messages so they cannot be read by any person other than the intended recipient. Ordinary text — or plain text — and other data are transformed into coded form by encryption and translated back to plain text or data by decryption. 2) The discipline that embodies the principles, means, and methods for the transformation of data in order to hide their semantic content, prevent their unauthorized use, or prevent their undetected modification.

FISCAM, ISACA, Centers for Medicare & Medicaid Services (CMS), Workgroup for Electronic Data Interchange, US National Information Assurance (IA) Glossary, PCI-DSS, Sedona Conference, NIST 800 Series, FIPS Pubs

Cryptology

The study and mathematics of secret codes and ciphers. It includes communications security and communications intelligence. Sometimes used interchangeably with cryptography. See also cipher, cryptography.

Workgroup for Electronic Data Interchange, US National Information Assurance (IA) Glossary, NIST 800 Series

Cryptonet

Stations holding a common key.

US National Information Assurance (IA) Glossary

Cryptoperiod

Time span during which each key setting remains in effect.

US National Information Assurance (IA) Glossary, NIST 800 Series

Cryptosecurity

Component of COMSEC resulting from the provision of technically sound cryptosystems and their proper use.

US National Information Assurance (IA) Glossary

Cryptosynchronization

Process by which a receiving decrypting cryptographic logic attains the same internal state as the transmitting encrypting logic.

US National Information Assurance (IA) Glossary

Cryptosystem

Associated INFOSEC items interacting to provide a single means of encryption or decryption.

US National Information Assurance (IA) Glossary

Cryptosystem analysis

Process of establishing the exploitability of a cryptosystem, normally by reviewing transmitted traffic protected or secured by the system under study.

US National Information Assurance (IA) Glossary

Cryptosystem evaluation

Process of determining vulnerabilities of a cryptosystem.

US National Information Assurance (IA) Glossary

Cryptosystem review

Examination of a cryptosystem by the controlling authority ensuring its adequacy of design and content, continued need, and proper distribution.

US National Information Assurance (IA) Glossary

Cryptosystem survey

Management technique in which actual holders of a cryptosystem express opinions on the system's suitability and provide usage information for technical evaluations.

US National Information Assurance (IA) Glossary

Culture

A set of values that is shared by a group of people, including expectations about how people should behave. Ideas, beliefs, and practices. See also vision.

ITIL

Custodian

Person having control of a network, computer or specific electronic files.

Sedona Conference

Custodian de-duplication

Culls a document to the extent multiple copies of that document reside within the same custodian's data set. See also De-duplication.

Sedona Conference

Customer

A person of external or internal organization or entity who receives IT services. Someone who buys goods or services. The customer of an IT service provider is the person or group who defines and agrees with the service level targets. The term customers is also sometimes informally used to mean users, for example, "this is a customer focused organization".

CobiT, ISO/IEC 27001:2005, ITIL

Customer focus

Understanding and meeting the real needs of customers and users. This is done to maximize customer satisfaction and thus to obtain long term benefits for the IT service provider. Customer focus

can be displayed by the entire organization (see service culture) or by specific people or processes.

ITIL

Customer Information Control System (CICS)

CICS is a transaction processing system (like TCAM) designed for both online and batch activity. It is a transaction server that runs primarily on IBM mainframe systems under z/OS or VSE. CICS is available for other operating systems, notably OS/400, OS/2, and as the closely related IBM TXSeries software on AIX, Windows, and Linux, among others. CICS is used in bank teller applications, airline reservation systems, ATM systems etc. CICS first went on sale on July 8, 1969.

FISCAM

Customer Relationship Management (CRM)

Applications that help manage clients and contacts. Used in larger companies. Often a significant repository of sales, customer, and sometimes marketing data.

AIIM, Sedona Conference

Customer-added metadata

See User-added metadata.

Sedona Conference

Customer-managed use

The management of licenses by the customer or IT service provider. Licenses may also be managed by the supplier of the software (vendor managed use).

ITIL

Cyan

Cyan-colored ink reflects blue and green and absorbs red.

Sedona Conference

Cyan, Magenta, Yellow, and Black (CMYK)

A subtractive method used in four color printing and desktop publishing.

Sedona Conference

CyberSource Advanced Fraud Screen Enhanced by Visa

A real-time fraud-detection service that examines transactions generated from online stores. It estimates the level of risk associated with each transaction and provides merchants with risk scores, enabling them to more accurately identify potentially fraudulent orders.

VISA Glossary of Terms

Cyclic redundancy check

Error checking mechanism that checks data integrity by computing a polynomial algorithm based checksum.

US National Information Assurance (IA) Glossary

Cyclical Redundancy Check (CRC)

Used in data communications to create a checksum character at the end of a data block to ensure integrity of data transmission and receipt.

Sedona Conference, NIST 800 Series

Cylinder

The set of tracks on both sides of each platter in the hard drive that is located at the same head position.

Sedona Conference

Public key cryptographic algorithm

A cryptographic algorithm that uses two related keys, a public key and a private key. The two keys have the property that deriving the private key from the public key is computationally infeasible. Public key cryptography uses "key pairs," a public key and a mathematically related private key. Given the public key, it is infeasible to find the private key. The private key is kept secret while the public key may be shared with others. A message encrypted with the public key can only be decrypted with the private key. A message can be digitally signed with the private key, and anyone can verify the signature with the public key.

NIST 800 series, FIPS Pubs

Zeroization

A method of erasing electronically stored data, cryptographic keys, and CSPs by altering or deleting the contents of the data storage to prevent recovery of the data.

NIST 800 series, FIPS Pubs

D

Authorizing official designated representative

Individual selected by an authorizing official to act on their behalf in coordinating and carrying out the necessary activities required during the security certification and accreditation of an information system.

NIST 800 series

Damage assessment

Post-incident appraisal or determination of actual consequences to an organization including human, physical, economic, reputation and natural resource impacts.

Centers for Medicare & Medicaid Services (CMS)

Dashboard

A tool for setting expectations for an organization at each level and continuous monitoring of the performance against set targets.

CobiT

Data

Objects in their widest sense (i.e., external and internal), structured and non-structured, graphics, sound, etc. Facts and information that can be communicated and manipulated. All software is divided into two general categories: data and programs. Programs are collections of instructions for manipulating data. In database management systems data files are the files that store the database information. Other files, such as index files and data dictionaries, store administrative information, known as metadata.

CobiT, FISCAM, Centers for Medicare & Medicaid Services (CMS), ISO/IEC 27001:2005, Sedona Conference

Data access method

See access method.

FISCAM

Data administration

The function that plans for and administers the data used throughout the organization. This function is concerned with identifying, cataloging, controlling, and coordinating the information needs of the organization.

FISCAM, Centers for Medicare & Medicaid Services (CMS)

Data aggregation

Compilation of unclassified individual data systems and data elements that could result in the totality of the information being classified or of beneficial use to an adversary.

US National Information Assurance (IA) Glossary

Data analysis

Typically in large organizations where the quantum of data processed by the ERPs are extremely voluminous, analysis of patterns and trends prove to be extremely useful in ascertaining the efficiency and effectiveness of operations. Most ERPs provide opportunities for extraction and analysis of data, some with built-in tools through the use of third-party developed tools that interface with the ERP systems.

ISACA

Data center

See computer facility or computer room.

FISCAM, Centers for Medicare & Medicaid Services (CMS)

Data classification scheme

An enterprise wide schema for classifying data on factors such as criticality, sensitivity, and ownership. This is a high level control objective, and a part of defining the information architecture for the organization. There is no consensus in the security industry on how to describe various levels of sensitivity of information. Most organizations that have adopted a data classification scheme will usually find that Account and Transaction Information is within their existing classifications of "sensitive" or "confidential."

CobiT, Visa CISP, PCI-DSS

Data collection

See Harvesting.

Sedona Conference

Data communications

The transfer of information from one computer to another through a communications medium, such as telephone lines, microwave relay, satellite link, or physical cable. The transfer of data between functional units by means of data transmission according to a protocol.

FISCAM, ISACA, Centers for Medicare & Medicaid Services (CMS), FIPS Pubs

Data communications systems

Computer systems that transmit data over communications lines such as tele-

153

phone lines or cables. This would be defined as a part of a General Support System. See also General Support System, networks.

FISCAM

Data contamination

The introduction of data of one sensitivity level into data of a lower or different sensitivity level. An accidental or intentional violation of data integrity.

Centers for Medicare & Medicaid Services (CMS)

Data control

The function responsible for seeing that all data necessary for processing is present and that all output is complete and distributed properly. This function is generally responsible for reconciling record counts and control totals submitted by users with similar counts and totals generated during processing.

FISCAM, Centers for Medicare & Medicaid Services (CMS), ISO/IEC 27001:2005

Data custodian

Individuals and departments responsible for the storage and safeguarding of computerized information. This typically is within the IS organization.

ISACA

Data definition

Identification of all fields in the database, how they are formatted, how they are combined into different types of records, and how the record types are interrelated.

FISCAM

Data dictionary

A repository of information about data, such as its meaning, relationships to other data, origin, usage, and format. The dictionary assists company management, database administrators, systems analysts, and application programmers in effectively planning, controlling, and evaluating the collection, storage, and use of data. It also indicates which application programs use that data so that when a data structure is contemplated, a list of the affected programs can be generated. The data dictionary may be a stand-alone information system used for management or documentation purposes, or it may control the operation of a database. CobiT also references an enterprise data dictionary.

FISCAM, ISACA, Centers for Medicare & Medicaid Services (CMS), CobiT

Data diddling

Changing data with malicious intent before or during input to the system.

FISCAM, ISACA

Data element

A combination of characters or bytes referring to one separate piece of information, such as name, address, or age. A basic unit of information that has a unique meaning and subcategories (data items) of distinct value. Examples of data elements include gender, race, and geographic location.

Sedona Conference, NIST 800 Series

Data Encryption Algorithm (DEA)

The cryptographic engine that is used by the Triple Data Encryption Algorithm (TDEA).

NIST 800 series

Data Encryption Standard (DES)

A NIST Federal Information Processing Standard and a commonly used secret-key cryptographic algorithm for encrypting and decrypting data. DES has been used commonly for data encryption in the forms of software and hardware implementation. The conversion of data into an unintelligible form so that it is readable except by authorized users is called data encryption. The DES is an approved FIPS cryptographic algorithm which is as required by FIPS 140-1. The National Institute of Standards and Technology Data Encryption Standard was adopted by the U.S. Government as Federal Information Processing Standard (FIPS) Publication 46-1, which

allows only hardware implementations of the data encryption algorithm. See also private key cryptosystems.

NIST 800 series, Centers for Medicare & Medicaid Services (CMS), US National Information Assurance (IA) Glossary

Data extraction

The process of retrieving data from documents (hard copy or electronic). The process may be manual or electronic.

Sedona Conference

Data field

See Field.

Sedona Conference

Data file

See file.

FISCAM, Centers for Medicare & Medicaid Services (CMS)

Data filtering

The process of identifying for extraction specific data based on specified parameters.

Sedona Conference

Data flow

The flow of data from the input (in Internet banking, ordinarily user input at his/her desktop) to output (in Internet banking, ordinarily data in a bank's central database). Data flow includes traveling through the communication lines, routers, switches and firewalls as well as processing through various applications on servers which process the data from user input to storage in the organization's central database.

ISACA

Data flow control

Synonymous with information flow control.

US National Information Assurance (IA) Glossary

Data formats

The organization of information for display, storage or printing. Data is maintained in certain common formats so that it can be used by various programs, which may only work with data in a particular format, e.g. PDF, html.

Sedona Conference

Data harvesting

See Harvesting.

Sedona Conference

Data integrity

Data integrity is a requirement that information and programs are changed only in a specified and authorized manner. It is the property that data has not been altered in an unauthorized manner. Data integrity covers data in storage, during processing, and while in transit.

National Research Council - Computers at Risk, NIST 800 series, ISACA, Centers for Medicare & Medicaid Services (CMS), Workgroup for Electronic Data Interchange, US National Information Assurance (IA) Glossary

Data leakage

Siphoning out or leaking information by dumping computer files or stealing computer reports and tapes.

ISACA

Data mining

Data mining generally refers to techniques for extracting summaries and reports from an organization's databases and data sets. In the context of electronic discovery, this term often refers to the processes used to cull through a collection of electronic data to extract evidence for production or presentation in an investigation or in litigation.

Sedona Conference

Data oriented systems development

The purpose is to provide usable data rather than a function. The focus of the development is to provide ad hoc reporting for users by developing a suitable, accessible database of information.

ISACA

Data origin authentication

The verification that the source of data received is as claimed.

NIST 800 series, US National Information Assurance (IA) Glossary

Data owner

See owner.

FISCAM, ISACA, Centers for Medicare & Medicaid Services (CMS), CobiT

Data processing

The computerized preparation of documents and the flow of data contained in these documents through the major steps of recording, classifying, and summarizing. The process wherein computer and its programs organize/manipulate data and the flow of data.

FISCAM, Centers for Medicare & Medicaid Services (CMS)

Data processing center

See computer facility.

FISCAM

Data security

See security management function.

FISCAM, ISACA, Centers for Medicare & Medicaid Services (CMS), FIPS Pubs, US National Information Assurance (IA) Glossary

Data Security Standard (DSS)

The security standard utilized by the Payment Card Industry.

PCI-DSS

Data set

A named or defined collection of data. See also Production data set and Privilege data set.

Sedona Conference

Data structure

The relationships among files in a database and among data items within each file.

ISACA

Data terminal equipment (DTE)

ISACA

Data Transfer Device (DTD)

Fill device designed to securely store, transport, and transfer electronically both COMSEC and TRANSEC key, designed to be backward compatible with the previous generation of COMSEC common fill devices, and programmable to support modern mission systems.

US National Information Assurance (IA) Glossary

Data validation

Checking transaction data for any errors or omissions that can be detected by examining the data.

FISCAM, Centers for Medicare & Medicaid Services (CMS), ISO/IEC 27001:2005

Data warehouse

A generic term for a system used to store, retrieve, and manage large amounts of data. A database, often remote, containing recent snapshots of corporate data that can be used for analysis without slowing down day-to-day operations of the production database.

FISCAM

Database

A structured collection of related information about a subject organized in a useful manner that provides a base or foundation for procedures, such as retrieving information, drawing conclusions, or making decisions. Any collection of information that serves these purposes qualifies as a database, even if the information is not stored on a computer. In computing databases are sometimes classified according to their organizational approach with the most prevalent approach being the relational database - a tabular database in which data is defined so that it can be reorganized and accessed in a number of different ways. Another popular organizational structure is the distributed database which can be dispersed or replicated among different points in a network. Also, a database of this sort does not need to be a single physical database, but may consist of various data sources and tools that together meet the requirements. For example, configuration management database, capacity database, availability database, and application portfolio. SQL (Structured Query Language) is a standard computer language for making interactive queries from and updates to a database.

FISCAM, ISACA, Centers for Medicare & Medicaid Services (CMS), PCI-DSS, ITIL, Sedona Conference

Database administrator

The individual responsible for both the design of the database, including the structure and contents, and the access capabilities of application programs and users to the database. Additional responsibilities include operation, performance, integrity, and security of the database.

FISCAM, ISACA, PCI-DSS

Database administrator, or Doing Business As (DBA)

FISCAM, PCI-DSS

Database management (DBM)

Tasks related to creating, maintaining, organizing, and retrieving information from a database.

Centers for Medicare & Medicaid Services (CMS)

Database Management System (DBMS)

A software product that aids in controlling and using the data needed by application programs. Database Management Systems are a set of programs that control the organization, storage, and retrieval of data. DBMSs organize data in a database, manage all requests for database actions (such as queries or updates from users), and permit centralized control of security and data integrity. The database management system also controls the security and data integrity of the database.

FISCAM, Centers for Medicare & Medicaid Services (CMS), AIIM, Sedona Conference

Database replication

The process of creating and managing duplicate versions of a database. Replication not only copies a database but also synchronizes a set of replicas so that changes made to one replica are reflected in all the others. The beauty of replication is that it enables many users to work with their own local copy of a database but have the database updated as if they were working on a single centralized database. For database applications where geographically users are distributed widely, replication is often the most efficient method of database access.

ISACA

Database specifications

These are the requirements for establishing a database application. They include field definitions, field requirements, and reporting requirements for the individual information in the database.

ISACA

Datagram

A packet (encapsulated with a frame containing information) which is transmitted in a packet-switching network from source to destination.

ISACA

Daubert (challenge)

Daubert v. Merrell Dow Pharmaceuticals, 509 U.S. 579 (1993), addresses the admission of scientific expert testimony to ensure that the testimony is reliable before considered for admission pursuant to Rule 702. The court assesses the testimony by analyzing the methodology and applicability of the expert's approach. Faced with a proffer of expert scientific testimony, the trial judge must determine first, pursuant to Rule 104(a), whether the expert is proposing to testify to (1) scientific knowledge that (2) will assist the trier of fact to understand or determine a fact at issue. This involves preliminary assessment of whether the reasoning or methodology is scientifically valid and whether it can be applied to the facts at issue. Daubert suggests a open approach and provides a list of four potential factors: (1) whether the theory can be or has been tested; (2) whether the theory has been subjected to peer review or publication; (3) known or potential rate of error of that particular technique and the existence and maintenance of standards controlling the technique's operation; and (4)consideration of general acceptance within the scientific community. 509 U.S. at 593-94.

Sedona Conference

De-duplication

De-duplication ("De-duping") is the process of comparing electronic records based on their characteristics and removing or marking duplicate records within the data set. The definition of "duplicate records" should be agreed upon, i.e., whether an exact copy from a different location (such as a different mailbox, server tapes, etc.) is considered to be a duplicate. De-duplication can be selective, depending on the agreed-upon criteria. See also Case de-duplication, Content comparison, Cross-custodian de-duplication, Custodian de-duplication, Data verification, Digital fingerprint, File level binary comparison, Hash coding, Horizontal de-duplication, Metadata comparison, and Production de-duplication.

Sedona Conference

De-fragment ("de-frag")

Use of a computer utility to reorganize files so they are more contiguous on a hard drive or other storage medium, if the files or parts thereof have become fragmented and scattered in various locations within the storage medium in the course of normal computer operations. Used to optimize the operation of the computer, it will overwrite information in unallocated space. See Fragmented.

Sedona Conference

De-shading

Removing shaded areas to render images more easily recognizable by OCR. De-shading software typically searches for areas with a regular pattern of tiny dots.

Sedona Conference

De-skewing

The process of straightening skewed (tilted) images. De-skewing is one of the image enhancements that can improve OCR accuracy. Documents often become skewed when scanned or faxed.

Sedona Conference

De-speckling

Removing isolated speckles from an image file. Speckles often develop when a document is scanned or faxed.

Sedona Conference

Debt Collection Improvement Act (DCIA)

GAO/PCIE Financial Audit Manual

Debug

With software, to detect, locate, and correct logical or syntactical errors in a computer program.

FISCAM, Centers for Medicare & Medicaid Services (CMS)

Decentralization

The process of distributing computer processing to different locations within an organization.

ISACA

Decertification

Revocation of the certification of an information system item or equipment for cause.

US National Information Assurance (IA) Glossary

Decipher

Convert enciphered text to plain text by means of a cryptographic system.

US National Information Assurance (IA) Glossary

Decision support system (DSS)

An information system or analytic model designed to help managers and professionals be more effective in their decision-making.

FISCAM

Decode

Convert encoded text to plain text by means of a code.

US National Information Assurance (IA) Glossary

Decoy server

See honey pot.

ISACA

Decrypt

Generic term encompassing decode and decipher.

US National Information Assurance (IA) Glossary

Decryption

The process of translating a coded sequence of bytes back to its original sequence. A technique used to recover the original plaintext from the ciphertext such that it is intelligible to the reader. The decryption is a reverse process of the encryption.

Sedona Conference, ISACA, NIST 800 Series, FIPS Pubs

Decryption key

A piece of information, in a digitized form, used to recover the plaintext from the corresponding ciphertext by decryption.

ISACA

Dedicated mode

IS security mode of operation wherein each user, with direct or indirect access to the system, its peripherals, remote terminals, or remote hosts, has all of the following: 1) valid security clearance for all information within the system; 2) formal access approval and signed non-disclosure agreements for all the information stored and/or processed (including all compartments, subcom-partments, and/or special access programs); and 3) valid need-to-know for all information contained within the information system. When in the dedicated security mode, a system is specifically and exclusively dedicated to and controlled for the processing of one particular type or classification of information, either for full-time operation or for a specified period of time.

US National Information Assurance (IA) Glossary

Dedicated work area

Work space provided for sole use by a single organization, configured ready for use. See also active recovery site.

PAS 56

Default accounts

A system login account that has been predefined in a manufactured system to permit initial access when the system is first put into service.

PCI-DSS

Default classification

Temporary classification reflecting the highest classification being processed in an information system. Default classification is included in the caution statement affixed to an object.

US National Information Assurance (IA) Glossary

Default deny policy

A policy whereby access is denied unless it is specifically allowed. The inverse of default allow.

ISACA

Default password

The password used to gain access when a system is first installed on a computer or network device, usually associated with the default account. There is a large list published on the Internet and maintained at several locations. Failure to change these after the installation leaves the system vulnerable.

ISACA, PCI-DSS

Defense Information Systems Agency (DISA)

The Defense Information Systems Agency is a combat support agency responsible for planning, engineering, acquiring, fielding, and supporting global net-centric solutions to serve the needs of the President, Vice President, the Secretary of Defense, and other DoD Components, under all conditions of peace and war. The designated core missions of DISA are communications, joint command and control, defensive information operations, combat support computing, and joint interoperability support. See also http://www.disa.mil for more information.

de facto

Defense-in-depth

IA strategy integrating people, technology, and operations capabilities to establish variable barriers across multiple layers and dimensions of networks. Synonymous with security-in-depth.

US National Information Assurance (IA) Glossary

Definitive Hardware Store

One or more physical locations in which hardware configuration items are securely stored when not in use. All hardware in the DHS is under the control of change and release management and is recorded in the CMDB. The DHS contains spare parts, maintained at suitable revision levels, and may also include hardware that is part of a future release.

ITIL

Definitive Hardware Store or Department of Homeland Security (DHS)

See Definitive Hardware Store, Department of Homeland Security.

de facto

Definitive Software Library (DSL)

One or more locations in which the definitive and approved versions of all software configuration items are securely stored. The DSL may also contain associated CIs such as licenses and documentation. The DSL is a single logical storage area even if there are multiple locations. All software in the DSL is under the control of change and release management and is recorded in the CMDB. Only software from the DSL is acceptable for use in a release.

ITIL

Degauss

Degauss loosely means to erase. Degauss is to demagnetize a monitor or the read/write head in a disk or tape drive, to neutralize unwanted magnetism in order to erase information from a magnetic storage medium. More specifically, it is to apply a variable, alternating current (AC) field for the purpose of demagnetizing magnetic recording media. The process involves increasing the AC field gradually from zero to some maximum value and back to zero, which leaves a very low residue of magnetic induction on the media. See also clearing.

ISACA, Centers for Medicare & Medicaid Services (CMS), FIPS Pubs, US National Information Assurance (IA) Glossary

Delegated development program

INFOSEC program in which the Director, NSA, delegates, on a case by case basis, the development and/or production of an entire telecommunications product, including the INFOSEC portion, to a lead department or agency.

US National Information Assurance (IA) Glossary

Delete access

This level of access provides the ability to erase or remove data or programs.

FISCAM

Deleted data

Deleted data is data that existed on the computer as live data and which have been deleted by the computer system or end-user activity. Deleted data may remain on storage media in whole or in part until they are overwritten or "wiped." Even after the data itself have been wiped, directory entries, pointers or other information relating to the deleted data may remain on the computer. "Soft deletions" are data marked as deleted (and not generally available to the end-user after such marking), but not yet physically removed or overwritten. Soft-deleted data can be restored with complete integrity.

Sedona Conference

Deleted file

A file with disk space that has been designated as available for reuse; the deleted file remains intact until it is overwritten. Deleting files does not always necessarily eliminate the possibility of recovering all or part of the original data.

Sedona Conference, NIST 800 Series

Deletion

Deletion is the process whereby data is removed from active files and other data storage structures on computers and rendered inaccessible except through the use of special data recovery tools designed to recover deleted data. Deletion occurs on several levels in modern computer systems: (a) File level deletion renders the file inaccessible to the operating system and normal application programs and marks the storage space occupied by the file's directory entry and contents as free and available to re-use for data storage, (b) Record level deletion occurs when a record is rendered inaccessible to a database management system (DBMS) (usually marking the record storage space as available for re-use by the DBMS, although in some cases the space is never reused until the database is compacted) and is also characteristic of many e-mail systems (c) Byte level deletion occurs when text or other information is deleted from the file content (such as the deletion of text from a

word processing file); such deletion may render the deleted data inaccessible to the application intended to be used in processing the file, but may not actually remove the data from the file's content until a process such as compaction or rewriting of the file causes the deleted data to be overwritten.

Sedona Conference

Deliverable

Something that must be provided to meet a commitment in a service level agreement or a contract. Deliverable is also used in a more informal way to mean a planned output of any process.

ITIL

Delivery and support

This high-level domain is concerned with the actual delivery of required services which range from traditional operations over security and continuity aspects to training. In order to deliver services, the necessary support processes must be set up. This domain includes the actual processing of data by application systems, often classified under application controls.

CobiT

Delta release

A release that includes only those components of a release unit that have actually changed since the last release. A delta release is also referred to as a partial release. See also release type.

ITIL

Demand management

Optimizing the use of capacity by moving workload to less utilized times, servers, or places. Demand management often uses differential charging to encourage customers to use IT services at less busy times. Demand management also makes use of other techniques such as limiting the number of concurrent users.

ITIL

Demilitarized Zone (DMZ)

Commonly it is the network segment between the Internet and a private network. It allows access to services from the Internet and the internal private network while denying access from the Internet directly to the private network. Firewall protection is usually implemented for the DMZ network, and an additional firewall layer protects the internal private network. A typical DMZ contains one or more servers intended for public access (web server, e-mail server, etc.), and prevents direct connections to the internal network from public untrusted networks.

Workgroup for Electronic Data Interchange, ISACA, Centers for Medicare & Medicaid

Services (CMS), US National Information Assurance (IA) Glossary, NIST 800 Series

Deming cycle

See plan do check act.

ITIL

Democracy

The continuity and security of information systems should be compatible with the legitimate use and flow of data and information in a democratic society.

NIST 800 series

Demodulation

The process of converting an analog telecommunications signal into a digital computer signal.

ISACA

Denial of Service (DoS)

A denial-of-service assault against a computing resource. An action (or series of actions) that prevents any part of a system from functioning in accordance with its intended purpose. This includes any action that causes unauthorized destruction, modification, delay, or interruption of service. See also interdiction.

Network Frontiers, ISACA, Centers for Medicare & Medicaid Services (CMS), US National Information Assurance (IA) Glossary, NIST 800 Series

Department

Any department, organization, administration, or other financial reporting organization that is not part of a larger financial reporting organization other than the government as a whole. Used in distinguishing inter- and intradepartmental activity and balances.

GAO/PCIE Financial Audit Manual

Department of Homeland Security

The United States Department of Homeland Security (DHS), commonly known as Homeland Security, is a Cabinet department of the Federal Government of the United States with the responsibility of protecting the territory of the United States from terrorist attack and responding to natural disasters. The department was created from 22 existing federal agencies in response to the terrorist attacks of September 11, 2001. See also http://www.dhs.gov for more information.

de facto

Dependency

The direct or indirect reliance of one process or activity upon another.

ITIL

Deployment

The activity responsible for movement of new or changed hardware, software, documentation, process, etc. to the live environment. See also rollout.

ITIL

Depreciation

A measure of the reduction in value of an asset over its life. This is based on wearing out, consumption, or other reduction in the useful economic value.

ITIL

Descenders

Tthe portion of a character which falls below the main part of the letter (e.g. g, p, q).

Sedona Conference

Descriptive top-level specification

Top-level specification written in a natural language (e.g., English), an informal design notation, or a combination of the two. Descriptive top-level specification, required for a class B2 and B3 (as defined in the Orange Book, Department of Defense Trusted Computer System Evaluation Criteria, DoD 5200.28-STD) information system, completely and accurately describes a trusted computing base. See also formal top-level specification.

US National Information Assurance (IA) Glossary

Design materiality

The portion of planning materiality that the auditor allocates to line items or accounts. This amount should be the same for all line items or accounts except for certain offsetting balances. The auditor should set design materiality for the audit as one-third of planning materiality.

GAO/PCIE Financial Audit Manual

Design vulnerability

A weakness inherent in the design or specification of hardware or software whereby even a perfect implementation will result in a vulnerability.

CERT OCTAVE

Designated Approval/Accrediting Authority (DAA)

Official with the authority to formally assume responsibility for operating a system at an acceptable level of risk. This term is synonymous with authorizing official, designated accrediting authority, and delegated accrediting authority.

US National Information Assurance (IA) Glossary, NIST 800 series

Designing and Implementing Recordkeeping Systems (DIRKS)

DIRKS: A Strategic Approach to Managing Business Information (also known as the DIRKS Manual) provides government agencies with practical guidance on managing business information and records. It complies with the eight-step methodology recommended in the Australian Standard for Records Management, AS ISO 15489 – 2002. The DIRKS Manual is primarily for use by Australian Government agency information and records management project teams and consultants.

de facto

Desktop

Generally refers to an individual PC that is not built as a mobile computer (such as a notebook or laptop).

Sedona Conference

Desktop Publishing (DTP)

PC applications used to prepare direct print output or output suitable for printing presses.

Sedona Conference

Desktop workstation

Hosts on an organization's networks that staff members use to conduct business.

CERT OCTAVE

Destruction

The removal of an asset from existence; the asset cannot be recovered.

CERT OCTAVE, ISO 15489, ISO/IEC 27001:2005

Detailed Control Objectives (DCO)

DCOs are components of a particular control objective.

CobiT

Detailed IS controls

Controls over the acquisition, implementation, delivery and support of information systems and services. They are made up of application controls plus those general controls not included in pervasive controls.

ISACA

Detection

A stage in the incident lifecycle. Detection results in the incident becoming known to the service provider. Detection can be automatic or can be the result of a user logging an incident.

ITIL

Detection risk

The risk that the auditor will not detect a material misstatement that exists in an assertion. The risk that audit procedures will not detect a material misstatement that exists in the financial statements. The auditor determines the desired detection risk based on combined risk and audit risk. In statistical terms, beta risk or type II risk.

FISCAM, GAO/PCIE Financial Audit Manual, ISACA

Detective controls

These controls exist to detect and report when errors, omissions, and unauthorized uses or entries occur. A control that is used to identify events (undesirable or desired), errors, and other occurrences that an enterprise has determined to have a material effect on a process or end product.

ISACA, CobiT

Development

The process responsible for creating or modifying an IT service or application. Also used to mean the role or group that carries out development work.

ITIL

Development environment

An environment used to create or modify IT services or applications. Development environments are not typically subjected to the same degree of control as test environments or live environments. See also development.

ITIL

Diagnosis

A stage in the incident and problem lifecycles. The purpose of diagnosis is to identify a workaround for an incident or the root cause of a problem.

ITIL

Diagnostic script

A structured set of questions used by service desk staff to ensure they ask the correct questions, and to help them classify, resolve and assign incidents. Diagnostic scripts may also be made available to users to help them diagnose and resolve their own incidents.

ITIL

Dial back

Synonymous with call back.

US National Information Assurance (IA) Glossary

Dial-back

Used as a control over dial-up telecommunications lines. The telecommunications link established through dial-up into the computer from a remote location is interrupted so the computer can dial back to the caller. The link is permitted only if the caller is from a valid phone number or telecommunications channel. See also dial-in access controls.

ISACA

Dial-in access controls

Controls that prevent unauthorized access from remote users that attempt to access a secured environment. These controls range from dial-back controls to remote user authentication.

ISACA

Dial-up access

A means of connecting to another computer (or a network like the Internet) over a telecommunications line using a modem-equipped computer. See also dial-in access controls.

FISCAM, Centers for Medicare & Medicaid Services (CMS)

Dial-up security software

Software that controls access via remote dial-up. One method of preventing unauthorized users from accessing the system through an unapproved telephone line is through dial-back procedures in which the dial-up security software disconnects a call initiated from outside the network via dial-up lines, looks up the user's telephone number, and uses that number to call the user.

FISCAM

Dictionary attack

A brute force attack that uses common words as possible passwords.

Network Frontiers

Differential charging

A technique used in charging to support demand management by charging different amounts for the same IT service function at different times.

ITIL

Differential Power Analysis (DPA)

An analysis of the variations of the electrical power consumption of a cryptographic module, using advanced statistical methods and/or other techniques, for the purpose of extracting information correlated to cryptographic keys used in a cryptographic algorithm.

NIST 800 series, FIPS Pubs

Digital

Information stored as a string of ones and zeros. Opposite of analog.

Sedona Conference

Digital Asset Management (DAM)

AIIM

Digital Audio Disc (DAD)

Another term for compact disk.

Sedona Conference

Digital Audio Tape (DAT)

A magnetic tape generally used to record audio but can hold up to 40 gigabytes (or 60 CDs) of data if used for data storage. Has the disadvantage of being a serial access device. Often used for backup.

Sedona Conference

Digital certificate

A digital credential that attests to the identity of the individual listed on the certificate. This also contains the individual's public key used to verify messages sent by the individual. It is a unique code that typically is used to allow the authenticity and integrity of communicated data to be verified.

Workgroup for Electronic Data Interchange, ISACA, Sedona Conference

Digital certification

A process to authenticate (or certify) a party's digital signature, carried out by trusted third parties.

ISACA

Digital evidence

1) Electronic information stored or transferred in digital form. 2) An asymmetric key operation where the private key is used to digitally sign an electronic document and the public key is used to verify the signature. Digital signatures, when properly implemented provides the services of: 1) origin authentication, 2) data integrity, and 3) signer non-repudiation.

NIST 800 series, FIPS Pubs, FIPS Pubs

Digital fingerprint

A fixed-length hash code that uniquely represents the binary content of a file. See also Data Verification and File Level Binary Comparison and Hash Coding.

Sedona Conference

Digital Linear Tape (DLT)

A type of backup tape which can hold up to 80 GB depending on the data file format.

Sedona Conference

Digital Rights Management (DRM)

AIIM

Digital Signal Processor/Processing (DSP)

A special purpose computer (or technique) which digitally processes signals and electrical/analog waveforms.

Sedona Conference

Digital signature

An electronic signature based upon cryptographic methods of originator authentication, by using a set of rules and a set of parameters such that the identity of the signer and the integrity of the data can be verified. A digital signature is generated using the sender's private key or applying a one-way hash function. Digital signatures are easily transportable, cannot be imitated by someone else, and can be automatically time-stamped. The ability to ensure that the original signed message arrived means that the sender cannot easily repudiate it later. See also electronic signature.

21 CFR Part 11, FISCAM, ISACA, Centers for Medicare & Medicaid Services (CMS), Workgroup for Electronic Data Interchange, US National Information Assurance (IA) Glossary

Digital signature algorithm

Procedure that appends data to, or performs a cryptographic transformation of, a data unit. The appended data or cryptographic transformation allows reception of the data unit and protects against forgery, e.g., by the recipient.

US National Information Assurance (IA) Glossary, NIST 800 Series

Digital to Analog Converter (DAC)

Converts digital data to analog data.

Sedona Conference

Digital Versatile Disk (DVD)

See Digital Video disk.

AIIM, Sedona Conference

Digital Video Disk (DVD)

A plastic disk, like a CD, on which data can be written and read. DVDs are faster, can hold more information, and can support more data formats than CDs.

Sedona Conference

Digitize

The process of converting an analog value into a digital (numeric) representation.

Sedona Conference

Direct access

An access method for finding an individual item on a storage device and accessing it directly, without having to access all preceding records.

FISCAM

Direct Access Storage Device (DASD)

Any storage device, such as a hard disk, that provides the capability to access and/or manipulate data as required without having to access all preceding records to reach it. In contrast to direct or random access, sequential access devices, such as tape drives, require all preceding records to be read to reach the required data.

FISCAM

Direct cost

A cost of providing an IT service which can be allocated in full to a specific customer, cost center, project, etc. For example, cost of providing non-shared servers or software licenses. See also indirect cost.

ITIL

Direct reporting engagement

An engagement where management does not make a written assertion about the effectiveness of their control procedures, and the IS auditor provides an opinion about subject matter directly, such as the effectiveness of the control procedures.

ISACA

Direct shipment

Shipment of COMSEC material directly from NSA to user COMSEC accounts.

US National Information Assurance (IA) Glossary

Directory

A simulated file folder or container used to organize files and directories in a hierarchical or tree-like structure. UNIX and DOS use the term "directory," while Mac and Windows use the term "folder."

Sedona Conference

Disaster

A sudden, unplanned, calamitous event that brings about damage or loss. Any unexplained event that creates an organizational inability to provide critical business functions for a period of time.

Centers for Medicare & Medicaid Services (CMS), ISO/IEC 27001:2005

Disaster plan

See disaster recovery plan.

DIRKS

Disaster recovery

The response to an interruption in services by implementing a predetermined process to restore an organization's business functions according to relative criticality.

Centers for Medicare & Medicaid Services (CMS)

Disaster Recovery Plan (DRP)

Establishing (and implementing as needed) procedures to restore any loss of data and application processing capabilities. A written set of procedures setting out the measures to be taken to minimize the risks and effects of disasters such as fire, flood or earthquake etc, and to recover, save and secure the vital records should such a disaster occur. A written plan for processing critical applications in the event of a major hardware or software failure or destruction of facilities. See also continuity plan.

HIPAA, DIRKS, FISCAM, Centers for Medicare & Medicaid Services (CMS), US National Information Assurance (IA) Glossary, NIST 800 Series

Disaster recovery tapes

Portable media used to store data for backup purposes. See also Backup Data/Backup tapes.

Sedona Conference

Disc

See disk.

Sedona Conference

Disclosure

This term has two meanings, one for Information Assurance, and the second for the Payment Card Industry. 1) The viewing of confidential or proprietary information by someone who should not see the information. Activities of individuals (employees, third parties, clients, hackers) that involve improper systems access and sometime disclosure of information found thereon, but not serious enough to warrant criminal prosecution. 2) Merchants are required to inform cardholders about their policies for merchandise returns, service cancellations, and refunds. How this information is conveyed, or disclosed, varies for card-present and card-not present merchants, but in general, disclosure must occur before a cardholder signs a receipt to complete the transaction.

CERT OCTAVE, Centers for Medicare & Medicaid Services (CMS), ISO/IEC 27001:2005, VISA Glossary of Terms

Disconnection

The termination of an interconnection between two or more IT systems. A disconnection may be planned (e.g., due to changed business needs) or unplanned (i.e., due to an attack or other contingency).

NIST 800 series

Discovery

Discovery is the process of identifying, locating, securing and producing information and materials for the purpose of obtaining evidence for utilization in the legal process. The term is also used to describe the process of reviewing all materials which may be potentially relevant to the issues at hand and/or which may need to be disclosed to other parties, and of evaluating evidence to prove or disprove facts, theories or allegations. There are several ways to conduct discovery, the most common of which are interrogatories, requests for production of documents and depositions.

Sedona Conference

Discovery sampling

A form of attribute sampling that is used to determine a specified probability of finding at least one example of an occurrence (attribute) in a population.

ISACA

Discretionary Access Control (DAC)

Controls that regulate how users delegate access permissions or make files/information accessible to other users. The basis of this kind of security is that an individual user, or program operating on the user's behalf is allowed to specify explicitly the types of access other users (or programs executing on their behalf) may have to information under the user's control.

NIST 800 series, US National Information Assurance (IA) Glossary, FIPS Pubs

Disk

Round, flat storage media with layers of material which enable the recording of data.

Sedona Conference

Disk mirroring

A method of protecting data from a catastrophic hard disk failure or for long term data storage. As each file is stored on the hard disk, a "mirror" copy is made on a second hard disk or on a different part of the same disk. See also Mirror.

Disk Operating System (DOS)

AIIM

Disk Partition

A hard drive containing a set of consecutive cylinders.

Sedona Conference

Disk storage

High-density random access magnetic storage devices that store billions of bits of data on round, flat plates that are either metal or plastic.

FISCAM

Diskette

A removable and widely used data storage medium that uses a magnetically coated flexible disk of Mylar enclosed in a plastic case.

FISCAM, Centers for Medicare & Medicaid Services (CMS)

Diskless workstation

A workstation or PC on a network that does not have its own disk. Instead, it stores files on a network file server.

ISACA

Diskwipe

Utility that overwrites existing data. Various utilities exist with varying degrees of efficiency some wipe only named files or unallocated space of residual data, thus unsophisticated users who try to wipe evidence may leave behind files of which they are unaware.

Sedona Conference

Disposal

Implement policies and procedures to address the final disposition of regulated data and/or the hardware or electronic media on which it is stored. It includes a range of processes associated with implementing disposal appraisal decision such as the retention, deletion or destruction of records in or from recordkeeping systems. They may also include the migration or transmission of records between recordkeeping systems and the transfer of custody or ownership of records. See also Disposition.

HIPAA, DIRKS, ISO/IEC 27001:2005

Disposal authority

A legal document issued by the National Archives of Australia to authorize the disposal of Commonwealth records. It specifies classes of records and the minimum length of time they should be kept. Records disposal authorities (RDAs) apply to the records of a single organization while general disposal authorities (GDAs), such as the Administrative Functions Disposal Authority (AFDA), normally apply to all Commonwealth agencies.

DIRKS

Disposal classes

Classes of records performing or recording similar activities and therefore having the same retention period and disposal action.

DIRKS

Disposition

The final business action carried out on a record. Associated with implementing records retention, destruction, or transfer decisions which are documented in disposition authorities or other instruments. This action generally is to destroy the archive of the record.

Electronic record disposition can include "soft deletions" (See also Deletion), "hard deletions," "hard deletions with overwrites," "archive to long-term store," "forward to organization," and "copy to another media or format and delete (hard or soft)."

ISO 15489, ISO/IEC 27001:2005, Sedona Conference

Disruption

An unplanned event that causes the general system or major application to be inoperable for an unacceptable length of time (e.g., minor or extended power outage, extended unavailable network, or equipment or facility damage or destruction).

NIST 800 series

Distinguished name

Globally unique identifier representing an individual's identity.

US National Information Assurance (IA) Glossary

Distinguishing identifier

Information which unambiguously distinguishes an entity in the authentication process.

NIST 800 series, FIPS Pubs

Distributed data

Distributed data is that information belonging to an organization which resides on portable media and non-local devices such as remote offices, home computers, laptop computers, personal digital assistants ("PDAs"), wireless communication devices (e.g., Blackberry) and internet repositories (including e-mail hosted by internet service providers or portals and web sites). Distributed data also includes data held by third parties such as application service providers and business partners. Note: Information Technology organizations may define distributed data differently (for example, in some organizations distributed data includes any non-server-based data, including workstation disk drives).

Sedona Conference

Distributed data processing network

A system of computers connected together by a communications network. Each computer processes its data and the network supports the system as a whole. Such a network enhances communication among the linked computers and allows access to shared files.

ISACA

Distributed Denial of Service (DDoS)

A denial-of-service (DoS) attack from multiple sources. See also DoS attack.

Network Frontiers, ISACA, NIST 800 Series

Distributed processing

A mode of operation in which processing is spread among different computers that are linked through a communications network. See also distributed data processing network.

FISCAM

Dithering

In printing, dithering is usually called halftoning, and shades of gray are called halftones. The more dither patterns that a device or program supports, the more shades of gray it can represent. Dithering is the process of converting grays to different densities of black dots, usually for the purposes of printing or storing color or grayscale images as black and white images.

Sedona Conference

Do nothing

A recovery option. The service provider formally agrees with the customer that recovery of this IT service will not be performed.

ITIL

Document [as a noun]

A recorded information or object which can be treated as a unit, information in readable form. A document may be paper or electronic. A document may be comprised of a single page, a collection of pages or any file produced manually or by a software application, that constitutes a logical single communication of information. Examples include a letter, a spreadsheet or an e-mail. See also record.

ISO 15489, ITIL, Sedona Conference

Document date

The original creation date of a document. For an e-mail the document date is indicated by the date-stamp of the e-mail.

Document imaging

Process of capturing, storing, and retrieving documents regardless of original format, using micrographics and/or electronic imaging (scanning, OCR, ICR, etc.).

AIIM

Document imaging programs

Software used to store, manage, retrieve and distribute documents quickly and easily on the computer.

Sedona Conference

Document Interchange Architecture (DIA/DCA)

An IBM standard for transmission and storage of voice, text or video over networks.

Sedona Conference

Document Management (DM)

AIIM

Document management software

Software that controls and organizes documents throughout an enterprise. Incorporates document and content capture, workflow, document repositories, COLD/ERM and output systems, and information retrieval systems.

AIIM

Document metadata

Data about the document stored in the document, as opposed to document content. Often this data is not immediately viewable in the software application used to create/edit the document but often can be accessed via a "Properties" view. Examples include document author and company, and create and revision dates. Contrast with File system metadata and E-mail metadata. See also Metadata.

Sedona Conference

Document Type Declaration (DTD)

AIIM

Document Type Definition (DTD)

AIIM

Document Type or Doc Type

A typical field used in bibliographical coding. Typical doc type examples include letter, memo, report, article and others.

Sedona Conference

Doing Business As (DBA)

A merchant's legal business name as differentiated from the names of a company's principals or other entity that owns or manages the business. A DBA that is significantly different from the principals' or other entity's name can result in an unrecognizable merchant name, or descriptor, on a cardholder's monthly credit card statement, which can in turn lead to potential copy requests and chargebacks. Compliance validation levels are based on the transaction volume of a DBA or chain of stores (not of the corporation that owns several chains).

PCI-DSS, VISA Glossary of Terms

Dollar-unit sampling (DUS)

GAO/PCIE Financial Audit Manual

Domain

A logically distinct segment of a network that is managed as a single security area. The scope of operations for an application or system. CobiT defines domain as a grouping of control objectives into logical stages in the IT investment life cycle. See also security domain.

Network Frontiers, Centers for Medicare & Medicaid Services (CMS), CobiT, US Na-

tional Information Assurance (IA) Glossary, Sedona Conference, NIST 800 Series

Domain hijacking

The act of gaining control of a Web domain and hosting a different web site at that domain or leaving the domain unavailable to visitors; often connected to phishing.

Network Frontiers

Domain Name System (DNS)

A hierarchical database that is distributed across the Internet that allows names to be resolved into IP addresses (and vice versa) to locate services such as web and e-mail servers.

ISACA

Domino database

Another name for Lotus Notes Databases versions 5.0 or higher. See also NSF.

Sedona Conference

Dormant contract

A recovery option. The service provider takes out a contract with a supplier to provide required products or services within agreed times for an agreed price. The contract is invoked as part of a recovery plan, at which time an additional payment is made and the goods or service are provided.

ITIL

DoS attack

A denial of service attack prevents legitimate users from accessing system resource or the delaying of time-critical operations. The assault on the service is from a single source that floods it with so many requests that it becomes overwhelmed and is either stopped completely or operates at a significantly reduced rate.

NIST 800 series, ISACA

Dot pitch

Distance of one pixel in a CRT to the next pixel on the vertical plane. The smaller the number, the higher quality display.

Sedona Conference

Dots Per Inch (DPI)

The measurement of the resolution of display in printing systems. A typical CRT screen provides 96 dpi, which provides 9,216 dots per square inch (96x96). When a paper document is scanned, the resolution, or level of detail, at which the scanning was performed is expressed in DPI. Typically, documents are scanned at 200 or 300 DPI.

Sedona Conference

Dove hologram

A three-dimensional hologram of a dove in flight that appears on all valid Visa cards. When the card is tilted back and forth, the dove should appear to "fly." The dove hologram is one of the card security features that merchants should check to ensure a card-present transaction is valid. This hologram is good through 2010. For updated cards, the Dove hologram is a multiple-color animated dove that appears in the holographic magnetic stripe on the back of all valid updated Visa cards.

VISA Glossary of Terms

Download

Process of transferring data from a central computer to a personal computer or workstation. The act of transferring computerized information from one computer to another computer.

FISCAM, ISACA

Downtime

The time when a configuration item or IT service is not available during its agreed service time. The availability of an IT service is often calculated from agreed service time and downtime.

Network Frontiers, ITIL

Downtime report

A report that identifies the elapsed time when a computer is not operating correctly because of machine failure.

ISACA

Draft record

A draft record is a preliminary version of a record before it has been completed, finalized, accepted, validated or filed. Such records include working files and notes. Records and information management policies may provide for the destruction of draft records upon finalization, acceptance, validation or filing of the final or official version of the record. However, draft records generally must be retained if (1) they are deemed to be subject to a legal hold; or (2) a specific law or regulation mandates their retention and policies should recognize such exceptions.

Sedona Conference

Drag-and-drop

The movement of on-screen objects by dragging them with the mouse, and dropping them in another place.

Sedona Conference

Drive geometry

A computer hard drive is made up of a number of rapidly rotating platters that have a set of read/write heads on both sides of each platter. Each platter is divided into a series of concentric rings called tracks. Each track is further divided into sections called sectors, and each sector is subdivided into bytes. Drive geometry refers to the number and positions of each of these structures.

Sedona Conference

Driver

A driver is a computer program that controls various devices such as the keyboard, mouse, monitor, etc.

Sedona Conference

Drop accountability

Procedure under which a COMSEC account custodian initially receipts for COMSEC material, and provides no further accounting for it to its central office of record. Local accountability of the COMSEC material may continue to be required. See also accounting legend code.

US National Information Assurance (IA) Glossary

Dry-pipe fire extinguisher system

Refers to a sprinkler system that does not have water in the pipes during idle usage, unlike a fully charged fire extin- guisher system that has water in the pipes at all times. The dry-pipe system is activated at the time of the fire alarm, and water is emitted to the pipes from a water reservoir for discharge to the location of the fire.

ISACA

Dual control

A method of preserving the integrity of a process by requiring that several individuals independently take some action before certain transactions are completed.

PCI-DSS

Dual-use certificate

A certificate that is intended for use with both digital signature and data encryption services.

NIST 800 series

Due care

Diligence which a person would exercise under a given set of circumstances. Managers and their organizations have a duty to provide for information security to ensure that the type of control, the cost of control, and the deployment of control are appropriate for the system being managed.

ISACA, NIST 800 series

Due professional care

Diligence which a person, who possesses a special skill, would exercise under a given set of circumstances.

ISACA

Dumb terminal

A terminal that serves only as an input/output mechanism linking a user with the central computer. This type of terminal does not have an internal processor. Dumb terminals are dependent upon the main computer for processing. All entered data are accepted without further editing or validation.

FISCAM, ISACA

Dump

To transfer the contents of memory to a printer or disk storage. Programmers use memory dumps to debug programs.

FISCAM

Duplex

Two-sided page(s).

Sedona Conference

Duplex routing

The method or communication mode of routing data over the communication network. See also half and full duplex.

ISACA

Duplex Scanners vs. Double-Sided Scanning

Duplex scanners automatically scan both sides of a double-sided page, producing two images at once. Double-sided scanning uses a single-sided scanner to scan double-sided pages, scanning one collated stack of paper, then flipping it over and scanning the other side.

Sedona Conference

Duplicate digital evidence

A duplicate is an accurate digital reproduction of all data objects contained on the original physical item and associated media.

NIST 800 series

Duration

A field within a certificate that is composed of two subfields; "date of issue" and "date of next issue".

NIST 800 series

Dynamic analysis

Analysis that is performed in real time or in continuous form.

ISACA

Dynamic Currency Conversion Service (DCC)

An optional service, which is facilitated by a merchant at the point of sale with either a third party agent or through its merchant bank. The DCC allows a cardholder to see the transaction amount in his or her billing currency and the merchant's pricing currency. This way, the cardholder knows exactly how much the goods or services cost, and is able to make value judgments quickly and easily.

VISA Glossary of Terms

Dynamic Host Configuration Protocol (DHCP)

A network protocol that automatically assigns IP addresses to clients logging onto a TCP/IP network.

Network Frontiers, NIST 800 Series, NIST 800 Series

Dynamic Random Access Memory (DRAM)

A memory technology which is periodically "refreshed" or updated – as opposed to "static" RAM chips which do not require refreshing. The term is often used to refer to the memory chips themselves.

Sedona Conference

E

E-commerce

The processes by which organizations conduct business electronically with their customers, suppliers and other external business partners, using the Internet as an enabling technology. It therefore encompasses both business-to-business (B2B) and business-to-consumer (B2C) e-commerce models but does not include existing non-Internet e-commerce methods based on private networks.

ISACA

E-forms/Web forms

Forms designed, managed, and processed completely in an electronic environment.

AIIM

E-mail address

An electronic mail address. Internet e-mail addresses follow the formula: user-ID@domain-name; other e-mail protocols may use different address formats. In some e-mail systems, a user's e-mail address is "aliased" or represented by his or her natural name rather than a fully qualified e-mail address. For example, john.doe@abc.com might appear simply as John Doe.

Sedona Conference

E-mail metadata

Data stored in the e-mail about the e-mail. Often this data is not even viewable in the e-mail client application used to create the e-mail. The amount of e-mail metadata available for a particular e-mail varies greatly depending on the e-mail system. Contrast with File system metadata and Document metadata.

Sedona Conference

E-mail string

A series of e mails linked together by e-mail responses or forwards. The series of e-mail messages created through multiple responses and answers to an originating message. Also referred to as an e-mail "thread." Comments, revisions, attachments are all part of an e-mail string.

Sedona Conference

Easter egg

Hidden functionality within an application program, which becomes activated when an undocumented, and often convoluted, set of commands and keystrokes are entered. Easter eggs are typically used to display the credits for the development team and are intended to be non-threatening.

NIST 800 series

Eavesdropping

The action of unobserved listening to conversations between people or systems in order to obtain information. See also President Bush, National Security Agency.

Centers for Medicare & Medicaid Services (CMS)

Echo checks

Detects line errors by retransmitting data back to the sending device for comparison with the original transmission.

ISACA

Edit controls

Detects errors in the input portion of information that is sent to the computer for processing. The controls may be manual or automated and allow the user to edit data errors before processing.

ISACA

Editing

Editing ensures that data conform to predetermined criteria and enable early identification of potential errors.

ISACA

Education

Education integrates all of the assurance skills and competencies of the various functional specialties into a common body of knowledge . . . and strives to produce IT security specialists and professionals capable of vision and proactive response.

NIST 800 series

Effectiveness

Deals with information being relevant and pertinent to the business process as well as being delivered in a timely, correct, consistent, and usable manner. A measure of whether the objectives of a process, service, or activity have been achieved. An effective process or activity is one that achieves its agreed objectives. See also KPI.

CobiT, ITIL

Efficiency

Concerns the provision of information through the optimal (most productive and economical) use of resources. A measure of whether the right amount of resources have been used to deliver a process, service, or activity. An efficient process achieves its objectives with the minimum amount of time, money, people, or other resources. See also KPI.

CobiT, ITIL

Egress

Traffic leaving the network.

PCI-DSS

Egress filtering

The process of blocking outgoing packets that use obviously false Internet Protocol (IP) addresses, such as source addresses from internal networks.

NIST 800 series

Electronic access

The ability or the means necessary to read, write, modify, or communicate information or otherwise use system resources.

Workgroup for Electronic Data Interchange

Electronic archive

See archive.

Sedona Conference

Electronic authentication

The process of establishing confidence in user identities electronically presented to an information system.

NIST 800 series

Electronic Bill Presentment and Payment (EBPP)

AIIM

Electronic cash

An electronic form functionally equivalent to cash in order to make and receive payments in cyber banking.

ISACA

Electronic credentials

Digital documents used in authentication that bind an identity or an attribute to a subscriber's token.

NIST 800 series

Electronic Data Integration (EDI)

AIIM, FISCAM

Electronic Data Interchange (EDI)

A standard for the electronic exchange of business documents, such as invoices and purchase orders. Electronic data interchange (EDI) eliminates intermediate steps in processes that rely on the transmission of paper-based instructions and documents by performing them electronically, computer to computer. EDI transmissions can replace the use of standard documents, including invoices or purchase orders.

FISCAM, AIIM, Sedona Conference

Electronic discovery

The process of collecting, preparing, reviewing, and producing electronic documents in the context of the legal process. See also discovery.

Sedona Conference

Electronic document

Recorded information or an object which can be treated as a unit.

ISO 15489

Electronic document management

For paper documents, involves imaging, indexing/coding and archiving of scanned documents/images, and thereafter electronically managing them during all life cycle phases. Electronic documents are likewise electronically managed from creation to archiving and all stages in between.

Sedona Conference

Electronic Document Management System (EDMS)

A system to electronically manage documents during all life cycles. See also Electronic Document Management.

AIIM, Sedona Conference

Electronic evidence

Information and data of investigative value that is stored on or transmitted by an electronic device.

NIST 800 series

Electronic file processing

Generally includes extraction of metadata from files, identification of duplicates/de-duplication and rendering of data into delimited format.

Sedona Conference

Electronic Funds Transfer (EFT)

The exchange of money via telecommunications. EFT refers to any financial transaction that originates at a terminal and transfers a sum of money from one account to another.

ISACA

Electronic Funds Transfer System (EFTS)

A system of transferring money from one bank account directly to another without any paper money changing hands. EFT refers to any transfer of funds initiated through an electronic terminal, including credit card, ATM, Fedwire and point-of-sale (POS) transactions. It is used for both credit transfers, such as payroll payments, and for debit transfers, such as mortgage payments. Transactions are processed by the bank through the Automated Clearing House (ACH) network, the secure transfer system that connects all U.S. financial institutions. For payments, funds are transferred electronically from one bank account to the billing company's bank.

ISACA

Electronic image

An electronic or digital picture of a document (e.g. TIFF, PDF, etc.).

Sedona Conference

Electronic Image Management (EIM)

AIIM, Sedona Conference

Electronic Industries Association (EIA)

Sedona Conference

Electronic key entry

The entry of cryptographic keys into a cryptographic module using electronic methods such as a smart card or a key-loading device. (The operator of the key may have no knowledge of the value of the key being entered.)

NIST 800 series, FIPS Pubs

Electronic Key Management System (EKMS)

Interoperable collection of systems being developed by services and agencies of the U.S. Government to automate the planning, ordering, generating, distributing, storing, filling, using, and destroying of electronic key and management of other types of COMSEC material.

US National Information Assurance (IA) Glossary

Electronic mail message

A document created or received via an electronic mail system, including brief notes, formal or substantive narrative documents, and any attachments, such as word processing and other electronic documents, which may be transmitted with the message.

Sedona Conference

Electronic mail or e-mail

Electronic mail is the exchange of computer produced and stored messages. E-mail messages can be encoded in either ASCII or Unicode text formats, and can also attach any other document or application to the message as a sub-part of it. An individual using a terminal, PC or an application can access a network to send an unstructured message to another individual or group of people. An e-mail system requires a messaging system, which provides the store and forward capability, and a mail program that provides the user interface with send and receive functions. The Internet revolutionized e-mail by turning countless incompatible islands into one global system. The Internet initially served its own members, of course, but then began to act as a mail gateway between the major online services. It then became "the" messaging system for the planet.

de facto, ISACA, Centers for Medicare & Medicaid Services (CMS), Sedona Conference

Electronic media

Memory devices in computers (hard drives) and any removable/transportable digital memory medium, such as magnetic tape or disk, optical disk, or digital memory card; or Transmission media used to exchange information already in electronic storage media. Transmission media include, for example, the Internet (wide-open), extranet (using internet technology to link a business with information accessible only to collaborating parties), leased lines, dial-up lines, private networks, and the physical movement of removable/transportable electronic storage media. Certain transmissions, including paper, via facsimile, and of voice, via telephone, are not considered transmissions via electronic media because the information being exchanged did not exist in electronic form before the transmission.

HIPAA

Electronic messaging services

Services providing interpersonal messaging capability; meeting specific functional, management, and technical requirements; and yielding a business-quality electronic mail service suitable for the conduct of official government business.

US National Information Assurance (IA) Glossary

Electronic Protected Health Information (ePHI)

Individually identifiable health information (IIHI) transmitted or maintained in any electronic form or medium which is held by a CE or its business associate. Identifies the individual or offers a reasonable basis for identification. Is created or received by a CE or an employer. Relates to a past, present, or

future physical or mental condition, and provision of health care or payment for health care. See also regulated data, personally identifiable information, confidential data. See also Protected Health Information.

HIPAA

Electronic record

Any combination of text, graphics, data, audio, pictorial, or other information represented in digital forms that is created, modified, maintained, archived, retrieved, or distributed by a computer system. E-mail and associated attachments, are considered electronic records. Defined in evidentiary terms, information created, received, and maintained as evidence and information by an organization or person in pursuance of legal obligations or in transaction of business.

21 CFR Part 11, IRS Proc 97-22, NARA 1234.2, ISO 15489, Sedona Conference

Electronic Records Management (ERM)

AIIM

Electronic Records Management System (ERMS)

AIIM

Electronic security

Protection resulting from measures designed to deny unauthorized individuals information derived from the interception and analysis of non communications electromagnetic radiations.

US National Information Assurance (IA) Glossary

Electronic signature

A computer data compilation of any symbol or series of symbols executed, adopted, or authorized by an individual to be the legally binding equivalent of the individual's handwritten signature. A symbol, generated through electronic means, that can be used to 1) identify the sender of information and 2) ensure the integrity of the critical information received from the sender. An electronic signature may represent either an individual or an organization. Adequate electronic signatures are 1) unique to the signer, 2) under the signer's sole control, 3) capable of being verified, and 4) linked to the data in such a manner that if data are changed, the signature is invalidated upon verification. Traditional user identification code/password techniques do not meet these criteria. See also digital signature.

21 CFR Part 11, FISCAM, ISACA, Centers for Medicare & Medicaid Services (CMS), Workgroup for Electronic Data Interchange, US National Information Assurance (IA) Glossary

Electronic storage system

An electronic storage system is a system to prepare, record, transfer, index, store, preserve, retrieve, and reproduce files, organizational books and records.

IRS Proc 97-22

Electronic vaulting

A data recovery strategy that allows organizations to recover data within hours after a disaster. It includes recovery of data from an offsite storage media that mirrors data via a communication link. Typically used for batch/journal updates to critical files to supplement full backups taken periodically.

ISACA

Electronically generated key

Key generated in a COMSEC device by introducing (either mechanically or electronically) a seed key into the device and then using the seed, together with a software algorithm stored in the device, to produce the desired key.

US National Information Assurance (IA) Glossary

Electronically Stored Information (ESI)

Sedona Conference

Electrostatic printing

Paper is exposed to electron charge. Toner sticks to the charged pixels.

Sedona Conference

Elliptic Curve Cryptography (ECC)

Approach to public-key cryptography based on elliptic curves over finite fields.

PCI-DSS

Em

In any print, font or size is equal to the width of the letter "M" in that font and size.

Sedona Conference

Embedded audit module

Integral part of an application system that is designed to identify and report specific transactions or other information based on pre-determined criteria. Identification of reportable items occurs as part of real-time processing. Reporting may be real-time online or may use store and forward methods. Also known as integrated test facility or continuous auditing module.

ISACA

Embedded computer

Computer system that is an integral part of a larger system.

US National Information Assurance (IA) Glossary

Embedded cryptographic system

Cryptosystem performing or controlling a function as an integral element of a larger system or subsystem.

US National Information Assurance (IA) Glossary

Embedded cryptography

Cryptography engineered into an equipment or system whose basic function is not cryptographic.

US National Information Assurance (IA) Glossary

Emergency change

A change that must be introduced as soon as possible. For example, to resolve a major incident or implement a security patch. The change management process will normally have a specific procedure for handling emergency changes. See also change advisory board/emergency committee.

ITIL

Emergency Coordinator

The system member responsible for assessing emergency situations and making decisions to respond.

Centers for Medicare & Medicaid Services (CMS)

Emergency mode operation plan

Establish (and implement as needed) procedures to enable continuation of critical business processes for protection of the security of regulated data while operating in emergency mode.

HIPAA

Emergency response

Initial response to any incident, focused on protecting human life and the organization's assets.

PAS 56

Emissions Security (EMSEC)

Protection resulting from measures taken to deny unauthorized individuals information derived from intercept and analysis of compromising emanations from crypto-equipment or an information system. See also TEMPEST.

US National Information Assurance (IA) Glossary

Encapsulated PostScript (EPS)

Uncompressed files for images, text and objects. Only print on PostScript printers.

Sedona Conference

Encapsulating Security Payload

A security protocol that authenticates packets from servers, ensures that messages are not tampered with while in route, and encrypts the packet payload ensuring confidentiality.

Network Frontiers

Encapsulating Security Payload or External Service Provider (ESP)

See Encapsulating Security Payload, External Service Provider.

ITIL, de facto

Encapsulation [of objects]

Encapsulation is the technique used by layered protocols in which a lower layer protocol accepts a message from a higher layer protocol and places it in the data portion of a frame in the lower layer.

ISACA

Encipher

Convert plain text to cipher text by means of a cryptographic system.

US National Information Assurance (IA) Glossary

Enclave

Collection of computing environments connected by one or more internal networks under the control of a single authority and security policy, including personnel and physical security.

US National Information Assurance (IA) Glossary

Enclave boundary

Point at which an enclave's internal network service layer connects to an external network's service layer, i.e., to another enclave or to a Wide Area Network (WAN).

US National Information Assurance (IA) Glossary

Encode

Convert plain text to cipher text by means of a code.

US National Information Assurance (IA) Glossary

Encrypt

Generic term encompassing encipher and encode.

US National Information Assurance (IA) Glossary

Encrypted key

A cryptographic key that has been encrypted using an Approved security function with a key encrypting key, a PIN, or a password in order to disguise the value of the underlying plaintext key.

NIST 800 series, FIPS Pubs

Encrypted network

A network on which messages are encrypted (e.g. using DES, AES, or other appropriate algorithms) to prevent reading by unauthorized parties.

NIST 800 series

Encryption

The transformation of data into a form readable only by using the appropriate key, held only by authorized parties. The use of an algorithmic process (scrambling) to transform data into a form in which there is a low probability of assigning meaning without use of a confidential process or key. Therefore, it is a three-step process of taking an un-encrypted message (plaintext), applying a mathematical function to it (encryption algorithm with a key), and producing an encrypted message (ciphertext).

HIPAA, FISCAM, ISACA, Centers for Medicare & Medicaid Services (CMS), PCI-DSS, Workgroup for Electronic Data Interchange, Sedona Conference, NIST 800 Series, FIPS Pubs

Encryption algorithm

Set of mathematically expressed rules for rendering data unintelligible by executing a series of conversions controlled by a key.

US National Information Assurance (IA) Glossary

Encryption certificate

A certificate containing a public key that is used to encrypt electronic messages, files, documents, or data transmissions, or to establish or exchange a session key for these same purposes.

NIST 800 series

Encryption key

A piece of information, in a digitized form, used by an encryption algorithm to convert the plaintext to the ciphertext and decrypt data. The number of bits in the encryption key is a rough measure of the encryption strength; generally, the more bits in the encryption key, the more difficult it is to break.

ISACA, Sedona Conference

End document number or End doc#

The last single page image of a document.

Sedona Conference

End Of File (EOF)

A distinctive code which uniquely marks the end of a data file.

Sedona Conference

End user computing

Any development, programming, or other activity where end users create or maintain their own systems or applications.

FISCAM, ISACA

End users

Employees who have access to computer systems and networks that process, store, or transmit information. This is the largest and most heterogeneous group of employees. It consists of everyone, from an executive with a desktop system to application programmers to data entry clerks. End users can also be third parties, such as suppliers or clients.

Centers for Medicare & Medicaid Services (CMS), Network Frontiers

End-item accounting

Accounting for all the accountable components of a COMSEC equipment configuration by a single short title.

US National Information Assurance (IA) Glossary

End-to-end

In entirety, from start to finish.

PAS 56

End-to-end encryption

Encryption of information at its origin and decryption at its intended destination without intermediate decryption.

US National Information Assurance (IA) Glossary, NIST 800 Series

End-to-end security

Safeguarding information in an information system from point of origin to point of destination.

US National Information Assurance (IA) Glossary

Endorsed For Unclassified Cryptographic Item (EUCI)

Unclassified cryptographic equipment that embodies a U.S. Government classified cryptographic logic and is endorsed by NSA for the protection of national security information. See also type 2 product.

US National Information Assurance (IA) Glossary

Endorsement

NSA approval of a commercially developed product for safeguarding national security information.

US National Information Assurance (IA) Glossary

Endorser

A small printer in a scanner that adds a document-control number or other endorsement to each scanned sheet.

Sedona Conference

Engagement letter

Formal document which defines the IS auditor's responsibility, authority, and accountability for a specific assignment.

ISACA

Enhanced Parallel Port (EPP)

Also known as Fast Mode Parallel Port. A new, industry standard parallel port, having higher transfer times competitive with SCSI.

Sedona Conference

Enhanced Small Device Interface (ESDI)

A defined, common electronic interface for transferring data between computers and peripherals, particularly disk drives.

Sedona Conference

Enhanced titles

A meaningful/descriptive title for a document. The opposite of Verbatim titles.

Sedona Conference

Enterprise

A group of individuals working together for a common purpose, typically within the context of an organizational form such as corporation, public agency, charity, or trust.

CobiT

Enterprise Application Integration (EAI)

AIIM

Enterprise architecture

Business-oriented technology road map for the attainment of business goals and objectives. The framework for how software, computing, storage and networking systems should integrate and operate to meet the changing needs across an entire business.

CobiT, Sedona Conference

Enterprise architecture for IT

IT's delivery response, provided by clearly defined processes using its resources (applications, information, infrastructure and people).

CobiT

Enterprise Content Management (ECM)

Enterprise Content Management (ECM) is the technologies, tools, and methods used to capture, manage, store, preserve, and deliver information, content, and documents related to organizational processes. ECM enables four key business drivers: Continuity, Collaboration, Compliance, and Costs.

AIIM, Sedona Conference

Enterprise data dictionary

The name, type, range of values, source, system of record, and authorization for access for each data element used in the enterprise. It indicates which application programs use that data so that when a data structure is contemplated, a list of the affected programs can be generated. See also data dictionary.

CobiT

Enterprise governance

A broad and wide-ranging concept of corporate governance covering associated organizations such as global strategic alliance partners.

ISACA

Enterprise Resource Planning (ERP)

First, it denotes the planning and management of resources in an enterprise. Second, it denotes a software system that can be used to manage whole business processes, integrating purchasing, inventory, personnel, customer service, shipping, financial management, and other aspects of the business. An ERP system typically is based on a common database, various integrated business process application modules, and business analysis tools.

ISACA, AIIM

Entity

Either a subject (an active element that operates on information or the system state) or an object (a passive element that contains or receives information). Entity can also refer to the component parts of business activity referred to in descending order as an organization's functions, activities, and transactions. See also organization.

NIST 800 series, DIRKS, FIPS Pubs

Entrapment

Deliberate planting of apparent flaws in an information system for the purpose of detecting attempted penetrations.

US National Information Assurance (IA) Glossary

Entropy

A measure of the amount of uncertainty that an attacker faces to determine the value of a secret.

NIST 800 series

Environment

CMS defines this as the state of a computer, usually determined by which programs are running and basic hardware and software characteristics that affect the development, operation, and maintenance of a system. However, FIPS takes a broader view stating that it is the aggregate of external procedures, conditions, and objects affecting the development, operation, and maintenance of an information system. ITIL defines this as a subset of the IT infrastructure that is used for a particular purpose. For example, live environment, test environment, and build environment. It is possible for multiple environments to share a configuration item. For example, test and live environments may use different partitions on a single mainframe computer. Also used in the term physical environment to mean the accommodation, air conditioning, power system, etc.

Centers for Medicare & Medicaid Services (CMS), FIPS Pubs, ITIL, US National Information Assurance (IA) Glossary, NIST 800 Series

Environmental controls

This subset of physical access controls prevents or mitigates damage to facilities and interruptions in service. Smoke detectors, fire alarms and extinguishers, and uninterruptible power supplies are some examples of environmental controls.

FISCAM, Centers for Medicare & Medicaid Services (CMS)

Environmental system software

Software, which is required to operate the hardware equipment (sometimes referred to as OS Software) and software and utility programs that are used in the development of applications and/or databases.

Centers for Medicare & Medicaid Services (CMS)

Ephemeral keys

Short-lived cryptographic keys that are statistically unique to each execution of a key establishment process and meets other requirements of the key type (e.g., unique to each message or session).

NIST 800 series

Erasable optical drive

A type of optical drive that uses erasable optical discs.

Sedona Conference

Erasure

Process intended to render magnetically stored information irretrievable by normal means.

US National Information Assurance (IA) Glossary

Error

The Government Account Office defines this as unintentional misstatements or omissions of amounts or disclosures in financial statements. Error control deviations (compliance testing) or misstatements (substantive testing). More generically, an error is a design flaw or malfunction that causes a failure of one or more configuration items or IT ser-

vices. A mistake made by a person or a faulty process that impacts a CI or IT service is also an error. See also known error.

GAO/PCIE Financial Audit Manual, ISACA, ISO/IEC 27001:2005, ITIL

Error control

The activity responsible for managing known errors until they are resolved by the successful implementation of changes. See also problem control.

ITIL

Error detection code

A code computed from data and comprised of redundant bits of information designed to detect, but not correct, unintentional changes in the data.

NIST 800 series, FIPS Pubs

Error risk

The risk of errors occurring in the area being audited.

ISACA

Escalation

An activity that obtains additional resources when these are needed to meet service level targets or customer expectations. Escalation may be needed within any IT service management process but is most commonly associated with incident management, problem management, and the management of customer complaints. There are two types of escalation, functional escalation and hierarchical escalation.

ITIL

Escrow

Something (e.g., a document, an encryption key) that is "delivered to a third person to be given to the grantee only upon the fulfillment of a condition."

NIST 800 series, FIPS Pubs

Espionage

The covert act of spying through copying, reproducing, recording, photographing, interception, etc. to obtain information through unauthorized means.

Centers for Medicare & Medicaid Services (CMS)

Estimated Annual Frequency (EAF)

The estimated annual frequency is the number of times a threat will occur in a year.

Network Frontiers

Estimation

The use of experience to provide an approximate value for a metric or cost. Estimation is also used in capacity and availability management as the cheapest and least accurate modeling method.

ITIL

Ethernet

A popular network protocol and cabling scheme that uses a bus topology and CSMA/CD (carrier sense multiple access/collision detection) to prevent network failures or collisions when two devices try to access the network at the same time.

ISACA, Sedona Conference

Ethics

The information systems and the security of information systems should be provided and used in such a manner that the rights and legitimate interest of others are respected.

NIST 800 series, ISO/IEC 27001:2005

European Foundation for Quality Management (EFQM)

The EFQM excellence model was introduced at the beginning of 1992 as the framework for assessing organizations for the European quality award. It is now the most widely used organizational framework in Europe and it has become the basis for the majority of national and regional quality awards. See also http://www.efqm.org/ for more information.

ITIL

Evacuation

An organized withdrawal from a place or an area usually because of a crisis or emergency.

Centers for Medicare & Medicaid Services (CMS)

Evaluation Assurance Level (EAL)

Set of assurance requirements that represent a point on the Common Criteria predefined assurance scale.

US National Information Assurance (IA) Glossary

Evaluation criteria

A set of qualitative measures against which a risk is evaluated. Evaluation criteria define high, medium, and low impacts for an organization.

CERT OCTAVE

Event

An alert or notification created by any IT service, configuration item, or monitoring tool. For example, a notification that a batch job has completed. Events typically require IT operations personnel to take actions, and often lead to incidents being logged. See also event management.

ITIL, US National Information Assurance (IA) Glossary, NIST 800 Series

Event management

The process responsible for managing events throughout their lifecycle. Event management is one of the main activities of IT operations.

ITIL

Evidence

Information that tends to prove a fact. Not limited to the legal sense of the term. The information an auditor gathers in the course of performing an IS audit. Evidence is relevant if it pertains to the audit objectives and has a logical relationship to the findings and conclusions it is used to support.

DIRKS, ISACA

Evidentiary Image or Copy

See Forensic Copy.

Sedona Conference

Exabyte

A unit of 1000 petabytes. See also Byte.

Sedona Conference

Examination

A technical review that makes the evidence visible and suitable for analysis; tests performed on the evidence to determine the presence or absence of specific data.

NIST 800 series

Examination board

An organization accredited to develop and manage examinations. It service management examination boards are accredited by ICMB to develop ITIL examinations, based on a common syllabus, to accredit training organizations, and to award certificates. See also ISEB, EXIN.

ITIL

Examination Institute for Information Science (EXIN)

The Examination Institute for Information Science, is accredited by the ICMB as an examination board. See also http://www.exin-exams.com/ for more information.

ITIL

Exception criteria

Exception criteria refer to batch processes that return files or records as not meeting certain predefined criteria for processing.

Centers for Medicare & Medicaid Services (CMS)

Exception file

A list of lost, stolen, counterfeit, fraudulent, or otherwise invalid account numbers kept by individual merchants or their third-party processors. The exception file should be checked as part of the authorization process, particularly for transactions that are below a merchant's floor limit.

VISA Glossary of Terms

Exception report

An exception report is generated by a program that identifies transactions or data that appear to be incorrect. These items may be outside a predetermined range or may not conform to specified criteria. An exception report contains details of one or more KPIs or other important targets that have exceeded defined thresholds. Examples include SLA targets being missed or about to be missed and a performance metric indicating a potential capacity problem.

ISACA, ITIL

Exclusion zone

Geographical zone agreed between a client and a third party provider of work area recovery (WAR) resources within which the third party provider will not provide WAR services to another client.

PAS 56

Exculpatory evidence

Evidence that tends to decrease the likelihood of fault or guilt.

NIST 800 series

Executable code

The machine language code that is generally referred to as the object or load module.

ISACA

Execute access

This level of access provides the ability to execute a program.

FISCAM, Centers for Medicare & Medicaid Services (CMS)

Executive agency

An executive department specified in 5 U.S.C., SEC. 101; a military department specified in 5 U.S.C., SEC. 102; an independent establishment as defined in 5 U.S.C., SEC. 1041); and a wholly-owned Government corporation fully subject to the provisions of 31 U.S.C., CHAPTER 91.

FIPS Pubs, NIST 800 Series

Executive state

One of several states in which an information system may operate, and the only one in which certain privileged instructions may be executed. Such privileged instructions cannot be executed when the system is operating in other states. Synonymous with supervisor state.

US National Information Assurance (IA) Glossary

Exercise key

Key used exclusively to safeguard communications transmitted over-the-air during military or organized civil training exercises.

US National Information Assurance (IA) Glossary

Exercising

The critical testing of BCM strategies and BCPs, rehearsing the roles of team members and staff, and testing the recovery or continuity of an organization's systems (e.g. technology, telephony, administration) to demonstrate BCM competence and capability. An exercise may involve invoking business continuity procedures but is more likely to involve the simulation of a business continuity incident, announced or unannounced, in which participants role-play in order to assess what issues may arise, prior to a real invocation.

PAS 56, BS 25999

Exit

A predefined or in-house written routine that receives controls at a predefined point in processing. These routines provide an organization with flexibility to customize processing, but also create the opportunity to bypass security controls.

FISCAM

Expectation

The auditor's estimate of an account balance in an analytical procedure.

GAO/PCIE Financial Audit Manual

Expected misstatement

The dollar amount of misstatements the auditor expects in a population.

GAO/PCIE Financial Audit Manual

Expert system

Expert systems are the most prevalent type of computer systems that arise from the research of artificial intelligence. An expert system has a built in hierarchy of rules, which are acquired from human experts in the appropriate field. Once input is provided, the system should be able to define the nature of the problem and provide recommendations to solve the problem.

ISACA

Expired account

A budgetary account in which the balances are no longer available for incurring new obligations because the time available for incurring such obligations has expired. After 5 years, these accounts are canceled and are then considered to be closed accounts. See also closed accounts.

GAO/PCIE Financial Audit Manual

Exploit code

A program that allows attackers to automatically break into a system.

NIST 800 series

Exploitable channel

Channel that allows the violation of the security policy governing an information system and is usable or detectable by subjects external to the trusted computing base. See also covert channel.

US National Information Assurance (IA) Glossary

Export

Data extracted or taken out of one environment or application usually in a prescribed format, and usually for import into another environment or application.

Sedona Conference

Exposure

The potential compromise associated with an attack exploiting a corresponding vulnerability. The potential loss to an area due to the occurrence of an adverse event.

ISACA, Centers for Medicare & Medicaid Services (CMS), ISO/IEC 27001:2005

Exposure Factor (EF)

The percent of an asset lost due to a threat.

de facto

Extended Binary-Coded Decimal Interchange Code (EBCDIC)

An eight-bit code developed by IBM for representing 256 characters; used in most large computer systems.

FISCAM, ISACA

Extended Graphics Adapter (EGA)

See VGA.

Sedona Conference

Extended Industry Standard Architecture (EISA)

One of the standard buses used for PCs.

Sedona Conference

Extended Partitions

If a computer hard drive has been divided into more than four partitions, extended partitions are created. Under such circumstances each extended partition contains a partition table in the first sector that describes how it is further subdivided.

Sedona Conference

Extensible Markup Language (XML)

Promulgated through the World Wide Web Consortium, XML is a web-based application development technique that allows designers to create their own customized tags, thus, enabling the definition, transmission, validation and interpretation of data between applications and organizations. XML is a pared-down version of SGML, designed especially for Web documents. It allows designers to create their own customized tag, enabling the definition, transmission, validation, and interpretation of data between applications and between organizations.

ISACA, AIIM, Adobe, Sedona Conference

External connectivity

A computer or network connection to an outside, uncontrolled network that is unprotected by perimeter security, e.g., a modem connection to a network computer. See also external router.

Centers for Medicare & Medicaid Services (CMS)

External customer

A customer who works for a different business than the IT service provider. See also external service provider, internal customer.

ITIL

External router

The router at the extreme edge of the network under control, usually connected to an ISP or other service provider; also known as border router.

ISACA

External Service Provider

An IT service provider which is part of a different business to their customer. An

205

IT service provider may have both internal customers and external customers. See also internal service provider, application service provider, Internet service provider.

ITIL

Extraction resistance

Capability of crypto-equipment or secure telecommunications equipment to resist efforts to extract key.

US National Information Assurance (IA) Glossary

Extranet

Extension to the intranet allowing selected outside users access to portions of an organization's intranet. This type of access is often utilized in cases of joint defense, joint venture and vendor client relationships.

US National Information Assurance (IA) Glossary, Sedona Conference

F

Facilities

These are all the resources to house and support information systems. A physical location containing the equipment, supplies, communication lines (voice and data), and related data to perform transactions required under normal operating conditions. See also computer facility.

CobiT, Centers for Medicare & Medicaid Services (CMS), ISO/IEC 27001:2005

Facsimile (FAX)

A process of transmitting documents by scanning them to digital, converting to analog, transmitting over phone lines and reversing the process at the other end and printing.

Sedona Conference

Fail safe

Automatic protection of programs and/or processing systems when hardware or software failure is detected.

US National Information Assurance (IA) Glossary

Fail soft

Selective termination of affected nonessential processing when hardware or software failure is determined to be imminent.

US National Information Assurance (IA) Glossary

Fail-over

The transfer of service from an incapacitated primary component to its backup component.

ISACA

Fail-safe

Describes the design properties of a computer system that allow it to resist active attempts to attack or bypass it.

ISACA

Failure

Loss of ability to operate to specification or to deliver the required output. The term failure may be used when referring to IT services, processes, activities, configuration items, etc. A failure often causes an incident. See also error.

ITIL

Failure access

Type of incident in which unauthorized access to data results from hardware or software failure.

US National Information Assurance (IA) Glossary

Failure control

Methodology used to detect imminent hardware or software failure and provide fail safe or fail soft recovery.

US National Information Assurance (IA) Glossary

False acceptance

When a biometric system incorrectly identifies an individual or incorrectly verifies an impostor against a claimed identity

NIST 800 series, FIPS Pubs

False acceptance rate

The probability that a biometric system will incorrectly identify an individual or will fail to reject an impostor. The rate given normally assumes passive impostor attempts.

NIST 800 series, FIPS Pubs

False Match Rate (FMR)

Alternative to 'False Acceptance Rate'. Used to avoid confusion in applications that reject the claimant if their biometric data matches that of an applicant.

NIST 800 series, FIPS Pubs

False negative

A result that is not correct. This may be a result of performing a process incorrectly or using a process that is not accurate. In intrusion detection, an error that occurs when an attack is misdiagnosed as a normal activity.

ISACA, Sedona Conference

False Non Match Rate (FNMR)

Alternative to 'False Rejection Rate'. Used to avoid confusion in applications

that reject the claimant if their biometric data matches that of an applicant.

NIST 800 series, FIPS Pubs

False positive

A result that is not correct. This may be a result of performing a process incorrectly or using a process that is not accurate. In intrusion detection, an error that occurs when a normal activity is misdiagnosed as an attack.

ISACA, Sedona Conference, NIST 800 Series

False rejection

When a biometric system fails to identify an applicant or fails to verify the legitimate claimed identity of an applicant.

NIST 800 series, FIPS Pubs

False Rejection Rate (FRR)

The probability that a biometric system will fail to identify an applicant, or verify the legitimate claimed identity of an applicant.

NIST 800 series, FIPS Pubs

Fault

See error.

ITIL

Fault tolerance

A system's level of resilience to seamlessly react from hardware and/or software failure. The ability of an IT service or configuration item to continue to operate correctly after failure of a component part. See also resilience, countermeasure.

ISACA, ITIL

Fault tree analysis

A technique that can be used to determine the chain of events that leads to a problem. Fault tree analysis represents a chain of events using Boolean notation in a diagram.

ITIL

Feasibility study

A phase of an SDLC methodology that researches the feasibility and adequacy of resources for the development or acquisition of a system solution to meet a user need.

ISACA

Federal Accounting Standards Advisory Board (FASAB)

The mission of the FASAB is to promulgate federal accounting standards after considering the financial and budgetary information needs of citizens, congressional oversight groups, executive agencies, and the needs of other users of federal financial information. Accounting and financial reporting standards are essential for public accountability and for an efficient and effective functioning of our democratic system of government. Federal accounting standards and financial reporting play a major role in fulfilling the government's duty to be publicly accountable and can be used to assess 1) the government's accountability and its efficiency and effectiveness, and 2) the economic, political, and social consequences of the allocation and various uses of federal resources. See also http://www.fasab.gov for more information.

GAO/PCIE Financial Audit Manual

Federal Agencies' Centralized Trial Balance System (FACTS)

GAO/PCIE Financial Audit Manual

Federal agency

See agency.

FIPS Pubs

Federal Bridge Certification Authority (FBCA)

The Federal Bridge Certification Authority consists of a collection of Public Key Infrastructure components (Certificate Authorities, Directories, Certificate Policies and Certificate Practice Statements) that are used to provide peer-to-peer interoperability among Agency Principal Certification Authorities.

NIST 800 series

Federal bridge certification authority membrane

The Federal Bridge Certification Authority Membrane consists of a collection of Public Key Infrastructure components including a variety of Certification Authority PKI products, Databases, CA specific Directories, Border Directory, Firewalls, Routers, Randomizers, etc.

NIST 800 series

Federal Computer Incident Response Center (FedCIRC)

Established in 2003 to protect the nation's Internet infrastructure, US-CERT coordinates defense against and responses to cyber attacks across the nation. See also http://www.us-cert.gov for more information.

NIST 800 series, Workgroup for Electronic Data Interchange

Federal Credit Reform Act (FCRA)

GAO/PCIE Financial Audit Manual

Federal Employees' Retirement System (FERS)

A federal government retirement system which provides annuities to qualified employees who retire because of age and years of service, involuntary separation not for cause, or disability, to widows or widowers and minor children of employees who die and, in certain circum-stances, to the survivors of annuitants. Applies to employees hired since 1984. The Federal Employees Retirement System (FERS) replaced the Civil Service Retirement System effective 1987.

GAO/PCIE Financial Audit Manual

Federal Financial Institutions Examination Council (FFIEC)

The Council is a formal interagency body empowered to prescribe uniform principles, standards, and report forms for the federal examination of financial institutions by the Board of Governors of the Federal Reserve System (FRB), the Federal Deposit Insurance Corporation (FDIC), the National Credit Union Administration (NCUA), the Office of the Comptroller of the Currency (OCC), and the Office of Thrift Supervision (OTS) and to make recommendations to promote uniformity in the supervision of financial institutions. See also http://www.ffiec.gov for more information.

de facto

Federal Financial Management Improvement Act of 1996 (FFMIA)

GAO/PCIE Financial Audit Manual

Federal financial management systems requirements

One of the three requirements of FFMIA. They include the requirements of OMB Circulars A-127, A-123, and

A-130 and the JFMIP Federal Financial Management Systems Requirements series.

GAO/PCIE Financial Audit Manual

Federal Information Processing Standards (FIPS)

Federal Information Processing Standard (FIPS) issued by the National Institute of Standards and Technology after approval by the Secretary of Commerce pursuant to Section 111(d) of the Federal Property and Administrative Services Act of 1949, as amended by the Computer Security Act of 1987, Public Law 100-235. This is the publication that specifies a cryptographic algorithm for use by US Government organizations to protect sensitive information.

FIPS Pubs, Workgroup for Electronic Data Interchange, PCI-DSS, Sedona Conference, NIST 800 Series

Federal Information Security Management Act (FISMA)

Federal Information Security Management Act - requires agencies to integrate IT security into their capital planning and enterprise architecture processes at the agency, conduct annual IT security reviews of all programs and systems, and report the results of those reviews to the Office of Management and Budget (OMB).

FIPS Pubs, NIST 800 Series

Federal information system

An information system used or operated by an executive agency, by a contractor of an executive agency, or by another organization on behalf of an executive agency.

FIPS Pubs, NIST 800 Series

Federal Information System Controls Audit Manual (FISCAM)

GAO/PCIE Financial Audit Manual

Federal Information Systems Security Educators' Association (FISSEA)

An organization whose members come from federal agencies, industry, and academic institutions devoted to improving the IT security awareness and knowledge within the federal government and its related external workforce.

NIST 800 series

Federal Managers' Financial Integrity Act of 1982 (FMFIA)

GAO/PCIE Financial Audit Manual

Federal Public Key Infrastructure Policy Authority (FPKI PA)

The Federal PKI Policy Authority is a federal government body responsible for setting, implementing, and administering policy decisions regarding inter-agency PKI interoperability that uses the FBCA.

NIST 800 series

Federal Trade Commission (FTC)

N 1938, Congress passed the Wheeler-Lea Amendment, which included a broad prohibition against "unfair and deceptive acts or practices." Since then, the Commission also has been directed to administer a wide variety of other consumer protection laws, including the Telemarketing Sales Rule, the Pay-Per-Call Rule and the Equal Credit Opportunity Act. In 1975, Congress passed the Magnuson-Moss Act, which gave the FTC the authority to adopt trade regulation rules that define unfair or deceptive acts in particular industries. Trade regulation rules have the force of law. As you read through this booklet, you will learn about other laws that enable the FTC to help consumers. The FTC's work is performed by the Bureaus of Consumer Protection, Competition and Economics. That work is aided by the Office of General Counsel and seven regional offices. See also http://www.ftc.gov for more information.

de facto

Fiber optic cable

Glass fibers that transmit binary signals over a telecommunications network. Fiber optic systems have low transmission losses as compared to twisted-pair cables. They do not radiate energy or conduct electricity. They are free from corruption and lightning-induced interference, and they reduce the risk of wiretaps.

ISACA

Fiber Optics

Transmitting information by sending light pulses over cables made from thin strands of glass.

Sedona Conference

Field

A location in a record in which a particular type of data are stored. A name for an individual piece of standardized data, such as the author of a document, a recipient, the date of a document or any other piece of data common to most documents in an image collection, to be extracted from the collection. In a database, the smallest unit of data that can be named. A string of fields is a concatenated field or record. Examples include employee name, customer address, account number, product unit price, and product quantity in stock.

FISCAM, ISACA, Centers for Medicare & Medicaid Services (CMS), ISO/IEC 27001:2005, Sedona Conference

Field separator

A code that separates the fields in a record. For example, the CSV format uses a comma as the field separator.

Sedona Conference

File

A collection of data stored in computerized form under a specified name on electronic media.

FISCAM, ISACA, Centers for Medicare & Medicaid Services (CMS), ISO/IEC 27001:2005, Sedona Conference

File Allocation Table (FAT)

An internal data table on hard drives that keeps track of where the files are stored. If a FAT is corrupt, a drive may be unusable, yet the data may be retrievable with forensics. See also Cluster File.

Sedona Conference

File compression

See Compression.

Sedona Conference

File extension

Many systems, including DOS and UNIX, allow a filename extension that consists of one or more characters following the proper filename. For example, image files are usually stored as .bmp, .gif, .jpg or .tiff. Audio files are often stored as .aud or .wav. There are a multitude of file extensions identifying file formats. The filename extension should indicate what type of file it is; however, users may change filename extensions to evade firewall restrictions or for other reasons. Therefore, file types should be identified at a binary level rather than relying on file extensions. To research file types, See also (http://www.filext.com). Different applications can often recognize only a predetermined selection of file types. See also Format

Sedona Conference

File format

The organization or characteristics of a file that determine with which software programs it can be used. See also Format.

Sedona Conference

File infector virus

A virus that attaches itself to a program file, such as a word processor, spreadsheet application, or game.

NIST 800 series

File integrity checker

Software that generates, stores, and compares message digests for files to detect changes to the files.

NIST 800 series

File layout

Specifies the length of the file's record and the sequence and size of its fields. A file layout also will specify the type of data contained within each field. For example, alphanumeric, zoned decimal, packed and binary are types of data.

ISACA

File level binary comparison

Method of de-duplication using the digital fingerprint (hash) of a file. File Level Binary comparison ignores metadata, and can determine that "SHOPPING LIST.DOC" and "TOP SECRET.DOC" are actually the same document. See also Data verification, Digital fingerprint, Hash coding, and De-duplication.

Sedona Conference

File name anomaly

1) A mismatch between the internal file header and its external extension; 2) A file name inconsistent with the content of the file (e.g., renaming a graphics file with a non-graphical extension.

NIST 800 series

File permissions

Access attributes associated with a file or directory as defined in an ACL. Basic file permissions include the ability to read, write, and execute.

Centers for Medicare & Medicaid Services (CMS)

File Plan

A document containing the identifying number, title, description, and disposition authority of files held or used in an office.

Sedona Conference

File protection

Aggregate of processes and procedures designed to inhibit unauthorized access, contamination, elimination, modification, or destruction of a file or any of its contents.

US National Information Assurance (IA) Glossary

File security

Means by which access to computer files is limited to authorized users only.

US National Information Assurance (IA) Glossary

File server

A high-capacity disk storage device or a computer that stores data centrally for network users and manages access to that data. File servers can be dedicated so that no process other than network management can be executed while the network is available. File servers can be non-dedicated so that standard user applications can run while the network is available.

ISACA, Centers for Medicare & Medicaid Services (CMS), Sedona Conference

File sharing

Sharing files stored on the server among several users on a network.

Sedona Conference

File slack

The unused space on a cluster that exists when the logical file space is less than the physical file space.

Sedona Conference

File system

The engine that an operating system or program uses to organize and kept track of files. More specifically, the logical structures and software routines used to control access to the storage on a hard disk system and the overall structure in which the files are named, stored, and organized. The file system plays a critical role in computer forensics because the file system determines the logical structure of the hard drive, including its cluster size. The file system also determines what happens to data when the user deletes a file or subdirectory.

Sedona Conference

File system metadata

Data that can be obtained or extracted about a file from the file system storing the file. Examples include file creation time, last modification time, and last access time.

Sedona Conference

File transfer

The process of moving or transmitting a file from one location to another, as between two programs or from one computer to another.

Sedona Conference

File Transfer Protocol (FTP)

A protocol used to transfer files over a TCP/IP network (Internet, UNIX, etc.).

Sedona Conference, ISACA, NIST 800 series, PCI-DSS

Filename

The name of a file, excluding root drive and directory path information. Different operating systems may impose different restrictions on filenames, for example, by prohibiting use of certain characters in a filename or imposing a limit on the length of a filename. The filename extension should indicate what type of file it is. However, users often change filename extensions to evade firewall restrictions or for other reasons. Therefore, file types must be identified at a binary level rather than relying on file extensions. See also File extension and Full path.

Sedona Conference

Fill device

COMSEC item used to transfer or store key in electronic form or to insert key into a crypto-equipment.

US National Information Assurance (IA) Glossary

Filter (verb)

See Data filtering.

Sedona Conference

Filtering router

A router that is configured to control network access by comparing the attributes of the incoming or outgoing packets to a set of rules.

ISACA

FIN

A flag set in a packet to indicate that this packet is the final data packet of the transmission.

ISACA

Financial audit

An audit designed to determine the accuracy of financial records and information.

ISACA

Financial Audit Manual [GAO/PCIE] (FAM)

GAO/PCIE Financial Audit Manual

Financial information system

An information system that is used for one of the following functions: 1) collecting, processing, maintaining, transmitting, and reporting data about financial events, 2) supporting financial planning or budgeting activity, 3) accumulating and reporting cost information, or 4) supporting the preparation of financial statements.

FISCAM

Financial management

A common abbreviation of financial management for IT services.

ITIL

Financial management for IT services

The process responsible for managing an IT service provider's budgeting, accounting, and charging requirements.

ITIL

Financial Management Service (FMS)

GAO/PCIE Financial Audit Manual

Financial management system

Financial information systems and the financial portions of mixed systems (systems that support both financial and non-financial functions) that are necessary to support financial management.

FISCAM

Financial reporting control

A process, effected by management and other personnel, designed to provide reasonable assurance that transactions are properly recorded, processed, and summarized to permit the preparation of the financial statements and required supplementary stewardship information in accordance with GAAP, and that assets are safeguarded against loss from unauthorized acquisition, use, or disposition.

GAO/PCIE Financial Audit Manual

Financial Services Roundtable (FSR)

Mission Statement

The mission of The Financial Services Roundtable is to unify the leadership of large integrated financial services companies in pursuit of three primary objectives: 1) To be the premier forum in which leaders of the United States financial services industry determine and influence the most critical public policy issues that shape a vibrant, competitive marketplace and a growing national economy; 2) To promote the interests of member companies in federal legislative, regulatory, and judicial forums; and 3) To effectively communicate the benefits of competitive and integrated financial services to the American public. See also http://www.fsround.org for more information.

de facto

Financial statements

The components of a federal entity's annual financial statement (also referred to as the accountability report), which are, balance sheet, statement of net cost, statement of changes in net position, statement of budgetary resources, statement of financing, statement of cus-

todial activity (if applicable), and related notes.

GAO/PCIE Financial Audit Manual

Financial year

An accounting period covering 12 consecutive months. A financial year may start on any date, for example, April 1to March 31.

ITIL

Financial, budgetary, commercial, proprietary, and trade secret information

Information related to financial information and applications, commercial information received in confidence, or trade secrets (i.e., proprietary, contract bidding information, sensitive information about patents, and information protected by the Cooperative Research and Development Agreement). Also included is information about payroll, automated decision making, procurement, inventory, other financially related systems, and site operating and security expenditures.

Centers for Medicare & Medicaid Services (CMS)

Finger

A protocol and program that allows the remote identification of users logged into a system.

ISACA

FIPS approved security method

A security method (e.g., cryptographic algorithm, cryptographic key generation algorithm or key distribution technique, random number generator, authentication technique, or evaluation criteria) that is either a) specified in a FIPS, or b) adopted in a FIPS.

NIST 800 series, FIPS Pubs

FIPS Pub

An acronym for Federal Information Processing Standards Publication. FIPS publications (PUB) are issued by NIST after approval by the Secretary of Commerce.

NIST 800 series

FIREFLY

Key management protocol based on public key cryptography.

US National Information Assurance (IA) Glossary

Firewall

A network device for limiting the flow of network traffic into and out of a network. Firewalls are hardware and software components that protect one set of system resources (e.g., computers, networks) from attack by outside network users (e.g., Internet users) by blocking and checking all incoming network traffic. Firewalls permit authorized users to access and transmit privileged information and deny access to unauthorized users. In other words, a firewall enforces a boundary between two or more networks. An enterprise with an intranet that allows its workers access to the wider Internet installs a firewall to prevent outsiders from accessing its own private data resources and for controlling what outside resources its own users have access to.

FISCAM, ISACA, Centers for Medicare & Medicaid Services (CMS), PCI-DSS, Workgroup for Electronic Data Interchange, US National Information Assurance (IA) Glossary, Sedona Conference, VISA Glossary of Terms, NIST 800 Series

Firewall control proxy

The component that controls a firewall's handling of a call. The firewall control proxy can instruct the firewall to open specific ports that are needed by a call, and direct the firewall to close these ports at call termination.

NIST 800 series

Firewall environment

A firewall environment is a collection of systems at a point on a network that together constitute a firewall implementation. A firewall environment could consist of one device or many devices such as several firewalls, intrusion detection systems, and proxy servers.

NIST 800 series

219

Firewall platform

A firewall platform is the system device upon which a firewall is implemented. An example of a firewall platform is a commercial operating system running on a personal computer.

NIST 800 series

Firewall ruleset

A firewall ruleset is a table of instructions that the firewall uses for determining how packets should be routed between its interfaces. In routers, the ruleset can be a file that the router examines from top to bottom when making routing decisions.

NIST 800 series

Firmware

1) Memory chips with embedded program code that hold their content when power is turned off. 2) The programs and data components of a cryptographic module that are stored in hardware within the cryptographic boundary and cannot be dynamically written or modified during execution.

ISACA, US National Information Assurance (IA) Glossary, NIST 800 Series, FIPS Pubs

First line support

The first level in a hierarchy of support groups involved in the resolution of incidents. Each level contains more spe-cialist skills, or has more time or other resources. See also escalation.

ITIL

First time fix rate

A metric that measures the percentage of incidents resolved by first-line support without delay or escalation. Other definitions of this metric are possible, for example, some IT service providers define it as the percentage of incidents that are resolved during the initial user phone call.

ITIL

Fiscal year

Any yearly accounting period without regard to its relationship to a calendar year.

ISACA

Fishbone diagram

See cause/effect diagram.

ITIL

Fit for purpose

An informal term used to describe a process, configuration item, IT service, etc. that is capable of meeting its objectives or service levels. Being fit for purpose requires suitable design, implementation, control, and maintenance.

ITIL, PAS 56

Fixed COMSEC facility

COMSEC facility located in an immobile structure or aboard a ship.

US National Information Assurance (IA) Glossary

Fixed cost

A cost that does not vary with IT service usage. For example, the cost of server hardware. See also variable cost.

ITIL

Fixed facility

A permanent building, available for use when needed by an IT service continuity plan. See also recovery option, portable facility.

ITIL

Fixed price

A cost or charge agreed with a supplier or customer. This cost or charge remains the same, even if resource usage or time to deliver a project changes.

ITIL

Flatbed scanner

A flat-surface scanner that allows users to input books and other documents.

Sedona Conference

Flaw

Error of commission, omission, or oversight in an information system that may allow protection mechanisms to be bypassed.

US National Information Assurance (IA) Glossary

Flaw hypothesis methodology

System analysis and penetration technique in which the specification and documentation for an information system are analyzed to produce a list of hypothetical flaws. This list is prioritized on the basis of the estimated probability that a flaw exists, on the ease of exploiting it, and on the extent of control or compromise it would provide. The prioritized list is used to perform penetration testing of a system.

US National Information Assurance (IA) Glossary

Flooding

Type of incident involving insertion of a large volume of data resulting in denial of service.

US National Information Assurance (IA) Glossary

Floppy disk

A removable and widely used data storage medium that uses a magnetically coated flexible disk of Mylar enclosed in a plastic envelope.

FISCAM, Sedona Conference

Flowchart

A diagram of the movement of transactions, computer functions, media, and/or operations within a system. The processing flow is represented by arrows between symbolic shapes for operation, device, data file, etc. to depict the system or program.

FISCAM

Flying V

The stylized, embossed "V" located to the right of the Good Thru date on all valid Visa cards. The "flying V" is one of the card security features that should be checked by merchants to ensure that a card-present transaction is valid.

VISA Glossary of Terms

Folder

See Directory.

Sedona Conference

Follow the sun support

A methodology for using service desks and support groups around the world to provide seamless 24 ★ 7 service. Calls, incidents, problems, and service requests are passed between groups in different time zones.

ITIL

Foreign exchange risk

Foreign exchange risk is present when a financial asset or liability is denominated in a foreign currency or is funded by borrowings in another currency.

ISACA

Forensic copy

A forensic copy is an exact copy of an entire physical storage media (hard drive, CD-ROM, DVD-ROM, tape, etc.), including all active and residual data and unallocated space on the media. Compresses and encrypts to ensure authentication and protect chain of custody. Forensic copies are often called "image or imaged copies." See also Bit stream back up and Mirroring.

Sedona Conference, NIST 800 Series

Forensic specialist

A professional who locates, identifies, collects, analyzes and examines data while preserving the integrity and maintaining a strict chain of custody of information discovered.

NIST 800 series

Forensics

Computer forensics is the scientific examination and analysis of data held on, or retrieved from, computer storage media in such a way that the information can be used as evidence in a court of law. It may include the secure collection of computer data; the examination of suspect data to determine details such as origin and content; the presentation of computer based information to courts of law; and the application of a country's laws to computer practice. Forensics may involve recreating "deleted" or missing files from hard drives, validating dates and logged in authors/editors of documents, and certifying key elements of documents and/or hardware for legal purposes.

Sedona Conference

Form of production

The manner in which requested documents are produced. Used to refer both to file format (native vs. PDF or TIFF) and the media on which the documents are produced (paper vs. electronic).

Sedona Conference

Formal access approval

Process for authorizing access to classified or sensitive information with specified access requirements, such as Sensitive Compartmented Information (SCI) or Privacy Data, based on the specified access requirements and a determination of the individual's security eligibility and need-to-know.

US National Information Assurance (IA) Glossary

Formal development methodology

Software development strategy that proves security design specifications.

US National Information Assurance (IA) Glossary

Formal method

Mathematical argument which verifies that the system satisfies a mathematically described security policy.

US National Information Assurance (IA) Glossary

Formal proof

Complete and convincing mathematical argument presenting the full logical justification for each proof step and for the truth of a theorem or set of theorems.

US National Information Assurance (IA) Glossary

Formal security policy

Mathematically precise statement of a security policy.

US National Information Assurance (IA) Glossary

Formal top-level specification

Top-level specification written in a formal mathematical language to allow theorems, showing the correspondence of the system specification to its formal requirements, to be hypothesized and formally proven.

US National Information Assurance (IA) Glossary

Formal verification

Process of using formal proofs to demonstrate the consistency between formal specification of a system and formal security policy model (design verification) or between formal specification and its high-level program implementation (implementation verification).

US National Information Assurance (IA) Glossary

Format (noun)

The internal structure of a file, which defines the way it is stored and used. Specific applications may define unique formats for their data (e.g., "MS Word document file format"). Many files may only be viewed or printed using their originating application or an application designed to work with compatible formats. There are several common e-mail formats, such as Outlook and Lotus Notes. Computer storage systems commonly identify files by a naming convention that denotes the format (and therefore the probable originating application). For example, "DOC" for Microsoft Word document files; "XLS" for Microsoft Excel spreadsheet files; "TXT" for text files; "HTM" for Hypertext Markup Language (HTML) files such as web pages; "PPT" for Microsoft Powerpoint files; "TIF" for tiff images; "PDF" for Adobe images; etc. Users may choose alternate naming conventions, but this will likely affect how the files are treated by applications.

Sedona Conference

Format (verb)

Makes a drive ready for first use. Erroneously thought to "wipe" drive. Typically, only overwrites FAT, but not files on the drive.

Sedona Conference

Format checking

The application of an edit, using a predefined field definition to a submitted information stream; a test to ensure that data conform to a predefined format.

ISACA

Formatting function

The function that transforms the payload, associated data, and nonce into a sequence of complete blocks.

NIST 800 series

Forms processing

The ability for software to accept scanned forms and extract data from the boxes and lines to populate databases. Software usually includes the ability to drop out the form so that recognition accuracy improves. Intelligent document recognition automatically identifies document types from the layout and structure of the document.

AIIM, Sedona Conference

Forward cipher

One of the two functions of the block cipher algorithm that is determined by the choice of a cryptographic key.

NIST 800 series

Fragmented

In the course of normal computer operations when files are saved, deleted or moved, the files or parts thereof may be broken into pieces, or fragmented, and scattered in various locations on the computer's hard drive or other storage medium, such as removable discs. Data saved in contiguous clusters may be larger than contiguous free space, and it is broken up and randomly placed throughout the available storage space. See also De-fragment.

Sedona Conference

Frame relay

A packet-switched, wide-area-network technology that provides faster performance than older packet-switched WAN technologies such as X.25 networks because it was designed for today's reliable circuits and performs less rigorous error detection. Frame relay is best suited for data and image transfers. Because of its variable-length packet architecture, it is not the most efficient technology for real-time voice and video. In a frame-relay network, end nodes establish a connection via a permanent virtual circuit (PVC).

ISACA

Framework

See control framework.

CobiT, ISO/IEC 27001:2005

Fraud

A deception deliberately practiced to secure unfair or unlawful gain. Although fraud is a broad legal concept, the auditor is interested in fraudulent acts that cause a material misstatement of financial statements. Fraud is distinguished from error because fraud is intentional whereas error is unintentional. Two relevant types of misstatements are those arising from fraudulent financial reporting and those arising from misappropriation of assets.

GAO/PCIE Financial Audit Manual, Centers for Medicare & Medicaid Services (CMS), ISO/IEC 27001:2005

Fraud risk

The risk that activities will include deliberate circumvention of controls with the intent to conceal the perpetuation of irregularities. The unauthorized use of assets or services and abetting or helping to conceal.

ISACA

Fraudulent financial reporting

Intentional misstatements or omissions of amounts or disclosures in financial statements to deceive financial statement users. This may involve acts such as manipulation, falsification, or alteration of accounting records or supporting documents; misrepresentation or intentional omission of events, transactions, or other significant information in the financial statements; or intentional misapplication of accounting principles relating to amounts, classification, manner of presentation, or disclosure.

GAO/PCIE Financial Audit Manual

Frequency hopping

Repeated switching of frequencies during radio transmission according to a specified algorithm, to minimize unauthorized interception or jamming of telecommunications.

US National Information Assurance (IA) Glossary

Front-end security filter

Security filter logically separated from the remainder of an information system to protect system integrity. Synonymous with firewall.

US National Information Assurance (IA) Glossary

Full and accurate records

Full and accurate records must be: 1) Compliant, complying with the record-keeping requirements arising from the regulatory and accountability environment in which the organization operates. 2) Adequate for the purposes for which they are kept. 3) Complete, containing not only the content, but also the structural and contextual information necessary to document a transaction. 4) Meaningful, containing information and/or linkages that ensure the business context in which the record was created and used is apparent. 5) Comprehensive, documenting the complete range of the organization's business for which evidence is required. 6) Accurate, reflecting accurately the transactions that they document. 7) Authentic, enabling proof that they are what they purport to be and that their purported creators did indeed create them. 8) Inviolate, securely maintained to prevent unauthorized access, alteration, or removal.

DIRKS

Full cost

In cost accounting, the sum of all costs required by a cost object including the costs of activities performed by other organizations regardless of funding sources.

GAO/PCIE Financial Audit Manual, ITIL

Full duplex

A communications channel over which data can be sent and received simultaneously. Data communications devices which allow full speed transmission in both directions at the same time.

ISACA, Sedona Conference

Full maintenance

Complete diagnostic repair, modification, and overhaul of COMSEC equipment, including repair of defective assemblies by piece part replacement. See also limited maintenance.

US National Information Assurance (IA) Glossary

Full path

A path name description that includes the drive, starting or root directory, all attached subdirectories and ending with the file or object name.

Sedona Conference

Full release

A release that includes all components of a release unit including those that have not changed. See also release type.

ITIL

Full-text indexing and search

Every word in the document is indexed into a master word list with pointers to the documents and pages where each occurrence of the word appears.

Sedona Conference

Full-text search

The ability to search a data file for specific words, numbers and/or combinations or patterns thereof.

Sedona Conference

Function

The largest unit of business activity in an organization or jurisdiction. Functions represent the major responsibilities that are managed by the organization to fulfill its goals. Functions are high-level aggregates of the organization's activities. A discrete area of operational or housekeeping responsibility administered by an organization over a period. A function may be, or derive from, a substantive function of the organization (e.g. allocated through the Administrative Arrangements Orders), or it may be a construct of the organization's management to achieve the organization's goals. As used by ITIL, a function is an intended purpose of a configuration item, person, team, process, or IT service. For example, one function of an e-mail service may be to store and forward outgoing mails, one function of a business process may be to dispatch goods to customers. The term function also has two other meanings: 1) Perform the intended purpose correctly, "the computer is functioning." 2) Team or group of people, "the change management function."

DIRKS, ITIL

Function point analysis

A technique used to determine the size of a development task based on the number of function points. Function points are factors such as inputs, outputs, inquiries, and logical internal sites.

ISACA

Functional Administrators

Functional Administrators are those IT support staff who are assigned a particular business or operational unit function and the support of it. Most design departments will have IT specialists who know both design and how to support the IT systems that create those designs. HR teams will have an IT support person assigned to the HR system per se.

NIST 800 series

Functional escalation

Transferring an incident, problem, or change to a technical team with a higher level of expertise to assist in an escalation.

ITIL

Functional proponent

See network sponsor.

US National Information Assurance (IA) Glossary

Functional records

Records created by an organization to help carry out its unique business role. The functions and their associated records are specific to the organization, as opposed to housekeeping records that document functions common to all agencies. Also referred to as operational or unique records.

DIRKS

Functional records disposal schedule

A disposal schedule covering an agency's functional records.

DIRKS

Functional testing

Segment of security testing in which advertised security mechanisms of an information system are tested under operational conditions.

US National Information Assurance (IA) Glossary

Functions thesaurus

A keyword thesaurus, produced and maintained by an organization (which has implemented the keyword classification system) and which contains keywords, descriptors and forbidden terms. The thesaurus covers terms of a functional nature relating specifically to an organization's specific functions to provide comprehensive controlled vocabulary to describe paper and electronic records and recordkeeping systems. A thesaurus that reflects the unique functions of an organization.

DIRKS

Fund Balance with Treasury account (FBWT)

An asset account representing the unexpended spending authority in agencies' appropriations. Also serves as a mechanism to prevent agencies' disbursements from exceeding appropriated amounts.

GAO/PCIE Financial Audit Manual

Fuzzy Search

Subjective content searching (as compared to word searching of objective data). Fuzzy Searching lets the user find documents where word matching does not have to be exact, even if the words searched are misspelled due to optical character recognition (OCR) errors

Sedona Conference

G

Credit receipt

A receipt that documents a refund or price adjustment a merchant has made or is making to a cardholder's account; also called credit voucher.

VISA Glossary of Terms

Gap analysis

A gap analysis is the study of the differences between two different systems, or states of the systems, for determining how to get from the present state to the desired state.

de facto

Gateway

In a communications network, a network node equipped to interface with another network that uses different protocols. A computer that connects two dissimilar local area networks or connects a local area network to a wide area network, minicomputer, or mainframe. A gateway may perform network protocol conversion and bandwidth conversion. See also router.

FISCAM, ISACA, Centers for Medicare & Medicaid Services (CMS), US National Information Assurance (IA) Glossary

General controls or general computer controls

Controls, other than application controls, which relate to the environment within which computer-based application systems are developed, maintained, and operated, and which are therefore applicable to all applications. General controls are the structure, policies, and procedures that apply to an entity's overall computer operations. They include an organization wide security program, access controls, application development and change controls, segregation of duties, system software controls, and service continuity controls. The objectives of general controls are to ensure the proper development and implementation of applications, the integrity of program, and data files and of computer operations. Like application controls, general controls may be either manual or programmed. Examples of general controls include the development and implementation of an IS strategy and an IS security policy, the organization of IS staff to separate conflicting duties, and planning for disaster prevention and recovery.

FISCAM, GAO/PCIE Financial Audit Manual, ISACA, Centers for Medicare & Medicaid Services (CMS), CobiT

General Ledger (G/L)

GAO/PCIE Financial Audit Manual

General Packet Radio Service (GPRS)

Mobile data service available to users of GSM mobile phones. Recognized for efficient use of limited bandwidth. Particularly suited for sending and receiving small bursts of data, such as e-mail and web browsing.

PCI-DSS

General Risk Analysis (GRA)

GAO/PCIE Financial Audit Manual

General support system (GSS)

An interconnected set of information resources under the same direct management control that shares common functionality. An interconnected information resource under the same direct management control that shares common functionality. It normally includes hardware, software, information, data, applications, communications, facilities, and people. It provides support for a variety of users and/or applications. Individual applications supporting different business-related functions may run on a single GSS. Users may be from the same or different organizations. Normally, the purpose of a general support system is to provide processing or communication support. A system can be, for example, a LAN including smart terminals that supports a branch office, an agency-wide backbone, or a communications network. A departmental data processing center including its operating system and utilities, a tactical radio network, or shared information processing service organization.

Centers for Medicare & Medicaid Services (CMS), NIST 800 series, FIPS Pubs, Clinger-Cohen Act, OMB Circular A-130

Generalized audit software

A computer program or series of programs designed to perform certain automated functions. These functions include reading computer files, selecting data, manipulating data, sorting data, summarizing data, performing calculations, selecting samples and printing reports or letters in a format specified by the IS auditor. This technique includes software acquired or written for audit purposes and software embedded in production systems.

ISACA

Generally Accepted Accounting Principles (GAAP)

The accounting principles that the entity should use. For federal executive agencies, these are federal accounting standards following the hierarchy listed in SAS 91. The standards issued by FASB are the first level of the hierarchy. For government corporations, generally accepted accounting principles are commercial generally accepted accounting principles issued by FASB.

GAO/PCIE Financial Audit Manual

Generally Accepted Auditing Standards (GAAS)

GAO/PCIE Financial Audit Manual

Generally Accepted Internet Security Principles (GAISP)

The GAISP provides a means to unify and harmonize information security efforts and measure their success. It offers a translation of existing regulations, standards, and accepted practices into logical strategy and detailed tactics that can be implemented by any organization.

Information Systems Security Association

Generally Accepted Internet Security Principles Committee

Originally carried by the International Information Security Foundation (IISF), the GAISP has drawn from a wide array of existing guidelines, such as those created by the Organization for Economic Cooperation and Development (OECD) and the United Kingdom Department of Trade and Industry. As a global initiative, participation and support have been gained from respected groups like the International Information Systems Security Certification Consortium (ISC2), the International Standards Organization (ISO), the Institute of Internal Auditors (IIA) and the international Common Criteria effort. See also http://www.issa.org/gaisp for more information.

de facto

Generator

An independent source of electrical power usually fueled by diesel or natural gas.

Centers for Medicare & Medicaid Services (CMS)

Geographical disk mirroring

A data recovery strategy that takes a set of physically disparate discs and synchronously mirrors them over high performance communication lines. Any write to a disk on one side will result in a write on the other. The local write will not return until the acknowledgment of the remote write is successful.

ISACA

Ghost

See Bit stream back up.

Sedona Conference

Gigabyte (GB)

A unit of consisting of either 1,000 or 1,024 megabytes. In terms of image storage capacity, one gigabyte equals approximately 17,000 81/2" x 11" pages scanned at 300 dpi, stored as TIFF Group IV images. See also Byte.

Sedona Conference

Global Address List (GAL)

Directory of all Microsoft Exchange users and distribution lists to whom messages can be addressed. The administrator creates and maintains this list. The global address list may also contain public folder names. Entries from this list can be added to a user's personal address book.

Sedona Conference

Global Information Grid

The globally interconnected, end-to-end set of information capabilities, associated processes, and personnel for collecting, processing, storing, disseminating, and managing information on demand to war fighters, policy makers, and support personnel. (DoD Directive 8100.1, 19 Sept. 2002)

US National Information Assurance (IA) Glossary

Global Information Infrastructure (GII)

Worldwide interconnections of the information systems of all countries, international and multinational organizations, and international commercial communications.

US National Information Assurance (IA) Glossary

Global Positioning System (GPS)

de facto

Global System for Mobile Communications (GSM)

Popular standard for mobile phones Ubiquity of GSM standard makes international roaming very common between mobile phone operators, enabling subscribers to use their phones in many parts of the world.

PCI-DSS

GMT Timestamp

Identification of a file using Greenwich Mean Time as the central time authentication method.

Sedona Conference

Going rate

A charging policy in which charges are the same as those charged by other internal departments or internal departments of similar organizations.

ITIL

Good Thru date

The date after which a bankcard is no longer valid, embossed on the front of all valid Visa cards. The Good Thru date is one of the card security features that should be checked by merchants to ensure that a card-present transaction is valid. See also: Card expiration date.

VISA Glossary of Terms

Governance

The method by which an organization is directed, administered, or controlled.

CobiT

Government Accountability Office (GAO)

Effective July 7, 2004, the GAO's legal name became the Government Accountability Office. The change, which better reflects the modern professional services organization GAO has become, is the most visible provision of the GAO Human Capital Reform Act of 2004, Pub. L. 108-271, 118 Stat. 811 (2004). See also http://www.gao.gov for more information.

GAO/PCIE Financial Audit Manual

GPS Generated Timestamp

Timestamp identifying time as a function of its relationship to Greenwich Mean Time.

Sedona Conference

Gradual recovery

A recovery option which is also known as cold standby. Provision is made to recover the IT service in a period of time greater than 72 hours. Gradual recovery typically uses a portable or fixed facility that has environmental support and network cabling but no computer systems. The hardware and software are installed as part of the IT service continuity plan.

ITIL

Graduated security

A security system that provides several levels (e.g., low, moderate, high) of protection based on threats, risks, available technology, support services, time, human concerns, and economics.

NIST 800 series, FIPS Pubs

Graphical User Interface (GUI)

Pronounced "gooey." Presenting an interface to the computer user comprised of pictures and icons, rather than words and numbers.

Sedona Conference

Graphics Interchange Format (GIF)

CompuServe's native file format for storing images. Limited to 256 colors.

Sedona Conference

Gray scale

The use of many shades of gray to represent an image. Continuous-tone images, such as black-and-white photographs, use an almost unlimited number of shades of gray. Conventional computer hardware and software, however, can only represent a limited number of shades of gray (typically 16 or 256).

Sedona Conference

Greenwich Mean Time (GMT)

de facto

Groupware

Software designed to operate on a network and allow several people to work together on the same documents and files.

Sedona Conference

Guard

Mechanism limiting the exchange of information between systems.

US National Information Assurance (IA) Glossary, NIST 800 Series

Guessing entropy

A measure of the difficulty that an attacker has to guess the average password used in a system. In this document, entropy is stated in bits. When a password has n-bits of guessing entropy then an attacker has as much difficulty guessing the average password as in guessing an n-bit random quantity. The attacker is assumed to know the actual password frequency distribution.

NIST 800 series

Guided media

Those media in which a message flows through a physical media (e.g., twisted pair wire, coaxial cable, fiber optical cable). Guided media provides a closed path between sender and receiver.

Centers for Medicare & Medicaid Services (CMS)

Guideline

Recommended configurations, policies, or actions developed to provide assistance in complying with one or more policies or standards. A description of a particular way of accomplishing something that is less prescriptive than a procedure. The hallmark of a guideline is that it will have a set of general principles followed by a set of procedures that guide the user through the necessary steps that should be followed with respect to the given topic under consideration. See also regulation, standard, best practice, policy, procedure.

Centers for Medicare & Medicaid Services (CMS), CobiT, ITIL

H

Hacker

A person who attempts to enter a system without authorization from a remote location. An individual who attempts to access and/or compromise the confidentiality, integrity, or availability of organizational data or systems.

FISCAM, ISACA, Centers for Medicare & Medicaid Services (CMS), US National Information Assurance (IA) Glossary, Sedona Conference

Hacking

An unauthorized attempt to access and/or comprise a computer system and the data it contains.

Centers for Medicare & Medicaid Services (CMS), ISO/IEC 27001:2005

Half duplex

A communications channel that can handle only one signal at a time. The two stations must alternate their transmissions.

ISACA, Sedona Conference

Halftone

See Dithering.

Sedona Conference

Halon

A gas used to extinguish fires that is effective only in closed areas.

Centers for Medicare & Medicaid Services (CMS)

Hand scanner

A biometric device that is used to authenticate a user through palm scans.

ISACA

Handled

As in "data handled" that is stored, processed, or used in an ADP system or communicated, displayed, produced, or disseminated by an ADP system.

Centers for Medicare & Medicaid Services (CMS)

Handler

A type of program used in DDoS attacks to control agents distributed throughout a network. Also refers to an incident handler, which refers to a person who performs incident response work.

NIST 800 series

Handprint Character Recognition (HCR)

OCR technology designed to turn images of handprint characters into ASCII code.

AIIM

Handshaking

Signals transmitted back and forth over a communications network that establish a valid connection between two stations.

Network Frontiers

Handshaking procedures

Dialogue between two information systems for synchronizing, identifying, and authenticating themselves to one another.

US National Information Assurance (IA) Glossary

Haphazard sample

A sample consisting of sampling units selected without any conscious bias, that is, without any special reason for including or omitting items from the sample. It does not consist of sampling units selected in a careless manner, but is selected in a manner that can be expected to be representative of the population.

GAO/PCIE Financial Audit Manual

Hard copy key

Physical keying material, such as printed key lists, punched or printed key tapes, or programmable, read-only memories (PROM).

US National Information Assurance (IA) Glossary

Hard disk drive

See Hard drive.

Sedona Conference

Hard drive

The primary storage unit on PCs, consisting of one or more magnetic media platters on which digital data can be written and erased magnetically.

Sedona Conference

Harden

To configure a computer or other network device to resist attacks.

ISACA

Hardware

The physical components of information technology including the computers, peripheral devices such as printers, discs, and scanners, and cables, switches, and other elements of the telecommunications infrastructure. See also hardware asset, components, IT assets.

de facto

Hardware asset

Information technology physical devices (workstations, servers, etc.). See also hardware, IT assets, components.

CERT OCTAVE

Hardwired key

Permanently installed key.

US National Information Assurance (IA) Glossary

Harmonization

See unification.

de facto

Harvesting

The process of retrieving or collecting electronic data from storage media or devices; an E-discovery vendor "harvests" electronic data from computer hard drives, file servers, CDs, and backup tapes for processing and load to storage media or a database management system.

Sedona Conference

Hash

An algorithm that maps or translates one set of bits into another (generally smaller) so that a message yields the same result every time the algorithm is executed using the same message as input. It is computationally infeasible for a message to be derived or reconstituted from the result produced by the algorithm. It is computationally unfeasible to find two different messages that produce the same hash result using the same algorithm. Common hash algorithms include MD5 and SHA. See also Hash function.

ISACA, Workgroup for Electronic Data Interchange, Sedona Conference

Hash coding

To create a digital fingerprint that represents the binary content of a file unique to every electronically-generated document; assists in subsequently ensuring that data has not been modified. See also Data verification and Digital fingerprint and File level binary comparison.

Sedona Conference

Hash function

A function used to create a hash value from binary input. The hash is substantially smaller than the text itself, and is generated by the hash function in such a way that it is extremely unlikely that some other input will produce the same hash value. Approved hash functions satisfy the following properties: 1) One-Way. It is computationally infeasible to find any input that maps to any pre-specified output. 2) Collision Resistant. It is computationally infeasible to find any two distinct inputs that map to the same output.

Sedona Conference, NIST 800 Series, FIPS Pubs

Hash total

The total of any numeric data field on a document or computer file. This total is checked against a control total of the same field to facilitate accuracy of processing.

ISACA, US National Information Assurance (IA) Glossary

Hash-based Message Authentication Code (HMAC)

1) A symmetric key authentication method using hash functions. 2) A message authentication code that uses a cryptographic key in conjunction with a hash function.

NIST 800 series, FIPS Pubs

Hashing

Computation of a hash total. The process of using a mathematical algorithm against data to produce a numeric value that is representative of that data.

US National Information Assurance (IA) Glossary, NIST 800 Series

Hashword

Memory address containing hash total.

US National Information Assurance (IA) Glossary

Hazardous material

Any substance that poses a physical and/or health hazard. Health hazardous materials may be toxic, carcinogenic, corrosive, a sensitizer, or irritant. Physically hazardous materials may be flammable, explosive, unstable, water-reactive, an oxidizer, organic peroxide, combustible liquid, or compressed gas.

Centers for Medicare & Medicaid Services (CMS)

Head

Each platter on a hard drive contains a head for each side of the platter. The heads are devices which ride very closely to the surface of the platter and allow information to be read from and written to the platter.

Sedona Conference

Health plan

A covered entity that assumes the risk of paying for medical treatments, i.e., un-insured patient, self-insured employer, payer, or HMO.

HIPAA

Healthcare clearinghouse

A public or private CE that does either of the following (CEs, including but not limited to, billing services, re-pricing companies, community health management information systems, or community health information systems, and "value-added" networks and switches are health care clearinghouses if they perform these functions): 1) Processes or facilitates the processing of information received from another CE in a nonstandard format or containing nonstandard data content into standard data elements or a standard transaction. 2) Receives a standard transaction from another CE and processes or facilitates the processing of information into nonstandard format or nonstandard data content for a receiving CE.

HIPAA

Healthcare provider

A person who is trained and licensed to provide health care. Also, a place licensed to give health care. Doctors, nurses, hospitals, skilled nursing facilities, some assisted living facilities and

certain kinds of home health agencies are examples of health care providers.

HIPAA

Help desk

A point of contact for users to log incidents. A help desk is usually more technically focused than a service desk and does not provide a single point of contact for all interaction. The term help desk is often used as a synonym for service desk.

ITIL

Hewlett Packard Printer Control Language (HP-PCL)

Sedona Conference

Hewlett-Packard Graphics Language (HPGL)

Sedona Conference

Hexadecimal

A numbering system that uses a base of 16 and uses 16 digits: 0, 1, 2, 3, 4, 5, 6, 7, 8, 9, A, B, C, D, E and F, where F equals the decimal value of 15. Programmers use hexadecimal numbers as a more convenient way of representing binary numbers.

ISACA, Sedona Conference

Hidden files or data

Files or data not visible in the file directory; cannot be accessed by unauthorized or unsophisticated users. Some operating system files are hidden, to prevent inexperienced users from inadvertently deleting or changing these essential files. See also Steganography.

Sedona Conference

Hierarchical database

A database structured in a tree/root or parent/child relationship. Each parent can have many children, but each child may have only one parent.

ISACA

Hierarchical escalation

Informing or involving more senior levels of management to assist in an escalation.

ITIL

Hierarchical Storage Management (HSM)

Software that automatically migrates files from on-line to near-line storage media, usually on the basis of the age or frequency of use of the files.

Sedona Conference

High Assurance Guard (HAG)

An enclave boundary protection device that controls access between a local area network that an enterprise system has a requirement to protect, and an external network that is outside the control of the enterprise system, with a high degree of assurance.

US National Information Assurance (IA) Glossary, NIST 800 Series

High Density (HD)

A 5.25" HD Floppy disk holds 1.2 MB and a 3.5" holds 1.4 MB.

Sedona Conference

High impact system

An information system in which at least one security objective (i.e., confidentiality, integrity, or availability) is assigned a FIPS 199 potential impact value of high.

FIPS Pubs, NIST 800 Series

High level programming language

A programming language that provides a certain level of abstraction from the underlying machine language through the use of declarations, control statements, and other syntactical structures. In practice, the term refers to a computer language above assembly language.

FISCAM

High-Risk Chargeback Monitoring Program

A Visa program that notifies merchant banks when a high-risk merchant has a chargeback-to-transaction rate of over one percent.

VISA Glossary of Terms

High-risk merchant

A merchant that is at a high risk for chargebacks due to the nature of its business. As defined by Visa, high-risk merchants include direct marketers, travel services, outbound telemarketers, inbound teleservices, and betting establishments. See also High-Risk Chargeback Monitoring Program.

VISA Glossary of Terms

Hold

See Legal hold

Sedona Conference

Holorith

Encoded data on aperture cards or old-style punch cards that contained encoded data.

Sedona Conference

Home computer

Home personal computers that staff members use to access information remotely via an organization's networks.

CERT OCTAVE

Honey pot

A specially configured server, designed to attract intruders so that their actions do not affect production systems; also known as a decoy server.

ISACA

Honeypot

A host that is designed to collect data on suspicious activity and has no authorized users other than its administrators.

NIST 800 series

Horizontal de-duplication

A way to identify documents that are duplicated across multiple custodians or other production data sets. See also De-duplication.

Sedona Conference

Host

In the traditional context, this term refers to almost any kind of computer that provides data to attached or interconnected terminals. In a distributed network architecture, a client workstation (e.g. PC) is also considered a host as this device may serve as a source of information to other devices. See also host computer.

PCI-DSS, Workgroup for Electronic Data Interchange, Sedona Conference

Host computer

The main computer in a system of computers and terminals connected by communication links.

FISCAM

Host-based IDS

IDSs which operate on information collected from within an individual computer system. This vantage point allows host-based IDSs to determine exactly which processes and user accounts are involved in a particular attack on the Operating System. Furthermore, unlike network-based IDSs, host-based IDSs can more readily "see" the intended outcome of an attempted attack, because they can directly access and monitor the data files and system processes usually targeted by attacks.

NIST 800 Series

Hosting provider

Offer various services to merchants and other service providers. Services range from simple to complex; from shared space on a server to a whole range of "shopping cart" options; from payment applications to connections to payment gateways and processors; and for hosting dedicated to just one customer per server.

PCI-DSS

Hot site

A fully operational off site data processing facility equipped with both hardware and system software to be used in the event of a disaster. An alternate facility that has the equipment and resources to recover the business functions affected by the occurrence of a disaster. Hotsites may vary in type of facilities offered (such as data processing, communication, or any other critical business functions needing duplication).

FISCAM, ISACA, Centers for Medicare & Medicaid Services (CMS), NIST 800 Series

Hub

A central unit that repeats and/or amplifies data signals being sent across a network. A common connection point for devices in a network, hubs commonly are used to connect segments of a LAN. A hub contains multiple ports. When a packet arrives at one port, it is copied to the other ports so that all segments of the LAN can see all packets.

ISACA, Sedona Conference

Human resources (HR)

Human resources has at least two meanings depending on context. The original usage derives from political economy and economics, where it was traditionally called labor, one of three factors of production. The more common usage within corporations and businesses refers to the individuals within the firm and to the portion of the firm's organization that deals with hiring, firing, training, and other personnel issues.

Wikipedia, de facto

Hybrid scanner

A vulnerability evaluation tool that targets a range of services, applications, and operating system functions. Hybrid scanners may address Web servers (CGI, JAVA), database applications, registry information (e.g., Windows NT/2000), and weak password storage and authentication services. These are also known as specialty and targeted scanners.

CERT OCTAVE

Hyper Text Markup Language (HTML)

Developed by CERN of Geneva, Switzerland, Hyper Text Markup Language is the computer language used to create Web pages.. The document standard of choice of Internet. (HTML+ adds support for multi-media.) The tag-based ASCII language used to create pages on the World Wide Web - uses tags to tell a web browser to display text and images.

Sedona Conference, Workgroup for Electronic Data Interchange

Hyper Text Transfer Protocol (HTTP)

A communication protocol used to connect to servers on the World Wide Web. Its primary function is to establish a connection with a web server and transmit HTML pages to the client browser. HTTP defines how messages are formatted and transmitted, and what actions Web servers and browsers should take in response to various commands. For example, when you enter a URL in your browser, this actually sends an HTTP command to the Web server directing it to fetch and transmit the requested Web page.

ISACA, PCI-DSS, Sedona Conference

Hyper Text Transfer Protocol Secure (HTTPS)

A protocol for accessing a secure web server, whereby all data transferred is encrypted.

ISACA

Hyperlink

An electronic pathway that may be displayed in the form of highlighted text, graphics, or a button that connects one web page with another web page address. When clicked, the hyperlink changes the active view, possibly to another place within the same document or view, or to another document altogether, usually regardless of the application or environment in which the other document or view exists.

ISACA, Sedona Conference

Hypertext

A language which enables electronic documents that present information that can be connected together by links instead of being presented sequentially, as is the case with normal text.

ISACA, Sedona Conference

I

I/O appendage

See input/output appendage.

FISCAM

IA architecture

Activity that aggregates the functions of developing IA operational, system, and technical architecture products for the purpose of specifying and implementing new or modified IA capabilities within the IT environment. (DoD Directive 8100.1, 19 Sept 2002)

US National Information Assurance (IA) Glossary

IA-enabled information

Product or technology whose primary role is not

US National Information Assurance (IA) Glossary

Icon

In a GUI, a picture or drawing which is activated by "clicking" a mouse to command the computer program to perform a predefined series of events.

Sedona Conference

Identification

Identification of a user and is accomplished by techniques such as a secret code only known by a single person, biometrics of a person, a computer read-able identity card, or other methods. The process that enables recognition and validation of an entity by a system.

HIPAA, Centers for Medicare & Medicaid Services (CMS), ISO/IEC 27001:2005, US National Information Assurance (IA) Glossary, NIST 800 Series, FIPS Pubs

Identified requirements

A comprehensive list of implicit and explicit recordkeeping requirements, identified from documentary and oral sources in DIRKS Step C, that an organization may potentially decide to meet. An organization must subject these identified requirements to risk-based assessment to prioritize a subset that the organization will meet.

DIRKS, ISO/IEC 27001:2005

Identifier

A unique data string used as a key in the biometric system to name a person's identity and its associated attributes.

NIST 800 series, FIPS Pubs

Identity (ID)

Information that is unique within a security domain and which is recognized as denoting a particular organization, system, asset, or person within that domain. Since the legal names of persons are not necessarily unique, the identity of a person must include sufficient additional information to make the complete name unique.

NIST 800 series, ISO/IEC 27001:2005, PCI-DSS, NIST 800 Series, FIPS Pubs

Identity binding

Binding of the vetted claimed identity to the individual (through biometrics) according to the issuing authority.

NIST 800 series, FIPS Pubs

Identity management

A system that coordinates authentication and password management across network applications and resources.

Network Frontiers

Identity proofing

The process by which a Credentials Service Provider (CSP) and a Registration Authority (RA) validate sufficient information to uniquely identify a person.

NIST 800 series, FIPS Pubs

Identity registration

The process of making a person's identity known to the Personal Identity Verification (PIV) system, associating a unique identifier with that identity, and collecting and recording the person's relevant attributes into the system.

NIST 800 series, FIPS Pubs

Identity token

Smart card, metal key, or other physical object used to authenticate identity.

US National Information Assurance (IA) Glossary

Identity validation

Tests enabling an information system to authenticate users or resources.

US National Information Assurance (IA) Glossary

Identity verification

The process of confirming or denying that a claimed identity is correct by comparing the credentials (something you know, something you have, something you are) of a person requesting access with those previously proven and stored in the PIV Card or system and associated with the identity being claimed.

NIST 800 series, FIPS Pubs

Identity-based security policy

A security policy based on the identities and/or attributes of the object (system resource) being accessed and of the subject (user, group of users, process, or device) requesting access.

NIST 800 series

Idle standby

A fail-over process in which the primary node owns the resource group. The backup node runs idle only supervising the primary node. In case of a primary node outage, the backup node takes over. The nodes are prioritized, which means the surviving node with the highest priority will acquire the resource group. A higher priority node joining the cluster will thus cause a short service interruption.

ISACA

IDS sensor

Intrusion Detection System sensor monitors network activity and can alert personnel when suspicious activity occurs and shut down suspect connections automatically. See also intrusion detection system.

Network Frontiers

Image

An exact copy of what is on the storage medium. To image a hard drive is to make an identical copy of the hard drive, including empty sectors. Also known as creating a "mirror image" or "mirroring" the drive.

Centers for Medicare & Medicaid Services (CMS), Sedona Conference, NIST 800 Series

Image copy

See Forensic copy.

Sedona Conference

Image enabling

A software function that creates links between existing applications and stored images.

Sedona Conference

Image file format

See File format, format.

Sedona Conference

Image key

The name of a file created when a page is scanned in a collection.

Sedona Conference

Image processing

The process of electronically inputting source documents by taking an image of the document thereby eliminating the need for key entry. See also Native format

ISACA, Sedona Conference

Image Processing Card (IPC)

A board mounted in the computer, scanner or printer that facilitates the acquisition and display of images. The primary function of most IPCs is the rapid compression and decompression of image files.

Sedona Conference

Imitative communications deception

Introduction of deceptive messages or signals into an adversary's telecommunications signals. See also communications deception and manipulative communications deception.

US National Information Assurance (IA) Glossary

Immediate recovery

Previously called "hot stand-by," provides for the immediate restoration of services following any irrecoverable incident. It is important to distinguish between the previous definition of "hot stand-by" and "immediate recovery." Hot stand-by typically referred to availability of services within a short timescale such as 2 or 4 hours whereas immediate recovery implies the instant availability of services. See also active recovery site, dedicated work area.

ITIL

Impact

The effect of a threat on an organization's mission and business objectives. A measure of the effect of an incident, problem, or change on business processes. Impact is often based on how service levels will be affected. Impact and urgency are used to assign priority. See also impact code.

CERT OCTAVE, ISO/IEC 27001:2005, ITIL, BS 25999, NIST 800 Series

Impact code

A category used to represent impact. For example, major, minor, or catastrophic. See also priority.

ITIL

Impersonating

Form of spoofing.

US National Information Assurance (IA) Glossary

Impersonation

An attempt to gain access to a system by posing as an authorized user.

Centers for Medicare & Medicaid Services (CMS)

Implant

Electronic device or electronic equipment modification designed to gain unauthorized interception of information-bearing emanations.

US National Information Assurance (IA) Glossary

Implementation

The process of making a system operational in the organization.

FISCAM, Centers for Medicare & Medicaid Services (CMS), ISO/IEC 27001:2005

Implementation life cycle review

Refers to the controls that support the process of transformation of the organization's legacy information systems into the ERP applications. This would largely cover all aspects of systems implementation and configuration such as change management.

ISACA

Implementation vulnerability

A weakness resulting from an error made in the software or hardware implementation of a satisfactory design.

CERT OCTAVE

Import

Data brought into an environment or application which has been exported from another environment or application.

Sedona Conference

Inactive record

Inactive records are those Records related to closed, completed, or concluded activities. Inactive Records are no longer routinely referenced, but must be retained in order to fulfill reporting requirements or for purposes of audit or analysis. Inactive records generally reside in a long-term storage format remaining accessible for purposes of business processing only with restrictions on alteration. In some business circumstances inactive records may be reactivated.

Sedona Conference

Inadvertent disclosure

Type of incident involving accidental exposure of information to an individual not authorized access.

US National Information Assurance (IA) Glossary

Inappropriate usage

A person who violates acceptable computing use policies.

NIST 800 series

Incident

Any adverse event whereby some aspect of computer security was or could be threatened involving the loss of data confidentiality, disruption of data or system integrity, or disruption or denial of availability. An occurrence that actually or potentially jeopardizes the confidentiality, integrity, or availability of an information system or the information the system processes, stores, or transmits or that constitutes a violation or imminent threat of violation of security policies, security procedures, or acceptable use policies. Any event which could affect an IT service in the future is also an incident. For example, failure of one disk from a mirror set. See also incident management, incident record.

Centers for Medicare & Medicaid Services (CMS), CobiT, ISO/IEC 27001:2005, FIPS Pubs, ITIL, US National Information Assurance (IA) Glossary, PAS 56, BS 25999, NIST 800 Series

Incident cost

A cost of providing an IT service which cannot be allocated in full to a specific customer. For example, cost of providing shared servers or software licenses. Indirect costs are divided into absorbed overhead and unabsorbed overhead. See also direct cost, overhead.

ITIL

Incident handling

The mitigation of violations of security policies and recommended practices.

NIST 800 series

Incident management

The process responsible for managing the lifecycle of all incidents. The primary objective of incident management is to return the IT service to customers as quickly as possible.

ITIL

Incident management plan

A clearly defined and documented plan of action for use at the time of an incident, typically covering the key personnel, resources, services and actions needed to implement the incident management process.

BS 25999

Incident record

A record containing the details of an incident. Each incident record documents the lifecycle of a single incident.

ITIL

Incident response plan

The documentation of a predetermined set of instructions or procedures to detect, respond to, and limit consequences of a malicious cyber attacks against an organization's IT systems(s).

NIST 800 series

Incident response procedure

Incident response involves detection, alert, triage, response (containment and eradication), recovery and follow-up. The goal of a systematic approach to handle security incidents is to resume system and business operations as soon as possible while preserving the incident's forensics information for further analysis and security process enhancements. A formal process or set of procedures to be followed after notification of a suspected system unauthorized action within a network or computer system.

Centers for Medicare & Medicaid Services (CMS)

Incomplete parameter checking

System flaw that exists when the operating system does not check all parameters fully for accuracy and consistency, thus making the system vulnerable to penetration.

US National Information Assurance (IA) Glossary

Incremental backup

The processes of making a copy of only the files that have changed since the last backup instead of backing up every file.

Centers for Medicare & Medicaid Services (CMS)

Incremental testing

Deliberately testing only the value-added functionality of a software component.

ISACA

Inculpatory evidence

Evidence that tends to increase the likelihood of fault or guilt.

NIST 800 series

Independence

Self-governance and freedom from conflict of interest and undue influence. The IS auditor should be free to make his/her own decisions, not influenced by the organization being audited and its people (managers and employers).

ISACA

Independence appearance

The outward impression of being self-governing and free from conflict of interest and undue influence.

ISACA

Independent attitude

Impartial point of view which allows the IS auditor to act objectively and with fairness.

ISACA

Independent verification and validation

An independent assessment of a system. The assessment assures that the products conform to the requirements and design, as documented, and fulfill the operational objectives.

Centers for Medicare & Medicaid Services (CMS)

Index

The searchable catalog of documents created by search engine software. Also called "catalog." Index is often used as a synonym for search engine.

Sedona Conference

Index/Coding fields

Database fields used to categorize and organize documents. Often user-defined, these fields can be used for searches.

Sedona Conference

Indexed Sequential Access Method (ISAM)

A disk access method that stores data sequentially, while also maintaining an index of key fields to all the records in the file for direct access capability.

ISACA

Indexed sequential file

A file format in which records are organized and can be accessed according to a pre-established key that is part of the record.

ISACA

Indexing

Identification of specific attributes of a document or database record to facilitate retrieval. The process of establishing access points to facilitate retrieval of records and/or information. Universal term for coding and data entry.

AIIM, ISO 15489, Sedona Conference

Indication

A sign that an incident may have occurred or may be currently occurring.

NIST 800 series

Indicator

Recognized action, specific, generalized, or theoretical, that an adversary might be expected to take in preparation for an attack.

US National Information Assurance (IA) Glossary

Individual

A citizen of the United States or an alien lawfully admitted for permanent residence. Agencies may, consistent with individual practice, choose to extend the protections of the Privacy Act and E-Government Act to businesses, sole proprietors, aliens, etc.

NIST 800 series

Individual accountability

Ability to associate positively the identity of a user with the time, method, and degree of access to an information system.

US National Information Assurance (IA) Glossary

Industry Standard Architecture (ISA)

Sedona Conference

Informal security policy

Natural language description, possibly supplemented by mathematical arguments, demonstrating the correspondence of the functional specification to the high-level design.

US National Information Assurance (IA) Glossary

Information

Knowledge communicated or received concerning some fact or circumstance. The meaning of data. Data are facts or subsets of information. Various groupings of data become information when they are seen in context and convey meaning to people. Therefore, information is communication or reception of knowledge, such as facts, data, or opinions, including numerical, graphic, or narrative forms, whether oral or maintained in any other medium, including computerized databases, paper, micro-film, or magnetic tape. In the world if e-discovery, information can mean either documents or data.

DIRKS, FISCAM, Centers for Medicare & Medicaid Services (CMS), OMB Circular A-130, ISO/IEC 27001:2005, FIPS Pubs, US National Information Assurance (IA) Glossary, Sedona Conference, NIST 800 Series

Information and communication

A component of internal control in addition to the control environment, risk assessment, monitoring, and control activities. The identification, capture, and exchange of information in a form and time frame that enable people to carry out their responsibilities. The accounting system and accounting manuals are examples of this component.

GAO/PCIE Financial Audit Manual

Information architecture

See IT architecture.

CobiT

Information asset

Documented (paper or electronic) information or intellectual assets used to meet the mission of the enterprise.

CERT OCTAVE

Information assurance

There are four basic properties of information, information processes, information systems, and information technology. 1) Confidentiality is a characteristic of information only being disclosed to authorized entities, processes, or persons at authorized times and in authorized manners. 2) Integrity is a characteristic of information, information processes, and information systems being complete and accurate. 3) Availability is a characteristic of information, information systems, and information technology being accessible and usable on a timely basis. 4) Accountability is a characteristic of responsibly interacting at a level commensurate with the sensitivity and criticality of information, information processes, information systems, and information technology. Furthermore, in order for information assurance to be guaranteed, these four properties must co-support each other. Loss of one characteristic can lead to loss of the other characteristics.

Network Frontiers, US National Information Assurance (IA) Glossary, NIST 800 Series

Information Assurance and Infrastructure Protection Directorate of the DHS (IAIP)

An organization within the Department of Homeland Security. IAD's mission involves detecting, reporting, and responding to cyber threats; making encryption codes to securely pass information between systems; and embedding IA measures directly into the emerging Global Information Grid. It includes building secure audio and video communications equipment, making tamper protection products, and providing trusted microelectronics solutions. It entails testing the security of customers' systems, providing OPSEC assistance, and evaluating commercial software and hardware against nationally set standards, to better meet our nation's IA needs. See also http://www.nsa.gov/ia/ for more information.

de facto

Information Assurance Manager (IAM)

See information systems security manager.

US National Information Assurance (IA) Glossary

Information Assurance Officer (IAO)

See information systems security officer.

US National Information Assurance (IA) Glossary

Information assurance product

Product or technology whose primary purpose is to provide security services (e.g., confidentiality, authentication, integrity, access control, non-repudiation of data) correct known vulnerabilities; and/or provide layered defense against various categories of non-authorized or malicious penetrations of information systems or networks. Examples include such products as data/network encryptors, firewalls, and intrusion detection devices.

US National Information Assurance (IA) Glossary

Information engineering

Data-oriented development techniques that work on the premise that data are at the center of information processing and that certain data relationships are significant to a business and must be represented in the data structure of its systems.

ISACA

Information environment

Aggregate of individuals, organizations, or systems that collect, process, or disseminate information, also included is the information itself.

US National Information Assurance (IA) Glossary

Information flow control

Procedure to ensure that information transfers within an information system are not made from a higher security level object to an object of a lower security level.

US National Information Assurance (IA) Glossary

Information Lifecycle Management (ILM)

Sedona Conference

Information Management System (IMS)

A general purpose system that allows users to access a database remotely.

FISCAM

Information Operations (IO)

Actions taken to affect adversary information and information systems while defending one's own information and information systems.

US National Information Assurance (IA) Glossary

Information owner

Official with statutory or operational authority for specified information and responsibility for establishing the controls for its generation, collection, processing, dissemination, and disposal.

FIPS Pubs, US National Information Assurance (IA) Glossary, NIST 800 Series

Information processing

Information processing describes the organized collection, initial storage, processing, transmission, dissemination, and long term storage in accordance with defined procedures that could be automated or manual.

Network Frontiers

Information Processing Facility (IPF)

See computer room, data center facility.

ISACA

Information resource

Information and related resources such as personnel, equipment, funds, and information technology. See also resource.

FISCAM, Centers for Medicare & Medicaid Services (CMS), FIPS Pubs, NIST 800 Series

Information resource management

See information systems management.

FISCAM

Information resource owner

See owner.

FISCAM, Centers for Medicare & Medicaid Services (CMS)

Information security

The preservation of confidentiality, integrity and availability of information; in addition, other properties such as authenticity, accountability, non-repudiation and reliability can also be involved. The protection of data against unauthorized disclosure, transfer, modification, or destruction, whether accidental or intentional to preserve the confidentiality, integrity, and availability of the system. See also information assurance.

Centers for Medicare & Medicaid Services (CMS), ISO/IEC 27001:2005, ISO/IEC 17799:2005, PCI-DSS, FIPS Pubs, NIST 800 Series

Information security event

An identified occurrence of a system, service, or network state indicating a possible breach of information security policy or failure of safeguards, or a previously unknown situation that may be security relevant.

ISO/IEC 27001:2005, ISO/IEC TR 18044:2004

Information Security Forum (ISF)

The Information Security Forum (ISF) is the world's leading independent authority on information security. By harnessing our world-renowned expertise and the collective knowledge and experience of our members - including 50% of Fortune 100 companies - the ISF delivers practical guidance and solutions to overcome wide-ranging security challenges impacting business information today. See also http://www.securityforum.org for more information.

de facto

Information security incident

A single or a series of unwanted or un-expected information security events that have a significant probability of compromising business operations and threatening information security.

ISO/IEC 27001:2005, ISO/IEC TR 18044:2004

Information security management

The process that ensures the confidentiality, integrity and availability of an organizations assets, information, data and IT services. Information security management usually has a wider scope than the service provider. It normally includes handling of paper, building access, phone calls, etc., for the entire organization.

ITIL

Information Security Management System (ISMS)

An information security management system (ISMS) is a system of management concerned with information security. It is that part of the overall management system, based on a business risk approach, to establish, implement, operate, monitor, review, maintain and improve information security. The design and implementation of an organization's ISMS is influenced by their needs and objectives, security requirements, the processes employed and the size and structure of the organization. These and their supporting systems are expected to change over time. It is expected that an ISMS implementation will be scaled in accordance with the needs of the organization, e.g. a simple situation requires a simple ISMS solution.

ISO/IEC 27001:2005

Information Security Manager

The information security manager is the role responsible for the information security management process in the IT service provider. The information security manager is responsible for fulfilling the security demands as specified in the information security policy and SLAs. The information security manager typically delegates the actual implementation to other personnel in the IT service provider. The information systems security officer and the information security manager work closely together.

ITIL

Information Security Officer

See Information Systems Security Officer.

ITIL

Information security policy

The policy that governs the organizations approach to information security management.

ITIL, US National Information Assurance (IA) Glossary, NIST 800 Series

Information security training and awareness

Training on organizational policies and procedures, security requirements, legal responsibilities, business controls, and correct, safe use of information processing facilities.

Centers for Medicare & Medicaid Services (CMS)

Information Services (IS)

GAO/PCIE Financial Audit Manual, Centers for Medicare & Medicaid Services (CMS), ISACA

Information sharing

The requirements for information sharing by an IT system with one or more other IT systems or applications, for information sharing to support multiple internal or external organizations, missions, or public programs.

NIST 800 series

Information system (IS)

Organized collections of hardware, software, supplies, policies, procedures and people, which store, process and provide access to information. The entire infrastructure, organization, personnel, and components for the collection, processing, storage, transmission, display, dissemination, and disposition of information. See also computer systems.

NIST 800 series, DIRKS, Centers for Medicare & Medicaid Services (CMS), ISO/IEC 27001:2005, FIPS Pubs, US National Information Assurance (IA) Glossary, PCI-DSS, Sedona Conference

Information system owner

Official responsible for the overall procurement, development, integration, modification, or operation and maintenance of an information system.

FIPS Pubs, NIST 800 Series

Information System Security Engineering (ISSE)

Information Systems Security Engineering (ISSE) is the art and science of discovering users' information protection needs and then designing and making information systems to safely resist the forces to which they may be subjected. ISSE should be an integral part of systems engineering and should support certification and accreditation processes, such as the Department of Defense (DoD) Information Technology Security Certification and Accreditation Process (DITSCAP). The ISSE process comprises the following eight activities:

1) discover Information Protection Needs, 2) Define System Security Requirements, 3) Design System Security Architecture, 4) Develop Detailed Security Design, 5) Implement System Security, 6) Assess Information Protection Effectiveness, 7) Plan Technical Effort, and 8) Manage Technical Effort.

US National Information Assurance (IA) Glossary

Information Systems Audit and Control Association (ISACA)

The Information Systems Audit and Control Association (ISACA) is a worldwide organization which provides up-to-date information for professionals in the converging disciplines of auditing, data processing, accounting, data security, and quality assurance. See also http://www.isaca.org for more information.

de facto

Information Systems Auditor

A person with specialized technical knowledge and skills who can understand the IS concepts discussed in the manual and apply them to the audit. See also auditor.

GAO/PCIE Financial Audit Manual

Information systems controls

Controls whose effectiveness depends on computer processing, including general, application, and user controls.

GAO/PCIE Financial Audit Manual

Information Systems Examination Board (ISEB)

The British computer society information systems examination board is accredited by the ICMB as an examination board. See also http://www.bcs.org/bcs/products/qualifications/iseb for more information.

ITIL

Information systems security

The protection afforded to information systems to preserve the availability, integrity, and confidentiality of the systems and information contained in the systems. Protection results from the application of a combination of security measures, including crypto security, transmission security, emission security, computer security, information security, personnel security, resource security, and physical security.

Centers for Medicare & Medicaid Services (CMS), US National Information Assurance (IA) Glossary

Information Systems Security Association (ISSA)

ISSA is a not-for-profit international organization of information security professionals and practitioners. It provides educational forums, publications, and peer interaction opportunities that enhance the knowledge, skill, and professional growth of its members. See also http://www.issa.org for more information.

de facto

Information systems security equipment modification

Modification of any fielded hardware, firmware, software, or portion thereof, under NSA configuration control. There are three classes of modifications: mandatory (to include human safety); optional/special mission modifications; and repair actions. These classes apply to elements, subassemblies, equipment, systems, and software packages performing functions such as key generation, key distribution, message encryption, decryption, authentication, or those mechanisms necessary to satisfy security policy, labeling, identification, or accountability.

US National Information Assurance (IA) Glossary

Information Systems Security Manager (ISSM)

Individual responsible for a program, organization, system, or enclave's information assurance program.

US National Information Assurance (IA) Glossary

Information Systems Security Officer (ISSO)

The person responsible for ensuring the security of an information system throughout its life cycle, from design through disposal. The Information Systems Security Officer is responsible for assessing the business risks and setting the information security policy. This role is the counterpart of the Information Systems Security Manager and resides in the customer organization. The Information Systems Security Officer and the Information Security Manager work closely together. This is roughly equivalent to the Chief Information Security Officer and Senior Agency Information Security Officer. See also security officer.

NIST 800 series, Centers for Medicare & Medicaid Services (CMS), ITIL, US National Information Assurance (IA) Glossary

Information systems security product

Item (chip, module, assembly, or equipment), technique, or service that performs or relates to information systems security.

US National Information Assurance (IA) Glossary

Information Technology (IT)

Processing information by computer. IT or Information Technology has probably been the most redefined term over the past few years. The definition has varied from simple automation of manual processes using microprocessors to computers to networks to desktop publishing to networking. FIPS 200 provides a much more in-depth definition whereby they define information technology as any equipment or interconnected system or subsystem of equipment that is used in the automatic acquisition, storage, manipulation, management, movement, control, display, switching, interchange, transmission, or reception of data or information by the executive agency. For purposes of the preceding sentence, equipment is used by an executive agency if the equipment is used by the executive agency directly or is used by a contractor under a contract with the executive agency which: 1) requires the use of such equipment; or 2) requires the use, to a significant extent, of such equipment in the performance of a service or the furnishing of a product. The term information technology includes computers, ancillary equipment, software, firmware and similar procedures, services (including support services), and related resources.

Centers for Medicare & Medicaid Services (CMS), CobiT, NIST 800 series, FIPS Pubs, ITIL, Sedona Conference

Information technology assets

Information technology assets are the individual elements of an information system and are classified into the staff, documents and records, applications and databases, operating systems, storage components, firmware and hardware, network, power and cooling, and facilities.

Network Frontiers

Information Technology infrastructure

The overall makeup of business-wide technology operations, including mainframe operations, standalone systems, e-mail, networks (WAN and LAN), internet access, customer databases, enterprise systems, application support, regardless of whether managed, utilized or provided locally, regionally, globally, etc., or whether performed or located internally or by outside providers (outsourced to vendors). The IT Infrastructure also includes applicable standard practices and procedures, such as backup procedures, versioning, resource sharing, retention practices, janitor program utilization, and the like.

Sedona Conference

Information Technology Laboratory (ITL)

NIST 800 series

Information type

A specific category of information (e.g., privacy, medical, proprietary, financial, investigative, contractor sensitive, security management) defined by an organization or in some instances by a specific law, Executive Order, directive, policy, or regulation.

FIPS Pubs, NIST 800 Series

Informed customer

A manager who works for the customer and is a specialist in dealing with and managing IT service providers. The informed customer is responsible for all aspects of managing the relationship with service providers.

ITIL

Infrastructure

Technology, human resources, and facilities that enable the processing of applications.

CobiT, ISO/IEC 27001:2005

Infrastructure service

An IT service that is not directly used by the business but is required by the IT service provider so they can provide other IT services. For example, directory services, naming services, or communication services. See also general support system.

ITIL

Ingress

Traffic entering the network.

PCI-DSS

Ingress filtering

The process of blocking incoming packets that use obviously false IP addresses, such as reserved source addresses.

NIST 800 series

Inherent risk

The susceptibility of an assertion to a material misstatement, assuming that there are no related internal controls. This is an auditor judgment.

FISCAM, GAO/PCIE Financial Audit Manual, ISACA

Inheritance [objects]

Inheritance refers to database structures that have a strict hierarchy (no multiple inheritance). Inheritance can initiate other objects irrespective of the class hierarchy, thus there is no strict hierarchy of objects.

ISACA

Initial Program Load (IPL)

A program that brings another program, often the operating system, into operation to run the computer. Also referred to as a bootstrap or boot program.

FISCAM, ISACA, Centers for Medicare & Medicaid Services (CMS)

Initialization Vector (IV)

A vector used in defining the starting point of an encryption process within a cryptographic algorithm.

NIST 800 series, FIPS Pubs

Initialize

Setting the state of a cryptographic logic prior to key generation, encryption, or other operating mode.

US National Information Assurance (IA) Glossary

Initiator

The entity that initiates an authentication exchange.

NIST 800 series

Input

Any information entered into a computer or the process of entering data into the computer.

FISCAM, Centers for Medicare & Medicaid Services (CMS), ISO/IEC 27001:2005

Input controls

Techniques and procedures used to verify, validate, and edit data to ensure that only correct data are entered into the computer.

ISACA

Input designs

Templates used to enable authors to more easily enter content into a system, typically customized, based on the type and format of content to be entered.

AIIM

Input device

Any peripheral that allows a user to communicate with a computer by entering information or issuing commands (e.g., keyboard).

Sedona Conference

Input/output appendage

A routine designed to provide additional controls for system input/output operations.

FISCAM

Inside threat

An entity with authorized access that has the potential to harm an information system through destruction, disclosure, modification of data, and/or denial of service.

NIST 800 series

Insource

Transferring the provision of IT services from an external service provider to an internal service provider. The term insourcing is used to mean running or managing IT services as an internal service provider. See also outsource.

ITIL

Inspectable space

Three dimensional space surrounding equipment that process classified and/or sensitive information within which TEMPEST exploitation is not considered practical or where legal authority to identify and remove a potential TEMPEST exploitation exists. Synonymous with zone of control.

US National Information Assurance (IA) Glossary

Inspector General (IG)

GAO/PCIE Financial Audit Manual

Instant Messaging (IM)

A form of electronic communication involving immediate correspondence between two or more online users. Peer-to-peer IM communications may not be stored on servers after receipt; logging of peer-to-peer IM messages is typically done on the client computer, and may be optionally enabled or disabled on each client.

de facto, Sedona Conference

Institute of Chartered Accountants in England & Wales (ICAEW)

The Institute of Chartered Accountants in England & Wales is the largest professional accountancy body in Europe with over 128,000 members.

The Institute was established by Royal Charter in 1880. It is now a key influencer on the international stage and the leading UK body of finance professionals offering world class qualifications. See also http://www.icaew.co.uk for more information.

de facto

Institute of Electrical and Electronics Engineers (IEEE)

Pronounced I-triple-E, IEEE is an organization composed of engineers, scientists, and students. The IEEE is best known for developing standards for the computer and electronics industry. See also http://www.ieee.org/portal/site for more information.

ISACA, Sedona Conference

Institute of Internal Auditors (IIA)

Established in 1941, The Institute of Internal Auditors (IIA) is an international professional association of more than 117,000 members with global headquarters in Altamonte Springs, Fla., United States. Throughout the world, the IIA is recognized as the internal audit profession's leader in certification, education,

research, and technological guidance. See also http://www.theiia.org for more information.

de facto

Institute of IT Service Managers

An independently governed professional body, specifically aimed at professionals in IT service management which "aims to promote and support the standing of its members by establishing high-standards of professional and ethical conduct, ensuring continuing professional development of its members in order to demonstrate their competence and commitment." See also http://www.iosm.com/ for more information.

ITIL

Integrated Drive Electronics (IDE)

An engineering standard for interfacing PC's and hard discs.

Sedona Conference

Integrated Services Digital Network (ISDN)

A public end-to-end digital telecommunications network with signaling, switching, and transport capabilities supporting a wide range of service accessed by standardized interfaces with integrated customer control. The standard allows transmission of digital voice, video, and data over 64 Kbps lines.

ISACA, Sedona Conference

Integrated Test Facilities (ITF)

Test data are processed in production systems. The data usually represent a set of fictitious entities such as departments, customers and products. Output reports are verified to confirm the correctness of the processing. See also integration testing.

ISACA

Integration

Measures, practices, and procedures for the continuity of information should be coordinated and integrated with each other and other measures, practices, and procedures of the organization so as to create a coherent system of continuity.

NIST 800 series

Integration testing

Testing of a build release to determine if related information system components perform to specification.

FISCAM, ITIL

Integrity

The authenticity, accuracy, and completeness of an asset. The property that data or information have not been altered or destroyed in an unauthorized manner. Information has integrity when it is timely, accurate, complete, and consistent. The security objective that generates the requirement for protection against either intentional or accidental attempts to violate data integrity (the property that data has not been altered in an unauthorized manner) or system integrity (the quality that a system has when it performs its intended function in an unimpaired manner, free from unauthorized manipulation). See also data integrity and system integrity.

HIPAA, NIST 800 series, CERT OCTAVE, CobiT, FISCAM, ISACA, Centers for Medicare & Medicaid Services (CMS), ISO/IEC 27001:2005, ISO/IEC 13335-1:2004, FIPS Pubs, ITIL, US National Information Assurance (IA) Glossary

Integrity check value

Checksum capable of detecting modification of an information system.

US National Information Assurance (IA) Glossary

Integrity controls

Implement security measures to ensure that electronically transmitted regulated data is not inadvertently modified or deleted without detection, until disposed of. Many information objects contain cyclic redundancy checks or checksums that indicate if the data has been corrupted while in storage or transit. These methods do not, however, protect against accidental or malicious modification of the data by an otherwise authorized user. Integrity proofing allows receivers of the object to verify that the information within it has not been modified and that the information comes from the claimed sender. As a type of checksum it is calculated from the original object and encrypted using asymmetric, or private/public key encryption technology. Any modification after this digital signature is applied will fail the subsequent verification process. Replacing a digital signature is, in practical terms, not possible when the secret key, i.e. the private key of the private/public key pair is unknown to the modifier.

HIPAA

Intellectual control

The control established over the informational content of records and archives resulting from ascertaining and documenting their provenance, and from the processes of arrangement and description.

DIRKS

Intellectual Property (IP)

Useful artistic, technical, and/or industrial information, knowledge or ideas that convey ownership and control of tangible or virtual usage and/or representation.

ISACA, NIST 800 Series

Intelligent Character Recognition (ICR)

The conversion of scanned images (bar codes or patterns of bits) to computer recognizable codes (ASCII characters and files) by means of software/programs which define the rules of and algorithms for conversion This is an advanced form of Optical Character Recognition technology that may include capabilities such as learning fonts during processing or using context to strengthen probabilities of correct recognition or that can recognize hand print characters.

AIIM, Sedona Conference

Intelligent terminal

A terminal with built-in processing capability. It has no disk or tape storage but has memory. The terminal interacts with the user by editing and validating data as they are entered prior to final processing.

ISACA

Inter-partition space

Unused sectors on a track located between the start of the partition and the partition boot record. This space is important because it is possible for a user to hide information here.

Sedona Conference

Interactive processing

A mode of operation in which users interact with the system as their programs and data are processed.

FISCAM

Interactive voice response (IVR)

A form of automatic call distribution that accepts user input, such as key presses and spoken commands, to identify the correct destination for incoming calls.

ITIL

Interconnection Security Agreement (ISA)

Written management authorization to interconnect information systems based upon acceptance of risk and implementation of established controls.

US National Information Assurance (IA) Glossary, NIST 800 Series

Interdepartmental amounts

Activity and balances between two different departments. The intradepartmental and interdepartmental amounts are subsets of intragovernmental activity and balances. See also department.

GAO/PCIE Financial Audit Manual

Interentity

Activities or balances between two or more agencies, departments, or bureaus.

GAO/PCIE Financial Audit Manual

Interest rate risk

Is the risk to earnings or capital arising from movements in interest rates. From an economic perspective, a bank focuses on the sensitivity of the value of its assets, liabilities, and revenues to changes in interest rates. Internet banking may attract deposits, loans, and other relationships from a larger pool of possible customers than other forms of marketing. Greater access to customers who primarily seek the best rate or term reinforces the need for managers to maintain appropriate asset/liability management systems which should include the ability to react quickly to changing market conditions.

ISACA

Interface

A connection between two devices, applications, or networks or a boundary across which two systems communicate. Interface may also refer to the portion of a program that interacts with the user.

FISCAM, Centers for Medicare & Medicaid Services (CMS), US National Information Assurance (IA) Glossary

Interface control document

Technical document describing interface controls and identifying the authorities and responsibilities for ensuring the operation of such controls. This document is baselined during the preliminary design review and is maintained throughout the information system lifecycle.

US National Information Assurance (IA) Glossary

Interface testing

A testing technique that is used to evaluate output from one application while the information is sent as input to another application.

ISACA

Interim Approval To Operate (IATO)

Temporary authorization granted by a DAA for an information system to process information based on preliminary results of a security evaluation of the system.

US National Information Assurance (IA) Glossary

Interim Approval To Test (IATT)

Temporary authorization to test an information system in a specified operational information environment within the timeframe and under the conditions or constraints enumerated in the written authorization.

US National Information Assurance (IA) Glossary

Interlaced

TV & CRT pictures must constantly be "refreshed". Interlace is to refresh every other line once/refresh cycle. Since only half the information displayed is updated each cycle, interlaced displays are less expensive than "non-interlaced". However, interlaced displays are subject to jitters. The human eye/brain can usually detect displayed images which are completely refreshed at less than 30 times per second.

Sedona Conference

Interleave

To arrange data in a noncontiguous way to increase performance. When used to describe disk drives, it refers to the way sectors on a disk are organized. In one-to-one interleaving, the sectors are placed sequentially around each track. In two-to-one interleaving, sectors are staggered so that consecutively numbered sectors are separated by an intervening sector. The purpose of interleaving is to make the disk drive more efficient. The disk drive can access only one sector at a time, and the disk is constantly spinning beneath.

Sedona Conference

Intermediate Certification Authority (CA)

A Certification Authority that is subordinate to another CA, and has a CA subordinate to itself.

NIST 800 series

Intermediate Distribution Frame (IDF)

Also known as a wiring closet; this is the room where the metal rack designated to connect telecommunications cables are located. The IDF consists of IT assets that provide the connection between inter-building cabling and intra-building cabling, i.e., between the MDF and local cabling runs out to devices.

Network Frontiers

Intermediate recovery

A recovery option which is also known as warm standby. Provision is made to recover the IT service in a period of time between 24 and 72 hours. Intermediate recovery typically uses a shared portable or fixed facility that has computer systems and network components. The hardware and software will need to be configured, and data will need to be restored as part of the IT service continuity plan.

ITIL

Internal administration

Information related to the internal administration of an agency. Includes personnel rules, bargaining positions, and advance information concerning procurement actions.

Centers for Medicare & Medicaid Services (CMS)

Internal connectivity

A computer or network connection to an organizational peer system within the defined security perimeter. See also domain.

Centers for Medicare & Medicaid Services (CMS)

Internal control

The policies, procedures, practices, and organizational structures designed to provide reasonable assurance that business objectives will be achieved and undesired events will be prevented or detected and corrected. A process, affected by organization management and other personnel, designed to provide reasonable assurance that 1) operations, including the use of organization resources, are effective and efficient; 2) financial reporting, including reports on budget execution, financial statements, and other reports for internal and external use, are reliable; and 3) applicable laws and regulations are followed. Internal control also includes the safeguarding of organization assets against unauthorized acquisition, use, or disposition. Internal control consists of five interrelated components that form an integrated process that can react to changing circumstances and conditions within the organization. These components include the control environment, risk assessment, control activities, information and communication, and monitoring. See also internal control structure.

FISCAM, GAO/PCIE Financial Audit Manual, ISACA, Centers for Medicare & Medicaid Services (CMS), CobiT

Internal control structure

The dynamic, integrated processes, effected by the governing body, management and all other staff, that are designed to provide reasonable assurance regarding the achievement of the following general objectives: effectiveness, efficiency and economy of operations; reliability of management; Compliance with applicable laws, regulations and internal policies. Management's strategies for achieving these general objectives are affected by the design and operation of the following components: control environment, information system, control procedures. See also internal control.

FISCAM, ISACA

Internal customer

A customer who works for the same business as the IT service provider. See also internal service provider, external customer.

ITIL

Internal penetrators or hackers

Authorized users of a computer system who overstep their legitimate access rights. This category is divided into masqueraders and clandestine users.

ISACA

Internal security controls

Hardware, firmware, or software features within an information system that restrict access to resources only to authorized subjects.

US National Information Assurance (IA) Glossary

Internal service provider

An IT service provider which is part of the same business as their customer. An internal service provider may have both internal customers and external customers. See also external service provider.

ITIL

Internal storage

The main memory of the computer's central processing unit.

ISACA

International Chamber of Commerce (ICC)

CC (International Chamber of Commerce) is the voice of world business championing the global economy as a force for economic growth, job creation and prosperity. ICC activities cover a broad spectrum, from arbitration and dispute resolution to making the case for open trade and the market economy system, business self-regulation, fighting corruption or combating commercial crime. See also http://www.iccwbo.org for more information.

de facto

International Federation of Accountants (IFAC)

IFAC is the global organization for the accountancy profession. It works with its 163 member organizations in 120 countries to protect the public interest by encouraging high quality practices by the world's accountants. IFAC members represent 2.5 million accountants employed in public practice, industry and commerce, government, and academe. Its structure and governance provide for the representation of its diverse constituencies and interaction with external groups that rely on or influence the work of accountants. See also http://www.ifac.org for more information.

de facto

International Information System Security Certification Consortium (ISC2)

The International Information Systems Security Certification Consortium, or ISC2, is internationally recognized for educating and certifying information security professionals throughout their careers. Their certification programs range from CISSPs through ISSAPs, ISSMP, and others. For more information see https://www.isc2.org.

Generally Accepted Information Security Principles, de facto

International Organization for Standardization (ISO)

The International Organization for Standardization (ISO) is the world's largest developer of standards. ISO is a non-governmental organization which is a network of the national standards institutes of 156 countries. Further information about ISO is available from http://www.ISO.org/.

ITIL, CobiT, AICPA, Centers for Medicare & Medicaid Services (CMS), PCI-DSS, Sedona Conference

International Standards Organization

See International Organization for Standardization (ISO).

Network Frontiers

273

International Telecommunication Union (ITU)

An international organization under the UN headquartered in Geneva concerned with telecommunications that develops international data communications standards; known as CCITT prior to March 1, 1993. See also http://www.itu.int.

Sedona Conference

Internet

When capitalized, the term "Internet" refers to the worldwide network of networks that all use the TCP/IP communications protocol and share a common address space. It supports services such as e-mail, the World Wide Web, file transfer, and Internet Relay Chat. Also known as "the net," "the information superhighway," and "cyberspace." When not capitalized, the term "internet" refers to two or more networks connected by a router.

FISCAM, ISACA, Centers for Medicare & Medicaid Services (CMS), Workgroup for Electronic Data Interchange, Sedona Conference

Internet banking

Use of the Internet as a remote delivery channel for banking services. Services include the traditional ones, such as opening an account or transferring funds to different accounts, and new banking services, such as electronic bill presentment and payment (allowing customers to receive and pay bills on a bank's web site).

ISACA

Internet Control Message Protocol (ICMP)

An extension to the Internet Protocol (IP) that supports packets containing error, control and informational messages. A set of protocols that allow systems to communicate information about the state of services on other systems. It is used, for example, in determining whether systems are up, maximum packet sizes on links, or whether a destination host/network/port is available. Hackers typically (abuse) use ICMP to determine information about the remote site.

ISACA

Internet Engineering Task Force (IETF)

The Internet standards setting organization with international affiliates from network industry representatives. This includes all network industry developers and researchers concerned with evolution and planned growth of the Internet. See also http://www.ietf.org for more information.

ISACA, PCI-DSS

Internet Inter-ORB Protocol (IIOP)

A protocol developed by the Object Management Group (OMG) to implement Common Object Request Broker Architecture (CORBA) solutions over the World Wide Web. CORBA enables modules of network-based programs to communicate with one another. These modules or program parts such as tables, arrays, and more complex program sub-elements are referred to as objects. Use of IIOP in this process enables browsers and servers to exchange both simple and complex objects. This significantly differs from HTTP which only supports the transmission of text.

ISACA

Internet packet spoofing

An attack using packets with spoofed source Internet packet (IP) addresses. This technique exploits applications that use authentication based on IP addresses. This technique also may enable an unauthorized user to gain root access on the target system.

ISACA

Internet Protocol (IP)

Specifies the format of packets and the addressing scheme. The standard protocol for transmission of data from source to destinations in packet switched communications networks and interconnected systems of such networks.

ISACA, Workgroup for Electronic Data Interchange, US National Information Assurance (IA) Glossary, PCI-DSS

Internet Protocol address

Also called an IP address. A string of four numbers separated by periods used to represent a computer on the Internet - a unique identifier for the physical location of the server containing the data. See also TCP/IP (e.g., 206-1432.001).

Sedona Conference, VISA Glossary of Terms

Internet Protocol security (IPsec)

An Institute of Electrical and Electronic Engineers (IEEE) standard, Request For Comments (RFC) 2411, protocol that provides security capabilities at the Internet Protocol (IP) layer of communications. IPsec's key management protocol is used to negotiate the secret keys that protect Virtual Private Network (VPN) communications, and the level and type of security protections that will characterize the VPN. The most widely used key management protocol is the Internet Key Exchange (IKE) protocol.

Network Frontiers, ISACA, PCI-DSS, NIST 800 series

Internet publishing

Specialized imaging software that allows documents to be published on the Internet.

Sedona Conference

Internet Security Alliance (ISA)

The Internet Security Alliance was created to provide a forum for information sharing and leadership on information security issues. It represents industry's interests to legislators and regulators and aims to identify and standardize best practices in Internet security and network survivability while creating a collaborative environment to develop and implement information security solutions. The alliance is a collaborative effort between Carnegie Mellon's Software Engineering Institute (SEI), its CERT Coordination Center (CERT/CC), and the Electronic Industries Alliance (EIA), a federation of trade associations. See also http://www.sei.cmu.edu for more information.

de facto

Internet Service Provider (ISP)

A third party that provides organizations with a variety of Internet and Internet-related services. ISPs may be a source of evidence through files (such as ISP e-mail) stored on ISP servers. See also Application Service Provider, Managed Service Provider.

ISACA, ITIL, Sedona Conference

Internetwork Packet Exchange/Sequenced Packet Exchange (IPX/SPX)

A networking protocol used by the Novell NetWare operating systems. Like UDP, IPX is a datagram protocol used for connectionless communications. IPX and SPX are derived from Xerox Network Services' IDP and SPP protocols. SPX is a transport layer protocol (layer 4 of the OSI Model) used in Novell Netware networks. The SPX layer sits on top of the IPX layer (layer 3 - the network layer) and provides connection-oriented services between two nodes on the network. SPX is used primarily by client/server applications. IPX and SPX both provide connection services similar to TCP/IP, with the IPX protocol having similarities to IP, and SPX having similarities to TCP.

Sedona Conference, Wikipedia

Internetwork private line interface

Network cryptographic unit that provides secure connections, singularly or in simultaneous multiple connections, between a host and a predetermined set of corresponding hosts.

US National Information Assurance (IA) Glossary

Interoperability

In FIPS 201, interoperability allows any Government facility or information system, regardless of the cardholder's parent organization, to authenticate cardholder's identity using the credentials stored on the Personal Identity Verification (PIV) card.

NIST 800 series, FIPS Pubs

Interruption

The limiting of an asset's availability; interruption refers mainly to services.

CERT OCTAVE, ISO/IEC 27001:2005

Intradepartmental amounts

Activity and balances within the same department. The intradepartmental and interdepartmental amounts are subsets of intragovernmental activity and balances. See also department.

GAO/PCIE Financial Audit Manual

Intragovernmental amounts

Activity and balances occurring within or between federal departments.

GAO/PCIE Financial Audit Manual

Intragovernmental Payment and Collection System (IPAC)

The primary method used by most federal agencies to electronically bill and/or pay for services and supplies within the government. Used to communicate to the Treasury and the trading partner agency that the online billing and/or payment for services and supplies has occurred.

GAO/PCIE Financial Audit Manual

Intranet

A private network that uses the infrastructure and standards of the Internet and World Wide Web but is isolated from the public Internet by firewall barriers.

ISACA

Intrusion

Any intentional violation of the security policy of a system. Unauthorized access to logical and physical resources.

ISACA, Centers for Medicare & Medicaid Services (CMS), US National Information Assurance (IA) Glossary

Intrusion detection

The process of monitoring the events occurring in a computer system or network and detecting signs of security problems.

ISACA

Intrusion Detection System (IDS)

Methods to track system activities to determine if current actions are consistent with the established policies and to identify to system administrators inconsistencies that may signal unauthorized access. An intrusion detection system (IDS) inspects network activity to identify suspicious patterns that may indicate a network or system attack from someone attempting to break into or compromise a system.

ISACA, Centers for Medicare & Medicaid Services (CMS), PCI-DSS, NIST 800 Series

Intrusion monitoring

In vulnerability analysis, gaining information by performing checks that affects the normal operation of the system, even crashing the system.

ISACA

Intrusion Prevention System (IPS)

Implementing the basic IDS, an intrusion prevention system is an in-line device; network traffic flows through it. Unlike the IDS, an IPS is able to block any traffic that appears to be an intrusion.

Network Frontiers, PCI-DSS, NIST 800 Series

Inverse cipher

Series of transformations that converts ciphertext to plaintext using the Cipher Key.

NIST 800 series, FIPS Pubs

Investigation

The review and analysis of system security features (e.g., the investigation of system control programs using flow charts, assembly listings, and related documentation) to determine the security provided by the operating system.

Centers for Medicare & Medicaid Services (CMS)

Investigation, intelligence related, and security information

Information related to investigations for law enforcement purposes; intelligence-related information that cannot be classified, but is subject to confidentiality and extra security controls. Includes security plans, contingency plans, emergency operations plans, incident reports, reports of investigations, risk or vulnerability assessments certification reports; does not include general plans, policies, or requirements.

Centers for Medicare & Medicaid Services (CMS), 14 CFR Part 191.5(D)

Investment adviser

A person or organization employed by an individual or mutual fund to manage assets or provide investment advice.

17 CFR 240.17a-3 & 4

Investment appraisals

The activity responsible for carrying out a cost benefit analysis to justify capital expenditure for a new or changed IT services. See also business case, cost effectiveness, return on investment, return on capital employed.

ITIL

Investment company

An investment company, commonly known as a mutual fund, invests the pooled funds of retail investors for a fee.

17 CFR 240.17a-3 & 4

Invocation

Initiation of the steps defined in a plan. For example, initiating the IT service continuity plan for one or more IT services.

ITIL, BS 25999

IP Address

An Internet Protocol address is a numeric code that uniquely identifies a particular computer on the Internet. The IP address is analogous to a house number for ordinary postal mail.

PCI-DSS, NIST 800 Series

IP Spoofing

See spoofing.

PCI-DSS

Irregularities

Intentional violations of established management policy or regulatory requirements. Deliberate misstatements or omissions of information concerning the area under audit or the organization as a whole; gross negligence or unintentional illegal acts.

ISACA

Ishikawa Diagram

See cause/effect diagram.

ITIL

ISIS and TWAIN scanner drivers

Specialized applications used for communication between scanners and computers.

Sedona Conference

ISO 17799

Code of practice for information security management from the International Organization for Standardization (ISO).

CobiT, ITIL

ISO 20000

ISO specification and code of practice for IT service management. ISO/IEC 20000 is aligned with ITIL best practice and supersedes BS 15000. See also standard.

ITIL

ISO 8583

An established standard for communication between financial systems.

PCI-DSS

ISO 9001:2000

Code of practice for quality management from the International Organization for Standardization (ISO). ISO 9001:2000 specifies requirements for a quality management system for any or-ganization that needs to demonstrate its ability to consistently provide product that meets customer and applicable regulatory requirements and aims to enhance customer satisfaction.

CobiT, ITIL

ISO 9660 CD format

The International Standards Organization format for creating CD-ROMs that can be read worldwide.

Sedona Conference

IT accounting

The process responsible for identifying actual costs of delivering IT services, comparing these with budgeted costs, and managing variance from the budget. See also charging.

ITIL

IT accounting system

The entire set of policy, tools, and process that support IT financial management.

ITIL

IT architecture

An integrated framework for evolving or maintaining existing IT and acquiring new IT to achieve the enterprise's strategic and business goals.

CobiT

IT Availability Metrics Model (ITAMM)

A model that helps to ensure all aspects of availability are considered when defining availability metrics and reports.

ITIL

IT Compliance Institute (ITCI)

The IT Compliance Institute (ITCi) strives to be a global authority on the role of technology in business governance and regulatory compliance. Through comprehensive education, research, and analysis related to emerging government statutes and affected business and technology practices, they help organizations overcome the challenges posed by today's regulatory environment and find new ways to turn compliance efforts into capital opportunities. See also http://www.itcinstitute.com for more information.

de facto

IT Directorate

Senior management within a service provider, charged with developing and delivering IT services. Most commonly used in UK government departments.

ITIL

IT governance

A structure of relationships and processes to direct and control the enterprise in order to achieve the enterprise's goals by adding value while balancing risk versus return over IT and its processes. See also governance, corporate governance.

ISACA

IT infrastructure

All of the hardware, software, networks, facilities, etc. that are required to develop, test, deliver, or support IT services. The term IT infrastructure includes all of the information technology but not the associated people, processes, and documentation.

ITIL

IT Infrastructure Library (ITIL)

The UK Office of Government Commerce (OGC) IT Infrastructure Library. A set of guides on the management and provision of operational IT services. A set of best practice guidance for IT service management. ITIL is owned by the OGC and is developed in conjunction with the ITSMF. ITIL consists of a series of publications giving guidance on the provision of quality IT services, and on the processes and facilities needed to support them. See also http://www.ogc.gov.uk/index.asp?id=2261 for more information.

CobiT, ITIL

IT investment dashboard

Charting of costs and returns of IT-enabled investment projects in terms of business values for an enterprise.

CobiT

IT operations

The process responsible for the day-to-day monitoring and management of one or more IT services and the IT infrastructure they depend on. The term IT operations is also used to refer to the group or department within an IT service provider responsible for IT operations. See also operations bridge, event management.

ITIL

IT policy

The "documentation of IT security decisions" in an organization. There are three basic types: 1) Program Policy—high-level policy used to create an organization's IT program, define its' scope within the organization, assign implementation responsibilities, establish strategic direction, and assign resources for implementation. 2) Issue-Specific Policies—address specific issues of concern to the organization, such as contingency planning, the use of a particular methodology for systems risk management, and implementation of new regulations or law. These policies are likely to require more frequent revision as changes in technology and related factors take place. 3) System-Specific Policies—address individual systems, such as establishing an access control list or in training users as to what system actions are permitted. These policies may vary from system to system within the same organization. In addition, policy may refer to entirely different matters, such as the specific managerial decisions setting an organization's electronic mail (e-mail) policy or fax security policy.

NIST 800 series

IT security architecture

A description of security principles and an overall approach for complying with the principles that drive the system design; i.e., guidelines on the placement and implementation of specific security services within various distributed computing environments.

NIST 800 series

IT security awareness

IT Security Awareness

NIST 800 series

IT security awareness and training program

Explains proper rules of behavior for the use of agency IT systems and information. The program communicates IT security policies and procedures that need to be followed.

NIST 800 series

IT security education

IT Security Education seeks to integrate all of the security skills and competencies of the various functional specialties into a common body of knowledge, adds a multidisciplinary study of concepts, issues, and principles (technological and social), and strives to produce IT security specialists and professionals capable of vision and pro-active response.

NIST 800 series

IT security goal

The five security goals are confidentiality, availability, integrity, accountability, and assurance. See also security goal.

NIST 800 series

IT security investment

An IT application or system that is solely devoted to security. For instance, intrusion detection systems (IDS) and public key infrastructure (PKI) are examples of IT security investments.

NIST 800 series

IT security metrics

Metrics based on IT security performance goals and objectives.

NIST 800 series

IT security training

IT Security Training strives to produce relevant and needed security skills and competencies by practitioners of functional specialties other than IT security (e.g., management, systems design and development, acquisition, auditing). The most significant difference between training and awareness is that training seeks to teach skills, which allow a person to perform a specific function, while awareness seeks to focus an individual's attention on an issue or set of issues. The skills acquired during training are built upon the awareness foundation, in particular, upon the security basics and literacy material.

NIST 800 series

IT service

A service provided to one or more customers by an IT service provider. An IT service is based on the use of information technology and supports the customer's business processes. An IT service is made up from a combination of people, processes, and technology and should be defined in a service level agreement.

ITIL

IT Service Continuity Management (ITSCM)

The process responsible for managing risks that could seriously impact IT services. ITSCM ensures that the IT service provider can always provide minimum agreed service levels, by reducing the risk to an acceptable level and planning for the recovery of IT services. ITSCM should be designed to support business continuity management and should be a part of the systems continuity plan.

ITIL, Network Frontiers

IT service continuity plan

A plan defining the steps required to recover one or more IT services. The plan will also identify the triggers for invocation, people to be involved, communications etc. The IT service continuity plan should be part of a business continuity plan and the systems continuity plan.

ITIL, Network Frontiers

IT Service Management (ITSM)

The implementation and management of quality IT services that meet the needs of the business. IT service management is performed by IT service providers through an appropriate mix of people, process, and information technology.

ITIL

IT Service Management Forum (ITSMF)

The IT service management forum is an independent organization dedicated to promoting a professional approach to IT service management. The ITSMF is a not-for-profit membership organization with representation in many countries around the world (ITSMF chapters). The ITSMF and its membership contribute to the development of ITIL and associated IT service management standards. See also http://www.itsmf.com/ for more information.

ITIL

IT service provider

A service provider that provides IT services to internal customers or external customers.

ITIL

IT steering group

A formal group that is responsible for ensuring that business and IT service provider strategies and plans are closely aligned. An IT steering group includes senior representatives from the business and the IT service provider.

ITIL

IT strategic plan

A long-term plan, i.e., three- to five-year horizon, in which business and IT management co-operatively describe how IT resources will contribute to the enterprise's strategic objectives (goals).

CobiT

IT strategy committee

Committee at the level of the board of directors to ensure the board is involved in major IT matters/decisions.

CobiT

IT tactical plan

A medium-term plan, i.e., six- to eighteen-month horizon, that translates the IT strategic plan direction into required initiatives, resource requirements, and ways in which resources and benefits will be monitored and managed.

CobiT

IT-related risk

The net mission/business impact (probability of occurrence combined with impact) from a particular threat source exploiting or triggering a particular information technology vulnerability. IT related-risks arise from legal liability or mission/business loss due to: 1. Unauthorized (malicious, non-malicious, or accidental) disclosure, modification, or destruction of information. 2. Non-malicious errors and omissions. 3. IT disruptions due to natural or man-made disasters. 4. Failure to exercise due care and diligence in the implementation and operation of the IT. See also risk.

NIST 800 series

ITIL Certification Management Board (ICMB)

The body responsible for the maintenance and ongoing development of the ITIL qualification scheme. See also http://www.ITIL.co.uk/ICMB.htm for further information.

ITIL

J

Jamming

Transmission of electronic signals that disrupt communication and the use of electronic data.

Centers for Medicare & Medicaid Services (CMS)

Janitor program

An application which runs at scheduled intervals to manage business information by deleting, transferring, or archiving on-line data (such as e-mail) which is at or past its scheduled active life. Janitor programs are sometimes referred to as "agents"—software that runs autonomously "behind the scenes" on user systems and servers to carry out business processes according to pre-defined rules. Janitor programs must include a facility to support disposition and process holds.

Sedona Conference

Java

Sun Microsystems' Java is a platform-independent, programming language for adding animation and other actions to websites.

Sedona Conference

Jaz drive

A removable disk drive. A Jaz drive holds up to 2 GB of data. Commonly used for backup storage as well as everyday use.

Sedona Conference

Job

A set of data that completely defines a unit of work for a computer. A job usually includes programs, linkages, files, and instructions to the operating system. A job is also that thing that you loathe to come to every day, but have to because you like to get paid so that you can eat.

FISCAM, Centers for Medicare & Medicaid Services (CMS), Network Frontiers, ISO/IEC 27001:2005

Job accounting software

Software that tracks the computer resources (e.g., processor time and storage) used for each job.

FISCAM

Job Control Language (JCL)

In mainframe computing, a programming language that enables programmers to specify batch processing instructions. The abbreviation JCL refers to the job control language used in IBM mainframes.

FISCAM

Job description

A document which defines the roles, responsibilities, skills, and knowledge required by a particular person. One job description can include multiple roles. For example, the roles of configuration manager and change manager may be carried out by one person.

ITIL

Job entry system (JES)

Software that allows the submission of programs from terminals (usually through online program development systems such as TSO) to the mainframe computer.

FISCAM

Job scheduling system

Software that queues the jobs submitted to be run on the mainframe. It uses job classes and other information provided by the person submitting the job to determine when the job will be run.

FISCAM

Joint Financial Management Improvement Program (JFMIP)

The joint undertaking of the U.S. Department of the Treasury, the U.S. Government Accountability Office, the Office of Management and Budget, and the Office of Personnel Management to improve financial management in the federal government. The source of government wide requirements for financial management systems software functionality that describes the basic elements of

an integrated financial management system including the core financial system.

GAO/PCIE Financial Audit Manual

Joint Photographic Experts Group (JPEG)

A compression algorithm for still images that is commonly used on the web.

Sedona Conference

Journal

A chronological record of data processing operations that may be used to reconstruct a previous or an updated version of a file. In database management systems, it is the record of all stored data items that have values changed as a result of processing and manipulation of the data.

Sedona Conference

Journal entry

A debit or credit to a general ledger account. See also manual journal entry.

ISACA

Journaling

A function of e-mail systems (such as Microsoft Exchange and Lotus Notes) that copies sent and received items into a second information store for retention or preservation. Because Journaling takes place at the information store (server) level when the items are sent or received, rather than at the mailbox (client) level, some message-related metadata, such as user foldering (what folder the item is stored in within the recipient's mailbox) and the status of the "read" flag, is not retained in the journaled copy. The Journaling function stores items in the system's native format, unlike e-mail archiving solutions, which use proprietary storage formats that are designed to reduce the amount of storage space required. Journaling systems also lack the sophisticated search and retrieval capabilities contained in e-mail archiving solutions.

Sedona Conference

Judgment fund

A permanent and indefinite appropriation that is available to pay final judgments, settlement agreements, and certain types of administrative awards against the United States when payment is not otherwise provided for. The Secretary of the Treasury certifies all payments from the fund.

GAO/PCIE Financial Audit Manual

Judgment sampling

Any sample that is selected subjectively or in such a manner that the sample selection process is not random or the sampling results are not evaluated mathematically.

ISACA

Jukebox

A mass storage device that holds optical disk s and loads them into a drive.

Sedona Conference

Jukebox Management Software (JMS)

Sedona Conference

Jump drive

See Key drive.

Sedona Conference

Junk mail

Transmitting e-mail to unsolicited recipients. U.S. federal law 47USC227 prohibits broadcasting junk faxes and e-mail, allowing recipients to sue the sender in Small Claims Court for $500 per copy. See also spam.

Centers for Medicare & Medicaid Services (CMS)

Just-In-Time supply chain (JIT)

System whereby dependencies for MCAs are provided when required, without requiring storage.

PAS 56

K

Kablooey

The point at which something bad happens to your IT assets.

The Backup Book

Kepner Tregoe Analysis

A structured approach to problem solving. The problem is analyzed in terms of what, where, when, and extent. Possible causes are identified. The most probable cause is tested. The true cause is verified.

ITIL

Kerberos

A widely used authentication protocol developed at the Massachusetts Institute of Technology (MIT). In "classic" Kerberos, users share a secret password with a Key Distribution Center (KDC). The user, Alice, who wishes to communicate with another user, Bob, authenticates to the KDC and is furnished a "ticket" by the KDC to use to authenticate with Bob. When Kerberos authentication is based on passwords, the protocol is known to be vulnerable to off-line dictionary attacks by eavesdroppers who capture the initial user-to-KDC exchange.

NIST 800 series

Kerning

Adjusting the spacing between two letters.

Sedona Conference

Key

A long stream of seemingly random bits used with cryptographic algorithms. In cryptography, a key is a variable value that is applied using an algorithm to a string or block of unencrypted text to produce encrypted text, or to decrypt encrypted text. The keys must be known or guessed to forge a digital signature or decrypt an encrypted message. The length of the key generally determines how difficult it will be to decrypt the text in a given message. See also cipher text, cipher key lock.

FISCAM, Centers for Medicare & Medicaid Services (CMS), ISO/IEC 27001:2005, PCI-DSS, Workgroup for Electronic Data Interchange, US National Information Assurance (IA) Glossary, NIST 800 Series

Key bundle

The three cryptographic keys (Key1, Key2, Key3) that are used with a Triple Data Encryption Algorithm mode.

NIST 800 series

Key classes of components

Types of devices that are important in processing, storing, or transmitting critical information. They represent related assets to critical assets.

CERT OCTAVE

Key Distribution Center (KDC)

COMSEC facility generating and distributing key in electrical form.

US National Information Assurance (IA) Glossary

Key drive

A small removable data storage device that uses flash memory and connects via a USB port. Key drives are also known as keychain drive, thumb drive, jump drive, USB flash drive. Can be imaged and may contain residual data.

Sedona Conference

Key escrow

1) A deposit of the private key of a subscriber and other pertinent information pursuant to an escrow agreement or similar contract binding upon the subscriber, the terms of which require one or more agents to hold the subscriber's private key for the benefit of the subscriber, an employer, or other party, upon provisions set forth in the agreement. 2) The processes of managing (e.g., generating, storing, transferring, auditing) the two components of a cryptographic key by two key component holders.

NIST 800 series, FIPS Pubs

Key escrow system

A system that entrusts the two components comprising a cryptographic key (e.g., a device unique key) to two key component holders (also called "escrow agents").

NIST 800 series, FIPS Pubs

Key exchange

Process of exchanging public keys (and other information) in order to establish secure communications.

US National Information Assurance (IA) Glossary, NIST 800 Series

Key expansion

Routine used to generate a series of Round Keys from the Cipher Key.

NIST 800 series, FIPS Pubs

Key field

Database fields used for document searches and retrieval.

Sedona Conference

Key generation material

Random numbers, pseudo-random numbers, and cryptographic parameters used in generating cryptographic keys.

NIST 800 series

Key Goal Indicator (KGI)

See Key Performance Indicator, critical success factor.

CobiT

Key list

Printed series of key settings for a specific cryptonet. Key lists may be produced in list, pad, or printed tape format.

US National Information Assurance (IA) Glossary

Key loader

A self-contained unit that is capable of storing at least one plaintext or encrypted cryptographic key or key component that can be transferred, upon request, into a cryptographic module.

NIST 800 series, FIPS Pubs

Key management

The use of encryption requires that encryption keys have to be managed inside an organization. Persons who need access to encrypted information require a key with the guarantee that it is the correct key. Safe distribution of keys is a necessary part of security and security administration. In the case of asymmetric encryption, where private/public key pairs are utilized, a person's private key may only be used on systems with strong authentication mechanisms in place to prevent misuse. The public keys a user maintains must have been distributed in a way that guarantees the key is the authentic public key of the intended communication partner. For this purpose Public Key Infrastructures (PKI) need to be implemented for the purposes of providing certification of the authenticity of one's private and public key pair. The PKI also provides certification of the authenticity of copies of one's public key so it can be relied upon as coming from an authorized source. See also digital signature.

HIPAA, Centers for Medicare & Medicaid Services (CMS), ISO/IEC 27001:2005, NIST 800 Series, FIPS Pubs

Key management infrastructure (KMI)

Framework and services that provide the generation, production, storage, protection, distribution, control, tracking, and destruction for all cryptographic key material, symmetric keys as well as public keys and public key certificates.

US National Information Assurance (IA) Glossary

Key management practices

The main management practices that the process owner needs to perform to achieve the process goals.

CobiT

Key pair

Two mathematically related keys having the properties that 1) one key can be used to encrypt a message that can only be decrypted using the other key, and 2) even knowing one key, it is computationally infeasible to discover the other key.

US National Information Assurance (IA) Glossary, NIST 800 Series

Key Performance Indicator (KPI)

A metric that is used to help manage a process, IT service, or activity. Many metrics may be measured, but only the most important of these are defined as KPIs and used to actively manage and report on the process, IT service, or activity. KPIs should be selected to ensure that efficiency, effectiveness, and cost effectiveness are all managed. See also critical success factor.

CobiT, ITIL, PAS 56

Key Production Key (KPK)

Key used to initialize a keystream generator for the production of other electronically generated key.

US National Information Assurance (IA) Glossary

Key recovery

Mechanisms and processes that allow authorized parties to retrieve the cryptographic key used for data confidentiality.

US National Information Assurance (IA) Glossary

Key stream

Sequence of symbols (or their electrical or mechanical equivalents) produced in a machine or auto-manual cryptosystem to combine with plain text to produce cipher text, control transmission security processes, or produce key.

US National Information Assurance (IA) Glossary

Key tag

Identification information associated with certain types of electronic key.

US National Information Assurance (IA) Glossary

Key tape

Punched or magnetic tape containing key. Printed key in tape form is referred to as a key list.

US National Information Assurance (IA) Glossary

Key transport

The secure transport of cryptographic keys from one cryptographic module to another module.

NIST 800 series, FIPS Pubs

Key updating

Irreversible cryptographic process for modifying key.

US National Information Assurance (IA) Glossary

Key wrap

A method of encrypting keys (along with associated integrity information) that provides both confidentiality and integrity protection using a symmetric key algorithm.

NIST 800 series

Key-Auto-Key (KAK)

Cryptographic logic using previous key to produce key.

US National Information Assurance (IA) Glossary

Key-Encryption-Key (KEK)

Key that encrypts or decrypts other key for transmission or storage.

US National Information Assurance (IA) Glossary

Key-entered transaction

A transaction that is manually keyed into a point-of-sale device.

VISA Glossary of Terms

Keyed-hash based message authentication code (HMAC)

A message authentication code tha

NIST 800 series, FIPS Pubs

Keying material

Key, code, or authentication information in physical or magnetic form.

US National Information Assurance (IA) Glossary

Keystroke monitoring

A specialized form of audit trail software or a specially designed device that records every key struck by a user and every character of the response that the AIS returns to the user. A process whereby computer system administrators view or record both the keystrokes entered by a computer user and the computer's response during a user-to-computer session.

Centers for Medicare & Medicaid Services (CMS), NIST 800 Series

Keyword search

A search of the text of documents in a database for documents containing one or more words that are specified by a user.

Sedona Conference

Keywords

Words designated by a user as important for searching purposes.

Sedona Conference

Kilobyte (KB)

A unit of 1,024 bytes. See also Byte.

Sedona Conference

Knowledge base

A database containing information about incidents, problems and known errors. The knowledge base is used to match new incidents with historical information improving resolution times and first time fix rates.

ITIL

Knowledge management

The process responsible for gathering, analyzing, storing and sharing knowledge information within an organization. The primary purpose of knowledge management is to improve efficiency by reducing the need to rediscover knowledge.

ITIL

Known error

A problem that has a documented root cause and a workaround. Known errors are created by problem control and are managed throughout their lifecycle by error control. Known errors may also be identified by development or suppliers.

See also known error record, knowledge base.

ITIL

Known error database

A database containing all known error records. This database is created by problem management and used by incident and problem management. See also knowledge base.

ITIL

Known error record

A record containing the details of a known error. Each known error record documents the lifecycle of a known error including the status, root cause, and workaround. In some implementations a known error is documented using additional fields in a problem record.

ITIL

Known misstatement

The amount of misstatement found by the auditor.

GAO/PCIE Financial Audit Manual

Kofax board

The generic term for a series of image processing boards manufactured by Kofax Imaging Processing. These are used between the scanner and the computer, and perform real-time image compression and decompression for faster image viewing, image enhancement, and cor-

rections to the input to account for conditions such as document misalignment.

Sedona Conference

L

Label

The marking of an item or information to reflect its information category and/or security classification. See also security label.

Centers for Medicare & Medicaid Services (CMS), US National Information Assurance (IA) Glossary, NIST 800 Series

Labeled security protections

Elementary-level mandatory access control protection features and intermediate-level discretionary access control features in a TCB that uses sensitivity labels to make access control decisions.

US National Information Assurance (IA) Glossary

Laboratory attack

Use of sophisticated signal recovery equipment in a laboratory environment to recover information from data storage media.

US National Information Assurance (IA) Glossary

Landscape mode

The image is represented on the page or monitor such that the width is greater than the height.

Sedona Conference

Laptop

Portable personal computers that staff members use to access information remotely via an organization's networks. See also notebook computer.

CERT OCTAVE

Laser Disk

Same as an optical CD, except 12" in diameter.

Sedona Conference

Laser printing

A beam of light hits an electrically charged drum and causes a discharge at that point. Toner is then applied which sticks to the non-charged areas. Paper is pressed against the drum to form the image and is then heated to dry the toner. Used in laser printers and copying machines.

Sedona Conference

Latency

The time it takes a system, drive, or network to respond. System latency is the time a system takes to retrieve data. Network latency is the time it takes for a packet to travel from source to the final destination.

ISACA, Sedona Conference

Latent data

Latent or ambient data are deleted files and other data that are inaccessible without specialized forensic tools and techniques. Until overwritten, these data reside on media such as a hard drive in unused space and other areas available for data storage.

Sedona Conference

Layer 2 Forwarding (L2F)

A tunneling protocol developed by Cisco Systems to support the creation of VPNs.

ISACA

Layer 2 Tunneling Protocol (L2TP)

An extension to PPP to facilitate the creation of VPNs. L2TP merges the best features of PPTP (from Microsoft) and L2F (from Cisco).

ISACA, PCI-DSS

Leading

The amount of space between lines of printed text.

Sedona Conference

Lear-line data storage

Storage in a system that is not a direct part of the network in daily use, but that can be accessed through the network. There is usually a small time lag between the request for data stored in near-line media and its being made available to an application or end-user. Making near-line data available will not require human intervention (as opposed

to "off-line" data which can only be made available through human actions).

Sedona Conference

Leased lines

A communication line permanently assigned to connect two points as opposed to a dial-up line that is only available and open when a connection is made by dialing the target machine or network. Also known as a dedicated line.

ISACA

Least privilege

The principle that each user is granted the most restrictive set of privileges needed for the performance of authorized tasks. The application of this principle limits the damage that can result from accident, error, or unauthorized use.

Centers for Medicare & Medicaid Services (CMS), US National Information Assurance (IA) Glossary, NIST 800 Series

Ledding

See Leading.

Sedona Conference

Legacy data

Legacy data is information the development of which an organization may have invested significant resources and has retained its importance, but has been created or stored by the use of software and/or hardware that has become obsolete or replaced ("legacy systems"). Legacy data may be costly to restore or reconstruct when required for investigation or litigation analysis or discovery.

Sedona Conference

Legacy system

A computer system consisting of older applications and hardware that was developed to solve a specific business problem. Many legacy systems do not conform to current standards but are still in use because they solve the problem well and replacing them would be too expensive.

FISCAM, Sedona Conference

Legal hold

A legal hold is a communication issued as a result of current or anticipated litigation, audit, government investigation or other such matter that suspends the normal disposition or processing of records. Legal holds can encompass business procedures affecting active data, including, but not limited to, backup tape recycling. The specific communication to business or IT organizations may also be called a "hold," "preservation order," "suspension order," "freeze notice," "hold order," or "hold notice."

Sedona Conference

Legal risk

The risk to earnings or capital arising from violations of, or nonconformance with, laws, rules, regulations, prescribed practices or ethical standards. Banks are subject to various forms of legal risk. This can include the risk that assets will turn out to be worth less or liabilities will turn out to be greater than expected because of inadequate or incorrect legal advice or documentation. In addition, existing laws may fail to resolve legal issues involving a bank; a court case involving a particular bank may have wider implications for banking business and involve costs to it and many or all other banks; and laws affecting banks or other commercial enterprises may change. Banks are particularly susceptible to legal risks when entering new types of transactions and when the legal right of a counter-party to enter into transactions is not established.

ISACA

Lempel-Ziv & Welch (LZW)

A common, lossless compression standard for computer graphics, used for most TIFF files. Typical compression ratios are 4/1.

Sedona Conference

Level coding

Used in Bibliographical coding to facilitate different treatment, such as prioritization or more thorough extraction of data, for different categories of documents, such as by type or source.

Sedona Conference

Level of Business Continuity (LBC)

Minimum level of continued output of products and/or services acceptable to an organization in achieving its business objectives. LBC can be influenced or dictated by regulation or legislation.

PAS 56

Level of concern

Rating assigned to an information system indicating the extent to which protection measures, techniques, and procedures must be applied. High, Medium, and Basic are identified levels of concern. A separate Level-of-Concern is assigned to each information system for confidentiality, integrity, and availability. See also adequate security.

US National Information Assurance (IA) Glossary

Level of protection

Extent to which protective measures, techniques, and procedures must be applied to information systems and networks based on risk, threat, vulnerability, system interconnectivity considerations, and information assurance needs. Levels of protection are: 1) Basic: information systems and net-works requiring implementation of standard minimum security countermeasures. 2) Medium: information systems and networks requiring layering of additional safeguards above the standard minimum security countermeasures. 3) High: information systems and networks requiring the most stringent protection and rigorous security countermeasures.

US National Information Assurance (IA) Glossary

LFP

IPRO Tech's image cross reference file; an ASCII delimited text file required for cross-reference of images to data.

Sedona Conference

Librarian

The individual responsible for the safeguard and maintenance of all program and data files.

ISACA

Library

In computer terms, a library is a collection of similar files such as data sets contained on tape and/or discs, stored together in a common area. Typical uses are to store a group of source programs or a group of load modules. In a library, each program is called a member. Libraries are also called Partitioned Data Sets (PDS). Library can also be used to refer to the physical site where magnetic media, such as a magnetic tape, is stored. These sites are usually referred to as tape libraries.

FISCAM, Centers for Medicare & Medicaid Services (CMS)

Library control/management

The function responsible for controlling program and data files that are either kept online or are on tapes and discs that are loaded onto the computer as needed.

FISCAM, Centers for Medicare & Medicaid Services (CMS)

Library copier

Software that can copy source code from a library into a program.

FISCAM

Library management software

Software that provides an automated means of inventorying software, ensuring that differing versions are not accidentally misidentified, and maintaining a record of software changes.

FISCAM, Centers for Medicare & Medicaid Services (CMS)

License management

The process responsible for the management of software licenses throughout their lifecycle.

ITIL

Life critical information

Information critical to life-support systems (i.e., information where inaccuracy, loss, or alteration could result in loss of life).

Centers for Medicare & Medicaid Services (CMS)

Life environment

A controlled environment containing live configuration items used to deliver IT services to customers.

ITIL

Lifecycle

The various stages in the life of a configuration item, incident, problem, change etc. The lifecycle defines the categories for status and the status transitions that are permitted. It is usually described in three stages: creation, maintenance and use, and archive to final disposition. For example: 1) The lifecycle of an application includes design, build, test, deploy, operate etc. 2) The lifecycle of an incident includes detect, respond, diagnose, repair, recover, restore. 3) The lifecycle of a server may include ordered, received, in test, live, disposed, etc.

ITIL, Sedona Conference

Lifecycle process or lifecycle model

Spans the entire time that a project/program including hardware and software is being planned, designed, developed, procured, installed, used, and retired from service. A framework containing the processes, activities, and tasks involved in the development, operation, and maintenance of a software product spanning the life of the system from the definition of its requirements to the termination of its use.

Centers for Medicare & Medicaid Services (CMS), ISO/IEC 12207

Lightweight Directory Access Protocol (LDAP)

A set of protocols for accessing information directories. It is based on the X.500 standard, but is significantly simpler. LDAP is a sibling protocol to HTTP and FTP and uses the LDAP:// prefix in its URL.

Network Frontiers, ISACA

Likelihood of occurrence

Estimation of the frequency or probability of a threat occurring based upon the ease of exploiting system vulnerabilities.

Centers for Medicare & Medicaid Services (CMS)

Likely misstatement

The auditor's best estimate of the amount of the misstatement in the tested population including known misstatement. For sampling applications

this amount is the projected misstatement.

GAO/PCIE Financial Audit Manual

Limit

Used in performing substantive analytical procedures, the limit is the amount of difference between the expectation and the recorded amount that the auditor will accept without investigation. Therefore, the auditor should investigate amounts that exceed the limit during analytical procedures.

GAO/PCIE Financial Audit Manual

Limit check

Tests of specified amount fields against stipulated high or low limits of acceptability. When both high and low values are used, the test may be called a range check.

ISACA

Limited background investigation

This investigation consists of a NACI, credit search, personal subject interview, and personal interviews by an investigator of subject's background during the most recent three years.

Centers for Medicare & Medicaid Services (CMS)

Limited maintenance

COMSEC maintenance restricted to fault isolation, removal, and replacement of plug-in assemblies. Soldering or unsoldering usually is prohibited in limited maintenance. See also full maintenance.

US National Information Assurance (IA) Glossary

Line conditioning

Elimination of unintentional signals or noise induced or conducted on a telecommunications or information system signal, power, control, indicator, or other external interface line.

US National Information Assurance (IA) Glossary

Line conduction

Unintentional signals or noise induced or conducted on a telecommunications or information system signal, power, control, indicator, or other external interface line.

US National Information Assurance (IA) Glossary

Line screen

The number of half-tone dots that can be printed per inch. As a general rule, newspapers print at 65 to 85 lpi.

Sedona Conference

Linear Tape-Open (LTO)

A type of backup tape which can hold as much as 400 GB of data, or 600 CDs depending on the data file format.

Sedona Conference

Link

See Hyperlink.

Sedona Conference

Link encryption

Link encryption encrypts all of the data along a communications path (e.g., a satellite link, telephone circuit, or T1 line). Since link encryption also encrypts routing data, communications nodes need to decrypt the data to continue routing.

US National Information Assurance (IA) Glossary, NIST 800 Series

Link or linkage editor

A utility program that combines several separately compiled modules into one, resolving internal references between them.

ISACA

Liquidity test

Is the risk to earnings or capital arising from a bank's inability to meet its obligations when they come due, without incurring unacceptable losses. Internet banking may increase deposit volatility from customers who maintain accounts solely on the basis of rate or terms.

ISACA

List-oriented

Information system protection in which each protected object has a list of all subjects authorized to access it.

US National Information Assurance (IA) Glossary

Live

Refers to an IT service or configuration item that is being used to deliver service to a customer.

ITIL

Load file

A file that relates to a set of scanned images and indicates where individual pages belong together as documents. A load file may also contain data relevant to the individual documents, such as metadata, coded data and the like. Load files must be obtained and provided in prearranged formats to ensure transfer of accurate and usable images and data.

Sedona Conference

Load library

A partitioned data set used for storing load modules for later retrieval.

FISCAM, Centers for Medicare & Medicaid Services (CMS)

Load module

The results of the link edit process. An executable unit of code loaded into memory by the loader.

FISCAM, Centers for Medicare & Medicaid Services (CMS)

Loader

A utility that loads the executable code of a program into memory for execution.

FISCAM

Local Area Network (LAN)

A group of computers and other devices dispersed over a relatively limited area and connected by a communications link that enables a device to interact with any other on the network. Local Area Networks (LAN) commonly include microcomputers and shared (often expensive) resources such as laser printers and large hard discs. Most modern LANs can support a wide variety of computers and other devices. Separate LANs can be connected to form larger networks. See also network.

FISCAM, Centers for Medicare & Medicaid Services (CMS), PCI-DSS, Sedona Conference

Local authority

Organization responsible for generating and signing user certificates.

US National Information Assurance (IA) Glossary

Local loop

The communication lines that provide connectivity between the telecommunications carrier's central office and the subscriber's facilities.

ISACA

Local Management Device/ Key Processor (LMD/KP)

EKMS platform providing automated management of COMSEC material and generating key for designated users.

US National Information Assurance (IA) Glossary

Local Registration Authority (LRA)

A Registration Authority with responsibility for a local community.

NIST 800 series

Lock and key protection system

Protection system that involves matching a key or password with a specific access requirement.

US National Information Assurance (IA) Glossary

Log

A record of a computer's, network's, or application's activity, used for system information, backup, and recovery. With respect to computer systems; to record an event or transaction usually sequenced in the order they occurred.

FISCAM, ISACA, Centers for Medicare & Medicaid Services (CMS), ISO/IEC 27001:2005

Log in

See log on.

Centers for Medicare & Medicaid Services (CMS)

Log off

The process of terminating a connection with a computer system or peripheral device in an orderly way.

FISCAM, ISACA, Centers for Medicare & Medicaid Services (CMS)

Log on

The process of establishing a connection with, or gaining access to, a computer system or peripheral device.

ISACA

Log or logging file

See log.

FISCAM, ISACA

Logging

The process of recording a pre-defined set of individual activities in electronic or paper format. The logging process can be automatic (computer system) or manual (logbook) and serves as the basis for establishing audit trails. See also log.

Centers for Medicare & Medicaid Services (CMS), ISO/IEC 27001:2005

Logic bomb

In programming, a form of sabotage in which a programmer inserts code that causes the program to perform a destructive action when some triggering event occurs, such as terminating the programmer's employment.

FISCAM, Centers for Medicare & Medicaid Services (CMS), US National Information Assurance (IA) Glossary

Logical access control

A technical means of controlling what information users can utilize, the programs they can run, and the modifications they can make. The policies, procedures, organizational structure and electronic access controls designed to restrict access to computer software and data files. The use of computer hardware and software to prevent or detect unauthorized access. For example, users may be required to input user identification numbers, passwords, or other identifiers that are linked to predetermined access privileges.

FISCAM, ISACA, Centers for Medicare & Medicaid Services (CMS)

Logical block

A logical block is the smallest unit of storage that can be allocated by the file system. A logical block is measured in bytes, and it may take several blocks to store a single file.

The Backup Book

Logical completeness measure

Means for assessing the effectiveness and degree to which a set of security and access control mechanisms meets security specifications.

US National Information Assurance (IA) Glossary

Logical file space

The actual amount of space occupied by a file on a hard drive. The amount of logical file space differs from the physical file space because when a file is created on a computer, a sufficient number of clusters (physical file space) are assigned to contain the file. If the file (logical file space) is not large enough to completely fill the assigned clusters (physical file space) then some unused space will exist within the physical file space.

Sedona Conference

Logical partition (LPAR)

Section of a disk which is not one of the primary partitions. Defined in a data block pointed to by the extended partition.

PCI-DSS

Logical security

See logical access control.

FISCAM

Logical volume

An area on the hard drive that has been formatted for files storage. A hard drive may contain a single or multiple volumes. A logical volume can be a physical disk or some subset of the physical disk space. A logical volume is also known as a disk partition.

The Backup Book, Sedona Conference

Logon

See log on.

FISCAM, ISACA

Long title

Descriptive title of a COMSEC item.

US National Information Assurance (IA) Glossary

Loss

The limiting of an asset's availability; the asset still exists but is temporarily unavailable. The unrecoverable business resources that are redirected interrupted or removed from a system. Such losses may be loss of life, financial, public image, facilities, or operational capability.

CERT OCTAVE, Centers for Medicare & Medicaid Services (CMS)

Lossless compression

Exact construction of image, bit-by-bit, with no loss of information.

Sedona Conference

Lossy compression

Reduces storage size of image by reducing the resolution and color fidelity while maintaining minimum acceptable standard for general use.

Sedona Conference

Low impact system

An information system in which all three security objectives (i.e., confidentiality, integrity, and availability) are assigned a FIPS 199 potential impact value of low.

FIPS Pubs, NIST 800 Series

Low probability of detection

Result of measures used to hide or disguise intentional electromagnetic transmissions.

US National Information Assurance (IA) Glossary

Low probability of intercept

Result of measures to prevent the inter-cept of intentional electromagnetic transmissions.

US National Information Assurance (IA) Glossary

M

Machine code

The program instructions that are actually read and executed by the computer's processing circuitry. See also machine language.

FISCAM

Machine language

The logical language a computer understands.

ISACA

Macro virus

A virus that attaches itself to documents and uses the macro programming capabilities of the document's application to execute and propagate.

NIST 800 series

Magenta

Used in four color printing. Reflects blue & red and absorbs green.

Sedona Conference

Magnetic card reader

A card reader that reads cards with a magnetizable surface on which data can be stored and retrieved.

ISACA

Magnetic Disk Emulation (MDE)

Software that makes a jukebox look and operate like a hard-drive such that it will respond to all the I/O commands ordinarily sent to a hard drive.

Sedona Conference

Magnetic Ink Character Recognition (MICR)

Used to electronically input, read and interpret information directly from a source document; requires the source document to have specially coded magnetic ink typeset. The process used by banks to encode checks.

ISACA, Sedona Conference

Magnetic remanence

Magnetic representation of residual information remaining on a magnetic medium after the medium has been cleared. See also clearing.

US National Information Assurance (IA) Glossary

Magnetic stripe

The magnetic stripe on the back of all credit cards is encoded with account information as specified in the credit card issuer's Operating Regulations. The stripe is "read" when a card is swiped through a POS terminal. On a valid card, the account number on the magnetic stripe matches the account number on the front of the cards.

VISA Glossary of Terms

Magnetic stripe data

Data encoded in the magnetic stripe used for authorization during a card-present transaction. Entities may not retain full magnetic stripe data subsequent to transaction authorization. Specifically, subsequent to authorization, service codes, discretionary data/CVV, and Visa reserved values must be purged; however, account number, expiration date, and name may be extracted and retained. See also Magnetic Stripe.

PCI-DSS

Magnetic-stripe reader

The component of a point-of-sale device that electronically reads the information on a payment card's magnetic stripe.

VISA Glossary of Terms

Magnetic/Optical storage media

Includes, but is not limited to, hard drives, backup tapes, CD-ROMs, DVD-ROMs, Jaz and Zip drives.

Sedona Conference

Magneto-Optical drive (MO)

A drive that combines laser and magnetic technology to create high-capacity erasable storage.

Sedona Conference

Mail Application Program Interface (MAPI)

A software standard that has become a popular e-mail interface used by MS Exchange, GroupWise, and other e-mail packages.

Sedona Conference

Mail order/telephone order (MOTO)

A merchant, market, or sales environment in which mail or telephone sales are the primary or a major source of income. Such transactions are frequently charged to customers' bankcard accounts. See also Card-not-present.

VISA Glossary of Terms

Mail server

A host computer that provides 'electronic post office' facilities to other electronic devices. Services may include authentication, distribution, filtering, forwarding, storage, and automated purging. The term may refer to just the application that performs these services, or a broad the entire solution including hardware and infrastructure.

Workgroup for Electronic Data Interchange

Mail Server Administrator

The individual(s) responsible for the design, implementation, oversight, and/or maintenance of the mail server.

Workgroup for Electronic Data Interchange

Mail spoofing

The practice of changing the header that contains information regarding the originator, the addressee, and other recipients so that it looks like the e-mail came from somewhere or someone else. Faking the sending address of a transmission in order to gain illegal entry into a secure system.

Centers for Medicare & Medicaid Services (CMS)

Mail Transfer Agent (MTA)

The MTA supports the receipt; transfer and forwarding of messages form one electronic mail server to another. Common MTAs include Microsoft's Exchange and sendmail.

Workgroup for Electronic Data Interchange

Mail User Agent (MUA)

An application used by an end user to access his or her mail server to read, compose, and send e-mail messages. Common MUAs include Microsoft Outlook, and Netscape Messenger.

Workgroup for Electronic Data Interchange

Mailbox

An area on a storage device where e-mail is placed. In e-mail systems, each user has a private mailbox. When the user receives e-mail, the mail system automatically puts it in the appropriate mailbox.

Sedona Conference

Main Distribution Frame (MDF)

The room where the telephone lines or cable lines come in from the outside and connect to the rest of the organization's telecommunications equipment.

Network Frontiers

Mainframe computer system

A multi-user computer designed to meet the computing needs of a large organization. The term refers to the large central computers developed in the late 1950s and 1960s to meet the accounting and information management needs of large organizations.

FISCAM, Centers for Medicare & Medicaid Services (CMS)

Mainframe systems

See mainframe computer.

Centers for Medicare & Medicaid Services (CMS)

Maintain

Retaining records in identifiable re-cordkeeping systems over time in accordance with appraisal decisions. Records that are required to be maintained should remain accessible, their integrity should be protected and, where necessary, they should meet the conditions or requirements identified in order to satisfy business needs, organizational accountability and community expectations. This may include migrating records across successive systems and other preservation strategies.

DIRKS

Maintainability

A measure of how quickly and effectively a configuration item or IT service can be restored to normal working after a failure. Maintainability is often measured and reported as MTTR. See also availability.

ITIL

Maintenance

Altering programs after they have been in use for a while. Periodic upkeep of computer systems including clearing of log files, installation of patches and sys-tem upgrades. Maintenance programming may be performed to add features, correct errors that were not discovered during testing, or update key variables (such as the inflation rate) that change over time. The process of retaining a hardware system or component in, or restoring it to, a state in which it can perform its required functions.

FISCAM, Centers for Medicare & Medicaid Services (CMS), IEEE Std 610.12-1990, ISO/IEC 27001:2005

Maintenance hook

Special instructions (trapdoors) in software allowing easy maintenance and additional feature development. Since maintenance hooks frequently allow entry into the code without the usual checks, they are a serious security risk if they are not removed prior to live implementation.

US National Information Assurance (IA) Glossary

Maintenance key

Key intended only for in-shop use.

US National Information Assurance (IA) Glossary

Major Application (MA)

An application that requires special attention due to the risk and magnitude of the harm resulting from the loss, misuse, or unauthorized access to or modification of information in the application. A breach in a major application might compromise many individual application programs, hardware, software, and telecommunications components. A major application can be either a major software application or a combination of hardware/software. Major Applications consist of data and customized application software only. Its sole purpose is to support a specific mission-related function. All Major Applications require "special management attention." The system security plan for a Major Application may be defined broadly enough to include hardware, software, networks, and even facilities where it is reasonable. This permits the systems to be bounded in reasonable ways for the purposes of security planning.

FISCAM, OMB Circular A-130, Centers for Medicare & Medicaid Services (CMS), FIPS Pubs, NIST 800 series, Clinger-Cohen Act

Major incident

The highest category of impact for an incident. A major incident results in significant disruption to the business. See also escalation.

ITIL

Major information system

An information system that requires special management attention because of its importance to an agency mission; its high development, operating, or maintenance costs; or its significant role in the administration of agency programs, finances, property, or other resources.

NIST 800 series, OMB Circular A-130

Make-available production

A process whereby what is usually a large universe of all potentially responsive documents are made available to the requestor; from this universe, the requestor then reviews and selects or tags the documents which they wish to obtain, and the producing party produces to the requestor only the selected documents. This is sometimes done under an agreement protecting against privilege and confidentiality waiver during the initial make available production; and the producing party, after the requestor has selected the documents they wish to obtain, reviews only the selected documents for privilege and confidentiality before the selected documents are physically produced to the requestor.

Sedona Conference

Malicious applets

Small application programs automatically downloaded and executed that perform an unauthorized function on an information system.

US National Information Assurance (IA) Glossary

Malicious code

Software or firmware intended to perform an unauthorized process that will have adverse impact on the confidentiality, integrity, or availability of an information system. See also Trojan horse.

US National Information Assurance (IA) Glossary, NIST 800 Series

Malicious code or software

Unauthorized subverting programs or code that have been introduced into organizational software with the intent to, and purpose of, causing damage to data, applications, or networks. Malicious code or software refers to viruses, worms, Trojan horses, logic bomb, and other "uninvited" software.

NIST 800 series, NIST 500-166, Centers for Medicare & Medicaid Services (CMS)

Malicious logic

Hardware, software, or firmware capable of performing an unauthorized function on an information system.

US National Information Assurance (IA) Glossary

Malware

Any type of malicious program such as virus, worm, Trojan horse, or blended threat. A program that is inserted into a system, usually covertly, with the intent of compromising the confidentiality, integrity, or availability of the victim's data, applications, or operating system or of otherwise annoying or disrupting the victim. See also malicious software.

PCI-DSS, NIST 800 Series

Man in the middle attack

An attack strategy in which the attacker intercepts the communications stream between two parts of the victim system and then replaces the traffic between the two components with the intruder's own, eventually assuming control of the communication.

ISACA

Man-in-the-middle Attack (MitM)

An attack on the authentication protocol run in which the attacker positions himself in between the claimant and verifier so that he can intercept and alter data traveling between them.

NIST 800 series

Managed Object (MO)

An abstract representation of a resource that is used for operational management of that resource. An MO is defined in terms of the attributes of the resource, operations that may be performed on it, notifications it may issue and relationships with other MOs. MOs differ from configuration items as their status is dynamic, and changes to their operational state do not need to be approved by the change management process.

ITIL

Managed Service Provider (MSP)

See Application Service Provider.

ISACA

Managed services

Used in ISO/IEC 20000 as a synonym for IT services, whether outsourced or not. See also Managed Service Provider, outsourced IT services.

ITIL

Management controls

Controls put in place to manage computer security systems or applications and the associated risks. The organization, policies, and procedures used to provide reasonable assurance that 1) programs achieve their intended result, 2) resources are used consistent with the organization's mission, 3) programs and resources are protected from waste, fraud, and mismanagement, 4) laws and regulations are followed, and 5) reliable and timely information is obtained, maintained, reported, and used for decision-making.

FISCAM, Centers for Medicare & Medicaid Services (CMS), FIPS Pubs, NIST 800 Series

Management information

Information that is used to support decision making by managers. Management information is often generated automatically by tools supporting the various IT service management processes. Management information often includes the values of KPIs such as "percentage of changes leading to incidents," or "first time fix rate."

ITIL

Management Information System (MIS)

An organized assembly of resources and procedures required to collect, process, and distribute data for use in decision making. The IT service that captures, processes, and provides management information. The term MIS is also informally used to mean the output of MIS including data and reports.

ISACA, ITIL, Sedona Conference

Management system

The framework of policy and processes that ensures an organization can achieve its objectives.

ITIL

Management's discussion and analysis (MD&A)

GAO/PCIE Financial Audit Manual

Mandatory Access Control (MAC)

A means of restricting access to system resources based on the sensitivity (as represented by a label) of the information contained in the system resource and the formal authorization (i.e., clearance) of users to access information of such sensitivity.

NIST 800 series, US National Information Assurance (IA) Glossary, PCI-DSS

Mandatory modification

Change to a COMSEC end-item that NSA requires to be completed and reported by a specified date. See also optional modification.

US National Information Assurance (IA) Glossary

Mandatory topography

The format and information required to be displayed on a PIV card. Also known as the Standard Topography.

NIST 800 series, FIPS Pubs

Manipulative communications deception

Alteration or simulation of friendly telecommunications for the purpose of deception. See also communications deception and imitative communications deception.

US National Information Assurance (IA) Glossary

Manual cryptosystem

Cryptosystem in which the cryptographic processes are performed without the use of crypto-equipment or auto-manual devices.

US National Information Assurance (IA) Glossary

Manual journal entry

A journal entry entered at a computer terminal. Manual journal entries can include regular, statistical, inter-company and foreign currency entries.

ISACA

Manual key transport

A non-electronic means of transporting cryptographic keys by physically moving a device, document or person containing or possessing the key or a key component.

NIST 800 series

Manual remote rekeying

Procedure by which a distant crypto-equipment is rekeyed electrically, with specific actions required by the receiving terminal operator. Synonymous with cooperative remote rekeying. See also automatic remote keying.

US National Information Assurance (IA) Glossary

Manual workaround

A workaround that requires manual intervention. A part of IT service continuity management as a recovery option. In other words, a manual workaround means that the business process operates without the use of IT services. This is a temporary measure and is usually combined with another recovery option. In reality, a manual workaround is a synonym for "I can't do my job because I forgot how to write with a pen."

ITIL, Network Frontiers

MAPI mail near-line

Documents stored on optical disk s or compact discs that are housed in the jukebox or CD changer and can be retrieved without human intervention.

Sedona Conference

Mapping

Diagramming data that are to be exchanged electronically; including how it is to be used and what business man-agement systems need it. It is a preliminary step for developing an applications link.

ISACA

Marginal cost

The cost of continuing to providing the IT service. Marginal cost does not include investment already made. For example, the cost of developing new software and delivering training. See also full cost, opportunity cost.

ITIL

Marginalia

Handwritten notes in the margin of the page in documents.

Sedona Conference

Market price

A charging policy in which charges are the same as those an external supplier would charge.

ITIL

Masking

A computerized technique of blocking out the display of sensitive information, such as passwords, on a computer terminal or report.

ISACA

Masqueraders

Attackers that penetrate systems by using user identifiers and passwords taken from legitimate users. See also hacker.

ISACA

Masquerading

When an unauthorized agent claims the identity of another agent it is said to be masquerading. See also spoofing.

US National Information Assurance (IA) Glossary, NIST 800 Series

Master boot record

See Boot sector.

Sedona Conference

Master console

In MVS environments, the master console provides the principal means of communicating with the system. Other Multiple Console Support (MCS) consoles often serve specialized functions but can have master authority to enter all MVS commands.

FISCAM, Centers for Medicare & Medicaid Services (CMS)

Master crypto-ignition key

Key device with electronic logic and circuits providing the capability for adding more operational CIKs to a keyset.

US National Information Assurance (IA) Glossary

Master file

In a computer, the most currently accurate and authoritative permanent or semi-permanent computerized record of information maintained over an extended period. A collection of records pertaining to information in a system such as customers, employees, products, and vendors. Master files contain information such as descriptive data, name and address, and summary information.

FISCAM, ISACA, Centers for Medicare & Medicaid Services (CMS)

Master File Table (MFT)

Index to files on a computer. If corrupt, a drive may be unusable, yet data may be retrievable using forensic methods.

Sedona Conference

Master secret

The master secret is used to generate symmetric keys, known as session keys, to establish a secure communications mode.

Network Frontiers

Mastering

Making many copies of a disk from a single master disk.

Sedona Conference

Match/matching

The process of comparing biometric information against a previously stored

317

template(s) and scoring the level of similarity.

NIST 800 series, FIPS Pubs

Material

When discussion physical assets, material refers to data processed, stored, or used in and information generated by an ADP system regardless of form or medium; e.g., programs, reports, data sets or files, records, and data elements. When referring to material measurement, material denotes a scale or significance that would threaten an organization's key objectives should it not occur.

Centers for Medicare & Medicaid Services (CMS), BS 25999, GAO/PCIE Financial Audit Manual, Institute of Internal Auditors

Material weakness

A material weakness is a reportable condition in which the design or operation of the internal controls does not reduce to a relatively low level the risk that losses, noncompliance, or misstatements in amounts that would be material in relation to the principal statements or to a performance measure or aggregation of related performance measures may occur and not be detected within a timely period by employees in the normal course of their assigned duties.

FISCAM

Materiality

An auditing concept regarding the relative importance of an amount or item. The magnitude of an item's omission or misstatement in a financial statement that, in the light of surrounding circumstances, makes it probable that the judgment of a reasonable person relying on the information would have been changed or influenced by the inclusion or correction of the item (FASB Statement of Financial Concepts No. 2). An item is considered as not material when it is not significant enough to influence decisions or have an effect on the financial statements. An expression of the relative significance or importance of a particular matter in the context of the organization as a whole. See also planning materiality, design materiality, and test materiality.

FISCAM, GAO/PCIE Financial Audit Manual, ISACA

Maturity

Indicates the degree of reliability or dependency the business can place on a process achieving the desired goals or objectives. See also maturity level, process maturity.

CobiT, ITIL

Maturity level

A named level in a maturity model such as the Carnegie Mellon Capability Maturity Model Integration. See also process maturity, CMMI.

ITIL

Maximum tolerable period of disruption

The duration after which an organization's viability will be irrevocably threatened if product and service delivery cannot be resumed.

BS 25999

MD5

Message-digest algorithm meant for digital signature applications where a large message has to be "compressed" in a secure manner before being signed with the private key.

Sedona Conference

Mean Time Between Failure (MTBF)

A metric for measuring and reporting reliability. MTBF is the average time that a configuration item or IT service can perform its agreed function without interruption. This is measured from when the CI or IT service starts working until it next fails.

ITIL, Sedona Conference

Mean Time Between Service Incident (MTBSI)

A metric used for measuring and reporting reliability. MTBSI is the mean time from when a system or IT service fails, until it next fails. MTBSI is equal to MTBF + MTTR.

ITIL

Mean Time to Repair (MTTR)

A metric for measuring and reporting maintainability. MTTR is the average time taken to restore a configuration item or IT service after a failure. MTTR is measured from when the CI or IT service fails until it is fully restored and delivering its normal functionality.

ITIL, Sedona Conference

Measures

See controls.

ISO/IEC 27001:2005

Mechanism to authenticate regulated data

Implement electronic mechanisms to corroborate that regulated data has not been altered or destroyed in an unauthorized manner. See also automated controls.

HIPAA

Media

The physical object such as discettes, magnetic tapes, optical discs, magnetic discs, Large-Scale Integration (LSI) memory chips, printouts (but not including display media), and other forms by which data is stored or transported. The risk to exposure is considered greater when data is in an electronically readable and transmittable form than when the same data is in paper-only form. This is due to the greater volume of information that can be sent in electronic form, the ease and convenience with which the information can be transmitted, and the potential that such information will be intercepted or inadvertently sent to the wrong person or entity.

Centers for Medicare & Medicaid Services (CMS), FIPS Pubs, Sedona Conference, NIST 800 Series

Media Access Control address

A hardware address that uniquely identifies each node of a network.

Network Frontiers

Media re-use

Implement procedures for removal of regulated data from electronic media before the media are made available for re-use.

HIPAA

Media sanitization

A general term referring to the actions taken to render data written on media unrecoverable by both ordinary and extraordinary means.

NIST 800 series

Meetings

Why the human race has never achieved its full potential.

de facto

Megabyte (MB)

A unit of approximately 1 million bytes or 1024 KB. See also Byte.

Sedona Conference

Member

An organization that is a member of the credit card issuing organization and which issues cards or signs merchants, or does both.

VISA Glossary of Terms

Memorandum of Understanding/Agreement (MOU/A)

A document established between two or more parties to define their respective responsibilities in accomplishing a particular goal or mission. In this guide, an MOU/A defines the responsibilities of two or more organizations in establishing, operating, and securing a system interconnection.

NIST 800 series

Memory

Data storage in the form of chips, or the actual chips used to hold data; "storage" is used to describe memory that exists on tapes or discs. See also RAM and ROM.

Sedona Conference

Memory dump

The act of copying raw data from one place to another with little or no formatting for readability. Usually, dump refers to copying data from main memory to a display screen or a printer. Dumps are useful for diagnosing bugs. After a program fails, one can study the dump and analyze the contents of memory at the time of the failure. Dumps are usually output in a difficult-to-read form (that is, binary, octal or hexadecimal), so a memory dump will not help unless each person knows exactly for what to look.

ISACA

Memory scavenging

The collection of residual information from data storage.

US National Information Assurance (IA) Glossary

Menu

A list of options, each of which performs a desired action such as choosing a command or applying a particular format to a part of a document.

Sedona Conference

Merchant

A business entity that accepts credit cards for payment.

VISA Glossary of Terms

Merchant agreement

The contract between a merchant and a merchant bank under which the merchant participates in the Visa payment system, accepts Visa cards for payment of goods and services, and agrees to abide by certain rules governing the acceptance and processing of credit card transactions. Merchant agreements may stipulate merchant liability with regard to chargebacks and may specify time frames within which merchants are to deposit transactions and respond to requests for information.

VISA Glossary of Terms

Merchant bank

A financial institution that enters into agreements with merchants to accept credit cards as payment for goods and services; also called acquirers or acquiring banks.

VISA Glossary of Terms

Merchant Chargeback Monitoring Program (MCMP)

A Visa program that alerts merchant banks when one of their merchants has a chargeback-to-transaction rate of over one percent. Merchants then work with the bank to reduce their chargeback rates to acceptable levels. Failure to reduce chargebacks can result in fines for a merchant.

VISA Glossary of Terms

Merge access

This level of access provides the ability to combine data from two separate sources.

FISCAM

Merged thesaurus

A merged keyword thesaurus is a single alphabetical list of both general and functional terms which is used to classify records according to the Keyword Classification System. See also thesaurus.

DIRKS

Message Authentication Code (MAC)

Data associated with an authenticated message allowing a receiver to verify the integrity of the message. A cryptographic checksum on data that uses a symmetric key to detect both accidental and intentional modifications of the data.

US National Information Assurance (IA) Glossary, PCI-DSS, NIST 800 series, FIPS Pubs

Message digest

A cryptographic checksum, typically generated for a file that can be used to detect changes to the file; Secure Hash Algorithm-1 (SHA-1) is an example of a message digest algorithm.

NIST 800 series

Message externals

Information outside of the message text, such as the header, trailer, etc.

US National Information Assurance (IA) Glossary

Message header

Message headers generally contain the identities of the author and recipients, the subject of the message, and the date the message was sent.

Sedona Conference

Message indicator

Sequence of bits transmitted over a communications system for synchronizing crypto-equipment. Some off-line cryptosystems, such as the KL-51 and one-time pad systems, employ message indicators to establish decryption starting points.

US National Information Assurance (IA) Glossary

Message switching

A telecommunications traffic controlling methodology in which a complete message is sent to a concentration point and stored until the communications path is established.

ISACA

Metadata

The data describing context, content, and structure of records and their management through time. Structured information that describes and/or allows us to find, manage, control, understand, or preserve other information over time. Metadata is information about a particular data set or document which describes how, when and by whom it was collected, created, accessed, modified and how it is formatted. Can be altered intentionally or inadvertently. Can be extracted when native files are converted to image. Some metadata, such as file dates and sizes, can easily be seen by users; other metadata can be hidden or embedded and unavailable to computer users who are not technically adept. Metadata is generally not reproduced in full form when a document is printed. See also Customer-added metadata, Document metadata, E-mail metadata, File system metadata, User-added metadata and Vendor-added metadata. For a thorough discussion of Metadata, The Sedona Guidelines: Best Practice Guidelines & Commentary for Managing Information & Records in the Electronic Age, Appendix D: Technical Appendix.

ISO 15489, DIRKS, Sedona Conference

Metadata comparison

A method of de-duplication that compares file metadata and ignores content. See also De-Duplication.

Sedona Conference

Methodology

The logic applied to define a process. The specific way of performing an operation that implies precise deliverables at the end of each stage.

Centers for Medicare & Medicaid Services (CMS)

Metric

A standard of measurement for performance against goal. Something that is measured and reported to help manage a process, IT service or activity. See also KPI.

CobiT, ITIL

Metrics

Tools designed to facilitate decision-making and improve performance and accountability through collection, analysis, and reporting of relevant performance-related data.

NIST 800 series

Micro Channel Architecture (MCA)

An IBM bus standard.

Sedona Conference

Microchip

Chip's little brother. See also chip.

FISCAM

Microcomputer

Any computer with its arithmetic-logic unit and control unit contained in one integrated circuit, called a microprocessor.

FISCAM

Microfiche

Sheet microfilm (4" by 6") containing reduced images of 270 pages or more in a grid pattern.

Sedona Conference

Microprocessor

An integrated circuit device that contains the miniaturized circuitry to perform arithmetic, logic, and control operations (i.e. contains the entire CPU on a single chip).

FISCAM

Microsoft Disk Operating System (MS-DOS)

Used in PCs as the control system.

Sedona Conference

Microwave transmission

A high-capacity line-of-sight transmission of data signals through the atmosphere which often requires relay stations.

ISACA

Middleware

Another term for an Application Programmer Interface (API). It refers to the interfaces that allow programmers to access lower- or higher-level services by providing an intermediary layer that includes function calls to the services.

ISACA

Midrange computer

A medium-sized computer with capabilities that fall between those of personal computers and mainframe computers.

FISCAM

Migrated data

Migrated Data is information that has been moved from one database or format to another.

Sedona Conference

Migration

The act of moving records from one system to another while maintaining the records' authenticity, integrity, reliability, and usability. A change from an older hardware platform, operating system, or software version to a newer one.

ISO 15489, FISCAM, Centers for Medicare & Medicaid Services (CMS), Sedona Conference

Mimicking

See spoofing.

US National Information Assurance (IA) Glossary

Min-entropy

A measure of the difficulty that an attacker has to guess the most commonly chosen password used in a system.

NIST 800 series

Minimum Background Investigation (MBI)

This investigation includes a NACI, a credit record search, a face-to-face personal interview between the investigator and the subject, and telephone inquiries to selected employers. The MBI is an enhanced version of the NACIC and can be used for selected public trust positions.

Centers for Medicare & Medicaid Services (CMS)

Minor application

An application, other than a major application, that requires attention to security due to the risk and magnitude of harm resulting from the loss, misuse, or unauthorized access to or modification of the information in the application. Minor applications are typically included as part of a general support system.

NIST 800 series

Mirrored site

See active recovery site.

Network Frontiers

Mirroring

The duplication of data for purposes of backup or to distribute Internet or network traffic among several servers with identical data. See also disk mirroring.

Sedona Conference

MIS Training Institute (MISTI)

Founded in 1978, the MIS Training Institute reports that it is the international leader in audit and information security training, with offices in the USA, UK, and Asia. The MIS's security and consulting division, the Information Security Institute (ISI), focuses exclusively on providing high-quality information security conferences, seminars, and consulting services. System Security Ltd., a UK division of MIS, provides hands-on audit and security training. For more information, see http://www.misti.com.

de facto

Misappropriation of assets

Theft of an entity's assets causing the financial statements not to be presented in conformity with GAAP.

GAO/PCIE Financial Audit Manual

Misnamed files

A technique used to disguise a file's content by changing the file's name to something innocuous or altering its extension to a different type of file, forcing the examiner to identify the files by file signature versus file extension.

NIST 800 series

Mission critical

The systems that support a core business process are called mission critical systems. The absence or failure of mission-critical systems could have a significant impact on the mission, operations and viability of the organization. Vital to the operation of an organization. In the past, mission critical information systems were implemented on mainframes and minicomputers. Increasingly, they are being designed for and installed on personal computer networks.

Centers for Medicare & Medicaid Services (CMS), NIST 800 Series

Mission Critical Activity (MCA)

Critical operational and/or business support, service or product related activity (provided internally or externally), including its dependencies and single points of failure, which enables an organization to achieve its business objective(s), taking into account seasonal trends and/or critical timing issues.

PAS 56

Mission critical information

Information designated as critical to an agency mission, includes vital statistics information for emergency operations.

Centers for Medicare & Medicaid Services (CMS)

Mission statement

The mission statement of an organization is a short but complete description of the overall purpose and intentions of that organization. It states what is to be achieved but not how this should be done.

ITIL

Misuse detection

Detection on the basis of whether the system activity matches that defined as bad.

ISACA

Misuse of government property

The use of computer systems for other than official business that does not involve a criminal violation but is not permissible under regulatory policies.

Centers for Medicare & Medicaid Services (CMS)

Mobile code

Software modules obtained from remote systems, transferred across a network, and then downloaded and executed on local systems without explicit installation or execution by the recipient.

US National Information Assurance (IA) Glossary, NIST 800 Series

Mobile code technologies

Software technologies that provide the mechanisms for the production and use of mobile code (e.g., Java, JavaScript, ActiveX, VBScript).

NIST 800 series

Mobile recovery solution

Work space (normally syndicated) transported to a location specified by an organization for the purposes of work area recovery.

PAS 56

Mobile site

A self-contained, transportable shell custom-fitted with the specific IT equipment and telecommunications necessary to provide full recovery capabilities upon notice of a significant disruption.

NIST 800 series

Mobile software agent

Programs that are goal-directed and capable of suspending their execution on one platform and moving to another platform where they resume execution.

NIST 800 series

Mode of operation

Description of the conditions under which an information system operates based on the sensitivity of information processed and the clearance levels, formal access approvals, and need-to-know of its users. Four modes of operation are authorized for processing or transmitting information: dedicated mode, system-high mode, compartmented/partitioned mode, and multilevel mode.

US National Information Assurance (IA) Glossary, NIST 800 Series

Modeling

The act of creating a simplified, abstract representation of a system for the purpose of describing, understanding and/or analyzing that system. Any technique used to predict the future behavior of an IT service, configuration item, or business process. Models are commonly used in financial management, capacity management and availability management. See also estimation, analytical modeling, simulation modeling.

DIRKS, ITIL

Modem

Short for modulator-demodulator. A device that allows digital signals to be transmitted and received over analog telephone lines. This type of device makes it possible to link a digital computer to the analog telephone system. It also determines the speed at which information can be transmitted and received.

FISCAM, ISACA, Centers for Medicare & Medicaid Services (CMS)

Moderate impact system

An information system in which at least one security objective (i.e., confidentiality, integrity, or availability) is assigned a FIPS 199 potential impact value of moderate, and no security objective is assigned a FIPS 199 potential impact value of high.

FIPS Pubs, NIST 800 Series

Modification

An unauthorized changing of an asset. Loss of integrity of an asset or asset group through the intentional or unintentional alteration of the asset or asset group.

CERT OCTAVE, Centers for Medicare & Medicaid Services (CMS)

Modulation

The process of converting a digital computer signal into an analog telecommunications signal.

ISACA

Modulator/Demodulator (MODEM)

A device translates digital data from a computer into analog signals (modulates) and transmits the information over telephones lines. Another modem at the receiving computer will receive the information, translate it back from analog to digital (demodulate) and store it.

Sedona Conference

Monetary unit sampling

A sampling technique that estimates the amount of overstatement in an account balance.

ISACA

Monitor

Any information collection mechanism utilized by an intrusion detection system.

ISACA

Monitoring

The fourth of the high-level control domains for CobiT, monitoring follows the belief that all IT processes need to be regularly assessed over time for their quality and compliance with control requirements. This domain thus addresses management's oversight of the organization's control process and independent assurance provided by internal and external audit or obtained from alternative sources. In general, monitoring is a component of internal control in addition to the control environment, risk assessment, information and communication, and control activities. The process by which management assesses internal control performance over time. It may include ongoing activities, separate evaluations, or a combination of both.

CobiT, GAO/PCIE Financial Audit Manual, Centers for Medicare & Medicaid Services (CMS), PCI-DSS

Monitoring policy

The rules outlining the way in which information is captured and interpreted.

ISACA

Monochrome

Displays capable of only two colors, usually black and white, or black and green.

Sedona Conference

Mosaic

A web browser popular before the introduction of Netscape and Internet Explorer.

Sedona Conference

Motive

A property of threat that defines whether an actor's intentions are deliberate or accidental. This only applies to human actors. Motive is also sometimes referred to as the objective of a threat actor.

CERT OCTAVE

Mount, Mounting

The process of making off-line data available for on-line processing. For example, placing a magnetic tape in a drive and setting up the software to recognize or read that tape. The terms "load" and "loading" are often used in conjunction with, or synonymously with, "mount" and "mounting" (as in "mount and load a tape"). "Load" may also refer to the process of transferring data from mounted media to another media or to an on-line system.

Sedona Conference

Moving Pictures Experts Group (MPEG)

de facto

MPEG-1 & -2

Two different standards for full motion video to digital compression and decompression techniques advanced by the Moving Pictures Experts Group. MPEG-1 compresses 30 frames/second of full-motion video down to about 1.5 Mbits/sec from several hundred megabytes. MPEG-2 compresses the same files down to about 3.0 Mbits/sec and provides better image quality.

Sedona Conference

Multi-hop problem

The security risks resulting from a mobile software agent visiting several platforms.

NIST 800 series

Multi-Security Level (MSL)

Capability to process information of different security classifications or categories by using periods processing or peripheral sharing.

US National Information Assurance (IA) Glossary

Multidisciplinary

Measures, practices, and procedures for the continuity of information systems should take account of and address all relevant considerations and viewpoints.

NIST 800 series

Multilevel device

Equipment trusted to properly maintain and separate data of different security categories.

US National Information Assurance (IA) Glossary

Multilevel mode

INFOSEC mode of operation wherein all the following statements are satisfied concerning the users who have direct or indirect access to the system, its peripherals, remote terminals, or remote hosts: a. some users do not have a valid security clearance for all the information processed in the information system; b. all users have the proper security clearance and appropriate formal access approval for that information to which they have access; and c. all users have a valid need-to-know only for information to which they have access.

US National Information Assurance (IA) Glossary

MultiLevel Security (MLS)

Concept of processing information with different classifications and categories that simultaneously permits access by users with different security clearances and denies access to users who lack authorization. See also cross domain solution.

US National Information Assurance (IA) Glossary

Multimedia

The combined use of different media; integrated video, audio, text and data graphics in digital form.

Sedona Conference

Multiple Virtual Storage (MVS)

An IBM mainframe operating system. It has been superseded by OS/390 for IBM 390 series mainframes.

FISCAM

Multiplexer

A device used for combining several lower-speed channels into a higher-speed channel.

ISACA

Multiplexing

The transmission of more than one signal across a physical channel.

ISACA

Multipurpose Internet Mail Extension (MIME)

A standard defined by the Internet Engineering Task Force Working Group specifying how attachments and encoding will be handled for Internet mail transmissions.

Workgroup for Electronic Data Interchange

Multipurpose Internet Mail Extensions (MIME)

An extensible mechanism for e-mail. A variety of MIME types exist for sending content such as audio using the Simple Mail Transfer Protocol (SMTP) protocol.

NIST 800 series

Multipurpose testing

Performing several tests, such as control tests, compliance tests, and substantive tests, on a common selection usually a sample.

GAO/PCIE Financial Audit Manual

Multisynch

Analog video monitors which can receive a wide range of display resolutions, usually including TV (NTSC). Color analog monitors accept separate red, green & blue (RGB) signals.

Sedona Conference

Mutation engine

A piece of software code that alters an application without affecting its purpose. Most often implemented in computer viruses.

Network Frontiers

Mutual authentication

Occurs when parties at both ends of a communication activity authenticate each other.

NIST 800 series

Mutual suspicion

Condition in which two information systems need to rely upon each other to perform a service, yet neither trusts the other to properly protect shared data.

US National Information Assurance (IA) Glossary

Mutual takeover

A fail-over process which is a two-way idle standby: two servers are configured so that both can take over the other node's resource group. Both must have enough CPU power to run both applications with sufficient speed, or performance losses must be taken into account until the failed node reintegrates. This also works nicely in three or more node configurations.

ISACA

N

N-line support

A generic term for any level of support group. See also first-line support, second-line support, third-line support.

ITIL

Name assertion

The process whereby verification of the individual's identity is achieved. This can be supplied during a registration process and passed in the authentication process.

Workgroup for Electronic Data Interchange

Naming authority

An organizational entity responsible for assigning distinguished names (DNs) and for assuring that each DN is meaningful and unique within its domain.

NIST 800 series

Naming conventions

Standards for naming computer resources, such as data files, program libraries, individual programs, and applications.

FISCAM

National Agency Check (NAC)

An integral part of all background investigations, the NAC consists of searches of OPM's Security/Suitability Investigations Index (SII), the Defense Clearance and Investigations Index (DCII), the FBI Identification Division's name and fingerprint files, and other files or indices when necessary.

Centers for Medicare & Medicaid Services (CMS)

National Association of Corporate Directors (NACS)

Founded in 1977, the National Association of Corporate Directors is the only non-profit membership organization dedicated exclusively to serving the corporate governance needs of directors and boards. NACD's mission is to achieve improved corporate governance through better board practice. By offering education, information, conducting independent research, and disseminating leading practices, NACD provides resources for increasing director and board effectiveness. See also http://www.nacdonline.org for more information.

de facto

National Cyber Security Alliance (NCSA)

A non-profit organization, the National Cyber Security Alliance (NCSA) is the go-to resource for cyber security awareness and education for home user, small business, and education audiences. A public-private partnership, NCSA sponsors include the Department of Homeland Security, Federal Trade

Commission, and many private-sector corporations and organizations. NCSA provides tools and resources to empower home users, small businesses, and schools, colleges, and universities to stay safe online. See also http://www.staysafeonline.info for more information.

de facto

National Cybercrime Training Partnership (NCTP)

The stated vision of the National Cybercrime Training Partnership (NCTP) is to develop a 21st century paradigm for law enforcement training in electronic and high-technology crime. This newly designed training paradigm must feature multilevel, multitiered, decentralized, and continuous training. See also http://www.nctp.org for more information.

de facto

National Information Assurance Partnership (NIAP)

A U.S. Government initiative originated to meet the security testing needs of both information technology (IT) consumers and producers. NIAP is a collaboration between the National Institute of Standards and Technology (NIST) and the National Security Agency (NSA) in fulfilling their respective responsibilities under Public Law (PL) 100-235 (Computer Security Act

of 1987). The partnership combines the extensive IT security experience of both agencies to promote the development of technically sound security requirements for IT products and systems and appropriate measures for evaluating those products and systems.

US National Information Assurance (IA) Glossary, NIST 800 Series

National Information Infrastructure (NII)

Nationwide interconnection of communications networks, computers, databases, and consumer electronics that make vast amounts of information available to users. It includes both public and private networks, the internet, the public switched network, and cable, wireless, and satellite communications.

US National Information Assurance (IA) Glossary

National Infrastructure Protection Center (NIPC)

The NIPC served as a national critical infrastructure threat assessment, warning, vulnerability, and law enforcement investigation and response entity. The NIPC provided timely warnings of international threats, comprehensive analysis and law enforcement investigation and response. Recently, the former National Infrastructure Protection Center (NIPC) was fully integrated into the Information Analysis and Infrastructure

Protection Directorate of the Department of Homeland Security (DHS). As such, the responsibilities of fulfilling the mission of physical and cyber critical infrastructure assessment and protection of the former NIPC are now being addressed by two new divisions. See also DHS.

NIST 800 series

National Institute of Standards and Technology (NIST)

From automated teller machines and atomic clocks to mammograms and semiconductors, innumerable products and services rely in some way on technology, measurement, and standards provided by the National Institute of Standards and Technology. Founded in 1901, NIST is a non-regulatory federal agency within the U.S. Commerce Department's Technology Administration. NIST's mission is to promote US innovation and industrial competitiveness by advancing measurement science, standards, and technology in ways that enhance economic security and improve our quality of life. See also http://www.nist.gov for more information.

NIST 800 series, PCI-DSS, Sedona Conference

National Security Agency (NSA)

The National Security Agency/Central Security Service is America's cryptologic organization. It coordinates, directs, and performs highly specialized activities to protect US government information systems and produce foreign signals intelligence information. A high technology organization, NSA is on the frontiers of communications and data processing. It is also one of the most important centers of foreign language analysis and research within the government. See also http://www.nsa.gov for more information.

de facto

National Security Emergency Preparedness Telecommunications Services

Telecommunications services that are used to maintain a state of readiness or to respond to and manage any event or crisis (local, national, or international) that causes or could cause injury or harm to the population, damage to or loss of property, or degrade or threaten the national security or emergency preparedness posture of the United States.

NIST 800 series, 47 CFR Part 64

National security information

Information that has been determined pursuant to Executive Order 12958 as amended by Executive Order 13292, or any predecessor order, or by the Atomic Energy Act of 1954, as amended, to require protection against unauthorized disclosure and is marked to indicate its classified status.

FIPS Pubs, US National Information Assurance (IA) Glossary

National security system

Any information system (including any telecommunications system) used or operated by an agency or by a contractor of an agency or other organization on behalf of an agency: 1) the function, operation, or use of which involves intelligence activities; involves cryptologic activities related to national security; involves command and control of military forces; involves equipment that is an integral part of a weapon or weapons system; or is critical to the direct fulfillment of military or intelligence missions (excluding a system that is to be used for routine administrative and business applications, for example, payroll, finance, logistics, and personnel management applications); or 2) is protected at all times by procedures established for information that have been specifically authorized under criteria established by an Executive Order or an Act of Congress to be kept classified in the interest of national defense or foreign policy.

FIPS Pubs, US National Information Assurance (IA) Glossary

Native format

Electronic documents have an associated file structure defined by the original creating application. This file structure is referred to as the "native format" of the document. Because viewing or searching documents in the native format may require the original application (for example, viewing a Microsoft Word document may require the Microsoft Word application), documents are often converted to a vendor-neutral format as part of the record acquisition or archive process. "Static" formats (often called "imaged formats"), such as TIFF or PDF, are designed to retain an image of the document as it would look viewed in the original creating application but do not allow metadata to be viewed or the document information to be manipulated.

Sedona Conference

Natural language search

A manner of searching that permits the use of plain language without special connectors or precise terminology, such as "Where can I find information on William Shakespeare?" as opposed to formulating a search statement (such as "information" and "William Shakespeare").

Sedona Conference

Near-line data

A term used to refer to data or a robotic storage device (robotic library) that houses removable media, uses robotic arms to access the media, and uses multiple read/write devices to store and retrieve records. Examples include optical discs.

Sedona Conference

Need to know

The necessity for access to, or knowledge or possession of, specific information required to carry out official duties.

Centers for Medicare & Medicaid Services (CMS)

Need to know determination

Decision made by an authorized holder of official information that a prospective recipient requires access to specific official information to carry out official duties.

US National Information Assurance (IA) Glossary

Need-to-know

Necessity for access to, or knowledge or possession of, specific official information required to carry out official duties.

US National Information Assurance (IA) Glossary

Needs assessment

A process that can be used to determine an organization's awareness and training needs. The results of a needs assessment can provide justification to convince management to allocate adequate resources to meet the identified awareness and training needs.

NIST 800 series

Netware

A popular local area network operating system developed by the Novell Corp.

ISACA

Network

A group of computers and associated devices that are connected by communications facilities in order to share resources. A network can involve permanent connections, such as cables, or temporary connections made through telephone or other communications links. A network can be as small as a local area network consisting of a few computers, printers, and other devices, or it can consist of many small and large computers distributed over a vast geographic area. A telecommunications medium and associated components responsible for the transmission of information. A local-area network (LAN) refers to connected computers and devices geographically close together (i.e. in the same building). A wide-area network (WAN) refers generally to a network of PC's or other devices, remote to each other, connected by telecommunications lines. Typically, a WAN may connect two or more LAN's together.

FISCAM, ISACA, Centers for Medicare & Medicaid Services (CMS), PCI-DSS, US National Information Assurance (IA) Glossary, Sedona Conference

Network Address Translation (NAT)

An Internet standard that allows a network to use one set of IP addresses for internal traffic and a second set of addresses for external traffic. The server, providing the NAT service, changes the source address of outgoing packets from the internal to the external address and reverses it for packets returning.

ISACA, PCI-DSS

Network administration

The function responsible for maintaining secure and reliable network operations. This function serves as a liaison with user departments to resolve network needs and problems.

FISCAM

Network Administrator

The person responsible for maintaining a LAN and assisting end users.

ISACA

Network architecture

The underlying structure of a computer network, including hardware, functional layers, interfaces, and protocols (rules) used to establish communications and ensure the reliable transfer of information. Because a computer network is a mixture of hardware and software, network architectures are designed to provide both philosophical and physical standards for enabling computers and other devices to handle the complexities of establishing communications links and transferring information without conflict. Various network architectures exist, among them the internationally accepted seven-layer Open Systems Interconnection model and International Business Machine (IBM) Systems Network Architecture. Both the Open Systems Interconnection model and the Systems Network Architecture organize network functions in layers, each layer dedicated to a particular aspect of communication or transmission and each requiring protocols that define how functions are carried out. The ultimate objective of these and other network architectures is the creation of communications standards that will enable computers of many kinds to exchange information freely.

FISCAM, Centers for Medicare & Medicaid Services (CMS)

Network components

Include, but are not limited to firewalls, switches, routers, wireless access points, network appliances, and other security appliances.

PCI-DSS

Network front-end

Device implementing protocols that allow attachment of a computer system to a network.

US National Information Assurance (IA) Glossary

Network gear

Refers to the actual hardware used in the operation of networks – for example routers, switches and hubs.

Sedona Conference

Network hop

An attack strategy in which the attacker successively hacks into a series of connected systems, obscuring his/her identify from the victim of the attack.

ISACA

Network infrastructure scanner

A vulnerability evaluation tool that focuses on the components of the network infrastructure, such as routers and intelligent switches, DNS (domain name system) servers, firewall systems, and intrusion detection systems.

CERT OCTAVE

Network interface

The point of interconnection for a single node to a network environment.

Centers for Medicare & Medicaid Services (CMS)

Network mapping

The process of identifying a network structure or architecture, including the placement and configuration of network components (servers, routers, firewalls, etc.).

Centers for Medicare & Medicaid Services (CMS)

Network mapping tools

Software used to search a network, identifying the physical connectivity of systems and networking components. The software also displays detailed information about the interconnectivity of networks and devices (routers, switches, bridges, hosts).

CERT OCTAVE

Network master control system

Software that controls the network providing monitoring information for reliability, stability, and availability of the network and traffic control and errors. These may also involve the use of special hardware.

FISCAM

Network Operating System (NOS)

See Operating System.

Sedona Conference

Network protocols

The rules and conventions for communication between devices. Protocol definitions include formatting rules that specify how data is packaged into messages, message acknowledgement conventions, and data compression conventions.

Centers for Medicare & Medicaid Services (CMS)

Network reference monitor

See reference monitor.

US National Information Assurance (IA) Glossary

Network security

See information systems security.

US National Information Assurance (IA) Glossary

Network security officer

See information systems security officer.

US National Information Assurance (IA) Glossary

Network security scan

Automated tool that remotely checks merchant or service provider systems for vulnerabilities. Non-intrusive test involves probing external-facing systems based on external-facing IP addresses and reporting on services available to external network (that is, services available to the Internet). Scans identify vulnerabilities in operating systems, services, and devices that could be used by hackers to target the company's private network.

PCI-DSS

Network sponsor

Individual or organization responsible for stating the security policy enforced by the network, designing the network security architecture to properly enforce that policy, and ensuring the network is implemented in such a way that the policy is enforced.

US National Information Assurance (IA) Glossary

Network system

System implemented with a collection of interconnected components. A network system is based on a coherent security architecture and design.

US National Information Assurance (IA) Glossary

Network Time Protocol (NTP)

Protocol for synchronizing the clocks of computer systems over packet-switched, variable-latency data networks.

PCI-DSS

Network topology diagrams

Electronic or paper documents used to display the logical or physical mapping of a network. These documents identify the connectivity of systems and networking components. They usually contain less detail than that provided by network mapping tools.

CERT OCTAVE

Network weaving

Penetration technique in which different communication networks are linked to access an information system to avoid detection and trace-back.

US National Information Assurance (IA) Glossary

Network-based IDS

IDSs which detect attacks by capturing and analyzing network packets. Listening on a network segment or switch, one network-based IDS can monitor the network traffic affecting multiple hosts that are connected to the network segment.

NIST 800 Series

Networking component

Devices important to an organization's networks. Routers, switches, and modems are all examples of this class of component.

CERT OCTAVE

Neural network

Neural networks are made up of interconnected processing elements called units, which respond in parallel to a set of input signals given to each.

Sedona Conference

New technology or controlled scientific information

Information related to new technology; scientific information that is prohibited from disclosure to certain foreign governments or that may require an export license from the Department of State and/or the Department of Commerce.

Centers for Medicare & Medicaid Services (CMS)

No-lone zone

Area, room, or space that, when staffed, must be occupied by two or more appropriately cleared individuals who remain within sight of each other. See also two-person integrity.

US National Information Assurance (IA) Glossary

Node

In a local area network, a connection point that can create, receive, or repeat a message. Nodes include repeaters, computers, file servers, and shared peripherals. In common usage, however, the term node is synonymous with workstation.

FISCAM, ISACA

Noise

Disturbances, such as static, in data transmissions that cause messages to be misinterpreted by the receiver.

ISACA

Non privileged access

Cannot bypass any security controls.

Centers for Medicare & Medicaid Services (CMS)

Non-computing security methods

Non-computing methods are security safeguards which do not use the hardware, software, and firmware of IT. Non-computing methods include physical security (controlling physical access to computing resources), personnel security, and procedural security.

NIST 800 series

Non-consumer users

Any user, excluding consumer customers, that accesses systems, including but not limited to, employees, administrators, and third parties. See also users.

PCI-DSS

Non-interlace

When each line of a video image is scanned separately. Computer monitors use non-interlaced video.

Sedona Conference

Non-intrusive monitoring

In vulnerability analysis, gaining information by performing standard system status queries and inspecting system attributes.

ISACA

Non-repudiation

The ability to prevent senders from denying that they have sent messages and receivers from denying that they have received messages. It is the provision of proof of the integrity and origin of the data which can be verified by a third party. Non-repudiation may be provided by a digital signature. See also non-reputable transactions.

FISCAM, ISACA, Workgroup for Electronic Data Interchange, NIST 800 Series

Non-reputable transactions

Transactions that cannot be denied after the fact.

ISACA

Non-rewriteable, non-erasable format

Originally this meant WORM disk or tape formats only. However, the SEC issued an Interpretive Release on May 7, 2000 that discusses this requirement. This release includes language permitting the use of a combination hardware and software system to meet this requirement. In order to meet this criterion, the hardware software combination must verify accuracy, serialize the media, and prove capacity to download indexes and records. See also secure storage.

17 CFR 240.17a-3 & 4, ISO/IEC 27001:2005

Non-Treasury Disbursing Office (NTDO)

GAO/PCIE Financial Audit Manual

Nonce

A value used in security protocols that is never repeated with the same key. For example, challenges used in challenge-response authentication protocols generally must not be repeated until authentication keys are changed, or there is a possibility of a replay attack. Using a nonce as a challenge is a different requirement than a random challenge, because a nonce is not necessarily unpredictable.

NIST 800 series

Nonrepudiation

Assurance the sender of data is provided with proof of delivery and the recipient is provided with proof of the sender's identity, so neither can later deny having processed the data.

US National Information Assurance (IA) Glossary

Nonsampling selection

A selection of items to reach a conclusion only on the items selected. Sometimes called a case study, the auditor using a nonsampling selection may not project the results to the population, but should be satisfied that there is a low risk of material misstatement in the untested items.

GAO/PCIE Financial Audit Manual

Normalization

The elimination of redundant data.

ISACA

North American Electric Reliability Council (NERC)

NERC's mission is to ensure that the bulk electric system in North America is reliable, adequate and secure. Since its formation in 1968, NERC has operated successfully as a self-regulatory organization, relying on reciprocity and the mutual self-interest of all those involved. See also http://www.nerc.com for more information.

de facto

Notebook

See laptop.

Network Frontiers

Notional charging

A charging policy where customers are sent bills for the IT services they have used, but money is not actually transferred. This is sometimes introduced to ensure that customers are aware of the costs they incur or as a stage during the introduction of real charging.

ITIL

NSF

Lotus Notes Format Database File (i.e. database.nsf) Can be either an e-mail database or the traditional type of fielded database.

Sedona Conference

NT File System (NTFS)

NT File System is the file system that Windows NT and XP operating systems use for storing and retrieving files on storage media.

Microsoft

Null

Dummy letter, letter symbol, or code group inserted into an encrypted message to delay or prevent its decryption or to complete encrypted groups for transmission or transmission security purposes.

US National Information Assurance (IA) Glossary

Numeric check

An edit check designed to ensure the data in a particular field is numeric.

ISACA

O

Object

A passive organization that contains or receives information. Note that access to an object potentially implies access to the information it contains. An object is defined by its interface, behaviors, and attributes which interact to produce a set of responses to input. The interface defines what the system will respond to and how it will respond. The behaviors are the internal processes that are set in motion in response to the input. The attributes are the defining qualities of the object per se. In programming terminology, an object is a freestanding block of code that defines the properties of some thing. Objects are created and used in a high-level method of programming called object-oriented programming (OOP). OOP involves giving programming objects characteristics that can be transferred to, added to, and combined with other objects to make a complete program.

NIST 800 series, US National Information Assurance (IA) Glossary, Sedona Conference

Object code

The machine code generated by a source code language processor such as an assembler or compiler. A file of object code may be immediately executable or it may require linking with other object code files, e.g., libraries, to produce a complete executable program.

FISCAM, ISACA, Centers for Medicare & Medicaid Services (CMS)

Object identifier

A specialized formatted number that is registered with an internationally recognized standards organization. The unique alphanumeric/numeric identifier registered under the ISO registration standard to reference a specific object or object class. In the federal government PKI they are used to uniquely identify each of the four policies and cryptographic algorithms supported.

NIST 800 series

Object Linking and Embedding (OLE)

A feature in Microsoft's Windows which allows each section of a compound document to call up its own editing tools or special display features. This allows for combining diverse elements in compound documents.

Sedona Conference

Object Management Group (OMG)

A consortium with more than 700 affiliates from the software industry. Its purpose is to provide a common framework for developing applications using object-oriented programming techniques. For example, OMG is known principally for promulgating the CORBA specification. See also http://www.omg.org for more information.

ISACA

Object orientation

An approach to system development where the basic unit of attention is an object, which represents an encapsulation of both data (an object's attributes) and functionality (an object's methods). Objects usually are created using a general template called a class. Classes are the basis for most design work in objects. Classes and their objects communicate in defined ways. Aggregate classes interact through messages which are directed requests for services from one class (the client) to another class (the server). A class may share the structure or methods defined in one or more other classes; a relationship known as inheritance.

ISACA

Object oriented system development

A system development methodology that is organized around "objects" rather than "actions," and "data" rather than "logic." Object-oriented analysis is an assessment of a physical system to determine which objects in the real world need to be represented as objects in a software system. Any object-oriented design is software design that is centered around designing the objects that will make up a program. Any object-oriented program is one that is composed of objects or software parts.

ISACA

Object reuse

Reassignment and re-use of a storage medium containing one or more objects after ensuring no residual data remains on the storage medium.

US National Information Assurance (IA) Glossary

Objective

The defined purpose or aim of a process, an activity or an organization as a whole. Objectives are usually expressed as measurable targets. The term objective is also informally used to mean a requirement.

ITIL

Objectivity

The ability to exercise judgment, express opinions and present recommendations with impartiality.

ISACA, ISO/IEC 27001:2005

Obligation ceiling

A limit set by Congress on the amount of obligations and expenditures the entity may incur even though the budget authority (such as an appropriation) is greater than this limit.

GAO/PCIE Financial Audit Manual

Off-card

Refers to data that is not stored within the PIV card or computation that is not done by the Integrated Circuit Chip (ICC) of the PIV card.

NIST 800 series, FIPS Pubs

Off-line attack

An attack where the attacker obtains some data (typically by eavesdropping on an authentication protocol run, or by penetrating a system and stealing security files) that he/she is able to analyze in a system of his/her own choosing.

NIST 800 series

Off-line cryptosystem

Cryptosystem in which encryption and decryption are performed independently of the transmission and reception functions.

US National Information Assurance (IA) Glossary

Off-the-shelf software

Software that is marketed as a commercial product, unlike custom programs that are privately developed for a specific client.

FISCAM

Office of General Counsel

Within the Government Accounting Office, the Office of General Counsel provides assistance to the auditor in 1) identifying provisions of laws and regulations to test, 2) identifying budget restrictions, and 3) identifying and resolving legal issues encountered in the financial statement audit, such as evaluating potential instances of noncompliance. See also http://www.ogc.doc.gov for more information.

GAO/PCIE Financial Audit Manual

Office of General Counsel or Office of Government Commerce (OGC)

See Office of General Counsel, Office of Government Commerce

GAO/PCIE Financial Audit Manual, ITIL

Office of Government Commerce

ITIL defines OGC as the Office of Government Commerce. OGC own the copyright to the ITIL publications. They are a UK government department that works with public sector organizations to help them improve their efficiency, gain better value for money from their commercial activities, and deliver improved success from programs and projects. See also http://www.ogc.gov.uk for more information.

ITIL

Office of Information Systems (OIS)

CMS office that ensures the effective management of CMS's information systems and resources. The office also develops and maintains central databases and statistical files and directs Medicare claims payment systems.

Centers for Medicare & Medicaid Services (CMS)

Office of Inspector General (OIG)

NIST 800 series

Office of Management and Budget (OMB)

OMB assists the President of the United States in the development and execution of his policies and programs. OMB has a hand in the development and resolution of all budget, policy, legislative, regulatory, procurement, e-gov, and management issues on behalf of the President. OMB is composed of divisions organized either by Agency and program area or by functional responsibilities. However, the work of OMB often requires a broad exposure to issues and programs outside of the direct area of assigned responsibility. See also http://www.whitehouse.gov/omb for more information.

GAO/PCIE Financial Audit Manual

Office of Personnel Management (OPM)

The United States' human resources agency. See also http://www.opm.gov for more information.

Network Frontiers

Office of Public Sector Information (OPSI)

OPSI are the publishers of the ITIL publications. They are a UK government department who provide online access to UK legislation, license the reuse of crown copyright material, manage the information fair trader scheme, maintain the government's information asset register, and provide advice and guidance on official publishing and crown copyright. See also http://www.opsi.gov.uk for more information.

ITIL

Official information

All information in the custody and control of a U.S. Government department or agency that was acquired by U.S. Government employees as a part of their official duties or because of their official status and has not been cleared for public release.

US National Information Assurance (IA) Glossary

Official record owner

See Record owner.

Sedona Conference

Offline data

The storage of electronic data outside the network in daily use (e.g., on backup tapes) that is only accessible through the off-line storage system, not the network.

Sedona Conference

Offline files

Computer file storage media not physically connected to the computer; typically tapes or tape cartridges used for backup purposes.

ISACA

Offline storage

Electronic records stored or archived on removable disk (optical, compact, etc.) or magnetic tape used for making disaster-recovery copies of records for which retrieval is unlikely. Accessibility to offline media usually requires manual intervention and is much slower than on-line or near-line storage depending on the storage facility. The major difference between near-line data and offline data is that offline data lacks an intelligent disk subsystem, and is not connected to a computer, network, or any other readily-accessible system.

Sedona Conference

Offsetting collections

Collections of a business- or market-oriented nature and intragovernmental transactions. If, pursuant to law, they are deposited to receipts accounts and are available for obligation, they are considered budget authority and referred to as offsetting receipts. Contract authority and immediate availability of offsetting receipts for use are the usual forms of budget authority for revolving funds.

GAO/PCIE Financial Audit Manual

Offsite storage facility

A storage facility located away from the building housing the primary Information Processing Facility (IPF) used for storage of computer media such as off-line backup data and storage files.

ISACA, Centers for Medicare & Medicaid Services (CMS)

On-card

Refers to data that is stored within the PIV card or computation that is done by the ICC of the PIV card.

NIST 800 series, FIPS Pubs

On-line

The old way of spelling online.

Network Frontiers

On-line attack

An attack against an authentication protocol where the attacker either assumes the role of a claimant with a genuine verifier or actively alters the authentication channel. The goal of the attack may be to gain authenticated access or learn authentication secrets.

NIST 800 series

On-Line Certificate/Certification Status Protocol (OCSP)

An on-line protocol used to determine the status of a public key certificate.

NIST 800 series, FIPS Pubs

One-part code

Code in which plain text elements and their accompanying code groups are arranged in alphabetical, numerical, or other systematic order, so one listing serves for both encoding and decoding. One-part codes are normally small codes used to pass small volumes of low-sensitivity information.

US National Information Assurance (IA) Glossary

One-time cryptosystem

Cryptosystem employing key used only once.

US National Information Assurance (IA) Glossary

One-time pad

Manual one-time cryptosystem produced in pad form.

US National Information Assurance (IA) Glossary

One-time tape

Punched paper tape used to provide key streams on a one-time basis in certain machine cryptosystems.

US National Information Assurance (IA) Glossary

One-way hash algorithm

Hash algorithms which map arbitrarily long inputs into a fixed-size output such that it is very difficult (computationally infeasible) to find two different hash inputs that produce the same output. Such algorithms are an essential part of the process of producing fixed-size digital signatures that can both authenticate the signer and provide for data integrity checking (detection of input modification after signature).

NIST 800 series

Online

A processing term that categorizes operations that are activated and ready for use. If a resource is online, it is capable of communicating with or being controlled by a computer. For example, a printer is online when it can be used for printing. An application is classified as online when users interact with the system as their information is being processed as opposed to batch processing. It typically refers to being connected to the Internet or other remote service.

FISCAM, Centers for Medicare & Medicaid Services (CMS), Sedona Conference

Online coding facility

See online program development software.

FISCAM

Online cryptosystem

Cryptosystem in which encryption and decryption are performed in association with the transmitting and receiving functions.

US National Information Assurance (IA) Glossary

Online data processing

Processing is achieved by entering information into the computer via a video display terminal. The computer immediately accepts or rejects the information as it is entered.

ISACA

Online debugging facility

Software that permits online changes to program object code with no audit trail. This type of software can activate programs at selected start points.

FISCAM

Online editors

See online program development software.

FISCAM

Online program development software

Software that permits programs to be coded and compiled in an interactive mode.

FISCAM

Online review

The culling process produces a dataset of potentially responsive documents which are then reviewed for a final selection of relevant or responsive documents and assertion of privilege exception as appropriate. Online review enables the culled dataset to be accessed via PC or other terminal device via a local network or remotely via the Internet. Often, the Online review process is facilitated by specialized software which provides additional features and functions which may include: collaborative access of multiple reviewers, security, user logging, search and retrieval, document coding, redaction, and privilege logging.

Sedona Conference

351

Online storage

The storage of electronic data as fully accessible information in daily use on the network or elsewhere.

Sedona Conference

Online system

Available for immediate use. It typically refers to being connected to the Internet or other remote service. When you connect via modem, you are online after you dial in and log on to your Internet provider with your username and password. When you log off, you are offline. With cable modem and DSL service, you are online all the time. A peripheral device (terminal, printer, etc.) that is turned on and connected to the computer is also online.

Centers for Medicare & Medicaid Services (CMS)

Online transaction monitor

In the mainframe environment, software that provides online access to the mainframe.

FISCAM

Online transaction processing

Online transaction processing records transactions as they occur.

FISCAM

Open storage

Storage of classified information within an accredited facility, but not in General Services Administration approved secure containers, while the facility is unoccupied by authorized personnel.

US National Information Assurance (IA) Glossary

Open systems

An environment in which system access is not controlled by the person responsible for the content of electronic records on the system. Systems for which detailed specifications of their components composition are published in a nonproprietary environment, thereby enabling competing organizations to use these standard components to build competitive systems. The advantages of using open systems include portability, interoperability and integration. An example is the UNIX operating system with versions available for a wide variety of hardware platforms.

21 CFR Part 11, DIRKS, ISACA

Open Systems Interconnection Model (OSI model)

Network Frontiers

Open Web Application Security Project (OWASP)

The Open Web Application Security Project (OWASP) is dedicated to finding and fighting the causes of insecure software. Everything here is free and open source. The OWASP Foundation is a 501c3 not-for-profit charitable organization that ensures the ongoing availability and support for our work. Participation in OWASP is free and open to all. For more information, see http://www.owasp.org/

PCI-DSS

Operate

To perform as expected. A process or configuration item is said to operate if it is delivering the required outputs. Operate also means to perform one or more operations. For example, to operate a computer is to do the day-to-day operations needed for it to perform as expected. See also operation, IT operations, business operations.

ITIL

Operating System (OS)

An Operating system provides the software platform which directs the overall activity of a computer, network or system, and on which all other software programs and applications can run. In many ways, choice of an operating system will effect which applications can be run. Operating systems perform basic tasks, such as recognizing input from the keyboard, sending output to the display screen, keeping track of files and directories on the disk and controlling peripheral devices such as disk drives and printers. For large systems, the operating system has even greater responsibilities and powers - becoming a traffic cop to makes sure different programs and users running at the same time do not interfere with each other. The operating system is also responsible for security, ensuring that unauthorized users do not access the system. Examples of operating systems are UNIX, DOS, Windows, LINUX, Macintosh, and IBM's VM. Operating systems can be classified in a number of ways, including: multi-user (allows two or more users to run programs at the same time - some operating systems permit hundreds or even thousands of concurrent users); multiprocessing (supports running a program on more than one CPU); multitasking (allows more than one program to run concurrently); multithreading (allows different parts of a single program to run concurrently); and real time (instantly responds to input - general-purpose operating systems, such as DOS and UNIX, are not real-time).

FISCAM, ISACA, Centers for Medicare & Medicaid Services (CMS), Sedona Conference

Operating System audit trails

Records of system events generated by a specialized operating system mechanism.

ISACA

Operating system scanner

A vulnerability evaluation tool that targets specific operating systems such as Windows NT/2000, Sun Solaris, Red Hat Linux, or Apple Mac OS.

CERT OCTAVE

Operation

A predefined activity or transaction. For example, loading a magnetic tape, accepting money at a point of sale, or reading data from a disk drive. See operate, IT operations, business operations.

ITIL

Operational

The lowest of three levels of planning and delivery (strategic, tactical, operational). Operational activities include the day-to-day or short term planning or delivery of a business process or IT service management process. The term operational is also used to refer to a configuration item or IT service being ready for use.

ITIL

Operational acceptance

Part of the release acceptance activity, responsible for ensuring that everything needed for IT operations is in place before the release is deployed. Operational acceptance often uses a checklist to ensure that all required documentation, IT operations processes, tools, and training are in place.

ITIL

Operational audit

An audit designed to evaluate the various internal controls, economy and efficiency of a function or department.

ISACA

Operational controls

The day-to-day security procedures and mechanisms to protect operational systems. The operational controls consist of the physical, environmental, and personnel security controls. These controls relate to managing the entity's business and include policies and procedures to carry out organizational objectives such as planning, productivity, programmatic, quality, economy, efficiency, and effectiveness objectives. Management uses these controls to provide reasonable assurance that the organization 1) meets its goals, 2) maintains quality standards, and 3) does what management directs it to do.

FISCAM, GAO/PCIE Financial Audit Manual, ISACA, Centers for Medicare & Medicaid Services (CMS), FIPS Pubs, NIST 800 Series

Operational cost

The cost resulting from running the IT services. Often repeating payments; for example, staff costs, hardware maintenance, and electricity (also known as "current expenditure" or "revenue expenditure"). See also capital costs.

ITIL

Operational Expenditure (OPEX)

See operational cost.

ITIL

Operational information

Information that requires protection during operations; usually time-critical information.

Centers for Medicare & Medicaid Services (CMS)

Operational key

Key intended for use over-the-air for protection of operational information or for the production or secure electrical transmission of key streams.

US National Information Assurance (IA) Glossary

Operational Level Agreement (OLA)

An internal agreement covering the delivery of services that support the IT organization in its delivery of services. For example, there could be an OLA with a facilities department to provide air conditioning or with the procurement department to obtain hardware in agreed times. An OLA may also be between two parts of the same IT service provider; for example, between the service desk and a support group. See also service level agreement.

CobiT, ITIL

Operational practice

Security practices that focus on technology-related issues. They include issues related to how people use, interact with, and protect technology.

CERT OCTAVE

Operational risk

The most important types of operational risk involve breakdowns in internal controls and corporate governance. Such breakdowns can lead to financial losses through error, fraud or failure to perform in a timely manner or cause the interests of the bank to be compromised in some other way, for example, by its dealers, lending officers or other staff exceeding their authority or conducting business in an unethical or risky manner. Other aspects of operational risk include major failure of information technology systems or events such as security problems or other disasters.

ISACA, PAS 56

Operational vulnerability

Information that describes the presence of a

US National Information Assurance (IA) Glossary

Operational waiver

Authority for continued use of unmodified COMSEC end-items pending the completion of a mandatory modification.

US National Information Assurance (IA) Glossary

Operations bridge

A physical location where IT services and IT infrastructure are monitored and managed. See also IT operations, event management.

ITIL

Operations code

Code composed largely of words and phrases suitable for general communications use.

US National Information Assurance (IA) Glossary

Operations Security (OPSEC)

Systematic and proven process by which potential adversaries can be denied information about capabilities and intentions by identifying, controlling, and protecting generally unclassified evidence of the planning and execution of sensitive activities. The process involves five steps: identification of critical information, analysis of threats, analysis of vulnerabilities, assessment of risks, and application of appropriate countermeasures.

US National Information Assurance (IA) Glossary

Operator console

A special terminal used by computer operations personnel to control computer and systems operations functions. These terminals typically provide a high level of computer access and should be properly secured.

ISACA

Opportunity cost

A cost that is used in deciding between investment choices. Opportunity cost represents the revenue that would have been generated by using the resources in a different way. For example, the opportunity cost of purchasing a new server may include the loss of interest that the money would otherwise have earned in the bank. See also full cost, marginal cost.

ITIL

Optical Character Recognition (OCR)

A technology process that translates and converts printed matter on an image into a format that a computer can manipulate (ASCII codes, for example) and, therefore, renders that matter text searchable. OCR software evaluates scanned data for shapes it recognizes as letters or numerals. All OCR systems include an optical scanner for reading text, and software for analyzing images. Most OCR systems use a combination of hardware (specialized circuit boards) and software to recognize characters, although some inexpensive systems operate entirely through software. Advanced OCR systems can read text in a large variety of fonts, but still have difficulty with handwritten text. OCR technology relies upon the quality of the imaged material, the conversion accuracy of the software, and the quality control process of the provider. The process is generally acknowledged to be only 80-85 percent accurate.

ISACA, AIIM, Sedona Conference

Optical disks

Computer media similar to a compact disk that cannot be rewritten. An optical drive uses a laser to read the stored data.

Sedona Conference

Optical jukebox

See Jukebox.

Sedona Conference

Optical Mark Recognition (OMR)

Detects presence, or absence, of marks in defined areas; used for processing questionnaires, standardized tests, etc.

AIIM

Optical scanner

An input device that reads characters and images that are printed or painted on a paper form into the computer.

ISACA

Optimize

Review, plan, and request changes in order to obtain the maximum efficiency and effectiveness from a process, configuration item, application, etc. See also continuous improvement.

ITIL

Optional modification

NSA-approved modification not required for universal implementation by all holders of a COMSEC end-item. This class of modification requires all of the engineering/doctrinal control of mandatory modification but is usually not related to security, safety, TEMPEST, or reliability. See also mandatory modification.

US National Information Assurance (IA) Glossary

Optional topography

A Personal Identity Verification (PIV) card having both the Standard Topography (Mandatory Topography) features and the Optional features as defined in FIPS 201 sections 4.1.4.3 and 4.1.4.4.

NIST 800 series, FIPS Pubs

Organization

CobiT states that it is the manner in which an enterprise is structured. However, an enterprise is indicative of a large group of people, and an organization can be any size. Examples of organizations that are not companies include international standards organization, ITSMF. The term organization is sometimes used to refer to any entity which has people, resources, and budgets. For example, a project or business unit. See also entity, agency, enterprise.

BS 25999, CobiT, FIPS Pubs, ITIL

Organization for Economic Cooperation and Development (OECD)

The OECD groups 30 member countries sharing a commitment to democratic government and the market economy. With active relationships with some 70 other countries, NGOs and civil society, it has a global reach. Best known for its publications and its statistics, its work covers economic and social issues from macroeconomics, to trade, education, development and science and innovation. The OECD plays a prominent role in fostering good governance in the public service and in corporate activity. The OECD produces internationally agreed instruments, decisions and recommendations to promote rules of the game in areas where multilateral agreement is necessary for individual countries to make progress in a globalized economy. See also http://www.oecd.org for more information.

de facto

Organizational maintenance

Limited maintenance performed by a user organization.

US National Information Assurance (IA) Glossary

Organizational Registration Authority (ORA)

Entity within the PKI that authenticates the identity and the organizational affiliation of the users.

US National Information Assurance (IA) Glossary

Organizational value

The measure of an asset's worth from strictly an internal perspective.

Network Frontiers

Organizational vulnerability

A weakness in organizational policy or practice that can result in unauthorized actions occurring. They are indications of missing or inadequate security practices.

CERT OCTAVE

Originator

See Author.

Sedona Conference

OST

A Microsoft Outlook information store that is used to save folder information that can be accessed offline.

Sedona Conference

Other federal agency information

Information, the protection of which is required by statute, or which has come from another Federal agency and requires release approval by the originating agency.

Centers for Medicare & Medicaid Services (CMS)

Other systems

Any system that is not determined to be a GSS or MA is referred to as an "other" system.

Centers for Medicare & Medicaid Services (CMS)

Outcome

A property of threat that defines the immediate outcome (disclosure, modification, destruction, loss, interruption) of violating the security requirements of an asset.

CERT OCTAVE

Output

In computing terms, output refers to data/information produced by computer processing, such as graphic display on a terminal or hard copy. In general business terms, output refers to any product or service generated from the consumption of resources. This can include information generated by the completion of a task or activity.

FISCAM, GAO/PCIE Financial Audit Manual, Centers for Medicare & Medicaid Services (CMS)

Output analyzer

Checks the accuracy of the results produced by a test run. There are three types of checks that an output analyzer can perform. First, if a standard set of test data and test results exists for a program, the output of a test run after program maintenance can be compared with the set of results that should be produced. Second, as programmers prepare test data and calculate the expected results, these results can be stored on a file and the output analyzer compares the actual results of a test run with the expected results. Third, the output analyzer can act as a query language; it accepts queries about whether certain relationships exist in the file of output results and reports compliance or noncompliance.

ISACA

Output devices

Peripheral equipment, such as a printer or tape drive, that provides the results of processing in a form that can be used outside the system.

FISCAM

Outside threat

An unauthorized entity from outside the domain perimeter that has the potential to harm an Information System through destruction, disclosure, modification of data, and/or denial of service.

NIST 800 series

Outsource

A formal agreement with a third party to perform an IS function for an organization. The term outsourcing is used to mean making use of an external service provider to manage IT services or acting as an external service provider to manage IT services. See also insource.

ISACA, ITIL

Over-the-air key distribution

Providing electronic key via over-the-air rekeying, over-the-air key transfer, or cooperative key generation.

US National Information Assurance (IA) Glossary

Over-the-air key transfer

Electronically distributing key without changing traffic encryption key used on the secured communications path over which the transfer is accomplished.

US National Information Assurance (IA) Glossary

Over-The-Air Rekeying (OTAR)

Changing traffic encryption key or transmission security key in remote crypto-equipment by sending new key directly to the remote crypto-equipment over the communications path it secures.

US National Information Assurance (IA) Glossary

Overall analytical procedures

Analytical procedures performed as an overall financial statement review during the audit reporting phase.

GAO/PCIE Financial Audit Manual

Overhead

See indirect cost.

ITIL

Overt channel

Communications path within a computer system or network designed for the authorized transfer of data. See also covert channel.

US National Information Assurance (IA) Glossary

Overwrite

To record or copy new data over existing data, as in when a file or directory is updated. Data that is overwritten cannot be retrieved.

Sedona Conference

Overwrite procedure

Process of writing patterns of data on top of the data stored on a magnetic medium.

US National Information Assurance (IA) Glossary

Owner

Manager or director with responsibility for a computer resource, such as a data file or application program. The individual who is responsible for making and communicating judgments and decisions on behalf of the organization with regard to the use, identification, classification, and protection of a specific information asset. See also system owner.

FISCAM, Centers for Medicare & Medicaid Services (CMS)

P

PAB

A Microsoft Outlook list of recipients created and maintained by an individual user for personal use. The personal address book is a subset of the global address list (GAL).

Sedona Conference

Package release

A single release that includes a number of full or delta releases. See also release type.

ITIL

PackBits

A compression scheme which originated with the Macintosh. Suitable only for black & white.

Sedona Conference

Packet

Data unit that is routed from source to destination in a packet-switched network. A packet contains both routing information and data. Transmission control protocol/Internet protocol (TCP/IP) is such a packet-switched network.

ISACA, Sedona Conference

Packet Assembler/Disassembler (PAD)

A communication device that formats outgoing data and strips data out of incoming packets. In cryptography, the one-time PAD is an encryption algorithm with text combined with a random key or "pad" that is as long as the plaintext and used only once. Additionally, if key is truly random, never reused, and, kept secret, the one-time pad is unbreakable.

PCI-DSS

Packet filtering

Controlling access to a network by analyzing the attributes of the incoming and outgoing packets and either letting them pass, or denying them, based on a list of rules. As packets arrive they are filtered by their type, source address, destination address, and port information contained in each packet, ensuring data is only allowed to enter or leave the computing environment if firewall rules allow it.

ISACA, Centers for Medicare & Medicaid Services (CMS)

Packet sniffer

Software that observes and records network traffic.

NIST 800 series

Packet switching

The process of transmitting messages in convenient pieces that can be reassembled at the destination.

ISACA

Page

A single image of the equivalent of "one piece of paper". One or several pages make up a "Document."

Sedona Conference

Page file/Paging file

A file used to temporarily store code and data for programs that are currently running. This information is left in the swap file after the programs are terminated, and may be retrieved using forensic techniques. Also referred to as a swap file.

Sedona Conference

Pantone Matching System (PMS)

A color standard in printing.

Sedona Conference

Parallel

Transmission of all the bits (e.g. in a character) at the same time. If the character has eight bits, there are eight wires. Faster and more expensive than serial where the eight bits would be sent, "sideways," one at a time.

Sedona Conference

Parallel simulation

Parallel simulation involves the IS auditor writing a program to replicate those application processes that are critical to an audit opinion and using this program to reprocess application system data. The results produced are compared with the results generated by the application system and any discrepancies identified.

ISACA

Parallel testing

The process of feeding test data into two systems, the modified system and an alternative system (possibly the original system) and comparing results.

ISACA

Parameter

A value that is given to a variable. Parameters provide a means of customizing programs.

FISCAM, Centers for Medicare & Medicaid Services (CMS)

Parameter Library (PARMLIB)

The partitioned data set that contains many initialization parameters that are used by an MVS operating system during an initial program load and by other system software components such as SMF that are invoked by operator command.

FISCAM

Parent organization

The organization that is applying for the Personal Identity Verification card on behalf of an applicant. Typically this is an organization for whom the applicant is working.

NIST 800 series, FIPS Pubs

Pareto Principle

A technique used to prioritize activities. The Pareto principle says that 80% of the value of any activity is created with 20% of the effort. See also the 80-20 rule.

ITIL

Parity

Bit(s) used to determine whether a block of data has been altered.

US National Information Assurance (IA) Glossary

Parity check

A general hardware control which helps to detect data errors when data are read from memory or communicated from one computer to another. A 1-bit digit (either 0 or 1) is added to a data item to indicate whether the sum of that data item's bit is odd or even. When the parity bit disagrees with the sum of the other bits, the computer reports an error. The probability of a parity check detecting an error is 50 percent.

ISACA

Partition

A partition is an individual section of computer storage media such as a hard drive. For example a single hard drive may be divided into several partitions. When a hard drive is divided into partitions, each partition is designated by a separate drive letter, i.e., C, D, etc.

Sedona Conference

Partition table

The partition table indicates each logical volume contained on a disk and its location.

Sedona Conference

Partition waste space

After the boot sector of each volume or partition is written to a track, it is customary for the system to skip the rest of that track and begin the actual useable area of the volume on the next track. This results in unused or "wasted" space on that track where information can be hidden. This "wasted space" can only be viewed with a low level disk viewer. However, forensic techniques can be used to search these "wasted space" areas for hidden information.

Sedona Conference

Partitioned Data Set

Independent groups of sequentially organized records, called members, in direct access storage. Each member has a name stored in a directory that is part of the data set and contains the location of the member's starting point. PDSs are generally used to store programs. As a result, many are often referred to as libraries.

FISCAM

Partitioned Data Set or Protected Distribution Systems (PDS)

See Partitioned Data Set, Protected Distribution Systems.

FISCAM, US National Information Assurance (IA) Glossary

Partitioned file

A file format in which the file is divided into multiple subfiles and a directory is established to locate each subfile.

ISACA

Partitioned security mode

Information system security mode of operation wherein all personnel have the clearance, but not necessarily formal access approval and need-to-know, for all information handled by an information system.

US National Information Assurance (IA) Glossary

Partnership

A relationship between two organizations which involves working closely together for common goals or mutual benefit. The IT service provider should have a partnership with the business and with third parties who are critical to the delivery of IT services.

ITIL

Pass-phrase

A long, difficult-to-crack series of words and characters that is used like a password.

Network Frontiers

Passive assault

In a passive assault, intruders attempt to learn some characteristic of the data being transmitted. They may be able to read the contents of the data so the privacy of the data is violated. Alternatively, although the content of the data itself may remain secure, intruders may read and analyze the plaintext source and destination identifiers attached to a message for routing purposes, or they may examine the lengths and frequency of messages being transmitted.

ISACA

Passive attack

An attack against an authentication protocol where the attacker intercepts data traveling along the network between the claimant and verifier, but does not alter the data (i.e. eavesdropping).

NIST 800 series

Passive response

A response option in intrusion detection in which the system simply reports and records the problem detected, relying on the user to take subsequent action.

ISACA

Password

A confidential character string used to authenticate an identity and prevent unauthorized access. Most often associated with user authentication. However, they are also used to protect data and applications on many systems, including PCs. Password-based access controls for PC applications are often easy to circumvent if the user has access to the operating system (and knowledge of what to do).

FISCAM, ISACA, Centers for Medicare & Medicaid Services (CMS), PCI-DSS, US National Information Assurance (IA) Glossary, Sedona Conference, NIST 800 Series, FIPS Pubs

Password character

Specialized security checker that tests user's passwords, searching for passwords that are easy to guess by repeatedly trying words from specially crafted dictionaries. Failing that, many password crackers can brute force all possible combinations in a relatively short period of time with current desktop computer hardware.

ISACA

Password protected

The ability to protect a file using a password access control, protecting the data contents from being viewed with the appropriate viewer unless the proper password is entered.

NIST 800 series

Patch

A quick-repair job for a piece of programming. During a software product's beta test distribution or try-out period and later after the product is formally released, problems will almost invariably be found. A patch is the immediate solution that is provided to users.

PCI-DSS

Patch management server

A computer that houses applications or software related to software patches.

Network Frontiers

Path

The hierarchical description of where a directory, folder, or file is located on a computer or network. In DOS and Windows systems, a path is a list of directories where the operating system looks for executable files if it is unable to find the file in the working directory. The list of directories can be specified with the PATH command. Path is also used to refer to a transmission channel, the path between two nodes of a network that a data communication follows, and the physical cabling that connects the nodes on a network.

Sedona Conference

Path histories

Maintaining an authenticatable record of the prior platforms visited by a mobile software agent, so that a newly visited platform can determine whether to process the agent and what resource constraints to apply.

NIST 800 series

Pattern matching

A generic term that describes any process that compares one file's content with another file's content.

Sedona Conference

Pattern recognition

Technology that searches data for like patterns and flags, and extracts the pertinent data, usually utilizing an algorithm. For instance, in looking for addresses, alpha characters followed by a comma and a space, followed by two capital alpha characters, followed by a space, followed by five or more digits, are usually the city, state and zip code. By programming the application to look for a pattern, the information can be electronically identified, extracted, or otherwise utilized or manipulated.

Sedona Conference

Payload

1) The code of a virus that damages a computer system. 2) The input data to the CCM generation-encryption process that is both authenticated and encrypted. 3) The actual amount of data within a TCP/IP packet.

Network Frontiers, NIST 800 Series

Payment Card Industry (PCI)

A collaboration between Visa and MasterCard, that incorporated the CISP requirements into the Payment Card Industry (PCI) Data Security Standards (DSS) or PCI DSS, to create a common industry standard that is accepted internationally by all major credit card issuers. Currently, Visa maintains the standard and compliance program of PCI DSS.

PCI-DSS

Payment cardholder environment

That part of the network that possesses cardholder data or sensitive authentication data.

PCI-DSS

Payment gateway

A system that provides services to Internet merchants for the authorization and clearing of online Visa transactions.

VISA Glossary of Terms

Payment system

A financial system that establishes the means for transferring money between suppliers and users of funds, ordinarily by exchanging debits or credits between banks or financial institutions.

ISACA

Penetration

The successful act of bypassing the security mechanisms of a system or application. Unauthorized act of bypassing the security mechanisms of a system.

Centers for Medicare & Medicaid Services (CMS), PCI-DSS, US National Information Assurance (IA) Glossary

Penetration testing

Security testing in which evaluators attempt to circumvent the security features of a system based on their understanding of the system design and implementation so the tester can report

on the vulnerabilities and suggest steps to improve security. A live test of the effectiveness of security defenses through mimicking the actions of real-life attackers. Posing as either internal or external unauthorized intruders (or both, in different phases of the test), the test team attempts to obtain privileged access, extract information, and demonstrate the ability to manipulate the computer in what would be unauthorized ways if it had happened outside the scope of the test.

ISACA, Centers for Medicare & Medicaid Services (CMS), PCI-DSS, US National Information Assurance (IA) Glossary

People

People include staff skills, awareness, and productivity to plan, organize, acquire, deliver, support, and monitor information systems and services.

CobiT

People asset

The people in the enterprise, including their skills, training, knowledge, and experience.

CERT OCTAVE

Per-call key

Unique traffic encryption key generated automatically by certain secure telecommunications systems to secure single voice or data transmissions. See also co-operative key generation.

US National Information Assurance (IA) Glossary

Percentage utilization

The amount of time that a component is busy over a given period of time. For example, if a CPU is busy for 1800 seconds in a one hour period, its utilization is 50%.

ITIL

Performance

The actual implementation or achievement of a process. A measure of what is achieved or delivered by a person, team or process. Within capacity management, performance is a measure of the overall time taken to carry out one or more transactions. See also response time, throughput, KPI.

CobiT, ITIL

Performance indicators

A set of metrics designed to measure the extent to which performance objectives are being achieved on an on-going basis. They can include service level agreements, critical success factors, customer satisfaction ratings, internal or external benchmarks, industry best practices, and international standards.

ISACA

Performance management

The ability to manage any type of measurement including employee, team, process, operational or financial measurements. The term connotes closed-loop control and regular monitoring of the measurement, including threshold detection, performance analysis and tuning, and implementing changes related to performance and capacity.

CobiT, ITIL

Performance measure controls

Policies and procedures used to assure that data used to support performance measures reported in the MD&A of the accountability report are properly recorded, processed, and summarized to permit preparation of performance information in accordance with criteria stated by management.

GAO/PCIE Financial Audit Manual

Performance measures

An indicator used to quantify efficiency and/or effectiveness. An example of a performance measure is a KPI.

PAS 56

Performance monitor

Software that tracks and records the speed, reliability, and other service levels delivered by a computer system.

FISCAM

Performance testing

Comparing the system's performance to other equivalent systems using well defined benchmarks.

ISACA

Perimeter

Encompasses all those components of the system that are to be accredited by the DAA, and excludes separately accredited systems to which the system is connected.

US National Information Assurance (IA) Glossary

Perimeter firewall/VPN gateway

A security appliance added to the boundary of the network to screen out illegitimate traffic based on network security policies.

Network Frontiers

Periods processing

Processing of various levels of classified and unclassified information at distinctly different times. Under the concept of periods processing, the system must be purged of all information from one processing period before transitioning to the next.

US National Information Assurance (IA) Glossary

Peripheral

Hardware unit that is connected to and controlled by a computer but external to the CPU. These devices provide input, output, or storage capabilities when used in conjunction with a computer.

FISCAM, ISACA

Peripheral Component Interface (PCI)

A high-speed interconnect local bus used to support multimedia devices.

Sedona Conference

Permanent [sometimes also called Private] Virtual Circuit (PVC)

ISACA

Permanent Virtual Circuit

A permanent connection between hosts in a packet switched network.

ISACA

Permuter

Device used in crypto-equipment to change the order in which the contents of a shift register are used in various nonlinear combining circuits.

US National Information Assurance (IA) Glossary

Personal Computer (PC)

In most organizations this is a misnomer because the desktop computer doesn't actually belong to the person, but rather, the organization. You wouldn't know that when cleaning out the number of personal files and applications found within most desktop computers though.

NIST 800 series, Network Frontiers, Sedona Conference

Personal Computer Memory Card International Association (PCMCIA)

Plug-in cards for computers (usually portables), which extend the storage and/or functionality.

Sedona Conference

Personal data or personally identifiable information

Data (and compiled information) about an individual including, but not limited to, education, financial transactions, medical history, qualifications, service data, criminal record, or employment history which ties the data to the individual's name or an identifying number, symbol, or other identifying particular assigned to the individual. Includes all information covered by the Privacy Act of 1974 (e.g., salary data, social security information, passwords, user identifiers (IDs), EEO, personnel profile (including home address and phone number), medical history, employment history (general and security clearance information), and arrest/criminal investigation history). For example, a finger print,

voice print, or a photograph. See also confidential information.

Centers for Medicare & Medicaid Services (CMS)

Personal Digital Assistant (PDA)

A small, usually hand-held, computer which "assists" business tasks.

Sedona Conference

Personal Identification Number (PIN)

A type of password (i.e., a secret number assigned to an individual) that, in conjunction with some means of identifying the individual, serves to verify the authenticity of the individual. PINs have been adopted by financial institutions as the primary means of verifying customers in an electronic funds transfer system (EFTS).

ISACA, Centers for Medicare & Medicaid Services (CMS), PCI-DSS, NIST 800 Series, FIPS Pubs

Personal Identity Verification Authorizing Official

An individual who can act on behalf of an agency to authorize the issuance of a credential to an applicant.

NIST 800 series, FIPS Pubs

Personal Identity Verification Card (PIV Card)

Physical artifact (e.g., identity card, "smart" card) issued to an individual that contains stored identity credentials (e.g., photograph, cryptographic keys, digitized fingerprint representation etc.) such that a claimed identity of the cardholder may be verified against the stored credentials by another person (human readable and verifiable) or an automated process (computer readable and verifiable).

NIST 800 series, FIPS Pubs

Personal Identity Verification Issuance Authority

An authorized identity card creator that procures FIPS approved blank identity cards, initializes them with appropriate software and data elements for the requested identity verification and access control application, personalizes the card with the identity credentials of the authorized subject, and delivers the personalized card to the authorized subject along with appropriate instructions for protection and use.

NIST 800 series, FIPS Pubs

Personal Identity Verification Requesting Official

An individual who can act on behalf of an agency to request a credential for an applicant.

NIST 800 series, FIPS Pubs

Personnel controls

This type of control involves screening individuals prior to their authorization to access computer resources. Such screening should be commensurate with the risk and magnitude of the harm the individual could cause.

FISCAM, Centers for Medicare & Medicaid Services (CMS)

Personnel security

Procedures that are established to ensure that all personnel who have access to sensitive information have the required authority as well as appropriate clearances. Procedures to ensure a person's background is as presented; provide assurance of necessary trustworthiness. See also personnel controls.

FISCAM, Centers for Medicare & Medicaid Services (CMS)

Pervasive IS controls

General controls which are designed to manage and monitor the IS environment and which, therefore, affect all IS-related activities.

ISACA

Petabyte (PB)

A unit consisting of 1,000 or 1,024 tera-bytes. See also Byte.

Sedona Conference

Phase change

A method of storing information on rewritable optical discs.

Sedona Conference

Phishing

A form of online scam that attempts to trick people into disclosing private information, such as credit card numbers; well-known brands are often used to lure subjects to spoofed Web sites, or even hijacked domains, that look legitimate. Once there subjects are prompted for personal information.

Network Frontiers, NIST 800 Series

Physical access control

This type of control involves restricting physical access to computer resources and protecting these resources from intentional or unintentional loss or impairment.

FISCAM, Centers for Medicare & Medicaid Services (CMS)

Physical and environmental control

Protective mechanisms in the area where application processing takes place or for the general support system (e.g., locks on terminals, physical barriers around the building and processing area, air-conditioning, etc.) Factors to address include physical access, fire safety, failure of supporting utilities, structural collapse, plumbing leaks, interception of data, and mobile and portable systems.

Centers for Medicare & Medicaid Services (CMS)

Physical disk

An actual piece of computer media, such as the hard disk or drive, floppy discs, CDROM discs, Zip discs, etc.

Sedona Conference

Physical file space

When a file is created on a computer, a sufficient number of clusters (physical file space) are assigned to contain the file. If the file (logical file space) is not large enough to completely fill the assigned clusters (physical file space) then some unused space will exist within the physical file space. This unused space is referred to as file slack and can contain unused space, previously deleted/overwritten files or fragments thereof.

Sedona Conference

Physical intrusion

Unauthorized access to or use of physical resources including but not limited to facilities, wiring closets, and power supplies.

Centers for Medicare & Medicaid Services (CMS)

Physical security

See physical access control.

FISCAM, Centers for Medicare & Medicaid Services (CMS), ISO/IEC 27001:2005

Physically isolated network

A network that is not connected to entities or systems outside a physically controlled space.

NIST 800 series

PICA

One sixth (1/6) of an inch. Used to measure graphics/fonts. There are 12 points per pica; 6 picas per inch; 72 points per inch.

Sedona Conference

Pick-up response

An authorization response instructing a card-present merchant to refuse a transaction and recover the card. In all circumstances, card recovery should only be attempted if it can be done by reasonable and peaceful means.

VISA Glossary of Terms

Picture element (PIXEL)

The smallest addressable unit on a display screen. The higher the resolution (the more rows of columns), the more information can be displayed.

Sedona Conference

Piggy-backing

A method of gaining unauthorized access to a restricted area by entering after an authorized person but before the door closes and the lock resets. Piggybacking can also refer to the process of electronically attaching to an authorized telecommunications link to intercept transmissions.

FISCAM, ISACA

Pin Verification Value (PVV)

Encoded in magnetic stripe of payment card.

PCI-DSS

Pitch

Characters (or dots) per inch, measured horizontally.

Sedona Conference

PKI digital signature

A document or file may be digitally signed using a party's private signature key, creating a "digital signature" that is stored with the document. Anyone can validate the signature on the document using the public key from the digital certificate issued to the signer. Validating the digital signature confirms who signed it, and ensures that no alterations have been made to the document since it was signed. Similarly, an e-mail message may be digitally signed using commonly available client software that implements an open standard for this purpose, such as Secure Multipurpose Internet Mail Extensions (S/MIME). Validating the signature on the e-mail can help the recipient know with confidence who sent it, and that it was not altered during transmission. See also Certificate.

Sedona Conference

Plain text

Unencrypted information.

US National Information Assurance (IA) Glossary

Plaintext

The least formatted and therefore most portable form of text for computerized documents. The original, pre-encrypted form of a message. See also cleartext.

ISACA, Workgroup for Electronic Data Interchange, Sedona Conference, NIST 800 Series, FIPS Pubs

Plaintext key

An unencrypted cryptographic key.

NIST 800 series, FIPS Pubs

Plan

A document which identifies a series of activities and the resources required to achieve an objective. For example, a plan to implement a new IT service or process. ISO/IEC 20000 requires a plan for the management of each IT service management process. See also project.

ITIL, ISO/IEC 27001:2005

Plan Do Check Act (PDCA)

A four stage cycle for process management, devised by W. Edwards Deming. Plan Do Check Act is also called the Deming cycle. Plan: design or revise processes that support the IT services. Do: implement the plan and manage the processes. Check: measure the processes and IT services, compare with objectives and produce reports. Act: plan and implement changes to improve the processes. See also Plan Do Check Act model.

ISO/IEC 27001:2005, ITIL

Plan Do Check Act model

Plan establishes policy, objectives, processes, and procedures relevant to managing risk and improving information security to deliver results in accordance with an organization's overall policies and objectives. Do implements and operate the policy, controls, processes, and procedures. Check assesses and, where applicable, measure process performance against ISMS policy, objectives and practical experience and report the results to management for review. Act takes corrective and preventive actions, based on the results of the internal ISMS audit and management review or other relevant information, to achieve continual improvement.

ISO/IEC 27001:2005

Plan of Action and Milestones (POA&M)

A document that identifies tasks needing to be accomplished. It details resources required to accomplish the elements of the plan, any milestones in meeting the tasks, and scheduled completion dates for the milestones.

NIST 800 series, OMB Memorandum 02-01

Planned downtime

Agreed time when an IT service will not be available. Planned downtime is often used for maintenance, upgrades, and testing. See also change slot, downtime.

ITIL

Planning

An activity responsible for creating one or more plans. For example, capacity planning.

ITIL

Planning and organization

A high-level IT control domain that covers strategy and tactics, and concerns the identification of the way IT can best contribute to the achievement of the business objectives. Furthermore, the realization of the strategic vision needs to be planned, communicated and managed for different perspectives. Finally, a proper organization as well as technological infrastructure must be put in place.

CobiT

Planning materiality

The auditor's judgment of the total amount of misstatements that would be material in relation to the financial statements to be audited; used for planning the audit scope. The auditor determines an appropriate base (usually the greater of assets, liabilities, revenues, or expenses); then the auditor multiplies by a percent, usually 3 percent.

GAO/PCIE Financial Audit Manual

Platform

The foundation technology of a computer system. Typically, a specific combination of hardware and operating system.

FISCAM

Platter

One of several components that make up a computer hard drive. Platters are thin, rapidly rotating discs that have a set of read/write heads on both sides of each platter. Each platter is divided into a series of concentric rings called tracks. Each track is further divided into sections called sectors, and each sector is sub-divided into bytes.

Sedona Conference

Point estimate

Most likely amount of the population characteristic based on the sample.

GAO/PCIE Financial Audit Manual

Point of Presence (PoP)

A phone number that represents the area in which the communications provider or Internet service provider (ISP) provides service.

ISACA

Point of Sale system (POS)

Point-of-sale systems enable capture of data at the time and place of transaction. POS terminals may include use of optical scanners for use with bar codes or magnetic card readers for use with credit cards. POS systems may be online to a central computer or may use stand-alone terminals or microcomputers that hold the transactions until the end of a specified period when they are sent to the main computer for batch processing.

ISACA, PCI-DSS

Point to Point Protocol (PPP)

A protocol used for transmitting data between two ends of a connection.

ISACA

Point to Point Tunneling Protocol (PPTP)

A protocol used to transmit data securely between two end points to create a VPN.

ISACA

Point-of-sale terminal

Part of a POS System, the electronic device used for authorizing and processing bankcard transactions at the point of sale.

VISA Glossary of Terms

Pointer

A pointer is an index entry in the directory of a disk (or other storage medium) that identifies the space on the disk in which an electronic document or piece of electronic data resides, thereby preventing that space from being overwritten by other data. In most cases, when an electronic document is "deleted," the pointer is deleted, which allows the document to be overwritten, but the document is not actually erased.

Sedona Conference

Policy

Organization-wide rules governing acceptable use of computing resources, security practices, and guiding development of operational procedures. A policy is a definitive plan or method of action to guide decisions and actions. Policies are always selected from the various possible alternatives in the light of organizational conditions and the impact they will have. Policies are meant to limit individual discretion to make decisions about which choices and actions (or behaviors) can be taken regarding the topic in question. Because of this, a policy's intended purpose is to influence and guide both present and future decision making to be in line with the philosophy, objectives and strategic plans established by the enterprise's management teams. In addition to policy content, policies need to describe the consequences of failing to comply with the policy, the means for handling exceptions, and the manner in which compliance with the policy will be checked and measured. In practice, an organizational policy is a formal document describing the organization's position on a particular aspect of compliance with regulations, standards, and guidelines. Therefore, it acts as an official statement of a position, plan or course of action established by an identified sponsoring authority, which is designed to influence, to provide direction and to determine decisions and actions with regard to a specific topic. Organizational standards, procedures and guidelines flow from policies. Policies come in two basic forms; high-level policy statements and detailed policies.

Network Frontiers, Centers for Medicare & Medicaid Services (CMS), CobiT, PCI-DSS, ITIL, NIST 800 Series

Policy Approving Authority

First level of the PKI Certification Management Authority that approves the security policy of each PCA.

US National Information Assurance (IA) Glossary

Policy Certification Authority (PCA)

Second level of the PKI Certification Management Authority that formulates the security policy under which it and its subordinate CAs will issue public key certificates.

US National Information Assurance (IA) Glossary

Policy guideline

An example of how a policy might be applied to a specific situation. An outline or checklist of detailed procedures recommended to satisfy a policy.

Centers for Medicare & Medicaid Services (CMS)

Policy Management Authority (PMA)

Body established to oversee the creation and update of Certificate Policies, review Certification Practice Statements, review the results of CA audits for policy compliance, evaluate non-domain policies for acceptance within the domain, and generally oversee and manage the PKI certificate policies. For the FBCA, the PMA is the Federal PKI Policy Authority.

NIST 800 series

Policy mapping

Recognizing that, when a CA in one domain certifies a CA in another domain, a particular certificate policy in the second domain may be considered by the authority of the first domain to be equivalent (but not necessarily identi-

cal in all respects) to a particular certificate policy in the first domain.

NIST 800 series

Polymorphic virus

A virus that changes it surface characteristics with each replication; functionality does not change.

Network Frontiers

Polymorphism [objects]

Polymorphism refers to database structures that send the same command to different child objects that can produce different results depending on their family hierarchical tree structure.

ISACA

Population

The items comprising a financial statement line item, account balance, or class of transactions from which selections are made for audit testing. The entire set of data from which a sample is selected and about which the IS auditor wishes to draw conclusions.

GAO/PCIE Financial Audit Manual, ISACA

Port

1) An interface between the CPU of the computer and a peripheral device that governs and synchronizes the flow of data between the CPU and the external device. 2) A physical entry or exit point

of a cryptographic module that provides access to the module for physical signals, represented by logical information flows (physically separated ports do not share the same physical pin or wire).

FISCAM, ISACA, Centers for Medicare & Medicaid Services (CMS), NIST 800 Series, FIPS Pubs

Port Address Translation (PAT)

Feature of a network address translation (NAT) device that translates transmission control protocol (TCP) or user datagram protocol (UDP) connections made to a host and port on an outside network to a host and port on an inside network.

PCI-DSS

Port scanning

Using a program to remotely determine which ports on a system are open (e.g., whether systems allow connections through those ports).

NIST 800 series

Portable Document Format (PDF)

An imaging file format technology developed by Adobe Systems. PDF captures formatting information from a variety of applications in such a way that they can be viewed and printed as they were intended in their original application by practically any computer, on multiple platforms, regardless of the specific application in which the original was created. PDF files may be text-searchable or image-only. Adobe® Reader, a free application distributed by Adobe Systems, is required to view a file in PDF format. Adobe® Acrobat, an application marketed by Adobe Systems, is required to edit, capture text, or otherwise manipulate a file in PDF format.

Sedona Conference

Portable facility

A prefabricated building, or a large vehicle, provided by a third party and moved to a site when needed by an IT service continuity plan. See also recovery option, fixed facility.

ITIL

Portable volumes

A feature that facilitates the moving of large volumes of documents without requiring copying multiple files. Portable volumes enable individual CDs to be easily regrouped, detached and reattached to different databases for a broader information exchange.

Sedona Conference

Portfolio

A grouping of programs, projects, services or assets selected, managed and monitored to optimize business return. See also portfolio management.

CobiT

Portfolio management

The process responsible for managing the portfolio of services. Portfolio management includes maximizing the value to the business of existing and proposed new IT services and identifying the need to create new IT services and retire IT services that are no longer of value. The detailed planning and implementation work is carried out as part of the service planning process.

ITIL

Portfolio of services

A published description of all IT services. The portfolio is maintained by the service provider and includes all IT services whether they are live, in development, or proposed new services. See also service catalogue, application portfolio.

ITIL

Portrait mode

A display where the height exceeds the width.

Sedona Conference

Positive control material

Generic term referring to a sealed authenticator system, permissive action link, coded switch system, positive enable system, or nuclear command and control documents, material, or devices.

US National Information Assurance (IA) Glossary

Post Implementation Review (PIR)

A review that takes place after a change or a project has been implemented. A PIR determines if the change or project was successful and identifies opportunities for improvement.

ITIL

Posting

The process of actually entering transactions into computerized or manual files. Such transactions might immediately update the master files or may result in memo posting, in which the transactions are accumulated over a period of time, then applied to master file updating.

ISACA

Potential impact

The loss of confidentiality, integrity, or availability could be expected to have a limited adverse effect, a serious adverse effect, or a severe or catastrophic adverse effect on organizational operations, organizational assets, or individuals.

FIPS Pubs, NIST 800 Series

Practice statement

A formal statement of the practices followed by an authentication entity (e.g., RA, CSP, or verifier); typically the specific steps taken to register and verify identities, issue credentials and authenticate claimants.

NIST 800 series

Precision

The difference between the point estimate and the upper or lower limit. Thus, precision tells the auditor how close the point estimate could be from the true population amount.

GAO/PCIE Financial Audit Manual

Precursor

A sign that an attacker may be preparing to cause an incident.

NIST 800 series

Predicated rules

A predicate rule includes any requirements set forth in the Federal Food, Drug and Cosmetic Act, the PHS Act (Public Health Service Act), or any FDA regulation (GxP: GLP, GMP, GCP, etc.). Predicate rules mandate what records must be maintained, the content of records, whether signatures are required, how long records must be maintained, etc.

21 CFR Part 11

Preliminary analytical procedures

Analytical procedures performed during the audit planning phase.

GAO/PCIE Financial Audit Manual

Premaster secret

A client-generated, 48-byte secret key that is encrypted under the public key from the server's certificate.

Network Frontiers

Preproduction model

Version of INFOSEC equipment employing standard parts and suitable for complete evaluation of form, design, and performance. Preproduction models are often referred to as beta models.

US National Information Assurance (IA) Glossary

Preservation

The processes and operations involved in ensuring the technical and intellectual survival of authentic records through time. The range of activities associated with maintaining archival materials in a useable state, either in their original physical form or in some other useable way. Preservation encompasses a wide range of areas – from storage materials and conditions, to handling issues, to the unique problems associated with the preservation of electronic records. Intensive "hands on" conservation, the function most associated with preservation, is really only a small part of the picture. See also Spoliation.

ISO 15489, DIRKS, Sedona Conference

Preservation Notice

See Legal hold.

Sedona Conference

Preservation Order

See Legal hold.

Sedona Conference

President's Council on Integrity and Efficiency (PCIE)

The President's Council on Integrity and Efficiency (PCIE) and the Executive Council on Integrity and Efficiency (ECIE) were established by Executive Order 12805, May 11, 1992, to: 1) address integrity, economy, and effectiveness issues that transcend individual Government agencies, and 2) increase the professionalism and effectiveness of IG personnel throughout the Government. See also

http://www.ignet.gov/pcieecie1.html for more information.

GAO/PCIE Financial Audit Manual

Pretty Good Privacy (PGP)

A popular homegrown public key cryptosystem first released in 1991. Originally freeware, both free and commercial versions are available.

Workgroup for Electronic Data Interchange

Preventive controls

These controls are designed to prevent or restrict an error, omission, or unauthorized intrusion. An internal control that is used to prevent undesirable events, errors, and other occurrences that an organization has determined could have a negative material effect on a process or end product.

ISACA, CobiT

Price Risk

Is the risk to earnings or capital arising from changes in the value of portfolios of financial instruments. Price risk arises from market making, dealing, and position taking in interest rate, foreign exchange, equity and commodities markets. Banks may be exposed to price risk if they create or expand deposit brokering, loan sales, or securitization programs as a result of Internet banking activities.

ISACA

Pricing

Pricing is the activity for establishing how much customers will be charged. See also billing, charging process.

ITIL

Primary Account Number (PAN)

The payment card number (credit or debit) that identifies the issuer and the particular cardholder account. Also called Account Number.

PCI-DSS

Principal

An entity whose identity can be authenticated.

NIST 800 series, FIPS Pubs

Principal Accrediting Authority (PAA)

Senior official with authority and responsibility for all intelligence systems within an agency.

US National Information Assurance (IA) Glossary

Principal Certification Authority (CA)

The Principal Certification Authority is a CA designated by an Agency to interoperate with the FBCA. An Agency may designate multiple Principal CAs to interoperate with the FBCA.

NIST 800 series

Principal statements

See financial statements.

GAO/PCIE Financial Audit Manual

Print On Demand (POD)

Document images are stored in electronic format and are available to be quickly printed and in the exact quantity required, long or short runs.

Sedona Conference

Print suppression

Eliminating the display of characters in order to preserve their secrecy.

US National Information Assurance (IA) Glossary

Printed number

A four-digit number that is printed below the first four digits of the printed or embossed account number on all valid Visa cards. The four-digit printed number should begin with a "4", and be the same as the first four digits of the account number above it. The printed four-digit number is one of the card security features that merchants should check to ensure that a card-present transaction is valid.

VISA Glossary of Terms

Printout

A printed version of text of data, another term for which is hard copy.

Sedona Conference

Prioritized Requirements

The subset of implicit and explicit re-cordkeeping requirements identified from sources in DIRKS Step C that an organization prioritizes as essential to meet after it has undertaken a risk-based assessment.

DIRKS

Priority

A category used to identify the relative importance of an incident, problem or change. Priority is based on impact and urgency and is used to identify required times for actions to be taken. For example, the SLA may state that priority 2 incidents must be resolved within 12 hours.

ITIL

Privacy

Freedom from unauthorized intrusion. The right of individuals to control or influence information that is related to them in terms of who may collect or store it and to whom that information may be disclosed. The individual's right to privacy must be protected in Federal Government information activities involving personal information. Such information is to be collected, maintained, and protected so as to preclude intrusion into the privacy of individuals and the unwarranted disclosure of personal information.

ISACA, OMB Circular A-130, Centers for Medicare & Medicaid Services (CMS), NIST 800 Series

Privacy Act

The privacy to which individuals are entitled under 5 U.S.C. Section 552a but that has not been specifically authorized under criteria established by an Executive Order or an Act of Congress to be kept secret in the interest of national defense or foreign policy.

Centers for Medicare & Medicaid Services (CMS)

Privacy Act data

Personal data, which includes information pertaining to an individual's health or physical condition, job performance, investigatory or personal information about individuals that could cause embarrassment or damage to their reputations.

Centers for Medicare & Medicaid Services (CMS)

Privacy impact assessment

An analysis of how information is handled: 1) to ensure handling conforms to applicable legal, regulatory, and policy requirements regarding privacy; 2) to determine the risks and effects of collecting, maintaining and disseminating information in identifiable form in an electronic information system; and 3) to examine and evaluate protections and alternative processes for handling information to mitigate potential privacy risks.

NIST 800 series, OMB Memorandum 03-22

Privacy system

Commercial encryption system that affords telecommunications limited protection to deter a casual listener, but cannot withstand a technically competent cryptanalytic attack.

US National Information Assurance (IA) Glossary

Private Key

The private part of a two-part, public key cryptography system which is kept secret and never transmitted over a net-

work. Used to create digital signatures and, depending upon the algorithm, to decrypt messages or files encrypted (for confidentiality) with the corresponding public key. Depending on the algorithm, the private key may be used to: 1) compute the corresponding public key, 2) compute a digital signature that may be verified by the corresponding public key, 3) decrypt data that was encrypted by the corresponding public key, or 4) compute a piece of common shared data, together with other information.

Network Frontiers, ISACA, NIST 800 Series, FIPS Pubs

Private key cryptographic systems

Used in data encryption, it uses a secret key to encrypt the plaintext to the ciphertext. It also uses the same key to decrypt the ciphertext to the corresponding plaintext. In this case, the key is symmetric such that the encryption key is equivalent to the decryption key.

ISACA

Private network

A network that is connected to the Internet but is isolated from the Internet with security measures allowing use of the network only by persons within the private network.

Sedona Conference

Privilege

The level of trust with which a system object is imbued.

ISACA

Privilege data set

The universe of documents identified as responsive and/or relevant, but withheld from production on the grounds of attorney-client privilege or work product.

Sedona Conference

Privileged access

Can bypass, modify, or disable the technical or operational system security controls.

Centers for Medicare & Medicaid Services (CMS)

Privileged accounts

Individuals who have access to set "access rights" for users on a given system. Sometimes referred to as system or network administrative accounts.

NIST 800 series

Privileged user

Individual who has access to system control, monitoring, or administration functions (e.g., system administrator, system ISSO, maintainers, system programmers, etc.

US National Information Assurance (IA) Glossary

Privileges

Set of access rights permitted by the access control system. The rights to alter, circumvent, override, or bypass the operating system or system security measures. See also privilege.

FISCAM, Centers for Medicare & Medicaid Services (CMS)

Proactive problem management

Part of the problem management process. The objective of proactive problem management is to identify problems that might otherwise be missed. Proactive problem management analyzes incident records and uses data collected by other IT service management processes to identify trends or significant problems.

ITIL

Probable

The chance of the future confirming event(s) occurring is likely for pending or threatened litigation and unasserted claims. For other contingencies, the future event or events are more likely than not to occur.

GAO/PCIE Financial Audit Manual

Probe

Attempt to gather information about an information system or its users.

Centers for Medicare & Medicaid Services (CMS), US National Information Assurance (IA) Glossary

Problem

Unknown underlying cause of one or more incidents. The root cause of one or more incidents. See also problem management, problem record.

CobiT, ITIL

Problem control

Part of the problem management process. Problem control is the activity responsible for identifying the root cause and developing a workaround or structural solution for a problem. See also error control.

ITIL

Problem management

The process responsible for managing the lifecycle of all problems. The primary objectives of problem management are to prevent incidents from happening and to minimize the impact of incidents that cannot be prevented. Problem management includes problem control, error control, and proactive problem management.

ITIL

Problem record

A record containing the details of a problem. Each problem record documents the lifecycle of a single problem.

ITIL

Procedure

A step-by-step description of tasks required to support and carry out organizational policy. The extended portion of a policy that states the general process that will be performed to accomplish a goal. Procedures are the step-by-step documented form of controls, or the course of action to be taken to perform a given task as a series of steps followed in a definite regular order ensuring the consistent and repetitive approach to actions.

Network Frontiers, ISACA, Centers for Medicare & Medicaid Services (CMS), CobiT, PCI-DSS, ITIL

Process

Generally, a collection of procedures influenced by the organization's policies and standards that takes inputs from a number of sources, including other processes, manipulates the inputs, and produces outputs, including other processes, for process customers. A process may include any of the roles, responsibilities, tools and management controls required. Processes have clear business reasons for existing, accountable owners, clear roles and responsibilities around the execution of the process, and the means to measure performance. See also business process, vital business function, value chain.

CobiT, ITIL

Process approach

An organization needs to identify and manage many activities in order to function effectively. Any activity using resources and managed in order to enable the transformation of inputs into outputs can be considered to be a process. Often the output from one process directly forms the input to the next process. The application of a system of processes within an organization, together with the identification and interactions of these processes, and their management, can be referred to as a "process approach.".

ISO/IEC 27001:2005

Process control

The activity of planning and regulating a process, with the objective of performing it in an effective, efficient, and consistent manner.

ITIL

Process manager

A role responsible for operational management of a process. The process manager's responsibilities include planning and coordination of all activities required to carry out, monitor and report on the process. There may be several process managers for one process, for example, regional change managers or IT service continuity managers for each data center. The process manager role is often assigned to the person who carries out the process owner role, but the two roles may be separate in larger organizations.

ITIL

Process maturity

A measure of how reliable, efficient and effective a process is, and of how well it is integrated with other processes. The most mature processes are formally aligned to business objectives and strategy and are supported by a framework for continuous improvement.

ITIL

Process owner

A role responsible for ensuring that a process is fit for purpose. The process owner's responsibilities include sponsorship, design, and change management of the process and its metrics. This role is often assigned to the same person who carries out the process manager role, but the two roles may be separate in larger organizations.

ITIL

Processing

The execution of program instructions by the computer's central processing unit.

FISCAM, Centers for Medicare & Medicaid Services (CMS)

Processing data

In the context of this document, synonymous with Image processing.

Sedona Conference

Processor

In Payment Card Industry terminology, a Member, or credit card issuer-approved non-member acting as the agent of a Member, that provides authorization, clearing, or settlement services for merchants and processors: authorizing processors, clearing processors, and V.I.P. system users. See also: VisaNet processor.

VISA Glossary of Terms

Production

The process of delivering to another party, or making available for that party's review, documents deemed responsive to a discovery request.

Sedona Conference

Production control and scheduling

Methods used for the marking, handling, processing, storage, and disposal of input and output information and media, as well as labeling and distribution procedures for the information and media. The function responsible for monitoring the information into, through, and as it leaves the computer operations area and for determining the succession of programs to be run on the computer. Often, an automated scheduling package is utilized in this task.

FISCAM, Centers for Medicare & Medicaid Services (CMS)

Production data

The data that supports the agency's operational information processing activities. It is maintained in the production environment as opposed to the test environment. This is not the same as the e-discovery term of Production data set.

FISCAM

Production data set

The universe of documents identified as responsive to document requests and not withheld on the grounds of attorney-client privilege or work product.

Sedona Conference

Production de-duplication

Removal of a document if multiple copies of that document reside within the same production set. For example, if two identical documents are both marked responsive, non-privileged, production de-duplication ensures that only one of those documents is produced. See also De-duplication.

Sedona Conference

Production environment

The system environment where the organization performs its operational information processing activities.

FISCAM, Centers for Medicare & Medicaid Services (CMS)

Production model

INFOSEC equipment in its final mechanical and electrical form.

US National Information Assurance (IA) Glossary

Production number

Often referred to as the BATES number. A sequential number assigned to every page of a production for tracking and reference purposes. Often used in conjunction with a suffix or prefix to identify the producing party, the litigation, or other relevant information. See also Bates number.

Sedona Conference

Production programs

Programs that are being used and executed to support authorized organizational operations. Programs that are used to process live or actual data that were received as input into the production environment. Such programs are distinguished from "test" programs which are being developed or modified but have not yet been authorized for use by management.

FISCAM, ISACA, Centers for Medicare & Medicaid Services (CMS)

Production software

See production programs.

ISACA

Products and services

The beneficial outcomes provided to customers or recipients, for example manufactured items, car insurance, regulatory compliance and community nursing.

BS 25999

Professional competence

Proven level of ability, often linked to qualifications issued by relevant professional bodies and compliance with their codes of practice and standards.

ISACA

Profile

A set of rules that describes the nature and extent of access to available resources for a user or a group of users with similar duties, such as accounts payable clerks. See also standard profile and user profile.

FISCAM, Centers for Medicare & Medicaid Services (CMS)

Profiling

Measuring the characteristics of expected activity so that changes to it can be more easily identified.

NIST 800 series

Profit center

A business unit which charges for services provided. A profit center can be created with the objective of making a profit, recovering costs, or running at a loss. An IT service provider can be run as a cost center or a profit center.

ITIL

Program

A set of related instructions that, when followed and executed by a computer, perform operations or tasks. Application programs, user programs, system programs, source programs, and object programs are all software programs. A structured grouping of interdependent projects that includes the full scope of business, process, people, technology and organizational activities that are required (both necessary and sufficient) to achieve a clearly specified business outcome. See also Application, Software.

FISCAM, Centers for Medicare & Medicaid Services (CMS), CobiT, ITIL, Sedona Conference

Program Evaluation and Review Technique (PERT)

A project management technique used in the planning and control of system projects.

ISACA

Program flowcharts

Program flowcharts show the sequence of instructions in a single program or subroutine. The symbols used should be the internationally accepted standard. Program flowcharts should be updated when necessary.

ISACA

Program library

See library.

FISCAM, Centers for Medicare & Medicaid Services (CMS)

Program library software

A system that allows control and maintenance of programs for tracking purposes. The systems usually provide security, check out controls for programs, and on-line directories for information on the programs.

FISCAM

Program narratives

Program narratives provide a detailed explanation of program flowcharts, including control points and any external input.

ISACA

Program Properties Table (PPT)

A facility provided by IBM to identify programs that require special properties when invoked in an MVS environment. Although special properties may be required for an application to run efficiently, certain special properties also have security implications because they may allow the programs to bypass security authorization checking.

FISCAM

Programme

See the second definition of program.

CobiT

Programmer

A person who designs, codes, tests, debugs, and documents computer programs.

FISCAM, Centers for Medicare & Medicaid Services (CMS)

Project

A structured set of activities concerned with delivering to the enterprise a defined capability (that is necessary but not sufficient to achieve a required business outcome) based on an agreed-upon schedule and budget.

CobiT

Project Management Body of Knowledge (PMBOK)

A project management standard developed by the Project Management Institute (PMI).

CobiT

Project Management Institute (PMI)

The Project Management Institute is focused on the needs of project management professionals worldwide with more than 200,000 professionals in 125 countries. See also http://www.pmi.org for more information.

CobiT

Project Management Officer (PMO)

CobiT

Project Manager

Acts on behalf of the entire organization when planning, directing, or controlling the project within an authorized cost and timeframe. Agrees on the terms of reference to be used. Sets up the project program and plans. Reviews and controls the costs and progress of the project. Liaises between all parties involved. Reports on all progress and costs. Conducts a post-implementation review. Therefore, the project manager should possess good leadership qualities, a good understanding of the organization's business processes and business management, and have solid IT experience in information security, asset management, and contingency practices and planning.

CERT OCTAVE, Centers for Medicare & Medicaid Services (CMS), ISACA, ISO/IEC 27001:2005

Project Officer

CMS official (generally located in central office business components) responsible for the oversight of other business partners. These include Common Working File (CWF) Host Sites, Durable Medical Equipment Regional Carriers (DMERCs), standard claims processing system maintainers, Regional Laboratory Carriers, and claims processing data centers.

Centers for Medicare & Medicaid Services (CMS)

Project sponsor

Considered for acquisition the person responsible for high-level decisions, such as changes to the scope and/or

budget of the project, and whether or not to implement.

ISACA

Project team

Group of people responsible for a project whose terms of reference may include the development, acquisition, implementation, or maintenance of an application system. The team members may include line management, operational line staff, external contractors, and IS auditors.

ISACA

Projected misstatement

An estimate of the misstatement in a population, based on the misstatements found in the examined sample items; represents misstatements that are probable. The projected misstatement includes the known misstatement.

GAO/PCIE Financial Audit Manual

Projected Service Availability (PSA)

A document that identifies the effect of planned changes on agreed service levels, based on the Forward Schedule of Change (FSC).

ITIL

PRojects IN Controlled Environments (PRINCE2)

The standard UK government methodology for project management. See also http://www.OGC.gov.UK/prince2/ for more information.

ITIL

Promiscuous code

Allows the network interface to capture all network traffic irrespective of the hardware device to which the packet is addressed.

ISACA

Proof of Possession Protocol (PoP Protocol)

A protocol where a claimant proves to a verifier that he/she possesses and controls a token (e.g., a key or password).

NIST 800 series

Properties

Fields of electronic information, or "metadata," associated with a record or document such as creation date, author, date modified, blind cc's and date received.

Sedona Conference

Property, plant, and equipment (PP&E)

GAO/PCIE Financial Audit Manual

Proportionality

Systems continuity levels, costs, measures, practices, and procedures should be appropriate and proportionate to the value of and degree of reliance on the information systems and to the severity, probability, and extent of potential harm.

NIST 800 series

Proprietary

Privately owned, based on trade secrets, privately developed technology, or specifications that the owner refuses to divulge, thus preventing others from duplicating a product or program unless an explicit license is purchased.

FISCAM, Centers for Medicare & Medicaid Services (CMS)

Proprietary information

Material and information relating to or associated with a company's products, business, or activities, including but not limited to financial information; data or statements; trade secrets; product research and development; existing and future product designs and performance specifications; marketing plans or techniques; schematics; client lists; computer programs; processes; and know-how that has been clearly identified and properly marked by the company as proprietary information, trade secrets, or company confidential information. The information must have been developed by the company and not be available to the Government or to the public without restriction from another source.

US National Information Assurance (IA) Glossary

Protected Distribution Systems

Wire line or fiber optic distribution system used to transmit unencrypted classified national security information through an area of lesser classification or control.

US National Information Assurance (IA) Glossary

Protected Health Information (PHI)

PHI is any information created or received by a healthcare provider and re-lating to past, present, or future physical or mental health condition of an individual.

Workgroup for Electronic Data Interchange

Protection domain

The area of the system that the intrusion detection system is meant to monitor and protect.

ISACA

Protection philosophy

Informal description of the overall design of an information system delineating each of the protection mechanisms employed. Combination of formal and informal techniques, appropriate to the evaluation class, used to show the mechanisms are adequate to enforce the security policy.

US National Information Assurance (IA) Glossary

Protection profile

Common Criteria specification that represents an implementation-independent set of security requirements for a category of Target of Evaluations (TOE) that meets specific consumer needs.

US National Information Assurance (IA) Glossary

Protection ring

One of a hierarchy of privileged modes of an information system that gives certain access rights to user programs and processes that are authorized to operate in a given mode.

US National Information Assurance (IA) Glossary

Protection Strategy

Defines the strategies that an organization uses to enable, initiate, implement, and maintain its internal security. It tends to incorporate long-term, organization-wide initiatives.

CERT OCTAVE

Protection strategy practice

Actions that help initiate, implement, and maintain security within an organization. A protection strategy practice is also called a security practice.

CERT OCTAVE

Protective distribution system

Wire line or fiber optic system that includes adequate safeguards and/or countermeasures (e.g., acoustic, electric, electromagnetic, and physical) to permit its use for the transmission of unencrypted information.

NIST 800 series

Protective packaging

Packaging techniques for COMSEC material that discourage penetration, reveal a penetration has occurred or was attempted, or inhibit viewing or copying of keying material prior to the time it is exposed for use.

US National Information Assurance (IA) Glossary

Protective technologies

Special tamper-evident features and materials employed for the purpose of detecting tampering and deterring attempts to compromise, modify, penetrate, extract, or substitute information processing equipment and keying material.

US National Information Assurance (IA) Glossary

Protocol

In data communications and networking, a standard that specifies the format of data as well as the rules to be followed when performing specific functions such as establishing a connection and exchanging data. The rules by which a network operates and controls the flow and priority of transmissions.

FISCAM, ISACA, Centers for Medicare & Medicaid Services (CMS), PCI-DSS, US National Information Assurance (IA) Glossary, Sedona Conference

Protocol converter

Hardware devices, such as asynchronous and synchronous transmissions, that convert between two different types of transmission.

ISACA

Protocol data unit

A unit of data specified in a protocol and consisting of protocol information and, possibly, user data.

NIST 800 series, FIPS Pubs

Protocol entity

Entity that follows a set of rules and formats (semantic and syntactic) that determines the communication behavior of other entities.

NIST 800 series, FIPS Pubs

Protocol run

An instance of the exchange of messages between a claimant and a verifier in a defined authentication protocol that results in the authentication (or authentication failure) of the claimant.

NIST 800 series

Protocol stack

A set of utilities that implement a particular network protocol. For instance, in Windows machines a TCP/IP stack consists of TCP/IP software, sockets software, and hardware driver software.

ISACA

Prototyping

A system development technique in which a working model of a new computer system or program is created for testing and refinement. Prototyping enables users and developers to reach agreement on system requirements. Prototyping uses programmed simulation techniques to represent a model of the final system to the user for advisement and critique. The emphasis is on end-user screens and reports. Internal controls are not a priority item since this is only a model.

FISCAM, ISACA

Provider

Any Medicare provider (e.g., hospital, skilled nursing facility, home health organization, outpatient physical therapy, comprehensive outpatient rehabilitation facility, end-stage renal disease facility, hospice, physician, non-physician provider, laboratory, supplier, etc.) providing medical services covered under Medicare Part B. Any organization, institution, or individual that provides health care services to Medicare beneficiaries. Physicians, ambulatory surgical centers, and outpatient clinics are some of the providers of services covered under Medicare Part B.

HIPAA

Providing agency

The agency providing services, products, goods, transfer funds, investments, debt, and/or incurring the reimbursable costs. This includes bureaus, departments, and/or programs within agencies. The providing agency is the seller. The providing agency is the agency transferring out funds to another agency (transfers-out) when appropriations are transferred without the exchange of goods or services.

GAO/PCIE Financial Audit Manual

Proximity search

For text searches, the ability to look for words or phrases within a prescribed distance of another word or phrase, such as "accident" within 5 words of "tire."

Sedona Conference

Proxy

Software agent that performs a function or operation on behalf of another application or system while hiding the details involved. A proxy is an application that "breaks" the connection between client and server. The proxy accepts certain types of traffic entering or leaving a network and processes it and forwards it. This effectively closes the straight path between the internal and external networks. Making it more difficult for an attacker to obtain internal addresses and other details of the organization's internal network. Proxy servers are available for common Internet services; for example, an Hyper Text Transfer Protocol (HTTP) proxy used for Web access, and an Simple Mail Transfer Protocol (SMTP) proxy used for e-mail.

US National Information Assurance (IA) Glossary, NIST 800 Series

Proxy agent

A proxy agent is a software application running on a firewall or on a dedicated proxy server that is capable of filtering a protocol and routing it to between the interfaces of the device.

NIST 800 series

Proxy Server

A server that acts as an intermediary between two computer systems engaged in network communication. The proxy server accepts service requests to and from client computers (computers placed behind and protected by the proxy server), and makes the connection to the desired destination on behalf of the requesting party. Typical proxies accept a connection from a user, make a decision as to whether or not the user or client IP address is permitted to use the proxy, perhaps perform additional authentication, and complete a connection to a remote destination on behalf of the user.

ISACA, Centers for Medicare & Medicaid Services (CMS), NIST 800 Series

Pseudonym

A subscriber name that has been chosen by the subscriber that is not verified as meaningful by identity proofing.

NIST 800 series

Pseudorandom number generator (PRNG)

An algorithm that produces a sequence of bits that are uniquely determined from an initial value called a seed. The output of the PRNG "appears" to be random, i.e., the output is statistically indistinguishable from random values. A cryptographic PRNG has the additional property that the output is unpredictable, given that the seed is not known.

NIST 800 series

PST

A Microsoft Outlook e-mail store. Multiple .pst files may exist and contain archived e-mail.

Sedona Conference

Public access controls

A subset of access controls that apply when an organization application promotes or permits public access. These controls protect the integrity of the application and public confidence in the application and include segregating the information made directly available to the public from official organization records.

FISCAM, Centers for Medicare & Medicaid Services (CMS)

Public Company Accounting Oversight Board (PCAOB)

The PCAOB is a private-sector, non-profit corporation, created by the Sarbanes-Oxley Act of 2002, to oversee the auditors of public companies in order to protect the interests of investors and further the public interest in the preparation of informative, fair, and independent audit reports. See also http://www.pcaobus.org for more information.

de facto

Public Display of Affection (PDA)

A sure-fire way to get "canned" or at least brought up on sexual harassment charges in most organizations.

Network Frontiers

Public domain software

Software that has been distributed with an explicit notification from the program's author that the work has been released for unconditional use, including for-profit distribution or modification by any party under any circumstances.

FISCAM, Centers for Medicare & Medicaid Services (CMS), US National Information Assurance (IA) Glossary

Public information

Data available to the general population. The disclosures of this information are not expected to seriously or adversely impact the agency. Examples include general organizational information on the organization's website, public brochures, and pamphlets. This includes information contained in press releases approved by the Office of Public Affairs or other official sources.

Centers for Medicare & Medicaid Services (CMS)

Public key

The published part of a two-part, public key cryptography system. In an asymmetric cryptographic scheme, the key that may be widely published to enable the operation of the scheme. The public key is uniquely associated with an entity and may be made public. In an asymmetric (public) cryptosystem, the public key is associated with a private key. The public key may be known by anyone and, depending on the algorithm, may be used to: 1) verify a digital signature that is signed by the corresponding private key, 2) encrypt data that can be decrypted by the corresponding private key, or 3) compute a piece of shared data.

NIST 800 series, Network Frontiers, ISACA, FIPS Pubs

Public key certificate

A digital document issued and digitally signed by the private key of a Certification Authority that binds the name of a subscriber to a public key. The certificate indicates that the subscriber identified in the certificate has sole control and access to the private key. It contains the name of a user, the public key component of the user, and the name of the issuer who vouches that the public key component is bound to the named user.

US National Information Assurance (IA) Glossary, NIST 800 Series, FIPS Pubs

Public Key Cryptography (PKC)

Encryption system using a linked pair of keys. What one key encrypts, the other key decrypts.

US National Information Assurance (IA) Glossary

Public Key Cryptography Standard (PKCS)

Specifications used in the deployment of public-key cryptography.

Workgroup for Electronic Data Interchange

Public key cryptosystem

Used in data encryption, it uses an encryption key as a public key to encrypt the plaintext to the ciphertext. It uses the different decryption key as a secret key to decrypt the ciphertext to the corresponding plaintext. In contrast to a private key cryptosystem, the decryption key should be secret; however, the encryption key can be known to everyone. In a public key cryptosystem, two keys are asymmetric, such that the en-

cryption key is not equivalent to the decryption key.

ISACA

Public Key Infrastructure (PKI)

A system that authentically distributes users' public keys using certificates. The framework established to issue, maintain, and revoke public key certificates accommodating a variety of security technologies, including the use of software.

Workgroup for Electronic Data Interchange, Centers for Medicare & Medicaid Services (CMS), US National Information Assurance (IA) Glossary, NIST 800 Series, FIPS Pubs

Public network

Network established and operated by a telecommunications provider or recognized private company, for specific purpose of providing data transmission services for the public. Data must be encrypted during transmission over public networks as hackers easily and commonly intercept, modify, and/or divert data while in transit. Examples of public networks in scope of PCI DSS include the Internet, GPRS, and GSM.

PCI-DSS, Sedona Conference

Public seed

A starting value for a pseudorandom number generator. The value produced by the random number generator may be made public. The public seed is often called a "salt".

NIST 800 series

Public trust positions

Positions that have the potential for action or inaction by their incumbents to affect the integrity, efficiency, or effectiveness of assigned Government activities. The potential for adverse effects includes action or inaction that could diminish public confidence in the integrity, efficiency, or effectiveness of assigned Government activities, whether or not actual damage occurs.

Centers for Medicare & Medicaid Services (CMS), 5 CFR Part 731

Public/private key

A cryptographic method that uses a two-part key (code) that is made up of public and private components. To encrypt messages, the published public keys of the recipients are used. To decrypt the messages, the recipients use their unpublished private keys known only to them.

Network Frontiers, Workgroup for Electronic Data Interchange

Purge

Rendering sanitized data unrecoverable by laboratory attack methods.

NIST 800 series

Purging

Rendering stored information unrecoverable. See also Sanitize, degauss.)

US National Information Assurance (IA) Glossary

Q

QUADRANT

Short name referring to technology that provides tamper-resistant protection to crypto-equipment.

US National Information Assurance (IA) Glossary

Quality

The ability of a product, service, or process to provide the intended value. For example, a hardware component can be considered to be of high quality if it performs as expected and delivers the required reliability. Process quality also requires an ability to monitor effectiveness and efficiency and to improve them if necessary. See also quality management system.

ITIL

Quality Assurance (QA)

The function that reviews software project activities and tests software products throughout the software lifecycle to determine if 1) the software project is adhering to its established plans, standards, and procedures, and 2) the software meets the functional specifications defined by the user. See also Quality Control.

FISCAM, Centers for Medicare & Medicaid Services (CMS), ITIL

Quality Control (QC)

Steps taken to ensure that results of a given task, product or service are of sufficiently high quality; the operational techniques and activities that are used to fulfill requirements for quality. In document handling and management processes, this includes image quality (resolution, skew, speckle, legibility, etc.), and data quality (correct information in appropriate fields, validated data for dates, addresses, names/issues lists, etc.). See also Quality Assurance.

Sedona Conference

Quality Management System (QMS)

A system that outlines the policies and procedures necessary to improve and control the various processes that will ultimately lead to improved business performance. The set of processes responsible for ensuring that all work carried out by an organization is of a suitable quality to reliably meet business objectives or service levels. See also ISO 9000.

CobiT, ITIL

Quarter Inch Cartridge (QIC)

Digital recording tape, 2000 feet long, with an uncompressed capacity of 5 GB.

Sedona Conference

Query

The process of extracting data from a database and presenting it for use.

FISCAM, Sedona Conference

Query By Image Content (QBIC)

An IBM search system for stored images which allows the user to sketch an image, and then search the image files to find those which most closely match. The user can specify color and texture – such as "sandy beaches" or "clouds".

Sedona Conference

Queue

A group of items that is waiting to be serviced or processed. For example, a print queue holds files that are waiting to be printed.

ISACA, Sedona Conference

Quick ship

A recovery solution provided by recovery and/or hardware vendors and includes a pre-established contract to deliver hardware resources within a specified number of hours after a disaster occurs. This solution usually provides organizations with the ability to recover within 72 hours or greater.

ISACA

Quick win

An improvement activity which is expected to provide a return on invest-ment in a short period of time with relatively small cost and effort. See also Pareto principle.

ITIL

R

RACI chart

Illustrates who is responsible, accountable, consulted, and informed within in a standard organizational framework. See also RACI model.

CobiT

RACI model

The RACI model is a relatively straightforward tool that can be used for identifying roles and responsibilities during an organizational change process. After all, transformation processes do not process themselves; people have to "do" something to make the processes happen. Therefore it is useful to describe what should be done by whom to make a transformation process happen. R = Responsible - owns the problem/project. A = to whom "R" is Accountable - who must sign off (Approve) on work before it is effective. C = to be Consulted - has information and/or capability necessary to complete the work. I = to be Informed - must be notified of results, but need not be consulted. Typical steps in a RACI process: 1) Identify all of the processes/activities involved and list them down the left hand side of the chart. 2) Identify all of the roles and list them along the top of the chart. 3) Complete the cells of the chart: identify who has the R, A, C, I for each process. 4) Every process should preferably have one and only one "R" as a general principle. A gap occurs when a process exists with no "R" (no role is responsible), an overlap occurs when multiple roles exist that have an "R" for a given process. 5) Resolve overlaps. Every process in a role responsibility map should contain one and only one "R" to indicate a unique process owner. In the case of multiple "R"s, there is a need to "zoom in" and further detail the sub processes associated with "obtain resource commitment" to separate the individual responsibilities. 6) Resolve gaps. The simpler case to address is the resolution of a gap. Where no role is identified that is "responsible" for a process, the individual with the authority for role definition must determine which existing role is responsible or new role that is required, update the RACI map and clarify with the individual(s) that assume that role.

Network Frontiers

RACI Model and RACI chart (RACI)

See RACI chart, RACI model.

Network Frontiers

Random Access Memory (RAM)

Hardware inside a computer that retains memory on a short-term basis and stores information while the computer is in use. It is the "working memory" of the computer into which the operating system, startup applications and drivers are loaded when a computer is turned on, or where a program subsequently started up is loaded, and where thereafter, these applications are executed. RAM can be read or written in any section with one instruction sequence. It helps to have more of this "working space" installed when running advanced operating systems and applications. RAM content is erased each time a computer is turned off. See also Dynamic Random Access Memory DRAM.

ISACA, Sedona Conference

Random Number Generator (RNG)

A process used to generate an unpredictable series of numbers. Each individual value is called random if each of the values in the total population of values has an equal probability of being selected. Random Number Generators (RNGs) used for cryptographic applications typically produce a sequence of zero and one bits that may be combined into subsequences or blocks of random numbers. There are two basic classes: deterministic and nondeterministic. A deterministic RNG consists of an algorithm that produces a sequence of bits from an initial value called a seed. A nondeterministic RNG produces output that is dependent on some unpredictable physical source that is outside human control.

NIST 800 series, FIPS Pubs

Random sample

A sample selected so that every combination of the same number of items in the population has an equal chance of selection. A random sample should be selected by using computer software or a random number table. A systematic sample with a random start, although not technically meeting the definition, may generally be evaluated as if it were a random sample.

GAO/PCIE Financial Audit Manual

Randomizer

Analog or digital source of unpredictable, unbiased, and usually independent bits. Randomizers can be used for several different functions, including key generation or to provide a starting state for a key generator.

US National Information Assurance (IA) Glossary

Range check

Range checks ensure that data fall within a predetermined range. See also limit check.

ISACA

Rapid Application Development (RAD)

A methodology that enables organizations to develop strategically important systems faster, while reducing development costs and maintaining quality through the use of a series of proven application development techniques within a well-defined methodology.

ISACA

Raster/Rasterized

A method of representing an image with a grid (or "map") of dots. Typical raster file formats are GIF, JPEG, TIFF, PCX, BMP, etc.

Sedona Conference

Re-keying

To change the value of a cryptographic key that is being used in a cryptographic system application; this normally entails issuing a new certificate on the new public key.

PCI-DSS, NIST 800 Series

Read

Fundamental operation in an information system that results only in the flow of information from an object to a subject.

US National Information Assurance (IA) Glossary

Read access

This level of access provides the ability to look at and copy data or a software program.

FISCAM, Centers for Medicare & Medicaid Services (CMS), US National Information Assurance (IA) Glossary

Read Only Memory (ROM)

Random memory which can be read but not written or changed. Also, hardware, usually a chip, within a computer containing programming necessary for starting up the computer, and essential system programs that neither the user nor the computer can alter or erase. Information in the computer's ROM is permanently maintained even when the computer is turned off.

Sedona Conference

Real charging

A charging policy where actual money is transferred from the customer to the IT service provider in payment for the delivery of IT services. See also notional charging.

ITIL

Real time reaction

Immediate response to a penetration attempt that is detected and diagnosed in time to prevent access.

US National Information Assurance (IA) Glossary

Real-time analysis

Analysis that is performed on a continuous basis, with results gained in time to alter the run-time system.

ISACA

Real-time processing

An interactive online system capability that immediately updates computer files when transactions are initiated through a terminal.

ISACA

Real-time system

A computer and/or a software system that reacts to events before they become obsolete. This type of system is generally interactive and updates files as transactions are processed.

FISCAM, Centers for Medicare & Medicaid Services (CMS)

Realm

A community location that you are a part of identified usually by a server address, which enables you to receive and send secure e-mail.

Workgroup for Electronic Data Interchange

Reasonable assurance

A level of comfort short of a guarantee but considered adequate given the costs of the control and the likely benefits achieved.

ISACA

Reasonableness check

Compares data to predefined reasonability limits or occurrence rates established for the data.

ISACA

Reasonably possible

The chance of the future event or events occurring is more than remote but less than probable.

GAO/PCIE Financial Audit Manual

Reassessment

The continuity of information systems should be reassessed periodically as information systems and the requirements for their continuity vary over time.

NIST 800 series, ISO/IEC 27001:2005

Reassessment principle

Participants should review and reassess the security of information systems and networks and make appropriate modifications to security policies, practices, measures, and procedures.

OECD Guidelines for the Security of Information Systems and Networks

Receiving agency

The agency receiving services, products, goods, transfer funds, purchasing investments, and/or borrowing from Treasury (or other agency). This includes bureaus, departments, and/or programs within agencies. The receiving agency is the purchaser. The receiving agency is the agency receiving transfers of funds (transfers in) when appropriations are transferred without the exchange of goods or services.

GAO/PCIE Financial Audit Manual

Recipient usage period

The period of time during the cryptoperiod of a symmetric key when protected information is processed. The recipient usage period of the key is usually identical to the cryptoperiod of that key.

NIST 800 series

Reciprocal accounts

Corresponding SGL accounts that should be used by a providing and receiving agency to record like intragovernmental transactions. For example, the providing entity's accounts receivable would normally be reconciled to the reciprocal account, accounts payable, on the receiving entity's records.

GAO/PCIE Financial Audit Manual

Reciprocal agreement

Emergency processing agreements between two or more organizations with similar equipment or applications. Typically, participants promise to provide processing time to each other when an emergency arises.

ISACA, ITIL, PAS 56

Reciprocal work area

Work space provided by one organization for use by another in the event of a business continuity incident, by way of a reciprocal agreement.

PAS 56

Record

With regard to databases, a record is a unit of related data fields. The group of data fields that can be accessed by a program containing the complete set of information on a particular item. A records is also information, regardless of medium, detailing business transactions and maintained as evidence and information in pursuance of legal obligations. In general compliance terms, it is information created, received, and maintained as evidence and information by an organization or person, in pursuance of legal obligations or in the transaction of business. Records includes all books, papers, maps, photographs, machine readable materials, or other documentary materials, regardless of physical form or characteristics, made or received by an organization of the United States Government under Federal law or in connection with the transaction of public business and preserved or appropriate for preservation by that organization or its legitimate successor as evidence of the organization, functions, policies, decisions, procedures, operations, or other activities of the Government or because of the informational value of data in them. See also regulated data. A record is not necessarily the same as a document. All documents are potential records, but not vice versa. A record is essential for the business; documents are containers of "working information." Records are documents with evidentiary value.

Title 44 Section 3301 of Chapter 33, USC, "Definition of records", ISO 15489, DIRKS, FISCAM, ISACA, Centers for Medicare & Medicaid Services (CMS), ISO/IEC 27001:2005, FIPS Pubs, ITIL, Sedona Conference, NIST 800 Series

Record Custodian

A records custodian is an individual responsible for the physical storage and protection of records throughout their retention period. In the context of electronic records custodianship may not be a direct part of the records management function in all organizations. For example, some organizations may place this responsibility within their Information Technology Department, or they may assign responsibility for retaining and preserving records with individual employees.

Sedona Conference

Record lifecycle

The period of time between a record's creation and ending with appropriate disposition per NARA requirements.

Title 44 Section 2901 of Chapter 29, USC, "Definitions", Sedona Conference

Record Owner

The records owner is the subject matter expert on the contents of the record and is responsible for the lifecycle management of the record. This may be, but is not necessarily, the author of the record.

Sedona Conference

Record series

A description of a particular set of records within a file plan. Each category has retention and disposition data associated with it, applied to all record folders and records within the category.

DOD 5015.2-STD: June 2002, Sedona Conference

Record Submitter

The Record Submitter is the person who enters a record in an application or system. This may be, but is not necessarily, the author or the record owner.

Sedona Conference

Record Version

A particular form or variation of an earlier or original record. For electronic records the variations may include changes to file format, metadata or content.

Sedona Conference

Record, screen, and report layouts

Record layouts provide information regarding the type of record, its size and the type of data contained in the record. Screen and report layouts describe what information is provided and necessary for input.

ISACA

Recorded amount

The financial statement amount being tested by the auditor in the specific application of substantive tests.

GAO/PCIE Financial Audit Manual

Recordkeeping

Making and maintaining complete, accurate and reliable evidence of business transactions in the form of recorded information. Recordkeeping includes the following: 1)the creation of records in the course of business activity and the means to ensure the creation of adequate records; 2) the design, establishment, and operation of recordkeeping systems; and 3) the management of records used in business (traditionally regarded as the domain of records management) and as archives (traditionally regarded as the domain of archives administration).

DIRKS

Recordkeeping metadata

Structured or semi-structured information which enables the creation, management, and use of records through time and across domains. Recordkeeping metadata can identify, authenticate, and contextualize records and the peo-

ple, processes, and systems that create, manage, and use them.

DIRKS

Recordkeeping requirements

Identified needs for evidence arising from various internal and/or external sources that may be satisfied through appropriate recordkeeping action (such as creation, capture, maintenance, preservation, and access). The sources include legislative and other regulatory sources, industry codes of best practice, broader government interests, external clients or stakeholders, and the general public. An umbrella term that covers identified requirements and prioritized requirements.

DIRKS

Recordkeeping systems

Recordkeeping systems contain information which is linked to activities that they document. Their purpose is to capture, maintain and provide access to evidence over time, as required by the jurisdiction in which they are implemented and I accordance with common business practices. Recordkeeping systems include: 1) both records practitioners and records users; 2) a set of authorized polices, assigned responsibilities, delegations of authority, procedures, and practices; policy statements, procedures manuals, user guidelines, and other documents which are used to authorize and promulgate the policies, procedures, and practices; 3) the records themselves; 4) specialized information and records systems used to control the records; and 5) software, hardware and other equipment, and stationery. Recordkeeping systems may be distinguished from other types of information systems by the fact that they are organized to accomplish the specific functions of creating, storing, and accessing records for evidential purposes.

DIRKS

Records and Information Management (RIM)

Sedona Conference

Records continuum

The whole extent of a record's existence. Refers to a consistent and coherent regime of management processes from the time of the creation of records (and before creation, in the design of recordkeeping systems) through to the preservation and use of records as archives.

DIRKS

Records hold

See Legal hold.

Sedona Conference

Records Management (RM)

It is the field of management responsible for the efficient and systematic control of the creation, receipt, maintenance, use, and disposition of records, including processes for capturing and maintaining evidence of and information about business activities and transactions in the form of records. Also, records management are the policies and procedures that are to occur during a record's lifecycle. Enables an organization to assign a specific life cycle to individual pieces of information from creation, receipt, maintenance, and use to the ultimate disposition of records.

AIIM, DOD 5015.2-STD: June 2002, ISO 15489, DIRKS, Sedona Conference

Records Manager

The records manager is responsible for the implementation of a records management program in keeping with the policies and procedures that govern that program, including the identification, classification, handling and disposition of the organization's records throughout their retention life. The physical storage and protection of records may be a component of this individual's functions, but it may also be delegated to someone else. See also Records Custodian.

Sedona Conference

Records retention period

The length of time a given records series must be kept, expressed as either a time period (e.g., four years), an event or action (e.g., audit), or a combination (e.g., six months after audit).

Sedona Conference

Records Retention Schedule

A plan for the management of records listing types of records and how long they should be kept; the purpose is to provide continuing authority to dispose of or transfer records to historical archives.

Sedona Conference

Records store

See Repository for electronic records.

Sedona Conference

Records system

The information system which captures, manages and provides access to records through time.

ISO 15489, DIRKS

Recovery

Returning a configuration item or an IT service to a working state. Recovery of an IT service often includes recovering data to a known consistent state. After recovery, further steps may be needed before the IT service can be made avail-able to the users (restoration). See also restore.

ITIL, Sedona Conference

Recovery center

Third party provision of a shared fixed facility for use in recovery. See also recovery options.

ITIL

Recovery option

A strategy for responding to an interruption to service. Commonly used strategies are do nothing, manual workaround, reciprocal agreement, gradual recovery, intermediate recovery, immediate recovery. Recovery options may make use of dedicated facilities, or third party facilities shared by multiple businesses.

ITIL

Recovery Point Objective (RPO)

The point in time to which data is restored, which may include the loss of data. For example, if a backup is performed at midnight, and the data is used to restore the system the next day right before happy hour, any information added, deleted, or changed between midnight and the point of recovery will be lost. Recovery point objectives for each IT service should be negotiated, agreed and documented. See also Business Impact Analysis.

ISACA, ITIL, PAS 56

Recovery procedure

Actions necessary to restore data files of an IS and computational capability after a system failure.

Centers for Medicare & Medicaid Services (CMS)

Recovery procedures

Actions necessary to restore data files of an information system and computational capability after a system failure.

US National Information Assurance (IA) Glossary

Recovery testing

A test to check the system's ability to recover after a software or hardware failure.

ISACA

Recovery Time Objective (RTO)

The maximum time it takes to restore a system using backup data after the primary data has been corrupted or lost. The service level to be provided may be less than normal service level targets. Recovery Time Objectives for each IT service should be negotiated, agreed and documented. See also Business Impact Analysis, Recovery Point Objective.

ISACA, ITIL, PAS 56, BS 25999

RED

Designation applied to an information system, and associated areas, circuits, components, and equipment in which unencrypted national security information is being processed.

US National Information Assurance (IA) Glossary

RED signal

Any electronic emission (e.g., plain text, key, key stream, subkey stream, initial fill, or control signal) that would divulge national security information if recovered.

US National Information Assurance (IA) Glossary

Red team

Interdisciplinary group of individuals authorized to conduct an independent and focused threat-based effort as a simulated adversary to expose and exploit system vulnerabilities for the purpose of improving the security posture of information systems.

US National Information Assurance (IA) Glossary

Red, Green, Blue (RGB)

The three primary colors in the additive color family which create all the computer color video signals for a computer's color terminal.

Sedona Conference

RED/BLACK concept

Separation of electrical and electronic circuits, components, equipment, and systems that handle national security information (RED), in electrical form, from those that handle non-national security information (BLACK) in the same form.

US National Information Assurance (IA) Glossary

Redaction

A portion of an image or document is intentionally concealed to prevent disclosure of specific portions. Often done to avoid production of privileged or irrelevant materials.

Sedona Conference

Redo logs

Files maintained by a system, primarily a database management system, for the purposed of reapplying changes following an error or outage recovery.

ISACA

Redundancy

The term redundant also has a generic meaning of obsolete, or no longer needed. See also fault tolerance.

ITIL

Redundancy check

Detects transmission errors by appending calculated bits onto the end of each segment of data.

ISACA

Redundant Array of Independent Disks (RAID)

A method of storing data on servers that usually combines multiple hard drives into one logical unit thereby increasing capacity, reliability and backup capability. RAID systems may vary in levels of redundancy, with no redundancy being a single, non-mirrored disk as level 0, two discs that mirror each other as level 1, on up, with level 5 being one of the most common. RAID systems are more complicated to copy and restore.

Sedona Conference

Reengineering

A process involving the extraction of components from existing systems and restructuring these components to develop new systems or to enhance the efficiency of existing systems. Existing software systems thus can be modernized to prolong their functionality. An example of this is a software code translator that can take an existing hierarchical database system and transpose it to a relational database system. CASE includes a source code reengineering feature.

ISACA

Reference monitor

The security engineering term for IT functionality that 1) controls all access, 2) cannot be by-passed, 3) is tamper-resistant, and 4) provides confidence that the other three items are true.

NIST 800 series, US National Information Assurance (IA) Glossary

Refresh rate

The number of times per second a display (such as on a CRT or TV) is updated.

Sedona Conference

Region (of an image)

An area of an image file that is selected for specialized processing. Also called a "zone."

Sedona Conference

Registered Certification Body (RCB)

An organization that has been accredited to perform certification against a published standard such as ISO/IEC 17799 or ISO/IEC 20000.

ITIL

Registration

1) The act of giving a record a unique identity in a recordkeeping system. The purpose of registration is to provide evidence that a record has been created or captured in a recordkeeping system. It involves recording brief descriptive information about the record in a register and assigning the record a unique identifier. Registration should link the record to descriptive information about the context of the record and to other related records. In imaging, lining up a forms image to determine which fields are where. 2) Entering pages into a scanner such that they are correctly read. 3) The process through which a party applies to become a subscriber of a Credentials Service Provider (CSP) and a Registration Authority validates the identity of that party on behalf of the CSP.

ISO 15489, DIRKS, Sedona Conference, NIST 800 Series

Registration Authority (RA)

An organization responsible for identifying individuals and requesting certificates from a certificate authority. An entity that may be given responsibility for performing some of the administrative tasks necessary in the registration of subjects, such as confirming the subject's identity, validating that the subject is entitled to have the attributes requested in a certificate and verifying that the subject has possession of the private key associated with the public key requested for a certificate.

Centers for Medicare & Medicaid Services (CMS), ISACA, NIST 800 Series, FIPS Pubs

Regression testing

Selective retesting to detect faults introduced during modification of a system. Used to retest earlier program abends or logical errors that occurred during the initial testing phase.

FISCAM, ISACA

Regulated data

This is electronic information, whether in the form of e-mail, an instant message, a database or database record, or individual files that have been deemed by a law, regulation, or enforceable standard to fall within regulatory classifications. For Sarbanes-Oxley, regulated data is all data dealing with financial re-

porting. Healthcare and life sciences regulators use the term electronic protected health information. The payment card industry uses the term confidential information or personal information. US state and federal laws and regulations, as well as international laws and regulations use the terms confidential or personal information. See also electronic Protected Health Information (ePHI), electronic record, confidential information.

Sarbanes-Oxley, Basel II, 21 CFR Part 11, HIPAA, PCI-DSS, US Federal State, and International laws and regulations

Regulated organization

These are the organizations that have been targeted for regulatory compliance. See also covered organization, broker-dealer, transfer agent, transfer advisor, investment company, healthcare clearinghouse, healthcare provider, health plan, provider.

17 CFR 240.17a-4, HIPAA

Regulation

To regulate is to bring under the force of law or a governing authority. Everyone in his or her own country falls within the realm of their national, regional, and local laws. Hence, traditional regulators are those within the levels of government just mentioned. When governmental agencies create their Acts, they are codifying legal documents that resulted from deliberations of their legislative bodies. Those Acts are then documented as regulations, such as the Code of Federal Regulations that we have in the United States.

de facto

Regulatory value

Regulatory value is the measurement of an asset's worth from a regulatory perspective. This includes all legal requirements such as record retention, fines, penalties, legal counsel, and other direct costs for noncompliance.

Network Frontiers

Reimbursement activity

In intragovernmental activity, similar to goods or services except the amounts billed to the receiving entity by the providing entity are based on actual costs incurred instead of on fees.

GAO/PCIE Financial Audit Manual

Related parties

Affiliates, management of the entity, their immediate families, and other parties the entity deals with if one party controls or can significantly influence the management or operating policies of the other to an extent that one of the parties might be prevented from fully pursuing its own separate interests.

GAO/PCIE Financial Audit Manual

Relationship

A connection or interaction between two people or things. In business relationship management it is the interaction between the IT service provider and the business. In configuration management it is a link between two configuration items that identifies a dependency or connection between them. For example, applications may be linked to the servers they run on, IT services have many links to all the CIs that contribute to that IT service.

ITIL

Relationship process

The ISO/IEC 20000 process group that includes business relationship management and supplier management.

ITIL

Relative path

An implied path.

Sedona Conference

Release

A collection of hardware, software, documentation, processes or other components required to implement one or more approved changes to IT services. The contents of each release are managed, tested, and deployed as a single entity. See also full release, delta release, package release, release identification.

ITIL

Release acceptance

The activity responsible for testing a release, and its implementation and backout plans to ensure they meet the agreed business and IT operations requirements.

ITIL

Release identification

A naming convention used to uniquely identify a release. The release identification typically includes a reference to the configuration item and a version number. For example, Microsoft office 2003 SR2.

ITIL

Release management

The process responsible for planning, scheduling and controlling the movement of releases to test and live environments. The primary objective of release management is to ensure that the integrity of the live environment is protected and that the correct components are released. Release management works closely with configuration management and change management.

ITIL

Release mechanism

The methodology for deploying a release to its target environment. A release mechanism may include hardware and software tools as well as procedures.

ITIL

Release prefix

Prefix appended to the short title of U.S.-produced keying material to indicate its foreign releasability. "A" designates material that is releasable to specific allied nations and "U.S." designates material intended exclusively for U. S. use.

US National Information Assurance (IA) Glossary

Release process

The name used by ISO/IEC 20000 for the process group that includes release management. This group does not include any other processes.

ISO/IEC 27001:2005, ITIL

Release record

A record in the CMDB that defines the content of a release. A release record has relationships with all configuration items that are affected by the release.

ITIL

Release type

A category that is used to classify releases. A release type may be one of full, delta, or package release.

ITIL

Release unit

Components of an IT service that are normally released together. A release unit typically includes sufficient components to perform a useful function. For example, one release unit could be a desktop PC, including hardware, software, licenses, documentation, etc.; a different release unit may be the complete payroll application including IT operations procedures and user training. See also release type.

ITIL

Relevant audit evidence

Audit evidence is relevant if it pertains to the audit objectives and has a logical relationship to the findings and conclusions it is used to support.

ISACA

Reliability

The capability of hardware or software to perform as the user expects and to do so consistently without failures or erratic behavior. A measure of how long a configuration item or IT service can perform its agreed function without interruption. Usually measured as MTBF or MTBSI. See also availability.

FISCAM, Centers for Medicare & Medicaid Services (CMS), ISO/IEC 27001:2005, ITIL

Reliability of information

This relates to the provision of appropriate information for management to operate the organization and for management to exercise its financial and compliance reporting responsibilities.

CobiT

Reliable audit evidence

Audit evidence is reliable if, in the IS auditor's opinion, it is valid, factual, objective and supportable.

ISACA

Relying party

An entity that relies upon the subscriber's credentials, typically to process a transaction or grant access to information or a system.

NIST 800 series

Remanence

Residual information remaining on storage media after clearing. See also magnetic remanence and clearing.

US National Information Assurance (IA) Glossary

Remediation

The act of correcting a vulnerability or eliminating a threat. Three possible types of remediation are installing a patch, adjusting configuration settings, or uninstalling a software application.

NIST 800 series

Remediation plan

A plan to perform the remediation of one or more threats or vulnerabilities facing an organization's systems. The plan typically includes options to remove threats and vulnerabilities and priorities for performing the remediation.

NIST 800 series

Remote

The chance of the future event or events occurring is slight.

GAO/PCIE Financial Audit Manual

Remote access

The process of communicating with a computer located in another place over a communications link. For example, to use a computer, modem, and some remote access software to connect to a network from a distant location.

FISCAM, Centers for Medicare & Medicaid Services (CMS), US National Information Assurance (IA) Glossary, Sedona Conference, NIST 800 Series

Remote Authentication Dial-In User Service (RADIUS)

A type of service providing an authentication and accounting system often used for dial-up and remote access security.

ISACA, PCI-DSS

Remote Job Entry (RJE)

With respect to computer systems with locations geographically separate from the main computer center, submitting batch processing jobs via a data communications link. The transmission of Job Control Language (JCL) and batches of transactions from a remote terminal location.

FISCAM, ISACA

Remote logon

The act of gaining access to a machine across a network from a distant location through normal authentication methods. Generally, this implies a computer, a modem, and some remote access software to connect to the network.

Centers for Medicare & Medicaid Services (CMS)

Remote maintenance

Maintenance activities conducted by individuals communicating external to an information system security perimeter.

NIST 800 series

Remote Procedure Calls (RPC)

The traditional Internet service protocol widely used for many years on UNIX-based operating systems and supported by the Internet Engineering Task Force (IETF) that allows a program on one computer to execute a program on another (e.g., server). The primary benefit derived from its use is that a system developer need not develop specific procedures for the targeted computer system. For example, in a client-server arrangement, the client program sends a message to the server with appropriate arguments, and the server returns a message containing the results of the program executed. See also CORBA and DCOM, as two newer object-oriented methods for related RPC functionality.

ISACA

Remote rekeying

Procedure by which a distant crypto-equipment is rekeyed electrically. See also automatic remote rekeying and manual remote rekeying.

US National Information Assurance (IA) Glossary

Remote VPN user

A user connecting to your network from another location via a VPN (virtual private network) or private, encrypted channel through the Internet.

Network Frontiers

Render images

To take a native format electronic file and convert it to an image that appears as the original format file as if printed to paper.

Sedona Conference

Renew (a certificate)

The act or process of extending the validity of the data binding asserted by a public key certificate by issuing a new certificate.

NIST 800 series

Repair

The replacement or correction of a failed configuration item. Often measured as Mean Time To Repair (MTTR). See also maintainability, recovery, restoration of service.

ITIL

Repair action

NSA-approved change to a COMSEC end-item that does not affect the original characteristics of the end-item and is provided for optional application by holders. Repair actions are limited to minor electrical and/or mechanical improvements to enhance operation, maintenance, or reliability. They do not require an identification label, marking, or control but must be fully documented by changes to the maintenance manual.

US National Information Assurance (IA) Glossary

Report

Formatted output of a system providing specific information.

Sedona Conference

Report writer software

Software that allows access to data to produce customized reports.

FISCAM

Reportable condition

Reportable conditions include matters coming to the auditor's attention that, in the auditor's judgment, should be communicated because they represent significant deficiencies in the design or operation of internal controls which could adversely affect the entity's ability to meet its internal control objectives.

FISCAM

Repository

The central database that stores and organizes data. A database containing information and data relating to certificates as specified in a CP; may also be referred to as a directory.

ISACA, NIST 800 Series

Repository for Electronic Records

Repository for Electronic Records is a direct access device on which the electronic records and associated metadata are stored. (DoD 5015) Sometimes called a "records store" or "records archive."

Sedona Conference

Representment

A chargeback that is rejected and returned to a card issuer by a merchant bank on the merchant's behalf. A chargeback may be re-presented, or re-deposited, if the merchant or merchant bank can remedy the problem that led to the chargeback.

VISA Glossary of Terms

Repudiation

The denial by one of the parties to a transaction or participation in all or part of that transaction or of the content of communications related to that transaction.

ISACA

Reputational risk

The current and prospective effect on earnings and capital arising from negative public opinion. This affects the bank's ability to establish new relationships or services or continue servicing existing relationships. Reputation risk may expose the bank to litigation, financial loss, or a decline in its customer base. A bank's reputation can be damaged by Internet banking services that are poorly executed or otherwise alienate customers and the public. An Internet bank has a greater reputation risk as compared to a traditional brick-and-mortar bank since it is easier for its customers to leave and go to a different Internet bank and since it cannot discuss any problems with the customer in person.

ISACA

Request For Change (RFC)

A formal proposal for a change to be made. An RFC includes details of the proposed change and may be recorded on paper or electronically. The term RFC is often misused to mean a change record or the change itself.

ITIL

Request For Comments (RFC)

A document that has been approved by the IETF becomes an RFC and is assigned a unique number once published. If it gains enough interest, it may evolve into an Internet standard.

ISACA, PCI-DSS

Request For Proposal (RFP)

A document distributed to software vendors requesting them to submit a proposal to develop or provide a software product.

ISACA

Required Supplementary Information (RSI)

GAO/PCIE Financial Audit Manual

Required Supplementary Stewardship Information (RSSI)

GAO/PCIE Financial Audit Manual

Requirement

A formal statement of what is needed. For example, a service level requirement, a project requirement, or the required deliverables for a process. See also statement of requirements.

ITIL

Requirements definition

A phase of an SDLC methodology where the affected user groups define the requirements of the system for meeting the defined needs.

ISACA

Reserve keying material

Key held to satisfy unplanned needs. See also contingency key.

US National Information Assurance (IA) Glossary

Residual data

Residual Data (sometimes referred to as "Ambient Data") refers to data that is not active on a computer system. Residual data includes (1) data found on media free space; (2)data found in file slack space; and (3)data within files that has functionally been deleted in that it is not visible using the application with which the file was created, without use of undelete or special data recovery techniques. May contain copies of deleted files, Internet files and file fragments.

Sedona Conference

Residual risk

The risk associated with an event when the control is in place to reduce the effect or likelihood of that event being taken into account. The remaining qualitative or quantitative substantiation of potential risk or loss after all mitigating controls are applied. There is a residual risk associated with each threat.

NIST 800 series, ISACA, Centers for Medicare & Medicaid Services (CMS), ISO/IEC 27001:2005, ISO/IEC Guide 73:2002, US National Information Assurance (IA) Glossary, PAS 56

Residue

Data left in storage after information processing operations are complete, but before degaussing or overwriting has taken place.

US National Information Assurance (IA) Glossary

Resilience

The ability of a system or network to recover automatically or at least very quickly from any disruption, usually with minimal recognizable effect. For example, an armored cable will resist failure when put under stress. See also fault tolerance.

CobiT, ITIL, PAS 56, BS 25999

Resiliency measure

Activity or facility put in place to absorb the impact of an interruption, disruption or loss and to continue to provide a minimum acceptable level of service.

PAS 56

Resolution

An action taken to repair the root cause of an incident or problem or to implement a workaround. In ISO/IEC 20000, resolution processes is the process group that includes incident and problem management. See also workaround. In regards to images and imaging, see DPI.

ISO/IEC 27001:2005, ITIL, Sedona Conference

Resolution process

The ISO/IEC 20000 process group that includes incident management and problem management.

ISO/IEC 27001:2005, ITIL

Resource

Any function, device or collection of data in an organization that can be allocated for use by users or programs. Something that is needed to support computer operations including hardware, software, data, telecommunications services, computer supplies such as paper stock and preprinted forms, and other resources such as people, office fa-

cilities, and non-computerized records. See also asset.

FISCAM, Centers for Medicare & Medicaid Services (CMS), ITIL

Resource Access Control Facility (RACF)

An access control software package developed by IBM.

FISCAM

Resource Capacity Management (RCM)

The process responsible for understanding the capacity, utilization, and performance of configuration items. Data is collected, recorded and analyzed for use in the capacity plan. See also service capacity management.

ITIL

Resource encapsulation

Method by which the reference monitor mediates accesses to an information system resource. Resource is protected and not directly accessible by a subject. Satisfies requirement for accurate auditing of resource usage.

US National Information Assurance (IA) Glossary

Resource Owner

See owner.

FISCAM, Centers for Medicare & Medicaid Services (CMS)

427

Resource recovery solution

Plan of action that identifies the specific resource required to carry out recovery actions.

PAS 56

Responder

The entity that responds to the initiator of the authentication exchange.

NIST 800 series, FIPS Pubs

Response

Action taken to address an incident in order to assess the level of containment and control activity required.

PAS 56

Response principle

Participants should act in a timely and cooperative manner to prevent, detect, and respond to security incidents.

OECD Guidelines for the Security of Information Systems and Networks

Response time

A measure of the time taken to complete an operation or transaction. Used in capacity management as a measure of IT infrastructure performance and in incident management as a measure of the time taken to answer the phone or to start diagnosis.

ITIL

Responsibility

Responsibility is a broad term that defines obligations and expected behavior. It implies a proactive stance on the part of the responsible party and a causal relationship between the responsible party and a given outcome.

NIST 800 series, CobiT

Responsibility principle

All participants are responsible for the security of information systems and networks.

OECD Guidelines for the Security of Information Systems and Networks

Responsibility segment

In cost accounting, a significant organizational, operational, functional, or process component that has the following characteristics: 1) its manager reports to the entity's top management, 2) it is responsible for carrying out a mission, performing a line of activities or services, or producing one or a group of products, and 3) for financial reporting and cost management purposes, its resources and results of operations can be clearly distinguished, physically and operationally, from those of other segments of the entity.

GAO/PCIE Financial Audit Manual

Responsible individual

A trustworthy person designated by a sponsoring organization to authenticate individual applicants seeking certificates on the basis of their affiliation with the sponsor.

NIST 800 series

Responsiveness

A measurement of the time taken to respond to something. This could be response time of a transaction or the speed with which an IT service provider responds to an incident or request for change.

ITIL

Restoration

The process of planning for and implementing business recovery which enables the organization to return to a normal service level. See also restore, immediate recovery.

Centers for Medicare & Medicaid Services (CMS)

Restoration of service

See restore.

ITIL

Restore

Taking action to return an IT service to the users after repair and recovery from an incident. This is the primary objective of incident management. It is the process of transferring data from a backup medium (such as tapes) to an on-line system, often for the purpose of recovery from a problem, failure, or disaster. Restoration of archival media is the transfer of data from an archival store to an on-line system for the purposes of processing (such as query, analysis, extraction, or disposition of that data). Archival restoration of systems may require not only data restoration but also replication of the original hardware and software operating environment. Restoration of systems is often called "recovery".

ITIL, Sedona Conference

Retention period

See Records retention period and Records retention schedule.

Sedona Conference

Retention schedule

See Records retention schedule.

Sedona Conference

Retire

Withdraw an application, IT service etc. from use in the live environment. Something we'll never be able to do unless you buy many more books than you are currently buying.

ITIL, Network Frontiers

Return on Capital Employed (ROCE)

A measurement of the expected benefit of an investment. Calculated by dividing net profit before tax and interest by total assets minus current liabilities. This ratio is used by business analysts to judge the effectiveness of the organization as a whole. Any changes to IT services or products are expected to improve this figure. See also cost effectiveness, investment appraisal, Return On Investment.

ITIL

Return On Investment (ROI)

A measurement of the expected benefit of an investment. Calculated by dividing the average increase in financial benefit (taken over an agreed number of years) by the investment. See also cost effectiveness, return on capital employed.

ITIL

Return to normal

The phase of an IT service continuity plan during which full normal operations are resumed. For example, if an alternate data center has been in use, then this phase will bring the primary data center back into operation, and restore the ability to invoke IT service continuity plans again.

ITIL

Reverse engineering

A software engineering technique whereby an existing application system code can be redesigned and coded using computer-aided software engineering (CASE) technology. The process of analyzing a system to identify its intricacies and their interrelationships, and create depictions of the system in another form or at a higher level. Reverse engineering is usually undertaken in order to redesign the system for better maintainability or to produce a copy of a system without utilizing the design from which it was originally produced. For example, one might take the executable code of a computer program, run it to study how it behaved with different input, and then attempt to write a program which behaved the same or better.

Review: The culling process produces a dataset of potentially responsive documents which are then examined and evaluated for a final selection of relevant or responsive documents and assertion of privilege exception as appropriate. See also Online Review.

ISACA, Sedona Conference

Review

An evaluation of a change, problem, process, project, etc. Reviews are typically carried out at predefined points in the lifecycle, and especially after closure. The purpose of a review is to ensure that all deliverables have been provided and to identify opportunities for improvement. See also post implementation review, review and approval.

ITIL

Review and approval

The process whereby information pertaining to the security and integrity of an activity or network is collected, analyzed, and submitted to the appropriate organization for accreditation of the activity or network. See also review, post implementation review.

Centers for Medicare & Medicaid Services (CMS)

Revoke a certificate

To prematurely end the operational period of a certificate effective at a specific date and time.

NIST 800 series

Rewriteable technology

Storage devices where the data may be written more than once – typically hard drives, floppies and optical discs.

Sedona Conference

RFC 822

Standard that specifies a syntax for text messages that are sent among computer users, within the framework of e-mail.

Sedona Conference

Rijndael

Cryptographic algorithm specified in the Advanced Encryption Standard (AES).

NIST 800 series, FIPS Pubs

Ring topology

A type of LAN architecture in which the cable forms a loop with stations attached at intervals around the loop. Signals transmitted around the ring take the form of messages. Each station receives the messages and each station determines, on the basis of an address, whether to accept or process a given message. However, after receiving a message, each station acts as a repeater, retransmitting the message at its original signal strength.

ISACA

RIP

The procedures used to unbundle e-mail collections into individual e-mails during the e-discovery process while preserving authenticity and ownership.

Sedona Conference

Risk

The combination of the probability and severity of impact that results from successfully breaking through a vulnerability by a threat. The possibility of an act or event occurring that would have an adverse effect on the organization and its information systems. The possibility of suffering harm or loss. It is the potential for realizing unwanted negative consequences of an event. Risk refers to a situation where a person could do something undesirable or a natural occurrence could cause an undesirable outcome, resulting in a negative impact or consequence. The potential for harm or loss is best expressed as the answers to these four questions: What could happen? (What is the threat?) How bad could it be? (What is the impact or consequence?) How often might it happen? (What is the frequency?) How certain are the answers to the first three questions? (What is the degree of confidence? The key element among these is the issue of uncertainty captured in the fourth question. If there is no uncertainty, there is no "risk" per se. See also audit risk, inherent risk, control risk, detection risk, IT-related risk.

CERT OCTAVE, DIRKS, GAO/PCIE Financial Audit Manual, ISACA, Centers for Medicare & Medicaid Services (CMS), CobiT, NIST 800 series, FIPS Pubs, ITIL, US National Information Assurance (IA) Glossary, PAS 56, BS 25999

Risk acceptance

Formal process by which a management official agrees that no additional safeguards will be undertaken to control a specific risk. The decision to accept risk.

Centers for Medicare & Medicaid Services (CMS), ISO/IEC 27001:2005, ISO/IEC Guide 73:2002

Risk analysis

A component of internal control in addition to the control environment, monitoring, information and communication, and control activities. The process of identifying the risks to the system, determining the probability of occurrence, analyzing the related vulnerabilities of the system, the resulting impact, and the additional safeguards that mitigate this impact. Risk assessment forms the basis for determining how the risks should be managed. Part of risk management.

NIST 800 series, FISCAM, GAO/PCIE Financial Audit Manual, ISACA, Centers for Medicare & Medicaid Services (CMS), FIPS Pubs, ISO/IEC 27001:2005, ISO/IEC Guide 73:2002, PCI-DSS, US National Information Assurance (IA) Glossary

Risk appetite

Willingness of an organization to accept a defined level of risk. Different organizations at different stages of their existence will have different risk appetites.

PAS 56, BS 25999

Risk Assessment (RA)

The term risk assessment is used to characterize both the process and the result of analyzing and assessing risk. A part of risk management, risk assessment is the initial steps of risk management. Analyzing the value of assets to the business, identifying threats to those assets, and evaluating how vulnerable each asset is to those threats. See also CRAMM, risk analysis.

FISCAM, Centers for Medicare & Medicaid Services (CMS), ISO/IEC 27001:2005, ISO/IEC Guide 73:2002, NIST 800 series, ITIL, US National Information Assurance (IA) Glossary, PAS 56, BS 25999

Risk assessment principle

Participants should conduct risk assessments.

OECD Guidelines for the Security of Information Systems and Networks

Risk concentration

Concentration of MCAs within the same building or on the same site.

PAS 56

Risk evaluation

The process of comparing the estimated risk against given risk criteria to determine the significance of the risk. See also risk analysis.

Centers for Medicare & Medicaid Services (CMS), ISO/IEC 27001:2005, ISO/IEC 73:2002

Risk index

Difference between the minimum clearance or authorization of IS users and the maximum sensitivity (e.g.; classification and categories) of data processed by the system.

US National Information Assurance (IA) Glossary

Risk levels

The extent to which vulnerability could be exploited or the amount of damage that could be done. Risk levels are usually measured in a qualitative manner as high, moderate, or low.

Centers for Medicare & Medicaid Services (CMS)

Risk management

The ongoing process of identifying risks and implementing plans to address them. The total process of identifying, controlling, and mitigating information technology related risks. It includes risk analysis; cost-benefit analysis; and the selection, implementation, test, and se-

433

curity evaluation of safeguards. This overall system security review considers both effectiveness and efficiency, including impact on the mission/business and constraints due to policy, regulations, and laws. This term characterizes the overall process. The first, or risk analysis, phase includes identifying risks, risk-reducing measures, and the budgetary impact of implementing decisions related to the acceptance, avoidance, or transfer of risk. The second phase of risk management includes the process of assigning priority to, budgeting, implementing, and maintaining appropriate risk-reducing measures. Risk management is a continuous process of ever-increasing complexity. Risk management can be quantitative (based on numerical data) or qualitative. See also risk assessment, risk treatment, CRAMM.

CERT OCTAVE, NIST 800 series, FISCAM, Centers for Medicare & Medicaid Services (CMS), ISO/IEC 27001:2005, ISO/IEC Guide 73:2002, FIPS Pubs, ITIL, US National Information Assurance (IA) Glossary, PAS 56, BS 25999

Risk management program

The set of controls, processes and structures put in place to support risk management. See also risk mitigation plan.

PAS 56

Risk mitigation

Risk mitigation involves prioritizing, evaluating, and implementing the appropriate risk-reducing controls recommended from the risk assessment process.

NIST 800 series

Risk mitigation plan

A plan that is intended to reduce the risks to a critical asset. Risk mitigation plans tend to incorporate actions, or countermeasures, designed to counter the threats to the assets. See also risk reduction measure, countermeasure, control. See also risk management program.

CERT OCTAVE

Risk profile

Defines the range of risks that can affect an asset. Risk profiles contain categories that are grouped according to threat source (human actors using network access, human actors using physical access, system problems, other problems).

CERT OCTAVE, PAS 56

Risk reduction measure

See control, countermeasure.

ITIL

Risk tolerance

The level of risk an entity is willing to assume in order to achieve a potential desired result.

NIST 800 series

Risk treatment

The process of selection and implementation of measures/controls to modify risk. The part of risk management responsible for choosing and implementing an option for managing a risk. Options for risk treatments include: Applying cost effective controls to reduce the risk. Deciding to accept the risk Avoiding the risk by preventing the situation that could lead to it. Transferring the risk to a third party, for example, by taking out insurance.

ISO/IEC 27001:2005, ISO/IEC Guide 73:2002, ITIL

Roadmap

A central repository intended to provide summary, as well as detailed, information regarding approved CMS policies, processes, procedures, templates, resources and standards established for the successful engineering, implementation, maintenance and management of all CMS Information Technology (IT) projects. As such, the Roadmap provides active contributors on IT projects with an entry point to a wealth of information for successfully accomplishing the IT investment management process and Systems Development Life Cycle at CMS.

Centers for Medicare & Medicaid Services (CMS)

Role of a system

Once a system's role has been defined, the continuity requirements that are implicit in that role can be defined and then explicitly stated in terms of supporting the organization's mission.

NIST 800 series

Roles

A set of responsibilities defined in a process and assigned to a person or team. One person or team may have multiple roles, for example, the roles of configuration manager and change manager be carried out by a single person. See also job description.

ITIL

Rollout

Most often used to refer to complex or phased deployments. See also deployment.

ITIL

Root cause

The underlying or original cause of an incident or problem.

CobiT, ITIL

Root Cause Analysis (RCA)

The process of learning from consequences, typically of errors and problems. RCA typically concentrates on IT infrastructure failures. See also service outage analysis.

CobiT, ITIL

Root Certification Authority

In a hierarchical Public Key Infrastructure, the Certification Authority whose public key serves as the most trusted datum (i.e., the beginning of trust paths) for a security domain.

NIST 800 series

Root directory

The top level in a hierarchical file system. For example on a PC, the root directory of your hard drive, usually C:, contains all the second-level subdirectories on that drive.

Sedona Conference

Rootkit

A software suite designed to aid an intruder in gaining unauthorized administrative access to a computer system. After gaining root-level access to a host to conceal the attacker's activities on the host and permit the attacker to maintain root-level access to the host through covert means.

ISACA, NIST 800 Series

Rotary Camera

In microfilming, the papers are read "on the fly" with a camera that's synchronized to the motion.

Sedona Conference

Rotating standby

A fail-over process in which there are two nodes (as in idle standby but without priority). The node that enters the cluster first owns the resource group, and the second will join as a standby node.

ISACA

Round key

Round keys are values derived from the Cipher Key using the Key Expansion routine; they are applied to the State in the Cipher and Inverse Cipher.

NIST 800 series, FIPS Pubs

Router

A networking device that can send (route) data packets from one Local Area Network (LAN) or Wide Area Network (WAN) to another, based on addressing at the network layer (Layer 3) in the OSI model. Networks connected by routers can use different or similar networking protocols. As part of a LAN, a router receives transmitted messages and forwards them to their destination over the most efficient available route. Routers are usually capable of filtering packets based on parameters such as source addresses, destination addresses, protocol, and network applications (ports). Packet filtering routers, the simplest form of firewall protection, screen incoming and outgoing packets based on IP header information including source and destination addresses, protocol, source and destination port numbers.

Network Frontiers, FISCAM, ISACA, Centers for Medicare & Medicaid Services (CMS), PCI-DSS, Sedona Conference

RS-232 interface

Interface between data terminal equipment and data communications equipment employing serial binary data interchange.

ISACA

RSA

A public key cryptosystem developed by R. Rivest, A. Shamir, and L. Adleman. The RSA has two different keys, the public encryption key and the secret decryption key. The strength of the RSA depends on the difficulty of the prime number factorization. For applications with high-level security, the number of the decryption key bits should be greater than 512 bits. RSA is used for both encryption and digital signatures.

ISACA, PCI-DSS

Rule-based security policy

A security policy based on global rules imposed for all subjects. These rules usually rely on a comparison of the sensitivity of the objects being accessed and the possession of corresponding attributes by the subjects requesting access.

NIST 800 series

Rulebase

The list of rules and/or guidance that is used to analyze event data.

ISACA

Rules Of Behavior (ROB)

Guidelines describing permitted actions by users and their responsibilities when utilizing a computer system. ROB are the rules that have been established and implemented concerning use of, security in, and acceptable level of risk for the system. Rules will clearly delineate responsibilities and expected behavior of all individuals with access to the system. Rules should cover such matters as work at home, dial-in access, connection to the Internet, use of copyrighted works, unofficial use of federal government equipment, the assignment and limitation of system privileges and individual accountability. Rules for individual users of each general support system or application. These rules should clearly delineate responsibilities of and expectations for all individuals with access to the system. They should be consistent with system-specific policy. In addition, they should state the consequences of noncompliance. The rules should be in writing and will form the basis for security awareness and training.

Centers for Medicare & Medicaid Services (CMS)

Run

A popular, idiomatic expression for program execution.

FISCAM, Centers for Medicare & Medicaid Services (CMS)

Run instructions or run manual

A manual that provides application-specific operating instructions, such as instructions on job setup, console and error messages, job checkpoints, and re-start and recovery steps after system failures. It also identifies how to address problems that occur during processing.

FISCAM, ISACA, Centers for Medicare & Medicaid Services (CMS)

Run Length Encoded (RLE)

Compressed image format; supports only 256 colors; most effective on images with large areas of black or white.

Sedona Conference

Run to run totals

Provide verification that all transmitted data are read and processed.

ISACA

Running costs

See operational costs.

ITIL

Running down

A method of computer fraud involving a computer code that instructs the computer to remove small amounts of money from an authorized computer transaction by rounding down to the nearest whole value denomination and rerouting the rounded off amount to the perpetrator's account.

ISACA

S

S-box

Non-linear substitution table used in several byte substitution transformations and in the Key Expansion routine to perform a one for one substitution of a byte value.

NIST 800 series, FIPS Pubs

Sabotage

Malicious acts that can cause damage, destruction, interruption or loss of system assets. This could impact confidentiality, integrity, and availability.

Centers for Medicare & Medicaid Services (CMS)

Safeguard

1) Protection included to counteract a known or expected condition. 2) Incorporated countermeasure or set of countermeasures within a base release.

US National Information Assurance (IA) Glossary

Safeguarding controls

A security control or countermeasure employed to reduce the risk associated with a specific threat or group of threats. Internal controls to protect assets from loss due to unauthorized acquisition, use, or disposition arising from misstatements in processing transactions and handling the related assets.

This term represents a risk-reducing measure that acts to detect, prevent, or minimize loss associated with the occurrence of a specified threat or category of threats. Safeguards are also often described as controls or countermeasures. Safeguarding controls are considered part of financial reporting controls. Some safeguarding controls are operations controls.

GAO/PCIE Financial Audit Manual, Centers for Medicare & Medicaid Services (CMS)

Safeguarding statement

Statement affixed to a computer output or printout that states the highest classification being processed at the time the product was produced and requires control of the product, at that level, until determination of the true classification by an authorized individual. Synonymous with banner.

US National Information Assurance (IA) Glossary

Safeguards

Protective measures prescribed to meet the security requirements (i.e., confidentiality, integrity, and availability) specified for an information system. Safeguards may include security features, management constraints, personnel security, and security of physical structures, areas, and devices. Synonymous with security controls and countermeasures. See also safeguarding controls.

FIPS Pubs, NIST 800 Series

Salami technique

A method of computer fraud involving a computer code that instructs the computer to slice off small amounts of money from an authorized computer transaction and reroute this amount to the perpetrator's account.

ISACA

Sales receipt

The paper or electronic record of a bankcard transaction that a merchant submits to a merchant bank for processing and payment. In most cases, paper drafts are now generated by a merchant's POS terminal. When a merchant fills out a draft manually, it must include an imprint of the front of the card.

VISA Glossary of Terms

Salt

A non-secret value that is used in a cryptographic process, usually to ensure that the results of computations for one instance cannot be reused by an attacker.

NIST 800 series

SAM database

A database containing all data needed to support Software Asset Management.

The SAM database could be part of the CMDB.

ITIL

Sample

Items selected from a population to reach a conclusion about the population as a whole. Compare with nonsampling selection.

GAO/PCIE Financial Audit Manual

Sampling

The application of audit procedures to fewer than all items composing a population to reach a conclusion about the entire population. The auditor selects sample items in such a way that the sample and its results are expected to be representative of the population. Each item must have an opportunity to be selected, and the results of the procedures performed must be projected to the entire population. It can be a useful technique in addressing a number of issues relating to litigation, including decisions about what repositories of data are appropriate to search in a particular litigation, and determinations of the validity and effectiveness of searches or other data extraction procedures.

GAO/PCIE Financial Audit Manual, ISACA, Sedona Conference

Sampling interval

The amount between two consecutive sample items used in selecting the items in systematic sampling. In dollar-unit sampling, this amount may be determined by dividing the test materiality by a statistical risk factor.

GAO/PCIE Financial Audit Manual

Sampling rate

The frequency at which analog signals are converted to digital values during digitization. The higher the rate, the more accurate the process.

Sedona Conference

Sampling risk

The risk that the auditor's conclusion based on a sample might differ from the conclusion that would be reached by applying the test in the same way to the entire population. While sampling risk can be reduced to an acceptably low level by using an appropriate sample size and selection method, it can never be eliminated.

GAO/PCIE Financial Audit Manual, ISACA

Sanction

Sanction policies and procedures are actions taken against employees who are non-compliant with security policy.

Centers for Medicare & Medicaid Services (CMS)

Sandboxing

A method of isolating application modules into distinct fault domains enforced by software. The technique allows untrusted programs written in an unsafe language, such as C, to be executed safely within the single virtual address space of an application. Untrusted machine interpretable code modules are transformed so that all memory accesses are confined to code and data segments within their fault domain. Access to system resources can also be controlled through a unique identifier associated with each domain.

NIST 800 series

Sanitization

The elimination of information (confidential or otherwise) from a computer system or media associated with a computer system to permit the reuse of the computer system or media without the possibility that the old information could be accessed and read. See also degauss.

Centers for Medicare & Medicaid Services (CMS), PCI-DSS, FIPS Pubs, NIST 800 Series

Sanitize

To remove or edit classified or sensitive data so that what remains is of a lower classification or sensitivity than the original data. See also sanitization.

Workgroup for Electronic Data Interchange, US National Information Assurance (IA) Glossary

Scalability

The ability of an IT service, process, configuration item, etc. to perform its agreed function when the workload or scope changes. For example, multiple servers or additional storage can be easily added.

ITIL, Sedona Conference

Scale-to-Gray

An option to display a black and white image file in an enhanced mode, making it easier to view. A scale-to-gray display uses gray shading to fill in gaps or jumps (known as aliasing) that occur when displaying an image file on a computer screen. Also known as grayscale.

Sedona Conference

Scanner

An input device commonly used to convert paper documents into images. Scanner devices are also available to scan microfilm and microfiche.

Sedona Conference

Scanning

Sending packets or requests to another system to gain information to be used in a subsequent attack.

NIST 800 series

Scanning software

Software that enables a scanner to deliver industry standard formats for images in a collection. Enables the use of OCR and coding of the images.

Sedona Conference

Scavenging

The process of physical and electronic media searching for remnant (e.g., abandoned or discarded) data that may contain information of value. Physical searching is commonly referred to as "dumpster diving".

Centers for Medicare & Medicaid Services (CMS), US National Information Assurance (IA) Glossary

Scheduling

A method used in the Information Processing Facility (IPF) to determine and establish the sequence of computer job processing.

ISACA

Schema

A set of rules or conceptual model for data structure and content, such as a description of the data content and relationships in a database.

Sedona Conference

Scope

The boundary, or extent, to which a process, procedure, certification, contract etc. applies. For example, the scope of change management may include all live IT services and related configuration items, the scope of an ISO/IEC 20000 certificate may include all IT services delivered out of a named data center.

ISO/IEC 27001:2005, ITIL

Scoping guidance

Provides organizations with specific technology-related, infrastructure-related, public access-related, scalability-related, common security control-related, and risk-related considerations on the applicability and implementation of individual security controls in the control baseline.

NIST 800 series, FIPS Pubs

Screening router

A router configured to permit or deny traffic based on a set of permission rules installed by the administrator.

ISACA

Script test

A vulnerability evaluation tool that provides the same functionality as automated tools, but they usually have a singular function. If a large number of items are being evaluated, a corresponding number of scripts will be required. Scripts require a consistent review of the items being checked and must be routinely updated.

CERT OCTAVE

Scroll Bar

The bar on the side or bottom of a window that allows the user to scroll up and down through the window's contents. Scroll bars have scroll arrows at both ends, and a scroll box, all of which can be used to scroll around the window.

Sedona Conference

Search

See Compliance search, Concept search, Contextual search, Boolean search, Full-text search, Fuzzy search, Index, Keyword search, Pattern recognition, Proximity search, QBIC, Sampling, and Search Engine.

Sedona Conference

Search Engine

A program that enables search for keywords or phrases, such as on web pages throughout the World Wide Web.

Sedona Conference

Second-line support

The second level in a hierarchy of support groups involved in the resolution of incidents and investigation of problems. Each level contains more specialized skills or has more time or other resources. See also escalation.

ITIL

Secret key

A cryptographic key that is used with a secret key (symmetric) cryptographic algorithm, that is uniquely associated with one or more entities and is not be made public. The use of the term "secret" in this context does not imply a classification level, but rather implies the need to protect the key from disclosure.

NIST 800 series, FIPS Pubs

Secret Key (symmetric) Cryptographic Algorithm

A cryptographic algorithm that uses a single secret key for both encryption and decryption. This is the traditional method used for encryption. The same key is used for both encryption and decryption. Only the party or parties that exchange secret messages know the secret key. The biggest problem with symmetric key encryption is securely distributing the keys. Public key techniques are now often used to distribute the symmetric keys.

NIST 800 series, FIPS Pubs

Secret seed

A secret value that used to initialize a pseudorandom number generator. The resulting value from the random number generator remains secret or private.

NIST 800 series

Sector

A sector is normally the smallest individually addressable unit of information stored on a hard drive platter, and usually holds 512 bytes of information. Sectors are numbered sequentially starting with 1 on each individual track. Thus, Track 0, Sector 1 and Track 5, Sector 1 refer to different sectors on the same hard drive. The first PC Hard discs typically held 17 sectors per track. Today, they can hold thousands of sectors per track.

Sedona Conference

Secure communication protocol

A communication protocol that provides the appropriate confidentiality, authentication and content integrity protection.

NIST 800 series

Secure communications

Telecommunications deriving security through use of type 1 products and/or PDSs.

US National Information Assurance (IA) Glossary

Secure Hash Algorithm (SHA-1)

Secure Hash Algorithm, for computing a condensed representation of a message or a data file specified by FIPS PUB 180-1.

Sedona Conference, FIPS Pubs, NIST 800 Series

Secure hash standard

Specification for a secure hash algorithm that can generate a condensed message representation called a message digest.

US National Information Assurance (IA) Glossary

Secure Multipurpose Internet Mail Extension (S/MIME)

A set of specifications for securing electronic mail. Secure/ Multipurpose Internet Mail Extensions (S/MIME) is based upon the widely used MIME standard and describes a protocol for adding cryptographic security services through MIME encapsulation of digitally signed and encrypted objects. The basic security services offered by S/MIME are authentication, non-repudiation of origin, message integrity, and message privacy. Optional security services include signed receipts, security labels, secure mailing lists, and an extended method of identifying the signer's certificate(s).

Workgroup for Electronic Data Interchange, NIST 800 Series

Secure Shell (SSH)

A program to log into another computer over a network, to execute commands in a remote machine, and to move files from one machine to another while providing strong authentication and secure communications over insecure channels. It is intended as a replacement for telnet, rlogin, rsh, and rcp.

Centers for Medicare & Medicaid Services (CMS), PCI-DSS

Secure Socket Layer (SSL)

The leading security protocol on the Internet. A protocol originally developed by Netscape Communications to provide a high level of security for its browser software. It has become accepted widely as a means of securing Internet message exchanges. It ensures confidentiality of the data in transmission using encryption. In a typical SSL session, the server sends its public key to the browser; the browser uses that public key to send a randomly generated secret key back to the original server in order to have a secret key exchange for that session.

Network Frontiers, ISACA, Centers for Medicare & Medicaid Services (CMS), PCI-DSS, Workgroup for Electronic Data Interchange

Secure Socket Layer and Transport Layer Security (SSL and TSL)

Secure Sockets Layer is a protocol developed by Netscape for transmitting private documents via the Internet. SSL works by using a public key to encrypt data that's transferred over the SSL connection. Most web browsers support SSL, and many web sites use the protocol to obtain confidential user information, such as credit card numbers. By convention, URLs that require an SSL connection start with "https:" instead of "http:." TLS is an Internet standard based on SSL version 3.0. There are only very minor differences between SSL and TLS.

NIST 800 series

Secure state

Condition in which no subject can access any object in an unauthorized manner.

US National Information Assurance (IA) Glossary

Secure storage

When the storage media is not physically protected against unauthorized access (which you can't do with a CD-ROM or a backup tape), special measures have to be taken to block unauthorized access. For example, if regulated data is stored on a CD-ROM or backup tape, then additional measures are needed to protect the data against access or compromise. The information stored on the media has to be protected using encryption to ensure confidentiality. The creator could use a key to encrypt the data onto the media, and the reader would then use its symmetric pair to decrypt the data. This could also be accomplished using asymmetric encryption with the creator encrypting the data onto the media using the intended reader's public key. Then, no one but that reader will be able to decrypt the information using his or her private key. See also key management.

HIPAA

Secure subsystem

Subsystem containing its own implementation of the reference monitor concept for those resources it controls. Secure subsystem must depend on other controls and the base operating system for the control of subjects and the more primitive system objects.

US National Information Assurance (IA) Glossary

Secure transfer

Secure transfer (the secure exchange of information objects) takes place between two organizations that have pre-established a trusted relationship between sender and receiver. When the exchange utilizes encryption to provide security the needed trust is linked to the keys used to encrypt and then decrypt the data, and where the keys came from. During the establishment of a connection for secure data transfer, the authentication of both parties has to be verified.

HIPAA

Securities & Exchange Commission (SEC)

The mission of the US Securities and Exchange Commission is to protect investors, maintain fair, orderly, and efficient markets, and facilitate capital formation. See also http://www.sec.gov for more information.

de facto

Security

Security is a system property. Security is much more that a set of functions and mechanisms. Information technology security is a system characteristic as well as a set of mechanisms which span the system both logically and physically. Therefore it is the protection of computer facilities, computer systems, and data stored on computer systems or transmitted via computer networks from loss, misuse, or unauthorized access. Computer security, as defined by Appendix III to OMB Circular A-130, involves the use of management, personnel, operational, and technical controls to ensure that systems and applications operate effectively and provide confidentiality, integrity, and availability. See also information security management.

NIST 800 series, FISCAM, OMB Circular A-130, Centers for Medicare & Medicaid Services (CMS), ITIL

Security accreditation

The official management decision given by a senior agency official to authorize operation of an information system and to explicitly accept the risk to agency operations (including mission, functions, image, or reputation), agency assets, or individuals, based on the implementation of an agreed-upon set of security controls.

NIST 800 series

Security administrator (SA)

Person who is responsible for managing the security program for computer facilities, computer systems, and/or data that are stored on computer systems or transmitted via computer networks.

Centers for Medicare & Medicaid Services (CMS)

Security architecture

A description of security principles and an overall approach for complying with the principles that drive the system design; i.e., guidelines on the placement and implementation of specific security services within various distributed computing environments.

NIST 800 series

Security Assertion Markup Language (SAML)

Security Assertion Markup Language (SAML) is an XML-based framework for authentication and authorization information.

Workgroup for Electronic Data Interchange, NIST 800 Series

Security attribute

A security-related quality of an object. Security attributes may be represented as hierarchical levels, bits in a bit map, or numbers. Compartments, caveats, and release markings are examples of security attributes.

NIST 800 series

Security authorization

The official management decision given by a senior agency official to authorize operation of an information system and to explicitly accept the risk to agency operations (including mission, functions, image, or reputation), agency assets, or individuals, based on the implementation of an agreed-upon set of security controls.

NIST 800 series

Security awareness

The general, collective awareness of an organization's personnel on the importance of security and security controls.

Centers for Medicare & Medicaid Services (CMS), ISO/IEC 27001:2005

Security category

The characterization of information or an information system based on an assessment of the potential impact that a loss of confidentiality, integrity, or availability of such information or information system would have on organizational operations, organizational assets, or individuals.

FIPS Pubs, NIST 800 Series

Security certification

A formal testing of the security safeguards implemented in the computer system to determine whether they meet applicable requirements and specifications. To provide more reliable technical information, certification is often performed by an independent reviewer, rather than by the people who designed the system.

Centers for Medicare & Medicaid Services (CMS), NIST 800 series

Security component

Devices that have security as their primary function. A firewall is an example of a security component.

CERT OCTAVE

Security control baseline

The set of minimum security controls defined for a low-impact, moderate-impact, or high-impact information system.

FIPS Pubs, NIST 800 Series

Security control enhancements

Statements of security capability to: 1) build in additional, but related, functionality to a basic control; and/or 2) increase the strength of a basic control.

NIST 800 series

Security controls

The management, operational, and technical controls (i.e., safeguards or countermeasures) prescribed for an information system to protect the confidentiality, integrity, and availability of the system and its information.

FIPS Pubs, US National Information Assurance (IA) Glossary, NIST 800 Series

Security design and implementation principle

Participants should incorporate security as an essential element of information systems and networks.

OECD Guidelines for the Security of Information Systems and Networks

Security domain

A set of subjects, their information objects, and a common security policy. A scope or environment of trust that shares a single security policy and a single management.

NIST 800 series, Centers for Medicare & Medicaid Services (CMS), ISO/IEC 27001:2005, FIPS Pubs

Security Fault Analysis (SFA)

Assessment, usually performed on IS hardware, to determine the security properties of a device when hardware fault is encountered.

US National Information Assurance (IA) Glossary

Security Features Users Guide (SFUG)

Guide or manual explaining how the security mechanisms in a specific system work.

US National Information Assurance (IA) Glossary

Security filter

IS trusted subsystem that enforces security policy on the data passing through it.

US National Information Assurance (IA) Glossary

Security goal

The IT security goal is to enable an organization to meet all mission/business objectives by implementing systems with due care consideration of IT-related risks to the organization, its partners, and its customers. The five security goals are integrity, availability, confidentiality, accountability, and assurance (which is a balance of the other four). See also security objectives.

NIST 800 series

Security Hash Algorithm (SHA)

A family or set of related cryptographic hash functions. SHA-1 is most commonly used function. Use of unique salt value in the hashing function reduces the chances of a hashed value collision.

PCI-DSS

Security impact analysis

The analysis conducted by an agency official, often during the continuous monitoring phase of the security certification and accreditation process, to determine the extent to which changes to the information system have affected the security posture of the system.

NIST 800 series

Security in depth

Synonymous with defense in depth.

US National Information Assurance (IA) Glossary

Security incident

A computer security incident is any adverse event whereby some aspect of computer security could be threatened; loss of data confidentiality, disruption of data or system integrity, or disruption or denial of availability.

Centers for Medicare & Medicaid Services (CMS), ISO/IEC 27001:2005

Security inspection

Examination of an information system to determine compliance with security policy, procedures, and practices.

US National Information Assurance (IA) Glossary

Security kernel

Hardware, firmware, and software elements of a trusted computing base implementing the reference monitor concept. Security kernel must mediate all accesses, be protected from modification, and be verifiable as correct.

US National Information Assurance (IA) Glossary

Security label

Information representing the sensitivity of a subject or object, such as UNCLASSIFIED or its hierarchical classification (CONFIDENTIAL, SECRET, TOP SECRET) together with any applicable nonhierarchical security categories (e.g., sensitive compartmented information, critical nuclear weapon design information).

US National Information Assurance (IA) Glossary, NIST 800 Series, FIPS Pubs

Security level

A hierarchical indicator of the degree of sensitivity to a certain threat. It implies, according to the security policy being enforced, a specific level of protection.

NIST 800 series, FIPS Pubs

Security level designation

A rating based on the sensitivity of data (i.e., the need to protect data from unauthorized disclosure, fraud, waste, or abuse) and the operational criticality of data processing capabilities (i.e., the consequences were data processing capabilities to be interrupted for some period of time or subjected to fraud or abuse). There are four security level designations for data sensitivity and four security level designations for operational criticality. The highest security level designation for any data or process within an AIS is assigned for the overall security level designation.

Centers for Medicare & Medicaid Services (CMS)

Security management

The process of establishing and maintaining security in a computer or network system. The stages of this process include prevention of security problems, detection of intrusions, investigation of intrusions, and resolution. In network management controlling access to the network and resources, finding intrusions, identifying entry points for intruders, and repairing or otherwise closing those avenues of access. This includes the application of computer code intended to repair or lessen the impact of vulnerabilities within application software. See also information security management.

ISACA, Centers for Medicare & Medicaid Services (CMS), ISO/IEC 27001:2005, ITIL

Security management function

The function responsible for the development and administration of an entity's information security program. This includes assessing risks, implementing appropriate security policies and related controls, establishing a security awareness and education program for employees, and monitoring and evaluating policy and control effectiveness.

FISCAM

Security management principle

Participants should adopt a comprehensive approach to security management.

OECD Guidelines for the Security of Information Systems and Networks

Security manager

See information security manager.

ITIL

Security net control station

Management system overseeing and controlling implementation of network security policy.

US National Information Assurance (IA) Glossary

Security objective

Confidentiality, integrity, or availability.

NIST 800 series, FIPS Pubs

Security objectives

The five security objectives are integrity, availability, confidentiality, accountability, and assurance.

NIST 800 series, ISO/IEC 27001:2005, FIPS Pubs

Security officer

The person who takes primary responsibility for the security related affairs of the organization. See also information security officer.

PCI-DSS, ITIL

Security patch

Computer code intended to repair or lessen the impact of vulnerabilities within application software.

Centers for Medicare & Medicaid Services (CMS)

Security perimeter

The boundary that defines the area of security concern and security policy coverage.

ISACA, ISO/IEC 27001:2005, US National Information Assurance (IA) Glossary, NIST 800 Series

Security plan

A written plan that clearly describes the entity's security program and policies and procedures that support it. The plan and related policies should cover all major systems and facilities and outline the duties of those who are responsible for overseeing security (the security management function) as well as those who own, use, or rely on the entity's computer resources. See also system security plan.

FISCAM, Centers for Medicare & Medicaid Services (CMS), FIPS Pubs, NIST 800 Series

Security policy

The statement of required protection of the information objects that documents an organization's philosophy of managing, protecting, and distributing its computing and information assets. The set of security rules enforced by the system's security features. In business, a security policy is a document that states in writing how a company plans to protect the company's physical and Information

Technology assets. A security policy is often considered to be a "living document," meaning that the document is never finished, but is continuously updated as technology and employee requirements change. See also information security policy.

NIST 800 series, ISACA, Centers for Medicare & Medicaid Services (CMS), ISO/IEC 27001:2005, PCI-DSS

Security practice

Actions that help initiate, implement, and maintain security within an organization. A security practice is also called a protection strategy practice.

CERT OCTAVE

Security principle

A strategic objective in an information security policy. Common security principles include confidentiality, integrity and availability. Other objectives such as non-repudiation and accountability can also be security principles.

ITIL

Security profile

See profile.

FISCAM, Centers for Medicare & Medicaid Services (CMS)

Security program

The security program is an entity-wide program for security planning and management that forms the foundation of an entity's security control structure and reflects senior management's commitment to addressing security risks. The program should establish a framework and continuing cycle of activity for assessing risk, developing and implementing effective security procedures, and monitoring the effectiveness of these procedures.

FISCAM, Centers for Medicare & Medicaid Services (CMS)

Security range

Highest and lowest security levels that are permitted in or on an information system, system component, subsystem, or network.

US National Information Assurance (IA) Glossary

Security requirements

Requirements outlining the qualities of information assets that are important to an organization. These requirements are derived from applicable laws, Executive Orders, directives, policies, standards, instructions, regulations, procedures, or organizational mission/business case needs to ensure the confidentiality, integrity, and availability of the information being processed, stored, or transmitted. In other words, these requirements are the types and levels of protection necessary for equipment, data, information, applications, and facilities to meet security policy. See also sensitivity.

CERT OCTAVE, Centers for Medicare & Medicaid Services (CMS), ISO/IEC 27001:2005, FIPS Pubs, US National Information Assurance (IA) Glossary, NIST 800 Series

Security requirements baseline

Description of the minimum requirements necessary for an IS to maintain an acceptable level of security.

Centers for Medicare & Medicaid Services (CMS), US National Information Assurance (IA) Glossary

Security risk

See transaction risk.

ISACA

Security safeguards

Protective measures and controls prescribed to meet the security requirements specified for an information system. Safeguards may include security features, management constraints, personnel security, and security of physical structures, areas, and devices. See also accreditation.

US National Information Assurance (IA) Glossary

Security service

A capability that supports one, or many, of the security goals. Examples of secu-

rity services are key management, access control, and authentication.

NIST 800 series

Security software

Software used to administer logical security. It usually includes authentication of users, access granting according to predefined rules, and monitoring and reporting functions. See also access control software.

FISCAM, ISACA, Centers for Medicare & Medicaid Services (CMS)

Security specification

A security specification is a detailed description of the safeguards required to protect a sensitive application (or any AIS asset).

Centers for Medicare & Medicaid Services (CMS), OMB Circular A-130, US National Information Assurance (IA) Glossary

Security tag

Information unit containing a representation of certain security-related information (e.g., a restrictive attribute bit map).

NIST 800 series, FIPS Pubs

Security target

Common Criteria specification that represents a set of security requirements to be used as the basis of an evaluation of an identified Target of Evaluation (TOE).

US National Information Assurance (IA) Glossary

Security Technical Implementation Guide (STIG)

The Cyber Security Research and Development Act requires NIST to develop, and revise as necessary, a checklist setting forth settings and option selections that minimize the security risks associated with each computer hardware or software system that, or is likely to become widely used within the Federal Government.

NIST 800 series

Security testing

Process to determine that an information system protects data and maintains functionality as intended.

US National Information Assurance (IA) Glossary

Security testing and evaluation (ST&E)

Making sure the modified/new system includes appropriate access controls and does not introduce any security holes that might compromise other systems. An examination and analysis of the security safeguards of a system as they have been applied in an operational environment in order to determine the se-

curity posture of the system. This process includes hands on functional testing, penetration testing and verification.

ISACA, Centers for Medicare & Medicaid Services (CMS), NIST 800 series, US National Information Assurance (IA) Glossary

Security threat

The ability to exploit a computer or network vulnerability.

Network Frontiers

Security training and awareness

See information security training and awareness.

Centers for Medicare & Medicaid Services (CMS)

Security vulnerability

An opening into a system or an opportunity to acquire information.

Network Frontiers

Seed key

Initial key used to start an updating or key generation process.

US National Information Assurance (IA) Glossary

Segregation of duties

The practice of dividing the steps in a system function among different individuals, so as to keep a single individual from subverting the process. A basic control that prevents or detects errors and irregularities by assigning responsibility for initiating transactions, recording transactions and custody of assets to separate individuals. To ensure that no single person has control of a transaction from beginning to end, two or more people are responsible for its execution. Commonly used in large IT organizations so that no single person is in a position to introduce fraudulent or malicious code without detection. This is intended to prevent one person from manipulating transactions for personal gain, however it will not stop both people who are in collusion.

ISACA, CobiT, Centers for Medicare & Medicaid Services (CMS), ISO/IEC 27001:2005, PCI-DSS, ITIL

Self checking digit

See check digit verification.

ISACA

Self-Monitoring, Analysis and Reporting Technology (S.M.A.R.T.)

Self-Monitoring, Analysis and Reporting Technology is implemented into all of the modern hard discs. A special program inside the disk constantly keeps tracking the condition of a range of the vital parameters; driver, disk heads, surface state, electronics, etc.

IBM

Senior Agency Information Security Officer

Official responsible for carrying out the Chief Information Officer responsibilities under FISMA and serving as the Chief Information Officer's primary liaison to the agency's authorizing officials, information system owners, and information system security officers.

FIPS Pubs

Senior management

A person or group of people who directs and controls an organization at the highest level. Senior management, especially in a large multinational organization, might not be directly involved; however senior management accountability through the chain of command is manifest. In a small organization, senior management might be the owner or sole proprietor.

BS 25999

Sensitive application

An application that processes sensitive data. An application of information technology that requires protection because it processes sensitive data, or because of the risk and magnitude of loss or harm that could result from improper operation, deliberates manipulation, or delivery interruption of the application.

Centers for Medicare & Medicaid Services (CMS), OMB Circular A-130

Sensitive authentication data

Security-related information (Card Validation Codes/Values complete track data, and PINs, and PIN Blocks) used to authenticate cardholders,) appearing in plaintext or otherwise unprotected form. disclosure, modification, or destruction of this information could compromise the security of a cryptographic device, information system, or cardholder information or could be used in a fraudulent transaction.

PCI-DSS

Sensitive But Unclassified Information

The categorization of information whose exposure could prove detrimental to a system, person or organization but will not create serious damage to national security if disclosed. Health Care information is an example of SBU data. See also confidential information.

Centers for Medicare & Medicaid Services (CMS)

Sensitive cardholder data

Data whose unauthorized disclosure may be used in fraudulent transaction. It includes, the account number, magnetic stripe data, CVC2/CVV2, and expiration date. See also confidential information.

PCI-DSS

Sensitive Compartmented Information (SCI)

Classified information concerning or derived from intelligence sources, methods, or analytical processes, which is required to be handled within formal access control systems established by the Director of Central Intelligence.

US National Information Assurance (IA) Glossary

Sensitive Compartmented Information Facility (SCIF)

Accredited area, room, or group of rooms, buildings, or installation where SCI may be stored, used, discussed, and/or processed.

US National Information Assurance (IA) Glossary

Sensitive data

Data that require protection due to the risk and magnitude of loss or harm that could result from inadvertent or deliberate disclosure, alteration, or destruction of the data. The term includes data whose improper use or disclosure could adversely affect the ability of an agency to accomplish its mission, proprietary data, records about individuals requiring protection under the Privacy Act, and data not releasable under the Freedom of Information Act.

Centers for Medicare & Medicaid Services (CMS), OMB Circular A-130, ISO/IEC 27001:2005

Sensitive information

Any information that, if lost, misused, accessed, or modified in an improper manner could adversely affect the national interest, the conduct of federal programs, or the privacy to which individuals are entitled under section 552a of title 5, United States Code (the Privacy Act), but which has not been specifically authorized under criteria established by an Executive Order or an Act of Congress to be kept secret in the interest of national defense or foreign policy.

FISCAM, Centers for Medicare & Medicaid Services (CMS), Computer Security Act of 1987, US National Information Assurance (IA) Glossary

Sensitive media

Any form in which sensitive information is stored including paper, discette, etc.

Centers for Medicare & Medicaid Services (CMS)

Sensitivity

The degree to which information, data, or a system requires protection to ensure confidentiality, integrity, and availability.

Centers for Medicare & Medicaid Services (CMS), ISO/IEC 27001:2005, NIST 800 Series

Sensitivity label

Information representing elements of the security label(s) of a subject and an object. Sensitivity labels are used by the trusted computing base (TCB) as the basis for mandatory access control decisions.

US National Information Assurance (IA) Glossary

Sensitivity levels

A graduated system of marking (e.g., low, moderate, high) information and information processing systems based on threats and risks that result if a threat is successfully conducted.

NIST 800 series, FIPS Pubs

Sensitivity of data

The need to protect data from unauthorized disclosure, fraud, waste, or abuse.

Centers for Medicare & Medicaid Services (CMS)

Sentencing

The process of identifying the disposal class a record belongs to and applying the disposal action specified in the relevant disposal authority to the record. Sentencing is the implementation of decisions made during appraisal.

DIRKS

Separation of duties

See segregation of duties.

Centers for Medicare & Medicaid Services (CMS), CobiT, PCI-DSS

Sequence check

Verifies that the control number follows sequentially and any control numbers out of sequence are rejected or noted on an exception report for further research (can be alpha or numeric and usually utilizes a key field).

ISACA

Sequential file

A computer file storage format in which one record follows another. Records can be accessed sequentially only. Sequential access is required with magnetic tape as the tape must be read linearly from one end to the other.

ISACA

Serial Line Internet Protocol (SLIP)

A connection to the Internet in which the interface software runs in the local computer, rather than the Internet's.

Sedona Conference

Serializes media

This requirement was originally intended for removable media. However, with new technology emerging, including magnetic disk, serialization must occur at the physical or logical level of a subsystem. The serialization requirement assists examiners in determining timing of record creation and also assists in controlling media inventory.

17 CFR 240.17a-4

Serif

The little cross bars or curls at the end of strokes on certain type fonts.

Sedona Conference

Server

A computer running administrative software that controls access to all or part of the network and its resources, such as disk drives or printers. A computer acting as a server makes resources available to computers acting as workstations on the network. For example, there are web servers that send out web pages, mail servers that deliver e-mail, list servers that administer mailing lists, FTP servers that hold FTP sites and deliver files to users who request them, and name servers that provide information about Internet host names. See also File Server.

CERT OCTAVE, FISCAM, ISACA, Centers for Medicare & Medicaid Services (CMS), PCI-DSS, ITIL, Sedona Conference

Service

Providing something of value to a customer that is not goods (physical things with material value). Examples of services include banking and legal support. Service is also used as a synonym for IT service. See also business service, service request.

ITIL

Service bureau

A computer facility or third party that provides data processing services to clients on a continual basis.

ISACA

Service Capacity Management (CPM)

The activity responsible for understanding the performance and capacity of IT services. The resources used by each IT service and the pattern of usage over time are collected, recorded, and analyzed for use in the capacity plan. See also business capacity management, resource capacity management.

ITIL

Service catalog

A document listing all IT services with summary information about their SLAs and customers. The service catalogue is created and maintained by the IT service provider and is used by all IT service management processes. See also portfolio of services.

ITIL

Service code

Three- or four-digit number on the magnetic-stripe that specifies acceptance requirements and limitations for a magnetic-stripe read transaction.

PCI-DSS

Service continuity controls

This type of control involves ensuring that when unexpected events occur, critical operations continue without interruption or are promptly resumed and critical and sensitive data are protected.

FISCAM, Centers for Medicare & Medicaid Services (CMS)

Service culture

A customer oriented culture. The major objectives of a service culture are customer satisfaction and helping the customer to achieve their business objectives. See also business IT alignment, customer focus.

ITIL

Service delivery

The core IT service management processes that have a tactical or strategic focus. In ITIL these are service level management, capacity management, IT service continuity management, availability management, and financial management for IT services. Service delivery is also used to mean the delivery of IT services to customers. See also service support.

ITIL

Service dependency modeling

A technique that is used to graphically represent the dependency of IT services on configuration items.

ITIL

Service desk

The single point of contact within the IT organization for users of IT services. A typical service desk manages incidents and service requests and also handles communication with the users. See also call center.

CobiT, ITIL

Service hours

An agreed time period when a particular IT service should be available. For example, "Monday-Friday 08:00 to 17:00 except public holidays and when we are playing WarCraft with it". Service hours should be defined in a service level agreement.

ITIL

Service Improvement Plan (SIP)

A formal plan to implement improvements to a process or IT service. A SIP is managed as part of a continuous improvement process.

ITIL

Service level

Measured and reported achievement against one or more service level targets. Service level is sometimes used as an informal term to mean service level target.

ITIL

Service Level Agreement (SLA)

Defined minimum performance measures at or above which the service delivered is considered acceptable. Written agreement between a service provider and the customer(s)/user(s) that documents agreed service levels for a service. The SLA describes the IT service, documents service level targets, and specifies the responsibilities of the IT service provider and the customer. A single SLA may cover multiple IT services or multiple customers. See also operational level agreement.

de facto, ITIL, ISACA, Sedona Conference

Service Level Agreement Monitoring Chart (SLAM Chart)

A SLAM chart is used to help monitor and report achievements against service level targets. A SLAM chart is typically color coded to show whether each agreed service level target has been met, missed, or nearly missed during each of the previous 12 months.

ITIL

Service Level Management (SLM)

The process responsible for negotiating service level agreements and ensuring that these are met. SLM is responsible for ensuring that all IT service management processes, operational level agreements, and underpinning contracts are appropriate for the agreed service level targets. SLM monitors and reports on service levels and holds regular customer reviews. See also service reporting.

ITIL

Service Level Requirement (SLR)

A customer requirement for an aspect of an IT service. SLRs are based on business objectives and are used to negotiate agreed service level targets. See also Service Level Agreement.

ITIL

Service level target

A commitment that is documented in a Service Level Agreement. Service level targets are based on Service Level Requirements, and are needed to ensure that the IT service design is fit for purpose. Service level targets should be measurable, and are usually based on KPIs. See also service level, SMART.

ITIL

Service Maintenance Objective (SMO)

The expected time that a configuration item will be unavailable due to planned maintenance activity. See also planned downtime.

ITIL

Service manager

A generic term that can be used to mean any manager within the IT service provider. Most commonly used to refer to a business relationship manager, a process manager, an account manager, or a senior manager with responsibility for IT services overall.

ITIL

Service Oriented Architecture

In computing, the term Service-oriented architecture (SOA) expresses a software architectural concept that defines the use of services to support the requirements of software users.

de facto

Service Outage Activity

An activity that identifies underlying causes of an IT service interruption. SOA identifies opportunities to improve the IT service provider's processes and tools and not just the IT infrastructure. SOA is a time constrained, project-like activity, rather than an ongoing process of analysis. See also root cause analysis.

ITIL

Service Outage Activity or Service Oriented Architecture

See Service Outage Activity, Service Oriented Architecture.

ITIL, de facto

Service planning

The process responsible for implementing and retiring IT services. Service planning includes understanding customer requirements and planning the lifecycle of an IT service. ISO/IEC 20000 calls this process "planning and implementing new or changed services." See also portfolio management.

ITIL

Service provider

The organization providing the outsourced service. External entity that provides services to the organization. Service provider is often used as an abbreviation for IT service provider.

ISACA, CobiT, ITIL, PCI-DSS

Service reporting

The process responsible for producing and delivering reports of achievement and trends against service levels. Service reporting should agree with the format, content, and frequency of reports provided to customers.

ITIL

Service request

A request from a user for information or advice, or for a standard change. For example, to reset a password or to provide standard IT services for a new user. Service requests are usually handled by a service desk and do not require an RFC to be submitted.

ITIL

Service Set Identifier (SSID)

SSID is a 32-character unique identifier attached to the header of packets sent over a wireless network that acts as a password when a mobile device tries to connect to the network. The SSID differentiates one WLAN from another; so all access points and all devices attempting to connect to a specific WLAN must use the same SSID.

Network Frontiers, PCI-DSS

Service support

The core IT service management processes that have an operational focus. These are incident management, problem management, configuration management, change management, and release management. Service support also includes the service desk. See also service delivery.

ITIL

Service user

The organization using the outsourced service.

ISACA

Serviceability

The ability of a third party supplier to meet the terms of their contract. This contract will include agreed levels of reliability, maintainability, or availability for a configuration item.

ITIL

Session control

The application of security mechanisms to network connections which are intended to prevent unauthorized persons from capturing or modifying network connection data or taking control of preestablished network connections.

Centers for Medicare & Medicaid Services (CMS)

Seven principles of the OECD Guidelines for the Security of Information Systems and Networks

See awareness, responsibility, response, risk assessment, security design and implementation, security management, and reassessment principles.

OECD Guidelines for the Security of Information Systems and Networks

Severity of impact

The degree of potential loss of confidentiality, integrity, and/or system availability.

Centers for Medicare & Medicaid Services (CMS)

SGML/HyTime

A multimedia extension to SGML, sponsored by DOD.

Sedona Conference

Shared secret

A secret used in authentication that is known to the claimant and the verifier.

NIST 800 series

Shell

The interface between the user and the system.

ISACA

Shielded enclosure

Room or container designed to attenuate electromagnetic radiation, acoustic signals, or emanations.

US National Information Assurance (IA) Glossary

Short title

Identifying combination of letters and numbers assigned to certain COMSEC materials to facilitate handling, accounting, and controlling.

US National Information Assurance (IA) Glossary

Shoulder surfing

The capture via observation of information as entered by authorized personnel. For example, stealing phone numbers or passwords.

Centers for Medicare & Medicaid Services (CMS)

Shred key

If the key for a particular message is "shredded" or disabled, the recipient of the message is no longer able to open the message. In some systems the sender can preset a time for the key to expire or manually change the key status at any time. In most key-based solutions, the message is stored in the encrypted state by most e-mail clients unless the user stores a copy of the decrypted message.

Workgroup for Electronic Data Interchange

Signature

A recognizable, distinguishing pattern associated with an attack, such as a binary string in a virus or a particular set of keystrokes used to gain unauthorized access to a system. See also Certificate.

Sedona Conference, NIST 800 Series

Signature certificate

A public key certificate that contains a public key intended for verifying digital signatures rather than encrypting data or performing any other cryptographic functions.

NIST 800 series

Signature generation

Uses a digital signature algorithm and a private key to generate a digital signature on data.

NIST 800 series

Signature panel

For original Visa Card-Good through 2010, the panel for cardholders' signatures on the back of all valid credit cards. Valid panels are white with the repeated word "VISA/MasterCard/etc." printed at an angle. It may also contain the full or truncated account number and the three digit CVV2, printed in reverse italics. The words "Not Valid Without Signature" or "Authorized signature" should also appear below or to the side of the panel on most credit cards. The signature panel is one of the card security features merchants should check to ensure that a card-present transaction is valid. For updated credit cards, a valid panel may have a horizontal stripe pattern or a custom design. The signature panel is one of the card security features merchants should check to ensure that a card-present transaction is valid.

VISA Glossary of Terms

Signature verification

Uses a digital signature algorithm and a public key to verify a digital signature.

NIST 800 Series

Signatures

Patterns indicating misuse of a system.

ISACA

Signed data

Data on which a digital signature is generated.

NIST 800 series, FIPS Pubs

Significant change

A physical, administrative, or technical modification that alters the degree of protection required. Examples include adding a local area network, changing from batch to on-line processing, adding dial-up capability, and increasing the equipment capacity of the installation.

Centers for Medicare & Medicaid Services (CMS)

Simple fail-over

A fail-over process in which the primary node owns the resource group. The backup node runs a non-critical application (e.g., a development or test environment) and takes over the critical resource group but not vice versa.

ISACA

Simple Mail Transport Protocol (SMTP)

The standard e-mail protocol on the Internet.

ISACA, Workgroup for Electronic Data Interchange, Sedona Conference

Simple Network Management Protocol (SNMP)

Supports monitoring of network-attached devices for any conditions that warrant administrative attention.

PCI-DSS

Simple Object Access Protocol (SOAP)

A platform-independent XML-based formatted protocol enabling applications to communicate with each other over the Internet. Use of this protocol may provide a significant security risk to web application operations, since use of SOAP piggybacks onto a web-based document object model and is transmitted via the web's HTTP service protocol (port 80) to penetrate server firewalls which are usually configured to accept port 80 and port 21 (FTP) requests. Web-based document models define how objects on a web page are associated with each other and how they can be manipulated while being sent from a server to a client browser. SOAP typically relies on XML for presentation formatting and also adds appropriate HTTP-based headers to send it.

ISACA

Simple security property

Bell-La Padula security model rule allowing a subject read access to an object, only if the security level of the subject dominates the security level of the object.

US National Information Assurance (IA) Glossary

Simplex

One-sided page(s).

Sedona Conference

Simulation modeling

A technique that creates a detailed model to predict the behavior of a configuration item or IT service. Simulation models can be very accurate but are expensive and time consuming to create. A simulation model is often created by using the actual configuration items that are being modeled, with artificial workloads or transactions. They are used in capacity management when accurate results are important. A simulation model is sometimes called a performance benchmark.

ITIL

Simultaneous peripheral operations online (SPOOL)

In the mainframe environment, a component of system software that controls the transfer of data between computer storage areas with different speed capabilities. Usually, an intermediate device, such as a buffer, exists between the transfer source and the destination (e.g., a printer).

FISCAM

Single Loss Expectancy (SLE)

This value is classically derived from the following algorithm to determine the monetary loss (impact) for each occurrence of a threatened event: [ASSET VALUE X EXPOSURE FACTOR = SINGLE LOSS EXPECTANCY]. The SLE is usually an end result of a business impact analysis (BIA). A BIA typically stops short of evaluating the related threats' ARO or its significance. The SLE represents only one element of risk, the expected impact, monetary or otherwise, of a specific threat event. Because the BIA usually characterizes the massive losses resulting from a catastrophic event, however improbable, it is often employed as a scare tactic to get management attention and loosen budgetary constraints, often unreasonably.

Network Frontiers, Centers for Medicare & Medicaid Services (CMS)

Single point keying

Means of distributing key to multiple, local crypto-equipment or devices from a single fill point.

US National Information Assurance (IA) Glossary

Single Point of Contact (SPOC)

Providing a single, consistent way to communicate with an organization or business unit. For example, a single point of contact for an IT service provider is usually called a service desk. Also, SPOC is a misspelling of a certain Vulcan's name.

ITIL

Single Point of Failure (SPOF)

A resource whose loss will result in the loss of service or production. Any configuration item that can cause an incident when it fails and for which a countermeasure has not been implemented. A SPOF may be a person, or a step in a process or activity, as well as a component of the IT infrastructure. See also failure.

ISACA, ITIL, PAS 56

Single sign on

An authentication process in a client/server relationship where the client can enter one name and password and have access to more than one application or access to a number of resources.

de facto

Single Sign-On (SSO)

See Single Sign-on

de facto

Single-hop problem

The security risks resulting from an mobile software agent moving from its home platform to another platform.

NIST 800 series

Single, In-Line Memory Module (SIMM)

A mechanical package (with "legs") used to attach memory chips to printed circuit boards.

Sedona Conference

Skewed

Tilted images. See also De-skewing.

Sedona Conference

Skimming

The replication of account information encoded on the magnetic stripe of a valid card and its subsequent use for fraudulent transactions in which a valid authorization occurs. The account information is captured from a valid card and then re-encoded on a counterfeit card. The term "skimming" is also used to refer to any situation in which electronically transmitted or stored account data is replicated and then re-encoded on counterfeit cards or used in some other way for fraudulent transactions.

VISA Glossary of Terms

Slack/Slack space

The unused space on a cluster that exists when the logical file space is less than the physical file space. Also known as file slack. A form of residual data, the amount of on-disk file space from the end of the logical record information to the end of the physical disk record. Slack space can contain information soft-deleted from the record, information from prior records stored at the same physical location as current records, metadata fragments, and other information useful for forensic analysis of computer systems.

Sedona Conference

Small Computer System Interface (SCSI)

Pronounced "skuzzy." A common, industry standard, electronic interface (highway) between computers and peripherals, such as hard discs, CD-ROM drives and scanners. SCSI allows for up to 7 devices to be attached in a chain via cables. As of this writing, the current

SCSI standard is "SCSI II," also known as "Fast SCSI."

Sedona Conference

Smart card

A credit card sized token that contains a microprocessor, memory, and possibly an embedded integrated circuit for authenticating a user of computer, banking, or transportation services. It can be used for a number of purposes including the storage of digital certificates or digital cash, or it can be used as a token to authenticate users.

FISCAM, ISACA, Centers for Medicare & Medicaid Services (CMS), Sedona Conference, NIST 800 Series

Sniff

The act of capturing network packets including those not necessarily destined for the computer running the sniffing software.

ISACA

Sniffer

A program that intercepts routed data and examines each packet in search of specific information such as passwords transmitted in clear text. See also packet sniffer.

FISCAM, Centers for Medicare & Medicaid Services (CMS), US National Information Assurance (IA) Glossary, NIST 800 Series

Sniffing

An attack capturing sensitive pieces of information, such as passwords, passing through the network. In network management, the process of capturing and decoding packets of information for troubleshooting and management purposes.

Network Frontiers, ISACA

Social engineering

Illegally entering a computer system by having persuaded an authorized person to reveal IDs, passwords and other confidential information. A method used by hackers to obtain passwords for unauthorized access. Typically, this involves calling an authorized user of a computer system and posing as a network administrator.

Network Frontiers, FISCAM, NIST 800 Series

Society for the Worldwide Interbank Financial Telecommunication (SWIFT)

Founded in Brussels in 1973, the Society for the Worldwide Interbank Financial Telecommunication (SWIFT) is a cooperative organization dedicated to the promotion and development of standardized global interactivity for financial transactions. SWIFT's original mandate was to establish a global communications link for data processing and a common language for international financial transactions. The Society operates a messaging service for financial messages, such as letters of credit, payments, and securities transactions, between member banks worldwide. SWIFT's essential function is to deliver these messages quickly and securely—both of which are prime considerations for financial matters. Member organizations create formatted messages that are then forwarded to SWIFT for delivery to the recipient member organization. SWIFT operates out of its Brussels headquarters and processes data at centers in Belgium and the United States. See also http://www.swift.com for more information.

ISACA

Software

A computer program or programs, in contrast to the physical environment on which programs run (hardware). The computer program that instructs computer hardware to perform an action. System software is the operating system that controls the basic functioning capabilities of the computer, network software enables multiple computers to communicate with one another, and language software is used to develop programs. See also software asset, program, and application.

FISCAM, ISACA, Centers for Medicare & Medicaid Services (CMS), ISO/IEC 27001:2005, Sedona Conference

Software application

See Software, Application.

Sedona Conference

Software asset

Software applications (operating systems, database applications, networking software, office applications, custom applications, etc.).

CERT OCTAVE

Software asset management

The process responsible for management, control, and protection of software assets throughout their lifecycle.

ITIL

Software assurance

Level of confidence that software is free from vulnerabilities, either intentionally designed into the software or accidentally inserted at anytime during its lifecycle, and that the software functions in the intended manner.

US National Information Assurance (IA) Glossary

Software Engineering Institute (SEI)

Since 1984, the Carnegie Mellon Software Engineering Institute (SEI) has served the nation as a federally funded research and development center. The SEI staff has advanced software engineering principles and practices and has served as a national resource in software engineering, computer security, and process improvement. As part of Carnegie Mellon University, which is well known for its highly rated programs in computer science and engineering, the SEI operates at the leading edge of technical innovation. See also http://www.sei.cmu.edu for more information.

CobiT

Software lifecycle

The phases in the life of a software product, beginning with its conception and ending with its retirement. These stages generally include requirements analysis, design, construction, testing (validation), installation, operation, maintenance, and retirement.

FISCAM, Centers for Medicare & Medicaid Services (CMS)

Software Process Improvement and Capability dEtermination (SPICE)

An independent, international quality management system for software development. See also Capability Maturity Model Integration, and http://www.sqi.gu.edu.au/spice/ for more information.

ITIL

Software security

General purpose (executive, utility, or software development tools) and applications programs or routines that protect data handled by a system.

Centers for Medicare & Medicaid Services (CMS)

Software system test and evaluation process

Process that plans, develops, and documents the quantitative demonstration of the fulfillment of all baseline functional performance, operational, and interface requirements.

US National Information Assurance (IA) Glossary

Software-based fault isolation

A method of isolating application modules into distinct fault domains enforced by software. The technique allows untrusted programs written in an unsafe language, such as C, to be executed safely within the single virtual address space of an application. Untrusted machine interpretable code modules are transformed so that all memory accesses are confined to code and data segments within their fault domain. Access to system resources can also be controlled through a unique identifier associated with each domain.

NIST 800 series

Source code

Human-readable program statements written in a high-level or assembly language, as opposed to object code, which is derived from source code and designed to be machine-readable. Source code is the language in which a program is written. Source code is translated into object code by assemblers and compilers. In some cases, source code may be converted automatically into another language by a conversion program. Source code is not executable by the computer directly. It must first be converted into a machine language.

FISCAM, ISACA, Centers for Medicare & Medicaid Services (CMS), ISO/IEC 27001:2005

Source code compare programs

Programs that provide assurance that the software being audited is the correct version of the software by providing a meaningful listing of any discrepancies between the two versions of the program.

ISACA

Source documents

The forms used to record data that have been captured. A source document may be a piece of paper, a turnaround document, or an image displayed for online data input.

ISACA

Source Lines of Code (SLOC)

Source lines of code are often used in deriving single-point software-size estimations.

ISACA

Spanning port

A port configured on a network switch to receive copies of traffic from one or more other ports on the switch.

ISACA

Special Access Program (SAP)

Sensitive program, approved in writing by a head of agency with original top secret classification authority, that imposes need-to-know and access controls beyond those normally provided for access to Confidential, Secret, or Top Secret information. The level of controls is based on the criticality of the program and the assessed hostile intelligence threat. The program may be an acquisition program, an intelligence program, or an operations and support program. (Joint Pub 1-02, 12 Apr2001)

US National Information Assurance (IA) Glossary

Special Access Program Facility (SAPF)

Facility formally accredited by an appropriate agency in accordance with DCID 6/9 in which SAP information may be processed.

US National Information Assurance (IA) Glossary

Special management attention

Some systems require "special management attention" to security due to the risk and magnitude of the harm that would result from the loss, misuse, unauthorized access to, or modification of the information in the system.

Centers for Medicare & Medicaid Services (CMS)

Special Publication (SP)

NIST 800 series

Specific Control Evaluation (SCE)

Evaluating the effectiveness of the design and operation of specific control activities. This process is documented on the SCE worksheet.

GAO/PCIE Financial Audit Manual

Specific, Measurable, Achievable, Relevant, Time-based (SMART)

An acronym for helping to remember that targets in service level agreements and project plans should be specific, measurable, achievable, relevant, and time-based.

ITIL

Specification

A formal definition of requirements document. A specification may be used to define technical or operational requirements and may be internal or external. Many public standards consist of a code of practice and a specification. The specification defines the standard against which an organization can be audited.

ITIL

Speckle

Imperfections in an image as a result of scanning paper documents that do not appear on the original. See also Despeckling.

Sedona Conference

Spillage

See classified information spillage.

US National Information Assurance (IA) Glossary

Splatter

Data that should be kept on one disk of a jukebox goes instead to multiple platters.

Sedona Conference

Split data systems

A condition in which each of an organization's regional locations maintains its own financial and operational data while sharing processing with an organization wide, centralized database. This permits easy sharing of data while maintaining a certain level of autonomy.

ISACA

Split DNS

An implementation of DNS intended to secure responses provided by the server such that different responses are given to internal vs. external users.

ISACA

Split knowledge

Separation of data or information into two or more parts, each part constantly kept under control of separate authorized individuals or teams so that no one individual or team will know the whole data. 2) A procedure whereby a crypto-graphic key is handled as multiple key components from the time that the key or the separate key components are generated until the key components are combined for use. Each key component provides no knowledge of the ultimate key. The key may be created and then split into the key components, or may be created as separate key components. The key components are output from the generating cryptographic module(s) to separate entities for individual handling, and subsequently input separately into the intended cryptographic module and combined to form the ultimate key. Note: A suitable combination function is not provided by simple concatenation; e.g., it is not acceptable to form an 80-bit key by concatenating two 40-bit key components.

US National Information Assurance (IA) Glossary, PCI-DSS, NIST 800 Series, FIPS Pubs

Split sales

The preparation of two or more sales receipts for the purchase of a single item, using a single cardholder account, in order to avoid authorization limits. Split sales are a violation of most credit card company Operating Regulations.

VISA Glossary of Terms

Split tender

The use of two forms of payment, or legal tender, for a single purchase. For example, when buying a big-ticket item, a cardholder might pay half by cash or check and then put the other half on his or her credit credit card. Individual merchants may set their own policies about whether or not to accept split-tender transactions.

VISA Glossary of Terms

Spoliation

Spoliation is the destruction of records which may be relevant to ongoing or anticipated litigation, government investigation or audit. Courts differ in their interpretation of the level of intent required before sanctions may be warranted. See also The Sedona Guidelines: Best Practice Guidelines & Commentary for Managing Information & Records in the Electronic Age, Guideline 3.

Sedona Conference

Spoofing

Faking the sending address of a transmission in order to gain illegal entry into a secure system. An attack in which an unauthorized person or process pretends to be an authorized person or process, whereby the intruder sends messages to a computer with an IP address indicating that the message is coming from a trusted computer.

ISACA, Centers for Medicare & Medicaid Services (CMS), PCI-DSS, US National

Information Assurance (IA) Glossary, NIST 800 Series, FIPS Pubs

Spool

A process of storing data to be printed in memory or in a file until the printer is ready to process it. An automated function that can be operating system or application based in which electronic data being transmitted between storage areas are spooled or stored until the receiving device or storage area is prepared and able to receive the information. This operation allows more efficient electronic data transfers from one device to another by permitting higher speed sending functions, such as internal memory, to continue on with other operations instead of waiting on the slower speed receiving device, such as a printer.

FISCAM, ISACA

Spread spectrum

Telecommunications techniques in which a signal is transmitted in a bandwidth considerably greater than the frequency content of the original information. Frequency hopping, direct sequence spreading, time scrambling, and combinations of these techniques are forms of spread spectrum.

US National Information Assurance (IA) Glossary

Spyware

Software that is secretly or surreptitiously installed into an information system to gather information on individuals or organizations without their knowledge; a type of malicious code.

NIST 800 Series

SQL injection

A form of attack on a database-driven Web site in which the attacker executes unauthorized SQL commands by taking advantage of insecure code on a system connected to the Internet. SQL injection attacks are used to steal information from a database from which the data would normally not be available and/or to gain access to an organization's host computers through the computer that is hosting the database.

PCI-DSS

Stakeholder

Those people and organizations who may affect, be affected by, or perceive themselves to be affected by, a decision or activity. Stakeholders may be interested in the activities, targets, resources, or deliverables. Stakeholders may include customers, partners, employees, shareholders, owners, etc. The term stakeholder may also include interested parties.

DIRKS, ITIL, BS 25999

Stand-aline computer

A personal computer that is not connected to any other computer or network, except possibly through a modem.

Sedona Conference

Stand-alone system

A system that does not require support from other devices or systems. Links with other computers, if any, are incidental to the system's chief purpose.

FISCAM, Centers for Medicare & Medicaid Services (CMS)

Standard

A published statement on a topic specifying characteristics, usually measurable, that must be satisfied or achieved in order to comply with the standard. Organizational standards are used to define the commonality of parts and processes. A standard can be: 1) an object or measure of comparison that defines or represents the magnitude of a unit; 2) a characterization that establishes allowable tolerances or constraints for categories of items; 3) a degree or level of required excellence or attainment. Standards are definitional in nature and established either to further understanding and interaction, or to acknowledge observed (or desired norms) of exhibited characteristics or behavior. Thus, standards may function to specify minimum performance levels or describe best practice. In general computing terms a standard is a set of detailed technical guidelines used as a means of establishing uniformity in an area of hardware or software development. Standards can be put in place to support a policy or a process, or as a response to an operational need. Like policies, standards must include a description of the manner in which noncompliance will be detected. Records management and recordkeeping standards are authoritative standards to which an organization is subject or which it chooses to adopt. Standards provide benchmarks for measuring performance and describe best practices in any or all aspects of recordkeeping. For the purposes of CMS, an Information Technology Standard is an officially categorized convention, methodology, or preferred product authorized for use within CMS. While ITIL states that standards are mandated, there is no legal precedence that they are. See also guideline.

DIRKS, FISCAM, Centers for Medicare & Medicaid Services (CMS), CobiT, ISO/IEC 27001:2005, ITIL, FIPS Pubs, NIST 800 Series

Standard change

A pre-approved change that is low risk, relatively common, and follows a procedure or work instruction. For example, password reset or provision of standard equipment to a new employee. RFCs are not required to implement a standard change, and they are logged and tracked using a different mechanism, such as a service request. See also change model.

ITIL

Standard costs

A predetermined calculation of the cost of carrying out a common operation. For example, a standard cost per desktop may be used rather than calculating the exact cost each time a desktop PC is provided to a user.

ITIL

Standard form

See standard form.

de facto

Standard General Ledger (SGL)

A uniform chart of accounts and guidance for standardizing federal agency accounting. Composed of five major sections: 1) chart of accounts; 2) account descriptions; 3) accounting transactions; 4) SGL attributes; and 5) report crosswalks. Prescribed by the Department of the Treasury in its Treasury Financial Manual.

GAO/PCIE Financial Audit Manual

Standard General Ledger at the transaction level

One of the three requirements of FFMIA. Implementing the SGL at the transaction level means that the entity's general ledger is in full compliance with the SGL chart of accounts descriptions and posting rules, that transactions from feeder systems are fed into the general ledger following SGL requirements through an automated or, in certain cases, a manual interface, that detail supporting these transactions can be traced back to the source transactions in the feeder systems, and that the feeder systems process transactions consistent with SGL account descriptions and posting rules.

GAO/PCIE Financial Audit Manual

Standard Generalized Markup Language (SGML)

An informal industry standard for open systems document management which specifies the data encoding of a document's format and content.

Sedona Conference

Standard Parallel Port (SPP)

See Centronics.

Sedona Conference

Standard profile

A set of rules that describes the nature and extent of access to each resource that is available to a group of users with similar duties such as accounts payable clerks.

FISCAM, Centers for Medicare & Medicaid Services (CMS)

Standard topography

The format and information required to be displayed on a PIV card. Also known as the Mandatory Topography.

NIST 800 series, FIPS Pubs

Standardize

Standardization is the process of optimizing resources (through limiting diversity) in order to improve efficiency. An example would be establishing a uniform criteria for information processes or assets to be added to information systems. Unification is a related term. See also standard.

de facto

Standby

Used to refer to resources that are not required to deliver the live IT services but are available to support IT service continuity plans. For example, a standby data center may be maintained to support hot standby, warm standby, or cold standby arrangements.

ITIL

Standing data

Permanent reference data used in transaction processing. These data are changed infrequently such as a product price file or a name and address file.

ISACA

Star topology

A type of LAN architecture that utilizes a central controller to which all nodes are directly connected. All transmissions from one station to another pass through the central controller which is responsible for managing and controlling all communication. The central controller often acts as a switching device.

ISACA

Start-up KEK

Key-encryption-key held in common by a group of potential communicating entities and used to establish ad hoc tactical networks.

US National Information Assurance (IA) Glossary

State

Intermediate Cipher result that can be pictured as a rectangular array of bytes.

NIST 800 series, FIPS Pubs

Statement of applicability

The documented statement describing the control objectives and controls that are relevant and applicable to the organization's ISMS. Control objectives and controls are based on the results and conclusions of the risk assessment and risk treatment processes, legal or regulatory requirements, contractual obligations, and the organization's business requirements for information security.

ISO/IEC 27001:2005

Statement of Federal Financial Accounting Concepts (SFFAC)

GAO/PCIE Financial Audit Manual

Statement of Federal Financial Accounting Standards (SFFAS)

GAO/PCIE Financial Audit Manual

Statement Of Requirements (SOR)

A document containing all requirements for a product purchase or a new or changed IT service. See also terms of reference.

ITIL

Statement on Auditing Standards (SAS)

GAO/PCIE Financial Audit Manual, AICPA, PCAOB

Statement on Standards for Attestation Engagements (SSAE)

GAO/PCIE Financial Audit Manual

Static analysis

Analysis of information that occurs on a noncontinuous basis; also known as interval-based analysis.

ISACA

Static keys

Static keys are relatively long-lived and are common to a number of executions of a given algorithm.

NIST 800 series

Statistical sampling

Sampling that uses the laws of probability for selecting and evaluating a sample from a population for the purpose of reaching a conclusion about the population.

GAO/PCIE Financial Audit Manual, ISACA

Status

The name of a required field in many types of record. It shows the current stage in the lifecycle of the associated configuration item, incident, problem, etc.

ITIL

Status accounting

See configuration status accounting.

ITIL

Status Bar

A bar at the bottom of a window that is used to indicate the status of a task. For example, when an e-mail message is sent, the status bar will fill with dots indicating that a message is being sent.

Sedona Conference

Steganography

The hiding of information within a more obvious kind of communication. Although not widely used, digital steganography involves the hiding of data inside a sound or image file. Steganalysis is the process of detecting steganography by looking at variances between bit patterns and unusually large file sizes.

Sedona Conference, NIST 800 Series

Stewardship information

Required supplementary stewardship information includes 1) stewardship property, plant, and equipment (property owned by the federal government including: heritage assets [PP&E of historical, natural, cultural, educational, or artistic significance], national defense PP&E [weapons systems and vessels], and stewardship land [land other than that acquired for, or in connection with, general PP&E]), 2) stewardship investments (items treated as expenses in calculating net cost but meriting special treatment to highlight their substantial investment and long-term-benefit nature, including: nonfederal physical property [grants provided for properties financed by the federal government but owned by the state and local governments], human capital [education and training programs financed by the federal government for the benefit of the public], and research and development [basic and applied]), 3) stewardship responsibilities (current services assessment showing receipt and outlay data on the basis of projections of future activities—required in the consolidated statements of the U.S. government only—and social insurance information), and 4) risk-assumed information on insurance and guarantee programs (generally, the present value of unpaid expected losses net of associated premiums).

GAO/PCIE Financial Audit Manual

Storage Area Network (SAN)

A high-speed subnetwork of shared storage devices. A storage device is a machine that contains nothing but a disk or discs for storing data. A SAN's architecture works in a way that makes all storage devices available to all servers on a LAN or WAN. As more storage devices are added to a SAN, they too will be accessible from any server in the larger network. In this case, the server merely acts as a pathway between the end user and the stored data. Because stored data does not reside directly on

any of a network's servers, server power is utilized for business applications, and network capacity is released to the end user. See also Network.

Sedona Conference

Storage device

A device capable of storing data. The term usually refers to mass storage devices, such as disk and tape drives.

CERT OCTAVE, Sedona Conference

Storage management

The process responsible for managing the storage and maintenance of data throughout its lifecycle.

ITIL

Storage Media

See Magnetic storage media, Optical storage media.

Sedona Conference

Storage object

Object supporting both read and write accesses to an information system.

US National Information Assurance (IA) Glossary

Strategic

The highest of three levels of planning and delivery (strategic, tactical, operational). Strategic activities include objective setting and long term planning to achieve the overall vision.

ITIL

Strategic Alignment Objectives Model (SOAM)

A diagram showing the relationships between deliverables and requirements. For example, IT services supporting business requirements, IT infrastructure supporting technical requirements.

ITIL

Strategic practice

Security practices that focus on organizational issues at the policy level. They include business-related issues as well as issues that require organization-wide plans and participation.

CERT OCTAVE

Strategic risk

The current and prospective effect on earnings or capital arising from adverse business decisions, improper implementation of decisions, or lack of responsiveness to industry changes.

ISACA

Strategy

The vision and direction for an organization, involving the setting of mission statements and identifying markets and objectives so that the raison d' être of the organization can be achieved. A strategic plan designed to achieve defined objectives. You can't come up with a strategy while you are in the middle of scrum, in case you were wondering.

ITIL, PAS 56

Stratification

Separation of a population into what the auditor believes are relatively homogeneous groups, each of which is referred to as a stratum, usually to improve sampling efficiency in a classical variables estimation sample.

GAO/PCIE Financial Audit Manual

Stratified sample

A classical variables estimation sample where the auditor first stratifies the population then selects a random sample from each stratum.

GAO/PCIE Financial Audit Manual

Strong authentication

Layered authentication approach relying on two or more authenticators to establish the identity of an originator or receiver of information.

US National Information Assurance (IA) Glossary

Strong cryptography

General term to indicate cryptography that is extremely resilient to cryptanalysis. That is, given the cryptographic method (algorithm or protocol), the cryptographic key or protected data is not exposed. The strength relies on the cryptographic key used. Effective size of the key should meet the minimum key size of comparable strengths recommendations. One reference for minimum comparable strength notion is NIST Special Publication 800-57, August, 2005 (http://csrc.nist.gov/publications/) or others that meet the following minimum comparable key bit security: 80 bits for secret key based systems (for example TDES), 1024 bits modulus for public key algorithms based on the factorization (for example, RSA), 1024 bits for the discrete logarithm (for example, Diffie-Hellman) with a minimum 160 bits size of a large subgroup (for example, DSA), 160 bits for elliptic curve cryptography (for example, ECDSA)

PCI-DSS

Structured programming

A top-down technique of designing programs and systems. It makes programs more readable, more reliable, and more easily maintained.

ISACA

Structured Query Language (SQL)

A standard fourth generation programming language (4GL - a programming language that is closer to natural language and easier to work with than a high-level language). The primary language used by both application programmers and end users in accessing relational databases.

Network Frontiers, PCI-DSS, Sedona Conference

Subassembly

Major subdivision of an assembly consisting of a package of parts, elements, and circuits that perform a specific function.

US National Information Assurance (IA) Glossary

Subject

1) An active organization, generally in the form of a person, process, or device, that causes information to flow among objects or changes the system state. 2) The person whose identity is bound to a particular credential.

NIST 800 series, US National Information Assurance (IA) Glossary

Subject matter

The specific information subject to the IS auditor's report and related procedures which can include things such as the design or operation of internal controls and compliance with privacy practices, standards, or specified laws and regulations.

ISACA

Subject security level

Sensitivity label(s) of the objects to which the subject has both read and write access. Security level of a subject must always be dominated by the clearance level of the user associated with the subject.

US National Information Assurance (IA) Glossary

Subjective coding

The coding of a document using legal interpretation as the data that fills a field, versus objective data that is readily apparent from the face of the document, such as date, type, author, addresses, recipients and names mentioned. Usually performed by paralegals or other trained legal personnel.

Sedona Conference

Subordinate Certification Authority (CA)

In a hierarchical PKI, a Certification Authority whose certificate signature key is certified by another CA, and whose activities are constrained by that other CA.

NIST 800 series

Subscriber

A party who receives a credential or token from a CSP and becomes a claimant in an authentication protocol.

NIST 800 series

Substantive analytical procedures

Analytical procedures used as substantive tests.

GAO/PCIE Financial Audit Manual

Substantive assurance

The auditor's judgment that the assurance provided by all substantive tests of an assertion will detect misstatements that exceed materiality. Not the same as confidence level.

GAO/PCIE Financial Audit Manual

Substantive testing

Substantive testing is performed to obtain evidence that provides reasonable assurance of whether the principal statements, and related assertions, are free of material misstatement. There are two general types of substantive tests: 1) substantive analytical procedures and 2) tests of details.

FISCAM, GAO/PCIE Financial Audit Manual, ISACA

Subsystem

A subsystem, like a system, is a collection of interacting hardware, software, and human components. In particular, a subsystem is a secondary or subordinate system, usually capable of operating independently of, or asynchronously with, a controlling system. A subsystem is analogous to a subdirectory in a file system which contains files and other subdirectories. Subsystems are often organized physically (e.g.,, a building that contains floors, each of which contains rooms) or functionally (e.g.,, a process that contains stamping stations, the conveyor system, and inspection stations). A single device can appear in multiple subsystems. The authority documents also define several categories of subsystems.

de facto, NIST 800 Series

Subtractive colors

Since the colors of objects are white light minus the color absorbed by the object, they are called subtractive. This is how ink on paper works. The subtractive colors of process ink are CMYK (Cyan, Magenta, Yellow and Black) and are specifically balanced to match additive colors (RGB).

Sedona Conference

Sufficient audit evidence

Audit evidence is sufficient if it is adequate, convincing and would lead another IS auditor to form the same conclusions.

ISACA

Suitable criteria

In agreed upon procedures engagements, suitable standards that have the attributes of objectivity, measurability, completeness, and relevance.

GAO/PCIE Financial Audit Manual

Summary of Controls (SoC)

The Summary of Controls is a list of relevant and applicable controls the organization uses as a framework for their ISMS.

ISO/IEC 17799:2005

Super DLT (SDLT)

A type of backup tape which can hold up to 220 GB or 330 CDs, depending on the data file format. See also DLT.

Sedona Conference

Super Video Graphics Adapter (SVGA)

A graphics adapter one which exceeds the minimum VGA standard of 640 by 480 by 16 colors. Can reach 1600 by 1280 by 256 colors.

Sedona Conference

Superencryption

Process of encrypting encrypted information. Occurs when a message, encrypted off-line, is transmitted over a secured, on-line circuit, or when information encrypted by the originator is multiplexed onto a communications trunk, which is then bulk encrypted.

US National Information Assurance (IA) Glossary

Superior Certification Authority (CA)

In a hierarchical PKI, a Certification Authority who has certified the certificate signature key of another CA, and who constrains the activities of that CA.

NIST 800 series

Supersession

Scheduled or unscheduled replacement of a COMSEC aid with a different edition.

US National Information Assurance (IA) Glossary

Supervisor Call (SVC)

A supervisor call instruction interrupts a program being executed and passes control to the supervisor so that it can perform a specific service indicated by the instruction.

FISCAM

Supervisor state

Synonymous with executive state of an operating system.

US National Information Assurance (IA) Glossary

Supplemental analytical procedures

Analytical procedures to increase the auditor's understanding of account balances and transactions when detail tests are used as the sole source of substantive assurance.

GAO/PCIE Financial Audit Manual

Supplier

A third party responsible for supplying goods or services that are required to deliver IT services. Examples of suppliers include commodity hardware and software vendors, network and telecom providers, and outsourcing organizations. See also underpinning contract, supply chain.

ITIL

Supplier management

Supplier management is one of the ISO/IEC 20000 relationship management processes. It is responsible for ensuring that all contracts with suppliers support the needs of the business and that all suppliers meet their contractual commitments. Supplier management is also responsible for understanding the entire supply chain which includes suppliers to the IT service provider's own major suppliers. See also supply chain.

ISO/IEC 27001:2005, ITIL

Supply chain

The activities in a value chain carried out by suppliers. A supply chain typically involves multiple suppliers, each adding value to the product or service.

ITIL

Support group

A group of people with technical skills. Support groups provide the technical support needed by all of the IT service management processes. See also n-line support, technical support.

ITIL

Support hours

The times or hours when support is available to the users. Typically this is the hours when the service desk is available. Support hours should be defined in a service level agreement and may be different from service hours. For example, service hours may be 24 hours a day, but the support hours may be 07:00 to 19:00.

ITIL, Network Frontiers

Suppression measure

Action, procedure, modification, or device that reduces the level of, or inhibits the generation of, compromising emanations in an information system.

US National Information Assurance (IA) Glossary

Surge suppressor

Filters out electrical surges and spikes.

ISACA

Surrogate access

See discretionary access control.

US National Information Assurance (IA) Glossary

Suspension Notice

See Legal hold.

Sedona Conference

Suspension Order

See Legal hold.

Sedona Conference

Swap File

A file used to temporarily store code and data for programs that are currently running. This information is left in the swap file after the programs are terminated, and may be retrieved using forensic techniques. Also referred to as a page file or paging file.

Sedona Conference

Switch

A device that channels incoming data from any of multiple input ports to the specific output port that will take the data toward its intended destination. A device that forwards packets between LAN devices or segments. LANs that use switches are called switched LANs.

Network Frontiers, ISACA

Syllabary

List of individual letters, combination of letters, or syllables, with their equivalent code groups, used for spelling out words or proper names not present in the vocabulary of a code. A syllabary may also be a spelling table.

US National Information Assurance (IA) Glossary

Symmetric encryption algorithm

Encryption algorithms using the same secret key for encryption and decryption.

NIST 800 series

Symmetric key

Encryption methodology in which the encryptor and decryptor use the same key, which must be kept secret. A cryptographic key that is used to perform both the cryptographic operation and its inverse, for example to encrypt and decrypt, or create a message authentication code and to verify the code.

US National Information Assurance (IA) Glossary, NIST 800 Series

Symmetric key encryption

Two trading partners both share one or more secrets. No one else can read their messages. A different key (or set of keys) is needed for each pair of trading partners. Same key is used for encryption and decryption. See also Private Key Cryptosystems.

ISACA

Symmetric or session key

A key used only once and for a limited time such as during transmission of a single message. This encryption methodology is dependent upon the sender and recipient using the identical key to encrypt and decrypt a message.

Workgroup for Electronic Data Interchange

SYN

A flag set in the initial setup packets to indicate that the communicating parties are synchronizing the sequence numbers used for the data transmission.

ISACA

Synchronous crypto-operation

Method of on-line crypto-operation in which crypto-equipment and associated terminals have timing systems to keep them in step.

US National Information Assurance (IA) Glossary

Synchronous transmission

Block-at-a-time data transmission.

ISACA

Syndicated or shared subscription work area

Work space shared by a limited number of organizations, configured for general occupation (not for a particular organization.

PAS 56

Syndication ratio

The number of times that a work area is sold by the third party providers at a resource recovery location. A work area's availability at the time of business continuity incident could be on a first-come-first-served basis or a reduced allocation basis.

PAS 56

System

A logical grouping of components designed to perform a defined function(s) or meet a defined objective(s). An interconnected set of information resources under the same direct management control which shares common functionality. A system normally includes hardware, software, information, data, applications, communications, and people: 1) A management system, including multiple processes that are planned and managed together; for example, a quality management system. 2) A database management system or operating system that includes many software modules that are designed to perform a set of related functions. See also computer systems, systems asset, system boundaries.

CERT OCTAVE, DIRKS, OMB Circular A-130, Centers for Medicare & Medicaid Services (CMS), FIPS Pubs, ITIL, Sedona Conference, NIST 800 Series

System access control

This system manages end user access to computers and the software residing within them in order to manage the need-to-know and need-to-do of users attempting to access, change, or delete regulatory data. See also authentication and access control.

HIPAA, Centers for Medicare & Medicaid Services (CMS), ISO/IEC 27001:2005

System acquisition process

The procedures established to purchase application software, or an upgrade, including evaluation of the supplier's financial stability, track record, resources, and references from existing customers.

ISACA

System Administration, Networking, and Security Institute (SANS)

The SANS (System Administration, Networking, and Security) Institute is a cooperative research and education organization through which more than 96,000 system administrators, security professionals, and network administrators share the lessons they are learning and find solutions to the challenges they face. SANS was founded in 1989. See http://www.sans.org for more information.

de facto, PCI-DSS

System Administrator (SysAdmin)

The person responsible for administering use of a multiuser computer system, communications system, or both.

FISCAM, Centers for Medicare & Medicaid Services (CMS), ISO/IEC 27001:2005, US National Information Assurance (IA) Glossary, Sedona Conference, NIST 800 Series

System analysis

The systems development phase in which systems specifications and conceptual designs are developed, based on end-user needs and requirements.

ISACA

System analyst

A person who designs systems.

FISCAM, Centers for Medicare & Medicaid Services (CMS)

System assets

Any software, hardware, data, administrative, physical, communications, or personnel resource within an information system.

US National Information Assurance (IA) Glossary

System backup

See backup.

Centers for Medicare & Medicaid Services (CMS)

System BIOS

The program that handles instructions and interfaces to initialize and operate input and output procedures for computer hardware.

Centers for Medicare & Medicaid Services (CMS)

System boundary analysis and documentation

The process of uniquely assigning information assets or resources to an information system defines the boundaries for that system. Organizations have a lot of flexibility in determining what constitutes the boundaries of any given information system. The rules of thumb are: 1) Each asset should generally be under the same direct management control; subsystems typically fall under the same management authority and are included within a single system. 2) Each asset should have the same function or mission objective and essentially the same operating characteristics and security needs. 3) Each asset should reside in the same general operating environment (or in the case of a distributed information system, reside in various locations with similar operating environments). 4) The components (assets, resources) do not need to be physically connected to be considered a part of the system.

Centers for Medicare & Medicaid Services (CMS), NIST 800 series, Institute of Internal Auditors, Information Technology Security Evaluation Criteria (ITSEC), ISSA's GAISP

System components

Any network component, server, or application included in or connected to the cardholder data environment. See also

system boundary analysis and documentation.

PCI-DSS

System configuration management information

Any information pertaining to the internal operations of a network or computer system, including but not limited to network and device addresses; system and protocol addressing schemes implemented at an agency; network management information protocols, community strings, network information packets, etc.; device and system passwords; device and system configuration information.

Centers for Medicare & Medicaid Services (CMS)

System designer

See system analyst.

FISCAM

System developer

See programmer.

FISCAM

System Development Life Cycle (SDLC)

The scope of activities associated with a system, encompassing the system's initiation, development and acquisition, implementation, operation and maintenance, and ultimately its disposal that instigates another system initiation.

NIST 800 series

System Development Life Cycle methodology

The period of time that begins when a system is conceived and ends when the system is no longer available for use. The policies and procedures that govern software development and modification as a software product goes through each phase of its life cycle. An approach used to plan, design, develop, test and implement an application system or a major modification to an application system. Typical phases include the feasibility study, requirements study, requirements definition, detailed design, programming, testing, installation, and post-implementation review, and operations and maintenance. Each phase consists of a well-defined set of activities whose products lead to the evolution of the activities and products of each successive phase.

FISCAM, ISACA, Centers for Medicare & Medicaid Services (CMS), FIPS Pubs, CobiT

System Development Lifecycle (SDLC)

See System Development Life Cycle methodology.

FISCAM, CobiT, Centers for Medicare & Medicaid Services (CMS), NIST 800 series

System development methodologies

Methodologies developed through software engineering to manage the complexity of system development. Development methodologies include software engineering aids and high-level design analysis tools. See also System Development Life Cycle methodology.

US National Information Assurance (IA) Glossary

System environment

The operational characteristics and layout of a system including purpose, application, and configuration.

Centers for Medicare & Medicaid Services (CMS)

System event auditing

The process of identifying, detecting, and logging a set of predefined system and user activities.

Centers for Medicare & Medicaid Services (CMS)

System exit

Special system software features and utilities that allow the user to perform complex system maintenance. Use of these exits often permits the user to operate outside of the security access control system.

ISACA

System flowcharts

System flowcharts are graphical representations of the sequence of operations in an information system or program. Information system flowcharts show how data from source documents flow through the computer to final distribution to users. Symbols used should be the internationally accepted standard. System flowcharts should be updated when necessary. See also system narratives.

ISACA

System high

Highest security level supported by an information system.

US National Information Assurance (IA) Glossary

System high mode

IS security mode of operation wherein each user, with direct or indirect access to the information system, its peripherals, remote terminals, or remote hosts, has all of the following: a. valid security clearance for all information within an information system; b. formal access approval and signed nondisclosure agreements for all the information stored and/or processed (including all compartments, subcompartments and/or special access programs); and c. valid need-to-know for some of the information contained within the information system.

US National Information Assurance (IA) Glossary

System identification

Documentation of the name, purpose, configuration and organization responsible for a GSS, MA, or "other" system.

Centers for Medicare & Medicaid Services (CMS)

System impact

The degree of harm or potential harm caused to a system.

Centers for Medicare & Medicaid Services (CMS)

System indicator

Symbol or group of symbols in an off-line encrypted message identifying the specific cryptosystem or key used in the encryption.

US National Information Assurance (IA) Glossary

System integrity

System integrity is a requirement that a system performs its intended function in an unimpaired manner, free from deliberate or inadvertent unauthorized manipulation of the system. It is the quality that a system has when it performs its intended function in an unimpaired manner, free from unauthorized manipulation of the system, whether intentional or accidental.

National Computer Security Center Pub. NCSC-TC-004-88, US National Information Assurance (IA) Glossary, NIST 800 Series

System interconnection

The direct connection of two or more IT systems for the purpose of sharing data and other information resources.

NIST 800 series

System interconnection and information sharing

The direct connection between various systems for the purpose of sharing information resources. See also data flow.

Centers for Medicare & Medicaid Services (CMS)

System interface

A shared boundary where interaction occurs; i.e., the boundary between two or more subsystems or devices.

Centers for Medicare & Medicaid Services (CMS)

System life cycle

See software life cycle, System Development Life Cycle methodology.

FISCAM, FIPS Pubs, Centers for Medicare & Medicaid Services (CMS)

System low

Lowest security level supported by an information system.

US National Information Assurance (IA) Glossary

System maintainer

The individual or group of individuals who have the responsibilities of continued maintenance (e.g. bug fixing, minor modifications/enhancements, performance tuning, and/or customer service) of an implemented system. A system maintainer may or may not also serve as the system developer for a given project and may also be termed the system administrator.

Centers for Medicare & Medicaid Services (CMS)

System management

The part of IT service management that focuses on the management of IT infrastructure rather than process.

ITIL

System management facility (SMF)

An IBM control program that provides the means for gathering and recording information that can be used to evaluate the extent of computer system usage.

FISCAM

System managers

The systems managers are the personnel who design and manage the computer systems. They are responsible for implementing the technical continuity controls for the computer systems and are also responsible for being familiar with continuity and security technology that relates to their system. See also system administrator, system owner.

NIST 800 series

System narratives

System narratives provide an overview explanation of system flowcharts with explanation of key control points and system interfaces.

ISACA

System of interest

Systems that are most closely linked to the critical asset.

CERT OCTAVE

System operational status

There are four levels of status a system might be in at any given time. New (The status of a development effort with the objective of producing a system which has not previously been implemented at the organization). Operational (The status of a system currently supporting a business function or meeting a business need). Undergoing major modification (The status of a system supporting a business function or meeting a business need which is subject to changes in its functionality or information security controls). Down (The system is unavailable for any given reason and not currently supporting business functions or business needs due to a system outage).

Centers for Medicare & Medicaid Services (CMS), Network Frontiers

System outage

An unplanned interruption in system availability as a result of computer hardware or software problems or operational problems. The opposite of availability.

Centers for Medicare & Medicaid Services (CMS)

System Owner

The individual within the organization who serves as the primary point of contact for the system being developed or maintained. The System owner/manager has true ownership and fiduciary responsibility for the system, especially from both a Privacy Act and system security standpoint, and is therefore generally at the Director or Deputy Director level. The official who is responsible for the operation and use of an automated information system.

Centers for Medicare & Medicaid Services (CMS), Network Frontiers

System perimeter scan

A non-intrusive test which involves probing external-facing systems and reporting on the services available to the external network (i.e. services available to the Internet).

PCI-DSS

System profile

Detailed security description of the physical structure, equipment component, location, relationships, and general operating environment of an information system.

US National Information Assurance (IA) Glossary

System Programmer

A person who develops and maintains system software.

FISCAM, Centers for Medicare & Medicaid Services (CMS)

System security

Refers to the concepts, techniques, technical measures, and administrative measures used to protect the hardware, software, and data of an information processing system from deliberate or inadvertent unauthorized acquisition, damage, destruction, disclosure, manipulation, modification, use, or loss. See also system security plan.

Centers for Medicare & Medicaid Services (CMS), FIPS Pubs, US National Information Assurance (IA) Glossary

System Security Administrator (SSA)

The person responsible for administering security on a multi-user computer system, communications system, or both.

Centers for Medicare & Medicaid Services (CMS)

System Security Coordinator (SSC)

Term used to designate the security officer in the 1992 ROM, MIM, and MCM. This business partner security officer had complete oversight and responsibility for all aspects of the security of the Medicare program.

Centers for Medicare & Medicaid Services (CMS)

System security engineering

See information systems security engineering.

US National Information Assurance (IA) Glossary

System security incident

Those incidents not classified as physical crimes, criminal violations, fraudulent activity, illegal access, and disclosure or misuse of government property. A systems security breach is any action involving a system, which if not corrected, could violate the provisions of the Privacy Act, Copyright laws, organizational security policy, or lead to a fraudulent act or criminal violation through use of a system. See also breach.

Centers for Medicare & Medicaid Services (CMS)

System Security Officer (SSO)

The position held by the business partner Security Officer with complete oversight and responsibility for all aspects of the security of the Medicare program.

Centers for Medicare & Medicaid Services (CMS), US National Information Assurance (IA) Glossary

System security plan

A document that provides an overview of the security requirements of the system describes controls in place to meet those requirements and delineates responsibilities and expected behavior of all individuals who access the system. Provides a basic overview of the security and privacy requirements of the subject system and the agency's plan for meeting those requirements.

Centers for Medicare & Medicaid Services (CMS), OMB Bulletin 90-08, FIPS Pubs, US National Information Assurance (IA) Glossary, NIST 800 Series

System security profile

Detailed security description of the physical structure, equipment component, location, relationships, and general operating environment of an information system.

Centers for Medicare & Medicaid Services (CMS)

System software

The set of computer programs and related routines designed to operate and control the processing activities of computer equipment. It includes the operating system and utility programs and is distinguished from application software.

FISCAM, ISACA, Centers for Medicare & Medicaid Services (CMS), ISO/IEC 27001:2005, NIST 800 Series, FIPS Pubs

System startup

See initial program load.

FISCAM

System testing

Testing to determine that the results generated by the enterprise's information systems and their components are accurate and the systems perform to specification. These test procedures typically are performed by the system maintenance staff in their development library.

FISCAM, ISACA, Centers for Medicare & Medicaid Services (CMS)

System-specific security control

A security control for an information system that has not been designated as a common security control.

NIST 800 series

Systematic sampling

A method of selecting a sample in which every Nth item is selected. See also random sample.

GAO/PCIE Financial Audit Manual

Systems analysis and design

The process used to develop a system. The systems development life cycle is the traditional methodology used by information system professionals to develop a new computer application. It includes three general phases; definition, construction, and implementation. The methodology defines the activities necessary for these three phases, as well as a framework for planning and managing a development project. Operations and maintenance are included in the implementation phase. See also System Development Life Cycle methodology.

DIRKS

Systems asset

Information systems that process and store information. See also program, application, IT asset.

CERT OCTAVE

Systems Security Policy Standards and Guidelines Handbook (SSPS&G Handbook)

Centers for Medicare & Medicaid Services (CMS)

T

Federal Bridge Certification Authority Operational Authority

The Federal Bridge Certification Authority Operational Authority is the organization selected by the Federal Public Key Infrastructure Policy Authority to be responsible for operating the Federal Bridge Certification Authority.

NIST 800 series

T1

A high speed, high bandwidth leased line connection to the Internet. T1 connections deliver information at 1.544 megabits per second.

Sedona Conference

T3

A high speed, high bandwidth leased line connection to the Internet. T3 connections deliver information at 44.746 megabits per second.

Sedona Conference

Table look up

Used to ensure that input data agree with predetermined criteria stored in a table.

ISACA

Tactical

The middle of three levels of planning and delivery (strategic, tactical, operational). Tactical activities include the medium term plans required to achieve specific objectives, typically over a period of weeks to months.

ITIL

Tagged Image File Format (TIFF)

One of the most widely used and supported graphic file formats for storing bit-mapped images, with many different compression formats and resolutions. File name has .TIF extension. Can be black and white, gray-scaled, or color. Images are stored in tagged fields, and programs use the tags to accept or ignore fields, depending on the application. The format originated in the early 1980's.

Sedona Conference

Tamper resistance

A system is said to be tamper resistant if it is difficult to modify or subvert, even for an assailant who has physical access to the system.

PCI-DSS

Tampering

An unauthorized modification that alters proper functioning of equipment or systems in a manner that degrades security or functionality.

Centers for Medicare & Medicaid Services (CMS), ISO/IEC 27001:2005, US National Information Assurance (IA) Glossary

Tape drive

A hardware device used to store or backup electronic data on a magnetic tape. Tape drives are usually used to back up large quantities of data due to their large capacity and cheap cost relative to other data storage options.

Sedona Conference

Tape library

The physical site or physical device where magnetic media is stored. See also Tape drive.

FISCAM, Centers for Medicare & Medicaid Services (CMS)

Tape Management System (TMS)

A system software tool that logs, monitors and directs computer tape usage.

ISACA

Taps

Wiring devices that may be inserted into communication links for use with analysis probes, LAN analyzers, and intrusion detection security systems. Also, the last bugle call.

ISACA, Network Frontiers

Targa Format (TGA)

This is a "scanned format" – widely used for color-scanned materials (24-bit) as well as by various "paint" and desktop publishing packages.

Sedona Conference

Target Of Evaluation (TOE)

IT product or system and its associated administrator and user guidance documentation that is the subject of an evaluation.

US National Information Assurance (IA) Glossary

Taxonomy

The science of categorization, or classification, of things based on a predetermined system. In reference to Web sites and portals, a site's taxonomy is the way it organizes its data into categories and subcategories, sometimes displayed in a site map.

Sedona Conference

Tcpdump

ISACA

Technical controls

The security controls (i.e., safeguards or countermeasures) for an information system that are primarily implemented and executed by the information system through mechanisms contained in the hardware, software, or firmware components of the system. Technical controls can also be found in software measures that ensure the confidentiality, availability, and integrity of a system and/or data. See also logical access control.

FISCAM, Centers for Medicare & Medicaid Services (CMS), FIPS Pubs, US National Information Assurance (IA) Glossary, NIST 800 Series

Technical infrastructure security

A connection-based Internet protocol that supports reliable data transfer connections. Packet data is verified using checksums and retransmitted if it is missing or corrupted. The application plays no part in validating the transfer.

ISACA

Technical non-repudiation

The contribution of public key mechanisms to the provision of technical evidence supporting a non-repudiation security service.

NIST 800 series

Technical Observation Post (TOP)

A technique used in service improvement, problem investigation, and availability management. Technical support staff meet to monitor the behavior and performance of an IT service and make recommendations for improvement.

ITIL

Technical support

The process responsible for the technical aspects of supporting IT services. Technical support defines the roles of support groups, as well as the tools, processes and procedures required. See also support group.

ITIL

Technical vulnerability information

Detailed description of a vulnerability to include the implementable steps (such as code) necessary to exploit that vulnerability.

US National Information Assurance (IA) Glossary

Technology

This definition of technology covers hardware, operating systems, database management systems, networking, multimedia, etc.

CobiT

Technology infrastructure plan

A plan for the maintenance and development of the technology infrastructure.

CobiT

Technology neutral

Not specific or dependent upon a particular protocol, methodology or manufacturer solution.

Workgroup for Electronic Data Interchange

Technology product

Security, but which provides security services as an associated feature of its intended operating capabilities. Examples include such products as security-enabled web browsers, screening routers, trusted operating systems, and security-enabled messaging systems.

US National Information Assurance (IA) Glossary

Technology vulnerability

A weakness in systems that can directly lead to unauthorized action. Technology vulnerabilities are present in and apply to network services, architecture, operating systems, and applications. Types of technology vulnerabilities include design, implementation, and configuration vulnerabilities.

CERT OCTAVE

Telecommunications

A general term for the electronic transmission of information of any type, such as data, television pictures, sound, or facsimiles, over any medium, such as telephone lines, microwave relay, satellite link, or physical cable.

FISCAM, ISACA, Centers for Medicare & Medicaid Services (CMS), US National Information Assurance (IA) Glossary

Telephone network protocol (TELNET)

Used to enable remote access to a server computer. Commands typed are run on the remote server.

ISACA, PCI-DSS

Telephony

Converting sounds into electronic signals for transmission.

Sedona Conference

Teleprocessing

Using telecommunications facilities for handling and processing of computerized information.

ISACA

Teleprocessing monitor

In the mainframe environment, a component of the operating system that provides support for on-line terminal access to application programs. This type of software can be used to restrict access to on-line applications and may provide an interface to security software to restrict access to certain functions within the application.

FISCAM

TEMPEST

Short name referring to investigation, study, and control of compromising emanations from IS equipment.

US National Information Assurance (IA) Glossary, FIPS Pubs, NIST 800 Series

TEMPEST test

Laboratory or on-site test to determine the nature of compromising emanations associated with an information system.

US National Information Assurance (IA) Glossary

TEMPEST zone

Designated area within a facility where equipment with appropriate TEMPEST characteristics (TEMPEST zone assignment) may be operated.

US National Information Assurance (IA) Glossary

Template

A biometric image data record.

NIST 800 series, FIPS Pubs

Templates

Sets of index fields for documents, providing framework for preparation.

Sedona Conference

Temporary file (Temp)

Temporary (or "temp") files are files stored on a computer for temporary use only, and are often created by Internet browsers. These temp files store information about Web sites that a user has visited, and allow for more rapid display of the Web page when the user revisits the site. Forensic techniques can be used to track the history of a computer's Internet usage through the examination of these temporary files. Temp files are also created by common office applications, such as word process or spreadsheet applications.

Sedona Conference

Terabyte

A unit of 1,000 or 1,024 gigabytes, or approximately a trillion bytes.

Sedona Conference

Terminal

A device for sending and receiving computerized data over transmission lines consisting of a video adapter, a monitor, and a keyboard.

FISCAM, ISACA, Centers for Medicare & Medicaid Services (CMS)

Terminal Access Controller Access Control System Plus (TACACS+)

An authentication protocol, often used by remote-access servers.

ISACA, PCI-DSS

Terms of Reference (TOR)

A document that confirms the client's and the IS auditor's acceptance of a review assignment. The TOR specifies the requirements, scope, deliverables, resources, and schedule for a project or activity. See also statement of requirements.

ISACA, ITIL

Terrorism

A deliberate and violent act taken by an individual or group whose motives go beyond the act of sabotage, generally toward some political or social sentiment/position. A weekend visit from my in-laws.

Centers for Medicare & Medicaid Services (CMS), Network Frontiers

Test

A test is used to verify that a configuration item, IT service, process, etc. meets its specification and is able to correctly deliver specific functional or service level requirements. There should be no negative effects on other processes or IT services.

ITIL

Test bed

Test environment containing the software, data, and simulations necessary for testing systems.

Centers for Medicare & Medicaid Services (CMS)

Test data

Simulated transactions that can be used to test processing logic, computations, and controls actually programmed in computer applications. Individual programs or an entire system can be tested. This technique includes Integrated Test Facilities (ITFs) and Base Case System Evaluations (BCSEs).

ISACA

Test environment

A controlled environment used to test configuration items, builds, IT services, processes etc.

ITIL

Test facility

A processing environment isolated from the production environment that is dedicated to testing and validating systems and/or their components.

FISCAM

Test generators

Software used to create data to be used in the testing of computer programs.

ISACA

Test key

Key intended for testing of COMSEC equipment or systems.

US National Information Assurance (IA) Glossary

Test materiality

The maximum misstatement that the auditor can tolerate in a population. This materiality is used in determining the extent of a specific substantive test. In statistical terms, margin or bound of error. Test materiality is design materiality, reduced when the audit is being performed at some, but not all, entity locations (requiring increased audit assurance for those locations visited); the area tested is deemed to be sensitive to the users of the financial statements; or the auditor expects to find a significant amount of misstatements.

GAO/PCIE Financial Audit Manual

Test programs

Programs that are tested and evaluated before approval into the production environment. Test programs, through a series of control moves, migrate from the test environment to the production environment and become production programs.

ISACA

The Technology Group for The Financial Services Roundtable (BITS)

BITS is a nonprofit, CEO-driven financial service industry consortium made up of 100 of the largest financial institutions in the US. BITS works to leverage the intellectual capital of its members, fostering collaboration to address emerging issues where financial services, technology, and commerce intersect. See also http://www.bitsinfo.org/ for more information.

de facto

Thesaurus

A thesaurus is a complex alphabetical listing of all terms derived from a classification scheme. Such tools act as a guide in the allocation of classification terms to individual records. In a thesaurus the meaning of the term is specified and hierarchical relationships to other terms are shown. A thesaurus should provide sufficient entry points to allow users to navigate from terms which are not to be used to the preferred terminology adopted by the organization. See also merged thesaurus.

DIRKS

Thin Client

A networked user computer that acts only as a terminal and stores no applications or user files. May have little or no hard drive space. See also Client.

Sedona Conference

Third party

A person, group, or business who is not part of the Service Level Agreement for an IT service, but is required to ensure successful delivery of that IT service. For example, a software supplier, a hardware maintenance company, or a facilities department. Requirements for third parties are typically specified in underpinning contracts or Operational Level Agreements. See also partnership.

ITIL

Third party review

An independent audit of the control structure of a service organization, such as a service bureau, with the objective of providing assurances to the users of the service organization that the internal control structure is adequate, effective and sound.

ISACA

Third-line support

The third level in a hierarchy of support groups involved in the resolution of incidents and investigation of problems. Each level contains more specialist skills

or has more time or other resources. See also escalation.

ITIL

Third-party processor

A non-member organization that performs transaction authorization and processing, account record keeping, and other day-to-day business and administrative functions for issuers and merchant banks.

VISA Glossary of Terms

Thread

A series of postings on a particular topic. Threads can be a series of bulletin board messages (for example, when someone posts a question and others reply with answers or additional queries on the same topic). A thread can also apply to chats, where multiple conversation threads may exist simultaneously.

Sedona Conference

Threat

Any circumstance or event that has the potential to cause harm to a system (whether intentional or unintentional) in the form of destruction, disclosure, modification of data, interruption, and/or denial of service. An indication of a potential undesirable event. The potential for a "threat source" to exploit (intentional) or trigger (accidental) a specific vulnerability. It refers to a situation in which a threat source could do something undesirable (an attacker initiating a denial-of-service attack against an organization's e-mail server) or a natural occurrence could cause an undesirable outcome (a fire damaging an organization's information technology hardware). Threats have defined properties (asset, actor, motive, access, outcome). For example, a fire is a threat that could exploit the vulnerability of flammable floor coverings. This term is commonly used in information security management and IT service continuity management but also applies to other areas such as problem and availability management.

CERT OCTAVE, NIST 800 series, ISACA, Centers for Medicare & Medicaid Services (CMS), PCI-DSS, FIPS Pubs, ITIL, US National Information Assurance (IA) Glossary

Threat agent/source

Either: 1) intent and method targeted at the intentional exploitation of a vulnerability; or 2) a situation and method that may accidentally trigger a vulnerability.

NIST 800 series

Threat analysis

The examination of threat sources against system vulnerabilities to determine the threats for a particular system in a particular operational environment.

Centers for Medicare & Medicaid Services (CMS), US National Information Assurance (IA) Glossary, NIST 800 Series

Threat assessment

Formal description and evaluation of threat to an information system.

US National Information Assurance (IA) Glossary, NIST 800 Series

Threat monitoring

Analysis, assessment, and review of audit trails and other information collected for the purpose of searching out system events that may constitute violations of system security.

US National Information Assurance (IA) Glossary

Threat profile

Defines the range of threats that can affect an asset. Threat profiles contain categories that are grouped according to threat source (human actors using network access, human actors using physical access, system problems, other problems).

CERT OCTAVE

Threat source

Either intent and method targeted at the intentional exploitation of a vulnerability, or the situation and method that may accidentally trigger a vulnerability. See also common threat sources.

NIST 800 series, FIPS Pubs

Threshold

The value of a metric which should cause an alert to be generated or management action to be taken. For example, "priority 1 incident not solved within 4 hours," "more than 5 soft disk errors in an hour," or "more than 10 failed changes in a month."

ITIL

Throughput

A measure of the number of transactions, or other operations, performed in a fixed time. For example, 5000 e-mails sent per hour, or 200 disk I/Os per second.

ITIL

Thumb Drive

See Key drive.

Sedona Conference

Thumbnail

A miniature representation of a page or item for quick overviews to provide a general idea of the structure, content and appearance of a document. A thumbnail program may be standalone or part of a desktop publishing or graphics program. Thumbnails take considerable time to generate, but provide a convenient way to browse through multiple images before retrieving the one needed. Programs often allow clicking on the thumbnail to retrieve it.

Sedona Conference

Ticket-oriented

IS protection system in which each subject maintains a list of unforgeable bit patterns called tickets, one for each object a subject is authorized to access. See also list-oriented.

US National Information Assurance (IA) Glossary

Tied users

Users who have no choice about whether to use the IT services provided by their internal service provider. See also untied users.

ITIL

TIFF Group III

A two-dimensional compression format for storing black and white images. Typically compresses at a 20-to-1 ratio for standard business documents. See also TIFF.

Sedona Conference

Time bomb

Resident computer program that triggers an unauthorized act at a predefined time.

US National Information Assurance (IA) Glossary

Time Sharing Option (TSO)

The time sharing option of MVS allows users to interactively share computer time and resources and also makes it easier for users to interact with MVS.

FISCAM

Time-compliance date

Date by which a mandatory modification to a COMSEC end-item must be incorporated if the item is to remain approved for operational use.

US National Information Assurance (IA) Glossary

Time-dependent password

Password that is valid only at a certain time of day or during a specified interval of time.

US National Information Assurance (IA) Glossary

Time-sharing

A technique that allows more than one individual to use a computer at the same time.

FISCAM

Timeliness

Public and private parties, nationally and internationally, should act in a timely coordinately manner to prevent and respond to breaches of security of information systems.

NIST 800 series

TOE Security Functions (TSF)

Set consisting of all hardware, software, and firmware of the TOE that must be relied upon for the correct enforcement of the TSP.

US National Information Assurance (IA) Glossary

TOE Security Policy (TSP)

Set of rules that regulate how assets are managed, protected, and distributed within the TOE.

US National Information Assurance (IA) Glossary

Toggle

A switch that is either on or off, and reverses to the opposite when selected.

Sedona Conference

Token

A physical device used to convey privilege or a capability through dynamic authentication, e.g., a handheld password generator. In authentication systems, some type of physical device (such as a card with a magnetic strip or a smart card) that must be in the individual's possession in order to gain access. The token itself is not sufficient; the user must also be able to supply something memorized, such as a personal identification number (PIN).

FISCAM, ISACA, Centers for Medicare & Medicaid Services (CMS), PCI-DSS, NIST 800 Series

Token Ring topology

A type of LAN ring topology in which a frame containing a specific format, called the token, is passed from one station to the next around the ring. When a station receives the token, it is allowed to transmit. The station can send as many frames as desired until a predefined time limit is reached. When a station either has no more frames to send or reaches the time limit, it transmits the token. Token passing prevents data collisions that can occur when two computers begin transmitting at the same time.

ISACA

Tolerable misstatement

See test materiality.

GAO/PCIE Financial Audit Manual

Tolerable rate

In attribute sampling for control testing, the maximum rate of deviation from a prescribed control that the auditor

would be willing to accept without altering the assessment of the effectiveness of the control. For tests of compliance with laws and regulations, the tolerable rate is the maximum rate of noncompliance that the auditor would accept in the population without reporting the noncompliance. In statistical terms, margin or bound of error.

GAO/PCIE Financial Audit Manual

Tool Kit Without An Interesting Name (TWAIN)

A universal toolkit with standard hardware/software drivers for multi-media peripheral devices.

Sedona Conference

Toolbar

The row of buttons right below the menu that perform special functions quickly and easily.

Sedona Conference

Top level management

The highest level of management in the organization, responsible for direction and control of the organization as a whole (such as director, general manager, partner, chief officer, and executive manager).

ISACA

Top secret

The highest level of information classification. The unauthorized disclosure of top-secret information will cause exceptionally great damage to the country's national security.

Centers for Medicare & Medicaid Services (CMS)

Top stratum item

An item in a dollar-unit sample that equals or exceeds the amount of the sampling interval or implicit sampling interval. Top stratum items are tested 100 percent.

GAO/PCIE Financial Audit Manual

Topology

The geometric arrangement of a computer system. Common topologies include a bus (network topology in which nodes are connected to a single cable with terminators at each end), star (local area network designed in the shape of a star, where all end points are connected to one central switching device, or hub), and ring (network topology in which nodes are connected in a closed loop; no terminators are required because there are no unconnected ends). Star networks are easier to manage than ring topology.

ISACA, Sedona Conference, NIST 800 Series

Total Cost of Ownership (TCO)

The life cycle cost view of an asset, which includes acquisition, setup, support, ongoing maintenance, service and all operating expenses. It focuses attention on the sum of all costs of owning an asset, as opposed to the initial or vendor cost, and is useful in outsourcing decisions. Total cost of ownership can be significantly higher than the purchase cost, and systems with a lower purchase cost can have higher total cost of ownership.

CobiT, ITIL

Total Quality Management (TQM)

A methodology for managing continuous improvement by using a quality management system. TQM establishes a culture involving all people in the organization in a process of continuous monitoring and improvement.

ITIL

Total risk

The potential for the occurrence of an adverse event if no mitigating action is taken (i.e., the potential for any applicable threat to exploit a system vulnerability).

NIST 800 series

Track

Each of the series of concentric rings contained on a hard drive platter.

Sedona Conference

Track data

See Track, Magnetic stripe data.

PCI-DSS

Tracking

The creating, capturing, and maintaining information about the movement and use of records.

ISO 15489

Tracking cookie

A cookie placed on a user's computer to track the user's activity on different Web sites, creating a detailed profile of the user's behavior.

NIST 800 series

Trading partner code

As assigned by the U.S. Department of the Treasury, trading partner code is the attribute defined within the accounting for a transaction used to identify the trading partner entity. The trading partner code is illustrated next to the SGL account and is a two-digit number.

GAO/PCIE Financial Audit Manual

Trading partners

As defined by the U.S. Department of the Treasury, trading partners are agencies, bureaus, programs, or other entities (within or between agencies/ departments) participating in transactions with each other.

GAO/PCIE Financial Audit Manual

Traditional INFOSEC program

Program in which NSA acts as the central procurement agency for the development and, in some cases, the production of INFOSEC items. This includes the Authorized Vendor Program. Modifications to the INFOSEC end-items used in products developed and/or produced under these programs must be approved by NSA.

US National Information Assurance (IA) Glossary

Traffic analysis

The inference of information from observation of traffic flows (presence, absence, amount, direction, and frequency).

NIST 800 series, US National Information Assurance (IA) Glossary

Traffic Encryption Key (TEK)

Key used to encrypt plain text or to superencrypt previously encrypted text and/or to decrypt cipher text.

US National Information Assurance (IA) Glossary

Traffic flow confidentiality

A confidentiality service to protect against traffic analysis.

NIST 800 series

Traffic padding

Generation of spurious communications or data units to disguise the amount of real data units being sent.

US National Information Assurance (IA) Glossary

Traffic-Flow Security (TFS)

Measure used to conceal the presence of valid messages in an on-line cryptosystem or secure communications system.

US National Information Assurance (IA) Glossary

Training and awareness

Training strives to produce relevant and needed (information) security skills and competencies. See also information security training and awareness.

Centers for Medicare & Medicaid Services (CMS), ISO/IEC 27001:2005, NIST 800 Series

Training assessment

An evaluation of the training efforts.

NIST 800 series

Training effectiveness

A measurement of what a given student has learned from a specific course or training event.

NIST 800 series

Training effectiveness evaluation

Information collected to assist employees and their supervisors in assessing individual students' subsequent on-the-job performance, to provide trend data to assist trainers in improving both learning and teaching, and to be used in return-on-investment statistics to enable responsible officials to allocate limited resources in a thoughtful, strategic manner among the spectrum of IT security awareness, security literacy, training, and education options for optimal results among the workforce as a whole.

NIST 800 series

Tranquility

Property whereby the security level of an object cannot change while the object is being processed by an information system.

US National Information Assurance (IA) Glossary

Transaction

This term has two definitions, one for Information Assurance and another for the Payment Card Industry. 1) The smallest unit of business activity. A transaction should be activity-based rather than subject- or topic-based. A transaction provides the basis for identifying, in detail, the records that meet the business needs of the organization. Typically, a transaction is applied to a calculation or event that then results in the updating of a holding or master file. Depending on the complexity of an organization's business activities, it may be necessary to group transactions on the basis of their similarities or to further dissect this level to obtain an appropriate degree of specificity for the organization's record keeping purposes. A particular instance in the performance of an activity. In some cases, the term transaction is used to cover a class of transactions that occur in the performance of an activity. 2) For the Payment Card Industry, the act between a cardholder and merchant that results in the sale of goods or services.

DIRKS, FISCAM, ISACA, Centers for Medicare & Medicaid Services (CMS), ITIL, VISA Glossary of Terms

Transaction data

Data related to an electronic payment. See also transaction, transaction file.

PCI-DSS

Transaction file

A group of one or more computerized records containing current business activity and processed with an associated master file. Transaction files are sometimes accumulated during the day and processed in batch production overnight or during off-peak processing periods.

FISCAM

Transaction log

A manual or automated log of all updates to data files and databases.

ISACA

Transaction protection

Also known as "automated remote journaling of redo logs." A data recovery strategy that is similar to electronic vaulting, except that instead of transmitting several transaction batches daily, the archive logs are shipped as they are created.

ISACA

Transaction risk

The current and prospective risk to earnings and capital arising from fraud, error, and the inability to deliver products or services, maintain a competitive position, and manage information. Security risk is evident in each product and service offered and encompasses product development and delivery, transaction processing, systems development, computing systems, complexity of products and services, and the internal control environment. A high level of security risk may exist with

Internet banking products, particularly if those lines of business are not adequately planned, implemented, and monitored.

ISACA

Transfer

The change of custody, ownership and/or responsibility for records. The moving of records from one location to another.

ISO 15489

Transfer agent

An agent employed by a corporation or mutual fund to maintain shareholder records, including purchase, sales, and account balances.

17 CFR 240.17a-3 & 4

Transfer cost

A cost type which records expenditure made on behalf of another part of the organization. For example, the IT service provider may pay for an external consultant to be used by the finance department and transfer the cost to them. The IT service provider would record this as a transfer cost.

ITIL

Transfers

Funding moved from one entity to another based on an agreement between the providing entity and the receiving entity.

GAO/PCIE Financial Audit Manual

Transmission Control Protocol (TCP)

A protocol within the TCP/IP protocol suite that is used when reliable packet delivery is essential; TCP requires confirmation of packet delivery for all transmitted packets.

Network Frontiers, ISACA, PCI-DSS

Transmission Control Protocol/Internet Protocol (TCP/IP)

A connection-based Internet protocol that supports reliable data transfer connections. Packet data is verified using checksums and retransmitted if it is missing or corrupted. The application plays no part in validating the transfer.

ISACA, Sedona Conference

Transmission media

The facility through which information already recorded electronically is passed between electronic systems (e.g. twisted pair cables, coaxial, or optical cables). To include: transmissions over open communication channels e.g. Internet, intranets, and leased lines.

Workgroup for Electronic Data Interchange

Transmission security

Implement a mechanism to encrypt regulated data whenever deemed appropriate.

HIPAA, US National Information Assurance (IA) Glossary

Transport Layer Security (TLS)

Designed with goal of providing data secrecy and data integrity between two communicating applications. TLS is successor of SSL.

PCI-DSS, NIST 800 Series

Trap door

Unauthorized electronic exits, or doorways, out of an authorized computer program into a set of malicious instructions or programs. A hidden software or hardware mechanism that can be triggered to permit system protection mechanisms to be circumvented. It is activated in some innocent-appearing manner; e.g., a special "random" key sequence at a terminal. Software developers often introduce trap doors in their code to enable them to re-enter the system and perform certain functions. See also back door.

ISACA, Centers for Medicare & Medicaid Services (CMS), US National Information Assurance (IA) Glossary

Treasury Financial Manual (TFM)

The Treasury Financial Manual (TFM) is Treasury's official publication for financial accounting and reporting of all receipts and disbursements of the federal government. Provides procedures for federal agencies to account for and reconcile transactions occurring within and between each other. Includes procedures for CFO Act agencies to reconcile and confirm with their trading partners intragovernmental activity and balances.

GAO/PCIE Financial Audit Manual

Treatment, Payment, or health care Operations (TPO)

Those services directly associated with: 1) the delivery of care, 2) the processing of healthcare claim forms, 3) receipt of payments and corollary duties and services.

Workgroup for Electronic Data Interchange

Trend analysis

Analysis of data to identify time related patterns. Trend analysis is used in problem management to identify common failures or fragile configuration items and in capacity management as a modeling tool to predict future behavior. It is also used as a management tool for identifying deficiencies in IT service management processes.

ITIL

Triple Data Encryption Standard (TDES)

See Triple DES

PCI-DSS

Trojan horse

A computer program that conceals harmful code. A Trojan horse usually masquerades as a useful program that a user would wish to execute. Unlike viruses, they do not replicate themselves, but they can be just as destructive to a single computer.

FISCAM, ISACA, Centers for Medicare & Medicaid Services (CMS), US National Information Assurance (IA) Glossary, NIST 800 Series

True resolution

The "true" optical resolution of a scanner is the number of pixels per inch (without any software enhancements).

Sedona Conference

Truncation

The practice of removing a data segment. Commonly, when account numbers are truncated, the first 12 digits are deleted, leaving only the last 4 digits.

PCI-DSS

Trust

Generally, the assumption that an entity will behave substantially as expected. Trust may apply only for a specific function. The key role of this term in an authentication framework is to describe the relationship between an authenticating entity and a Certificate Authority (CA). An authenticating entity must be certain that it can trust the CA to create only valid and reliable certificates, and users of those certificates rely upon the authenticating entity's determination of trust.

ISACA

Trust anchor

A public key and the name of a certification authority that is used to validate the first certificate in a sequence of certificates. The trust anchor public key is used to verify the signature on a certificate issued by a trust anchor certification authority. The security of the validation process depends upon the authenticity and integrity of the trust anchor. Trust anchors are often distributed as self-signed certificates.

NIST 800 series

Trust list

The collection of trusted certificates used by Relying Parties to authenticate other certificates.

NIST 800 series

Trusted agent

Entity authorized to act as a representative of an Agency in confirming Subscriber identification during the registration process. Trusted Agents do not have automated interfaces with Certification Authorities.

NIST 800 series

Trusted certificate

A certificate that is trusted by the Relying Party on the basis of secure and authenticated delivery. The public keys included in trusted certificates are used to start certification paths. Also known as a "trust anchor".

NIST 800 series

Trusted channel

Means by which a TOE Security Function (TSF) and a remote trusted IT product can communicate with necessary confidence to support the TOE Security Policy (TSP).

US National Information Assurance (IA) Glossary

Trusted computer system

Information system employing sufficient hardware and software assurance measures to allow simultaneous processing of a range of classified or sensitive information.

US National Information Assurance (IA) Glossary

Trusted computing base (TCB)

Totality of protection mechanisms within a computer system, including hardware, firmware, and software, the combination responsible for enforcing a security policy.

US National Information Assurance (IA) Glossary

Trusted distribution

Method for distributing trusted computing base (TCB) hardware, software, and firmware components that protects the TCB from modification during distribution.

US National Information Assurance (IA) Glossary

Trusted foundry

Facility where both classified and unclassified parts can be produced with an extra level of assurance that the parts have not been tampered.

US National Information Assurance (IA) Glossary

Trusted identification forwarding

Identification method used in IS networks whereby the sending host can verify an authorized user on its system is attempting a connection to another host. The sending host transmits the required user authentication information to the receiving host.

US National Information Assurance (IA) Glossary

Trusted path

Means by which a user and a TOE Security Function (TSF) can communicate with necessary confidence to support the TOE Security Policy (TSP). A mechanism by which a user (through an input device) can communicate directly with the security functions of the information system with the necessary confidence to support the system security policy. This mechanism can only be activated by the user or the security functions of the information system and cannot be imitated by untrusted software.

US National Information Assurance (IA) Glossary, NIST 800 Series

Trusted process

Processes certified as supporting a security goal.

ISACA, US National Information Assurance (IA) Glossary

Trusted recovery

Ability to ensure recovery without compromise after a system failure.

US National Information Assurance (IA) Glossary

Trusted software

Software portion of a trusted computing base (TCB).

US National Information Assurance (IA) Glossary

Trusted systems

Systems that employ sufficient hardware and software assurance measures to allow their use for processing of a range of sensitive or classified information.

ISACA

Trusted third party

A person or organization that performs a function or activity on behalf of a CE but is not part of the regulated organization's workforce. See also business associate.

17 CFR 240.17a-3 & 4, HIPAA

Trusted timestamp

A digitally signed assertion by a trusted authority that a specific digital object existed at a particular time.

NIST 800 series

Trustworthiness

The attribute of a person or organization that provides confidence to others of the qualifications, capabilities, and reliability of that entity to perform specific tasks and fulfill assigned responsibilities.

NIST 800 series

Trustworthy system

Computer hardware, software and procedures that: 1) are reasonably secure from intrusion and misuse; 2) provide a reasonable level of availability, reliability, and correct operation; 3) are reasonably suited to performing their intended functions; and 4) adhere to generally accepted security procedures.

NIST 800 series

TSEC nomenclature

System for identifying the type and purpose of certain items of COMSEC material.

US National Information Assurance (IA) Glossary

Tuning

The activity responsible for planning changes to make the most efficient use of resources. Tuning is part of performance management which also includes performance monitoring and implementation of the required changes.

ITIL

Tunneled password protocol

A protocol where a password is sent through a protected channel. For example, the TLS protocol is often used with a verifier's public key certificate to 1) authenticate the verifier to the claimant, 2) establish an encrypted session between the verifier and claimant, and 3) transmit the claimant's password to the verifier. The encrypted TLS session protects the claimant's password from eavesdroppers.

NIST 800 series

Tunneling

Technology enabling one network to send its data via another network's connections. Tunneling works by encapsulating a network protocol within packets carried by the second network.

US National Information Assurance (IA) Glossary

Tuple

A row or record consisting of a set of attribute value pairs (column or field) in a relational data structure.

ISACA

Twisted pairs

A pair of small, insulated wires that are twisted around each other to minimize interference from other wires in the cable. This is a low-capacity transmission medium.

ISACA

Two-factor authentication

An authentication process whereas a user authenticates using two different types of identification; for example, a smart card and a password. This type of authentication requires users to produce two credentials - something they have (e.g., smartcards or hardware tokens), and something they know (e.g., a password). In order to access a system, users must produce both factors.

Network Frontiers, PCI-DSS

Two-part code

Code consisting of an encoding section, in which the vocabulary items (with their associated code groups) are arranged in alphabetical or other systematic order, and a decoding section, in which the code groups (with their associated meanings) are arranged in a separate alphabetical or numeric order.

US National Information Assurance (IA) Glossary

Two-person control

Continuous surveillance and control of positive control material at all times by a minimum of two authorized individuals, each capable of detecting incorrect and unauthorized procedures with respect to the task being performed, and each familiar with established security and safety requirements.

US National Information Assurance (IA) Glossary

Two-Person Integrity (TPI)

System of storage and handling designed to prohibit individual access to certain COMSEC keying material by requiring the presence of at least two authorized individuals, each capable of detecting incorrect or unauthorized security procedures with respect to the task being performed. See also no-lone zone.

US National Information Assurance (IA) Glossary

Type I key

Generated and distributed under the auspices of NSA for use in a cryptographic device for the protection of classified and sensitive national security information.

US National Information Assurance (IA) Glossary

Type 1 product

Cryptographic equipment, assembly or component classified or certified by NSA for encrypting and decrypting classified and sensitive national security information when appropriately keyed. Developed using established NSA business processes and containing NSA approved algorithms. Used to protect systems requiring the most stringent protection mechanisms.

US National Information Assurance (IA) Glossary

Type 2 key

Generated and distributed under the auspices of NSA for use in a cryptographic device for the protection of unclassified national security information.

US National Information Assurance (IA) Glossary

Type 2 product

Cryptographic equipment, assembly, or component certified by NSA for encrypting or decrypting sensitive national security information when appropriately keyed. Developed using established NSA business processes and containing NSA approved algorithms. Used to protect systems requiring protection mechanisms exceeding best commercial practices including systems used for the protection of unclassified national security information.

US National Information Assurance (IA) Glossary

Type 3 key

Used in a cryptographic device for the protection of unclassified sensitive information, even if used in a Type 1 or Type 2 product.

US National Information Assurance (IA) Glossary

Type 3 product

Unclassified cryptographic equipment, assembly, or component used, when appropriately keyed, for encrypting or decrypting unclassified sensitive U.S. Government or commercial information, and to protect systems requiring protection mechanisms consistent with standard commercial practices. Developed using established commercial standards and containing NIST approved cryptographic algorithms/modules or successfully evaluated by the National Information Assurance Partnership (NIAP).

US National Information Assurance (IA) Glossary

Type 4 key

Used by a cryptographic device in support of its Type 4 functionality; i.e., any provision of key that lacks U.S. Government endorsement or oversight.

US National Information Assurance (IA) Glossary

Type 4 product

Unevaluated commercial cryptographic equipment, assemblies, or components that neither NSA nor NIST certify for any Government usage. These products are typically delivered as part of commercial offerings and are commensurate with the vendor's commercial practices. These products may contain either vendor proprietary algorithms, algorithms registered by NIST, or algorithms registered by NIST and published in a FIPS.

US National Information Assurance (IA) Glossary

Type certification

The certification acceptance of replica information systems based on the comprehensive evaluation of the technical and non-technical security features of an information system and other safeguards, made as part of and in support of the accreditation process, to establish the extent to which a particular design and implementation meet a specified set of security requirements.

US National Information Assurance (IA) Glossary

Typeface

There are over 10,000 typefaces available for computers. The general categories are: oldstyle (faces have slanted serifs, gradual thick to thin strokes and a slanted stress - the "O" appears slanted), modern (faces have thin, horizontal serifs, radical thick to thin strokes and a vertical street - the "O" does not appear to slant); slab serif (faces have thick, horizontal serifs, little or no thick-to-thin in the strokes and a vertical stress - the "O" appears vertical); sans serif (faces have no serifs), script (from elaborate handwriting styles to casual, free-form, unconnected letter forms), decorative unusual fonts (designed to be very different and attention getting).

Sedona Conference

U

U.S. person

U.S. citizen or a permanent resident alien, an unincorporated association substantially composed of U.S. citizens or permanent resident aliens, or a corporation incorporated in U.S., except for a corporation directed and controlled by a foreign government or governments.

US National Information Assurance (IA) Glossary

U.S.-controlled facility

Base or building to which access is physically controlled by U.S. individuals who are authorized U.S. Government or U.S. Government contractor employees.

US National Information Assurance (IA) Glossary

U.S.-controlled space

Room or floor within a facility that is not a U.S.-controlled facility, access to which is physically controlled by U.S. individuals who are authorized U.S. Government or U.S. Government contractor employees. Keys or combinations to locks controlling entrance to U.S.-controlled spaces must be under the exclusive control of U.S. individuals who are U.S. Government or U.S. Government contractor employees.

US National Information Assurance (IA) Glossary

Ultrafiche

Microfiche which can hold 1,000 documents/sheet as opposed to the normal 270.

Sedona Conference

Unabsorbed overhead

Indirect cost of providing an IT service, which cannot be fairly allocated to specific customers. For example, cost of providing an IT service manager, or other shared resource which is not measured. Unabsorbed overhead is normally recovered by applying a percentage uplift to the cost of all IT services. See also direct cost, indirect cost, absorbed overhead.

ITIL

Unallocated space

The area of computer media, such as a hard drive, that does not contain normally accessible data. Unallocated space is usually the result of a file being deleted. When a file is deleted, it is not actually erased, but is simply no longer accessible through normal means. The space that it occupied becomes unallocated space, i.e., space on the drive that can be reused to store new information. Until portions of the unallocated space are used for new data storage, in most instances, the old data remains and can be retrieved using forensic techniques.

Sedona Conference

Unauthorized access

A person gains logical or physical access without permission to a network, system, application, data, or other resource.

NIST 800 series, FIPS Pubs

Unauthorized disclosure

Exposure of information to individuals not authorized to receive it.

Centers for Medicare & Medicaid Services (CMS), ISO/IEC 27001:2005, US National Information Assurance (IA) Glossary, NIST 800 Series

Uncertainty

This term characterizes the degree, expressed as a percent, from 0% to 100%, to which there is less than complete confidence in the value of any element of the risk assessment. Uncertainty is typically measured inversely with respect to confidence, i.e., if confidence is low, uncertainty is high.

Centers for Medicare & Medicaid Services (CMS)

Unclassified

Information that is designated as neither sensitive nor classified. The public release of this information does not violate national security interests. Information that has not been determined pursuant to the United States E.O. 12958 or any predecessor order to require protection against unauthorized disclosure and that is not designated as classified. See also regulated data.

Centers for Medicare & Medicaid Services (CMS), US National Information Assurance (IA) Glossary

Underpinning Contract (UC)

A contract with an external third party that supports delivery of an IT service by the IT service provider to a customer. The third party provides goods or services that are required by the IT service provider to meet agreed service level targets in the SLA with their customer.

ITIL

Unification

A pattern matching technique used by the authors of the Unified Compliance Framework when determining which controls were in common with others and which were specific and should be listed as such. The pattern matching method that the authors used is fully described in many of the UCF books and papers under the title "what is the Unified Compliance Framework?".

Network Frontiers

Unified Compliance Framework (UCF)

The Unified Compliance Framework is original research conducted by Network Frontiers and Latham Watkins. The goal of the UCF is to harmonize or unify all information technology and information services related controls into a single body of work, thus making it immensely easier to be "compliant" in today's over-regulated world.

Network Frontiers

Unified Compliance Project (UCP)

The IT Compliance Institute, through their association with Network Frontiers, provides complimentary research, publishing media, and financial support for the Unified Compliance Framework.

de facto

Uniform Resource Indicators (URI)

A URL is a URI.

Sedona Conference

Uniform Resource Locators (URL)

The addressing system used in the World Wide Web and other Internet resources. The URL contains information about the method of access, the server to be accessed and the path of any file to be accessed. A URL looks like this: http://thesedonaconference.org/ publications_html. See also Address.

Sedona Conference

Uninterruptible Power Supply (UPS)

Provides short-term backup power from batteries for a computer system when the electrical power fails, rises, or drops to an unacceptable voltage level.

ISACA

Unit cost

The cost of providing a single item. For example, if a box of paper with 1,000 sheets costs $10, then each sheet costs 1 cent. Similarly if a CPU costs $1m a year and performs 1,000 jobs in a year, the unit cost for each job is $1,000.

ITIL

Unit testing

Testing individual program modules to determine if they perform to specification. The testing technique is used to test program logic within a particular program or module. The purpose of the test is to ensure that the program meets system development guidelines and does not abnormally end during processing.

FISCAM, ISACA

Unitization – Physical and Logical

The assembly of individually scanned pages into documents. Physical Unitization utilizes actual objects such as staples, paper clips and folders to determine pages that belong together as documents for archival and retrieval purposes. Logical unitization is the process of human review of each individual page in an image collection using logical cues to determine pages that belong together as documents. Such cues can be consecutive page numbering, report titles, similar headers and footers and other logical indicators. This process should also capture document relationships, such as parent and child attachments. See also Attachment.

Sedona Conference

Universal Description Discovery and Integration (UDDI)

A web-based version of the traditional phone book's yellow and white pages enabling businesses to be publicly listed in promoting greater e-commerce activities.

ISACA

Universal messaging system (UMS)

Sedona Conference

Universe

See population.

GAO/PCIE Financial Audit Manual

UNIX

A multitasking operating system originally designed for scientific purposes which has subsequently become a standard for midrange computer systems with the traditional terminal/host architecture. UNIX is also a major server operating system in the client/server environment.

FISCAM, ISACA, Centers for Medicare & Medicaid Services (CMS), Sedona Conference

Unix File System (UFS)

Unix File System is the file system that the UNIX operating system uses for storing and retrieving files on storage media. Every item in a UNIX file system can be defined as belonging to one of four possible types: ordinary files, directories, special files, or links. See also UNIX.

de facto

Unsigned card

A seemingly valid credit card that has not been duly signed by the legitimate cardholder. Merchants cannot accept an unsigned card until the cardholder has signed it, and the signature has been checked against valid government identification, such as a driver's license or passport.

VISA Glossary of Terms

Unsigned data

Data included in an authentication token, in addition to a digital signature.

NIST 800 series, FIPS Pubs

Untied users

Users who can choose whether to use the services provided by an internal service provider or to purchase services from another source. See also tied users.

ITIL

Untrusted process

Process that has not been evaluated or examined for adherence to the security policy. It may include incorrect or malicious code that attempts to circumvent the security mechanisms.

US National Information Assurance (IA) Glossary

Untrustworthy host

To the basic border firewall, add a host that resides on an untrusted network where the firewall cannot protect it. That host is minimally configured and carefully managed to be as secure as possible. The firewall is configured to require incoming and outgoing traffic to go through the untrustworthy host. The host is referred to as untrustworthy because it cannot be protected by the firewall; therefore, hosts on the trusted networks can place only limited trust in it.

ISACA

Update (a certificate)

The act or process by which data items bound in an existing public key certificate, especially authorizations granted to the subject, are changed by issuing a new certificate.

NIST 800 series

Update access

This access level includes the ability to change data or a software program.

FISCAM, Centers for Medicare & Medicaid Services (CMS)

Updating

Automatic or manual cryptographic process that irreversibly modifies the state of a COMSEC key, equipment, device, or system.

US National Information Assurance (IA) Glossary

Upgrade

New or better version of some hardware or software.

Sedona Conference

Upload

The process of transferring a copy of a file from a local computer to a remote computer by means of a modem or network. With a modem-based communications link, the process generally involves the requesting computer instructing the remote computer to prepare to receive the file on its disk and wait for the transmission to begin.

FISCAM, ISACA, Sedona Conference

Urgency

A measure of how long it will be until an incident, problem or change has a significant impact on the business. For example, a high impact incident may have low urgency, if the impact will not affect the business until the end of the financial year. Impact and urgency are used to assign priority.

ITIL

URL filter server

A computer that houses software that allows you to manage and restrict user access from select Web sites and content in compliance with your organization's policies.

Network Frontiers

Usability

The ease with which an application, product, or IT service can be used. Usability requirements are often included in a statement of requirements.

ITIL

Useful audit evidence

Audit evidence is useful if it assists the IS auditors in meeting their audit objectives.

ISACA

User

The person who uses a computer system and its application programs to perform tasks and produce results. Any organizational or programmatic entity that utilizes or receives service from an automated information system facility.

A user may be either internal or external to the agency organization responsible for the facility, but normally does not report to either the manager or director of the facility or to the same immediate supervisor.

FISCAM, Centers for Medicare & Medicaid Services (CMS), OMB Circular A-130, FIPS Pubs, ITIL, US National Information Assurance (IA) Glossary, NIST 800 Series

User account management

Involves 1) the process of requesting, establishing, issuing, and closing user accounts; 2) tracking users and their respective access authorizations; and 3) managing these functions.

NIST 800 series

User controls

Manual comparisons of computer output (generally totals) to source documents or other input (including control totals).

GAO/PCIE Financial Audit Manual

User Datagram Protocol (UDP)

A connectionless Internet protocol that is designed for network efficiency and speed at the expense of reliability. A data request by the client is served by sending packets without testing to verify if they actually arrive at the destination, not if they were corrupted in transit. It is up to the application to determine these factors and request retransmissions.

ISACA, PCI-DSS

User ID

See user identification.

PCI-DSS, US National Information Assurance (IA) Glossary

User identification (UID)

A unique identifier (character string) assigned to each authorized computer user.

Centers for Medicare & Medicaid Services (CMS)

User Identification, or Identifier (ID)

FISCAM, NIST 800 series

User initialization

A stage in the lifecycle of keying material; the process whereby a user initializes its cryptographic application (e.g., installing and initializing software and hardware).

NIST 800 series

User Partnership Program (UPP)

Partnership between the NSA and a U.S. Government agency to facilitate development of secure IS equipment incorporating NSA-approved cryptography. The result of this program is the authorization of the product or system to safeguard national security information in the user's specific application.

US National Information Assurance (IA) Glossary

User profile

A set of rules that describes the nature and extent of access to each resource that is available to each user.

FISCAM, Centers for Medicare & Medicaid Services (CMS)

User registration

A stage in the lifecycle of keying material; a process whereby an entity becomes a member of a security domain.

NIST 800 series

User representative

Individual authorized by an organization to order COMSEC keying material and interface with the keying system, provide information to key users, and ensure the correct type of key is ordered.

US National Information Assurance (IA) Glossary

User-added metadata

Data or work product created by a user while reviewing a document, including annotations and subjective coding information.

Sedona Conference

Utility program

Generally considered to be system software designed to perform a particular function (e.g., an editor or debugger) or system maintenance (e.g., file backup and recovery). Examples include sorting, backing up, and erasing data.

FISCAM, ISACA

Utility software

Computer programs provided by a computer hardware manufacturer or software vendor and used in running the system. This technique can be used to examine processing activities; to test programs, system activities and operational procedures; to evaluate data file activity; and to analyze job accounting data. See also utility program.

ISACA

V

V.32bis

The ITU (See also ITU) standard for 14.4 kbs modem communications.

Sedona Conference

V.34bis

The proposed ITU (See also ITU) standard for 28.8 kbs modem communications.

Sedona Conference

Vaccine

A program designed to detect computer viruses.

ISACA

Valid data element

A payload, an associated data string, or a nonce that satisfies the restrictions of the formatting function.

NIST 800 series

Validate

Confirm or ensure well grounded logic, and true and accurate determinations.

Sedona Conference

Validated products list

List of validated products that have been successfully evaluated under the National Information Assurance Partnership (NIAP) Common Criteria Evaluation and Validation Scheme (CCEVS).

US National Information Assurance (IA) Glossary

Validation

Process of applying specialized security test and evaluation procedures, tools, and equipment needed to establish acceptance for joint usage of an information system by one or more departments or agencies and their contractors.

US National Information Assurance (IA) Glossary, NIST 800 Series, FIPS Pubs

Validation controls

Controls, tests and evaluations that assess the level of compliance with security specifications and requirements. The process of evaluating a system or component during or at the end of the development process to determine whether it satisfies specified requirements.

FISCAM, Centers for Medicare & Medicaid Services (CMS)

Validity check

Programmed checking of data validity in accordance with predetermined criteria.

ISACA

Value Added Dealer (VAD)

Companies or people who sell computer hardware or software and "add-value" in the process. Usually, the value added is specific technical or marketing knowledge and/or experience.

Sedona Conference

Value Added Network (VAN)

A data communication network that adds processing services such as error correction, data translation, and/or storage to the basic function of transporting data.

ISACA

Value Added Reseller (VAR)

Companies or people who sell computer hardware or software and "add-value" in the process. Usually, the value added is specific technical or marketing knowledge and/or experience.

Sedona Conference

Value Added Specialty Distributor (VASD)

Companies or people who sell computer hardware or software and "add-value" in the process. Usually, the value added is specific technical or marketing knowledge and/or experience.

Sedona Conference

Value chain

A sequence of processes that creates a product or service that is of value to a customer. Each step of the sequence builds on the previous steps and contributes to the overall product or service. See also business IT alignment.

ITIL

Value for money

An informal measure of cost effectiveness. Value for money is often based on a comparison with the cost of alternatives. See also cost benefit analysis.

ITIL

Variable cost

A cost that depends on how much the IT service is used, how many products are produced, or something else that cannot be fixed in advance. See also fixed cost.

ITIL

Variable sampling

A sampling technique used to estimate the average or total value of a population based on a sample; a statistical model used to project a quantitative characteristic, such as a dollar amount.

ISACA

Variance

The difference between a planned value and the actual measured value. Commonly used in financial management, capacity management and service level management, but could apply in any area where plans are in place.

ITIL

Variant

A Configuration Item that is identical to another CI except for specific attributes. Variants are used to group similar CIs together for analysis. For example, it may be necessary to identify all users with a particular model of laptop, even though that laptop has a number of variants.

ITIL, US National Information Assurance (IA) Glossary

Vector

Representation of graphic images by mathematical formulas. For instance, a circle is defined by a specific position and radius.

Sedona Conference

Vendor managed user

The management of licenses by the supplier of the software. Licenses may also be managed by the customer or the IT service provider (customer managed use).

ITIL

Vendor-added metadata

Data created and maintained by the electronic discovery vendor as a result of processing the document. While some vendor-added metadata has direct value to customers, much of it is used for process reporting, chain of custody and data accountability. Contrast with Customer-added metadata.

Sedona Conference

Verbatim coding

Extracting data from documents in a collection in a way that matches exactly as the information appears in the documents.

Sedona Conference

Verification

Process of comparing two levels of an information system specification for proper correspondence (e.g., security policy model with top-level specification, top-level specification with source code, or source code with object code).

US National Information Assurance (IA) Glossary, NIST 800 Series, FIPS Pubs

Verification check

Checks that data are entered correctly.

ISACA

Verification of accuracy

The ability to prove a record is in its original format is essential for a regulated organization. There are a number of ways technology can assist. During an examination, an "explanation" of the how the technology ensures that the records are the originals will be requested.

17 CFR 240.17a-3 & 4

Verified by Visa

A Visa Internet payment authentication system that validates a cardholder's ownership of an account in real-time during an online payment transaction. When the cardholder clicks "Buy" at the checkout page of a participating merchant web site, a Verified by Visa screen automatically appears on the cardholder's desktop. The cardholder enters a password that allows the card issuer to verify his or her identity.

VISA Glossary of Terms

Verified name

A subscriber name that has been verified by identity proofing.

NIST 800 series

Verifier

An entity that verifies the claimant's identity by verifying the claimant's possession of a token using an authentication protocol. To do this, the verifier may also need to validate credentials that link the token and identity and check their status.

NIST 800 series, FIPS Pubs

Verifier impersonation attack

An attack where the attacker impersonates the verifier in an authentication protocol, usually to learn a password.

NIST 800 series

Version

A version is used to identify a specific baseline of a configuration item. Versions typically use a naming convention that enables the sequence or date of each baseline to be identified. For example, payroll application version 3 contains updated functionality from version 2. Within the world of Microsoft software, applications shouldn't be considered out of the beta stage until at least version 3. For records, see Record Version.

ITIL, Network Frontiers, Sedona Conference

Vertical de-duplication

A process through which duplicate data are eliminated within a single custodial or production data set. See also Content comparison, File level binary comparison, Horizontal de-duplication, Metadata comparison.

Sedona Conference

Victim

A machine or system that is attacked.

NIST 800 series

Video Display Terminal (VDT)

Generic name for all display terminals.

Sedona Conference

Video Electronics Standards Association (VESA)

Concentrates on computer video standards.

Sedona Conference

Video Graphics Adapter (VGA)

A PC industry standard, first introduced by IBM in 1987, for color video displays. The minimum dot (pixel) display is 640 by 480 by 16 colors. Then "Super VGA" was introduced at 800 x 600 x 16, then 256 colors. VGA can extend to 1024 by 768 by 256 colors. Replaces EGA, an earlier standard and the even older CGA. Newer standard displays can range up to 1600 by 1280.

Sedona Conference

Video Scanner Interface

A type of device used to connect scanners with computers. Scanners with this interface require a scanner control board designed by Kofax, Xionics or Dunord.

Sedona Conference

Virtual organizations

Organizations that have no official physical site presence and are made up of diverse geographically dispersed or mobile employees.

ISACA

Virtual Private Network (VPN)

A private network that is configured within a public network. A combination of tunneling, encryption, authentication, and access control technologies and services used to carry traffic over the Internet, a managed IP network, or a provider's backbone network to ensure the security of information transmitted. For years, common carriers have built VPNs that appear as private national or international networks to the customer, but physically share backbone trunks with other customers. VPNs enjoy the security of a private network via access control and encryption, while taking advantage of the economies of scale and built-in management facilities of large public networks.

Workgroup for Electronic Data Interchange, ISACA, Centers for Medicare & Medicaid Services (CMS), US National Information Assurance (IA) Glossary, PCI-DSS, Sedona Conference, NIST 800 Series

Virus

A malicious program that replicates and transmits itself by exploiting vulnerabilities in other programs. A program that "infects" computer files, usually executable programs, by inserting a copy of itself into the file. These copies are usually executed when the "infected" file is loaded into memory, allowing the virus to infect other files. Unlike the computer worm, a virus requires human involvement (usually unwitting) to propagate. See also worm. The main difference between a virus and a Trojan horse is that the hidden code in a computer virus can only replicate by attaching a copy of itself to other programs and may also include an additional "payload" that triggers when specific conditions are met.

FISCAM, ISACA, Centers for Medicare & Medicaid Services (CMS), PCI-DSS, US National Information Assurance (IA) Glossary, Sedona Conference, NIST 800 Series

Virus hoax

An urgent warning message about a nonexistent virus.

NIST 800 series

Virus scanning

The process employed by anti-virus software to check for, identify, isolate, and eradicate viruses, Trojan Horses, worms, and other forms of malicious code.

Centers for Medicare & Medicaid Services (CMS)

Virus signature

A pattern that identifies a known organization, such as a virus. Signatures also describe calculated numbers or character strings that correspond to a file.

Network Frontiers

Visa ReaderCleaner™

A specially treated card that effectively removes dirt, magnetic oxides, and other contaminants from concealed magnetic heads in POS devices. The heads should be kept clean so that Visa cards can be swiped and their magnetic stripes read quickly and easily, thus avoiding key-entered transactions.

VISA Glossary of Terms

VisaNet processor

A processor directly connected to VisaNet. See also: Processor.

VISA Glossary of Terms

Vision

A description of what the organization intends to become in the future. A vision is created by senior management and is used to help influence culture and strategic planning. Visions are also what you see after twenty hours of trouble-shooting.

ITIL

Vital Business Function (VBF)

A function of a business process which is critical to the success of the business. Vital business functions are an important consideration of business continuity management, IT service continuity management and availability management.

ITIL

Vital records

Those records without which an organization could not continue to operate, that is, those containing information needed to re-establish the organization in the event of a disaster. Vital records are those which protect the assets and interests of the organization as well as those of its clients and shareholders.

DIRKS, PAS 56, Sedona Conference

Voice authorization

An authorization obtained by telephoning a voice authorization center. See also Voice authorization center.

VISA Glossary of Terms

Voice authorization center

An operator-staffed center that handles telephone authorization requests from merchants who do not have electronic POS terminals or whose electronic terminals are temporarily not working, or for transactions where special assistance is required. Voice authorization centers also handle manual authorization requests and Code 10 calls.

VISA Glossary of Terms

Voice mail

A system of storing messages in a private recording medium where the called party can later retrieve the messages.

ISACA

Voice over Internet Protocol (VoIP)

Telephonic capability across an IP connection; increasingly used in place of standard telephone systems.

Sedona Conference

Volume

A volume is a specific amount of storage space on computer storage media such as hard drives, floppy discs, CD-ROM discs, etc. In some instances, computer media may contain more than one volume, while in others, one volume may be contained on more than one disk.

Sedona Conference

Volume Boot Sector

When a partition is formatted to create a volume, a volume boot sector is created to store information about the volume. One volume contains the operating system and its volume boot sector contains code used to load the operating system when the computer is booted up.

Sedona Conference

Vulnerability

A weakness in an information system, system security practices and procedures, administrative controls, internal controls, implementation, or physical layout that could be accidentally triggered or intentionally exploited by a threat to gain unauthorized access to information or disrupt processing and result in a violation of the system's compliance policy. There are three basic types of vulnerabilities (physical, technological, and operational). For example, an open firewall port, a password that is never changed, or a flammable carpet. A missing control is also considered to be a vulnerability.

CERT OCTAVE, NIST 800 series, ISACA, Centers for Medicare & Medicaid

Services (CMS), ISO/IEC 27001:2005, PCI-DSS, FIPS Pubs, ITIL, US National Information Assurance (IA) Glossary

Vulnerability analysis

Examination of information to identify the elements comprising a vulnerability.

US National Information Assurance (IA) Glossary

Vulnerability analysis or evaluation approach

Systematic examination of systems and applications in order to determine the adequacy of security measures, identify security deficiencies, and provide data from which to predict the effectiveness of proposed security measures. An approach for evaluating each infrastructure component, including who will perform the evaluation and the selected tool(s). ISACA's definition limits this analysis to the security state, but in practice CobiT does not. Vulnerability analysis leads to a vulnerability assessment.

CERT OCTAVE, ISACA, Centers for Medicare & Medicaid Services (CMS)

Vulnerability assessment

Formal description and evaluation of vulnerabilities of an information system.

US National Information Assurance (IA) Glossary, NIST 800 Series

Vulnerability assessment or summary

A summary of the technology vulnerabilities for each component that is evaluated. A vulnerability summary includes the susceptibility of a particular system to a specific attack and the opportunities that are available to a threat agent to mount that attack, the types of technology vulnerabilities found, when they need to be addressed, the potential effect on the critical assets, and how they can be addressed. See also vulnerability scan.

CERT OCTAVE, Centers for Medicare & Medicaid Services (CMS)

Vulnerability scan

An automated tool that checks a merchant or service provider's systems for vulnerabilities. The tool remotely reviews networks and Web applications based on the external-facing Internet protocol (IP) addresses. Scans identify vulnerabilities in operating systems, services, and devices that could be used by hackers to target the company's private network. See also vulnerability assessment.

PCI-DSS

W

Walkthroughs

Audit procedures to help the auditor understand the actual operation of significant aspects of accounting system processing and control techniques. Walkthroughs of financial reporting controls consist of tracing one or more transactions from initiation, through all processing, to inclusion in the general ledger; observing the processing and applicable controls in operation; making inquiries of personnel applying the controls; and examining related documents.

GAO/PCIE Financial Audit Manual

War dialer

Software packages that sequentially dial telephone numbers, recording any numbers that answer.

ISACA

Warez

A term widely used by hackers to denote illegally copied and distributed commercial software from which all copy protection has been removed. Warez often contains viruses, Trojans and other malicious code and thus is very risky to download and use (legal issues notwithstanding).

NIST 800 series

Warm site

A warm-site is similar to a hot-site; however, it is not fully equipped with all necessary hardware needed for recovery. It is an environmentally conditioned workspace that is partially equipped with IT and telecommunications equipment to support relocated IT operations in the event of a significant disruption.

ISACA, NIST 800 Series

Warm standby

See intermediate recovery.

ITIL

Warning banner

The Department of Justice has advised that an ambiguity in U.S. law makes it unclear whether keystroke monitoring is considered equivalent to an unauthorized telephone wiretap. The ambiguity results from the fact that current laws were written years before such concerns as keystroke monitoring or system intruders became prevalent. Additionally, no legal precedent has been set to determine whether keystroke monitoring is legal or illegal. System administrators conducting such monitoring might be subject to criminal and civil liabilities. The Department of Justice advises system administrators to protect themselves by giving notice to system users if keystroke monitoring is being conducted. Notice should include agency/organization policy statements, training on the subject, and a banner notice on each system being monitored.

Centers for Medicare & Medicaid Services (CMS), NIST 800 series

Waterfall development

Also known as traditional development, it is a very procedure-focused development cycle with formal sign-off at the completion of each level.

ISACA

WAV

File extension name for Windows sound files . ".WAV" files can reach 5 Megabytes for one minute of audio.

Sedona Conference

Web bug

Tiny images, invisible to a user, placed on web sites in such a way that they allow third parties to track use of web servers and collect information about the user, including IP address, Host name, browser type and version, operating system name and version, and web browser cookie.

NIST 800 series

Web defacement

A form of malicious hacking in which a Web site is vandalized; often the hacker will replace the site's normal content with a specific political or social message or will erase the content from the site entirely.

Network Frontiers

Web page

A viewable screen displaying information, presented through a web browser in a single view sometimes requiring the user to scroll to review the entire page. A bank web page may display the bank's logo, provide information about bank products and services, or allow a customer to interact with the bank or third parties that have contracted with the bank.

ISACA

Web risk assessment

Process for ensuring websites are in compliance with applicable policies.

US National Information Assurance (IA) Glossary

Web server

A computer that houses Website files and manages requests to and from the Internet.

Network Frontiers

Web Service Description Language

An XML-formatted language used to describe a web service's capabilities as collections of communication endpoints capable of exchanging messages. WSDL is the language that UDDI uses. See also Universal Description, discovery and Integration (UDDI).

ISACA

Web Services Description Language (WSDL)

ISACA

Web site

Consists of one or more web pages that may originate at one or more web server computers. A person can view the pages of a website in any order, as he or she would a magazine. May include different types of URIs (e.g., file transfer protocol sites, telnet sites, as well as World Wide Web sites). See also URI and URL.

ISACA, ISO/IEC 27001:2005, Sedona Conference

What You See Is What You Get (WYSIWYG)

Display and software technology which shows on the computer screen exactly what will print. Often requires a large, high-density monitor.

Sedona Conference

Whitebox testing

A testing approach that uses knowledge of a program/module's underlying implementation and code intervals to verify its expected behavior.

ISACA

Wide Area Network (WAN)

A group of computers and other devices dispersed over a wide geographical area that are connected by communications links.

FISCAM, ISACA, Centers for Medicare & Medicaid Services (CMS)

WiFi Protect Access (WPA)

Security protocol for wireless (WiFi) networks. Created in response to several serious weaknesses in the WEP protocol.

PCI-DSS

Windows NT

A version of the Windows operating system that supports preemptive multitasking.

ISACA

Wired Equivalent Privacy (WEP)

A security protocol, designed to provide the same level of security as that of a wired LAN, for wireless local area networks defined in the 802.11b or 11g standard. Does not provide adequate security against intentional eavesdropping (for example, cryptanalysis).

Network Frontiers, PCI-DSS, NIST 800 Series

Wireless Application Protocol (WAP)

A standard for providing cellular telephones, pagers, and other handheld devices with secure access to e-mail and text-based Web pages.

NIST 800 series

Wireless component

Devices, such as cell phones and wireless access points, that staff members may use to access information; for example, e-mail.

CERT OCTAVE

Wireless technology

Permits the active or passive transfer of information between separated points without physical connection. Active information transfer may entail a transmit and/or receive emanation of energy, whereas passive information transfer entails a receive-only capability. Currently wireless technologies use IR, acoustic, RF, and optical but, as technology evolves, wireless could include other methods of transmission.

US National Information Assurance (IA) Glossary

Wiretapping

The practice of eavesdropping on information being transmitted over telecommunications links. Usually illegal unless you are the President and your party can stop an impeachment vote.

ISACA, Network Frontiers

Work area recovery

The provision of (internal or external) pre-designated work space providing the minimum necessary equipment and services ready for occupation by business recovery teams at short notice.

PAS 56

Work factor

Estimate of the effort or time needed by a potential perpetrator, with specified expertise and resources, to overcome a protective measure.

US National Information Assurance (IA) Glossary

Work In Progress (WIP)

A status that means activities have started but are not yet complete. It is commonly used as a status for incidents, problems, changes, etc.

ITIL

Work instructions

A document containing detailed instructions that specify exactly what steps to follow to carry out an activity. A work instruction contains much more detail than a procedure and is only created if very detailed instructions are needed.

ITIL

Workaround

The process used to reduce or eliminating the impact of an incident or problem for which a full resolution is not yet available. For example, by restarting a failed configuration item. Workarounds for problems are documented in known error records. Workarounds for incidents that do not have associated problem records are documented in the incident record.

ITIL

Workflow, Ad Hoc

A simple manual process by which documents can be moved around a multi-user review system on an "as-needed" basis.

Sedona Conference

Workflow, Rule-Based

A programmed series of automated steps that route documents to various users on a multi-user review system.

Sedona Conference

Workflow/BPM

Automation of business processes, in whole or in part, where documents, information, or tasks are passed from one participant to another for action, according to a set of rules. A business process is a logically related set of workflows, worksteps, and tasks that provide a product or service to customers. BPM is a mix of Process Management/Workflow with Application Integration technology.

AIIM

Workgroup

A group of computer users connected to share individual talents and resources as well as computer hardware and software – often to accomplish a team goal.

Sedona Conference

Workload

The resources required to deliver an identifiable part of an IT service. Workloads may be categorized by users, groups of users, or functions within the IT service. This is used to assist in analyzing and managing the capacity, performance and utilization of configuration items and IT services. The term workload is sometimes used as a synonym for throughput.

ITIL

Workpaper (W/P)

GAO/PCIE Financial Audit Manual

Workstation

A microcomputer or terminal connected to a network. Workstation can also refer to a powerful, stand-alone computer with considerable calculating or graphics capability. See also desktop workstation, discless workstation.

FISCAM, Centers for Medicare & Medicaid Services (CMS), Workgroup for Electronic Data Interchange

World Bank (WB)

de facto

World Wide Web (WWW)

A sub-network of the Internet through which information is exchanged by text, graphics, audio, and video. All of the computers on the Internet which use HTML-capable software (Netscape, Explorer, etc.) to exchange data. Data exchange on the WWW is characterized by easy-touse graphical interfaces, hypertext links, images, and sound. Today the WWW has become synonymous with the Internet, although technically it is really just one component.

ISACA, Sedona Conference

World Wide Web Consortium (W3C)

An international consortium founded in 1994 of affiliates from public and private organizations involved with the Internet and the web. The W3C's primary mission is to promulgate open standards to further enhance the economic growth of Internet web services globally. See also http://www.w3.org for more information.

ISACA

Worm

A malicious program that replicates and transmits itself with dependency on other programs; typically exploits a single vulnerability although newer worms are exploiting multiple vulnerabilities. An independent computer program that reproduces by copying itself from one system to another across a network. Unlike computer viruses, worms do not require human involvement to propagate. A worm might duplicate itself in one computer so often that it causes the computer to crash. Sometimes written in separate segments, a worm is introduced surreptitiously into a host system either for fun or with intent to damage or destroy information.

Network Frontiers, FISCAM, ISACA, Centers for Medicare & Medicaid Services (CMS), US National Information Assurance (IA) Glossary, NIST 800 Series

WORM disks

Write Once Read Many discs. A popular archival storage media during the 1980s. Acknowledged as the first optical discs, they are primarily used to store archives of data that cannot be altered.

WORM discs are created by standalone PCs and cannot be used on the network, unlike CD-ROM discs. See also WORM.

Sedona Conference

Write

Fundamental operation in an IS that results only in the flow of information from a subject to an object.

Centers for Medicare & Medicaid Services (CMS), US National Information Assurance (IA) Glossary

Write access

Permission to write to an object in an information system.

Centers for Medicare & Medicaid Services (CMS), US National Information Assurance (IA) Glossary

Write-blocker

A device that allows investigators to examine media while preventing data writes from occurring on the subject media.

NIST 800 series

Write-Once, Read-Many (WORM)

Data storage devices (e.g. CD-ROM's) where the space on the discs can only be written once. The data is permanently stored. This is often today's primary media for archival information. Common disk sizes run from 5.25" (1.3 giga-bytes) to 12" (8 to 10 gigabytes) capacities. There is also a 14'" disk (13 to 15 gigabytes), only manufactured by Kodak's optical storage group. WORMs can also be configured into jukeboxes. There are various technologies. The expected viable lifetime of a WORM is at least 50 years. Since it's impossible to change, the government treats it just like paper or microfilm and it is accepted in litigation and other record-keeping applications. On the negative side, there is no current standard for how WORMs are written. The only ISO standard is for the 14" version, manufactured only by one vendor. A 5.25" standard is emerging from the European Computer Manufacturing Association but is not yet accepted. Further, WORM discs are written on both sides, but there are currently no drives that read both sides at the same time. As for speed, WORM is faster than tape or CD-ROM, but slower than magnetic. Typical disk access times run between 40 and 150 milliseconds (compared with 11 ms for fast magnetic discs and 300 ms for CD-ROM). Data transfer rates run between 1 and 2 MB/sec (compared with 5 to 10 for magnetic discs and 600KB/sec for CD-ROM).

Sedona Conference

X

X.25

A protocol for packet-switching networks.

ISACA, Sedona Conference

X.25 interface

An interface between data terminal equipment (DTE) and data circuit-terminating equipment (DCE) for terminals operating in the packet mode on some public data networks.

ISACA

X.500

Standard that defines how global directories should be structured. X.500 directories are hierarchical with different levels for each category of information, such as country, state and city.

ISACA

X.509 certificate

The International Organization for Standardization/International Telecommunication Union – Standardization Department (ISO/ITU-T) X.509 standard defined two types of certificates – the X.509 public key certificate, and the X.509 attribute certificate. Most commonly (including this document), an X.509 certificate refers to the X.509 public key certificate.

NIST 800 series

X.509 public key certificate

The public key for a user (or device) and a name for the user (or device), together with some other information, rendered unforgeable by the digital signature of the certification authority that issued the certificate, encoded in the format defined in the ISO/ITU-T X.509 standard.

NIST 800 series

Z

Zap

A generic term used to define a type of program that can alter data and programs directly, bypassing controls. Because of this ability, the ZAP and SuperZAP programs must be secured from casual or unauthorized use.

FISCAM

Zero fill

To fill unused storage locations in an information system with the representation of the character denoting "0."

US National Information Assurance (IA) Glossary

Zeroize

To remove or eliminate the key from a crypto-equipment or fill device.

US National Information Assurance (IA) Glossary

ZIP

A common file compression format that allows quick and easy storage for transport.

Sedona Conference

Zip drive

A floppy disk drive that can hold a large amount of data, usually as much as 750 megabytes or more. Often used for backing up hard discs.

Sedona Conference

Zombie

A computer system that has been covertly taken over in order to transmit phony messages that slow down service and disrupt the network.

Network Frontiers, NIST 800 Series

Zone OCR

An add-on feature of the imaging software that populates document templates by reading certain regions or zones of a document, and then placing the text into a document index.

Sedona Conference

Zone of control

Synonymous with inspectable space.

US National Information Assurance (IA) Glossary

Have we missed anything?

One of the biggest problems with a print book is that once it is printed, it is locked. And it isn't very interactive.

But *you* can change all of that. Register as an owner at http://www.glossarybook.com and there you'll find a listing of new and up-dated acronyms and terms, more spotlight definitions, and a way for you to suggest terms and acronyms as well.

SPOTLIGHT DEFINITIONS

Why only a few spotlight definitions? Actually, we have many more than this. They are set up and ready for you online as a part of this book's continual update process. Every time you get a new update of the book, you'll also get a new spotlight definition. They will be in both HTML format and PDF format so that you can add them to the back of this book easily.

We've provided a few samples so that you can see their format and style, and hopefully pique your interests in the updates heading your way.

Log on to www.complianceglossary.com and register as a book owner so that you can be kept up to date!

Accountable vs. Responsible

Many regulations, standards, guidelines, and best practices discuss accountability and responsibility, but most do not directly define these concepts. This is confounded by the fact that most common language dictionaries show that these two words are synonyms for each other. There is one compliance document that gives precise definitions of both, and that is CobiT 4. On Pg 15 of CobiT 4, it says "Accountable means 'the buck stops here' — this is the person who provides direction and authorizes an activity. Responsibility means the person who gets the task done." For **ISACA's CobiT accountable** means **authorizer** and **responsible** means **doer**. Most regulations, standards, and guidelines roughly agree with this definition, although it might not seem like it at first.

Frequently, readers will note that when the word "accountable" appears in documentation, it is alongside instructions for creating logs and audit trails. This is because most regulations, standards, guidelines, and best practices interpret accountability as having a system in place that lets the organization easily determine whom was doing what (and when) in a reliable fashion. Accountability then, is all about the answer to the question 'who has the right to do this?' as accountability is about *explainability*. The accountable person is the one who must sign off on the work being done or the person whom the logs point to for the actions taken. Accountability means you will not, or can not, repudiate the actions in question.

On the other hand, when responsibility is presented, it often appears alongside specific tasks, such as "take responsibility for control over financial reporting," meaning that someone has to *take ownership of* the task. Taking responsibility for a task means being *the direct cause* of the work being done, or being able to explain *how* the work was done – both point to ownership. A person who is responsible for control over financial reporting could directly implement appropriate financial reporting controls, or delegate the work to someone else or even a set of automated controls. Delegating the work would make another person accountable for that work, but not responsible for it. I.e. if this question was asked: "who or what performed a specific financial control?" the answer would be the person or automated process delegated to perform the task. Delegation would not, however, make the person or process who did the work responsible for it. In other words, if something went wrong, blame would be placed on the person whose responsibility it was to ensure there were appropriate controls over financial reporting.

An easy way to think about the general difference between responsibility and accountability then, is when someone is responsible for a project, they are the owner of the project. When someone is accountable for a project, it means they are the one whom the paper trail or electronic logs point to and must approve the actions being taken.

In any given project, ultimately *one* person must be responsible while multiple can be held accountable, or one person with is both responsible *and* accountable. But you can never have a case where there is someone who is accountable without having someone who is responsible. There *must* be at least one responsible party.

Application, Software, Program, and Utility

Software is an umbrella term for any written, coded commands that tell a computer what tasks to perform. The word software is often paired with the word program as in **software program**. The word pairing is interchangeable with the term **software, but program is slightly more specific than software because one can use the word software to mean a single program, or multiple programs.** Because of this slight difference, program rather than software is our base definition in the following term discussions.

Program

The common definition of program is an organized list of instructions that when executed, cause the computer to do a specific activity or activities. However in regulations, standards, best practices, and guidelines, program is sometimes used a bit differently. Instead of **program** being used to refer specifically to **instructions for a computer**, alternatively **program is often used to describe a list of events or instructions** for employees to follow. This includes security programs, training programs, etc. It *also* includes computer instructions, so be sure to examine the context of the documentation to determine what meaning is being invoked.

Utility

Utilities are defined as a particular type of program, particularly programs that perform specific tasks, usually pertaining to managing system or application resources. We'll get to a definition of application in a moment.

Application

An **application** is a program or group of programs designed for end users. Applications usually rest on top of systems software because it often cannot run without something like an operating system or system utilities.

When regulations, standards, best practices, and guidelines talk about applications, they often preface this term with the word 'major' or 'minor.' A **major application** is an application that requires special security because of the risk and magnitude of the harm that would result from any tampering or loss of the information contained in the application. A **minor application** is similar to a major application in that it is big enough to warrant security measures, but the risk and magnitude of harm resulting from tampering or loss of the information it contains would not severely impact the organization.

Entity, Department, Organization, Agency and Enterprise

Entity, department, organization, agency and enterprise sometimes sound like five ways to say the exact same thing. So what makes the five of these words unique, particularly when viewed in regulations, standards, best practices, and guidelines? Let's find out, beginning with a discussion of what an organization is.

Organization

The best way to think of an organization is as a collection of rights, privileges, obligations, and responsibilities that are balanced over time through conflict and resolution. In other words, an organization is a collection of relationships and interactions. Throughout time, these relationships and patterns of interaction become established as practices within the organization, for instance, a way of creating products, holding meetings, deploying technology. Over time, through both habit and repetition, these practices become institutionalized, thus forming the structure of the organization. As time goes by, people within the organization draw from this structure when interacting with each other. In simple terms, interactions form structure, and that structure influences interactions.

Entity

An organization can be an entity, however the term entity may also be used to describe a group within an organization such as a department, grouping of people or collection of controls. Entities are often described as being scalable and definable. Thus an entity can be any grouping of people or things that can be readily described and which does some type of work as a grouping that has an impact on the rest of the organization, or other entities immediately associated with it. While an entity can be an organization, it is most often used to describe a smaller aspect of an organization.

Department

A department can be considered an entity, but a department is not a scalable term as entity is. It's used to describe an official group of workers under the umbrella of something larger such as an organization.

Agency

An agency is a person, authority, territory, political subdivision of a state or territory, Indian tribe or entity that is authorized to oversee or to regulate a set of activities or system.

Enterprise

Enterprise is used in two ways. One common meaning of enterprise is a big organization that uses computers. When used in this way enterprise refers to every aspect of an organization, including its subsidiaries. The term enterprise can also mean a complicated project or undertaking requiring the input of many people or departments.

RACI charts: a structure for coordination

What in the world is a RACI chart? In the simplest of definitions, RACI stands for defining the roles of the person **responsible**, **accountable**, **consulted**, and **informed** during an operational process. For the world of compliance, CobiT 4[1] uses RACI charts throughout their documentation – and maybe you should to.

The RACI model is used by process management professionals the world over and is very useful to describe *what* should be done *by whom* during an operational process. A typical RACI chart is a grid with the person (or title) listed along the top and the activities listed along the left side as shown in the diagram below. For each activity, a person can be assigned any combination of an R, A, C, or I. The goal is to ensure that *somebody* is assigned both an "R" and an "A" for each activity (the same person can be assigned an "RA," meaning that they are both responsible and accountable).

	Person 1	Person 2	Person 3	Person 4
Activity 1	R		A	
Activity 2	A	R		C
Activity 3	A		C	R
Activity 4			A	R

RACI table

The typical steps in a RACI process are to:

1. **Identify all of the processes and activities** involved, listing them down the left side of the table.

---

[1] Control Objectives for Information and Related Technology: A framework, control objectives, and audit guidelines developed as a generally applicable and accepted standard for good practices for controls over information technology.

2. **Identify all of the roles or key staff** that would be needed to accomplish the mission or objective and then list them across the top of the table.

3. **Identify who** is responsible (R), then who is being held accountable (A), who must be consulted (C), and who must be informed (I).

4. **Resolve overlaps** between the people and activities, because there should only be one "R" and one "A" per activity. If there is overlap between people, one person will think the other is taking care of the issue and it will be dropped.

5. **Resolve gaps** for each of the activities, ensuring that there someone is assigned an "R" and an "A" per activity. This is just as important a step as resolving overlaps because someone has to be held responsible and accountable for each activity.

RACI versus RASCI and advanced charting

There's one addition to the RACI chart that some use, and that's the addition of the **support** function, making it a RASCI chart. The supporting role is one of helping to facilitate the execution of the task.

The other addition to the charting method is that of adding time commitments to the chart. By adding time expectations per activity, per role, the person assigned to the role and activity will have a much clearer sense of understanding about their commitment levels for the project overall, and the chart can then be easily turned into a GANTT chart or timeline of activities.

	Person 1	Person 2	Person 3	Person 4
Activity 1	R/5		A/2	
Activity 2	A/2	R/3		C/.5
Activity 3	RA/2		S/.5	
Activity 4			A/1	R/3

Advanced RASCI chart

RACI provides structure for policies and procedures

What this all boils down to is a methodology for the coordination of personnel when documenting policies and procedures. By coordinating the knowledge, talents, and political decision making capabilities of staff, team effort can be leveraged and divided into different key areas of policy and procedure activities.

Because policies and procedures define organizational roles, RACI charts become quite effective when documenting and communicating the assignment of those roles.

Authority documents: regulations, principles, standards, guidelines, best practices, policies, and procedures

When we say that we are "complying," we are saying that we are complying with authoritative rules that are not of our own creation. (OK, so some of you reading this are, in fact, responsible for creating these rules – that's why you bought this in the first place. But when you're creating these rules you are not you, but rather you are your organization. So you, as yourself, are obligated to comply with the rules created by you as your organization. Got it?) These authoritative rules can come in the form of regulations, principles, standards, guidelines, best practices, policies, and procedures. Which is which, and what makes one authoritative body a regulator and another a best practice author? Let's start with regulations and move from there.

⚡ Regulations are rules of law that, if not followed, can result in penalties. Regulations state *that* something must be done. Regulations are promulgated by governmental agencies to interpret or expand the reach of statutes.

⚡ Standards are rallying points created by well organized groups or are generally accepted within the industry. Standards rally the affected entities around *what* must be done.

⚡ Guidelines are detailed outlines and plans for determining a course of action. Guidelines *prioritize and direct* the course of action.

⚡ Best practices are programs, initiatives or activities which are considered leading edge or exceptional models for others to follow. Best practices *set the example* of *how to do* something the best way.

Collectively, we refer to these as **authority documents** throughout this book and throughout all of the other documentation within the Unified Compliance Framework.

Regulations

To regulate is to bring under *the force of law* or a *governing authority*. Everyone in his or her own country falls within the realm of the national, regional, and local laws. Hence, traditional regulators are those within the levels of government just mentioned. When governmental agencies create their acts, they are codifying legal documents that resulted from deliberations of their legislative bodies. Often, however, the acts passed by those legislative bodies establish broad principles rather than detailed prescriptions for the behavior of people and companies and delegate to regulators responsibility for filling in the details and gaps. The regulators are empowered to interpret how the laws are to be implemented and to establish rules for following those laws. Those rules are then documented as **regulations**, such as the Code of Federal Regulations that we have in the United States. These acts and regulations, therefore, *must* be followed under penalty of law.

Regulations are enforceable by law. Failure to follow regulations will result in penalties.

Contractual Standards and Self-Regulatory Structures

There is much confusion between "regulations" promulgated by government regulators as discussed above and the rules, standards and, yes, "regulations" promulgated by other so-called regulatory bodies and other organizations that *can* and *do* emerge to reign in our actions. Variously known as "self-regulatory bodies," "standards bodies," or by similar names, these organizations are not part of the government and do not have the force of law behind their requirements, but failure to comply with those requirements may well disqualify an entity from participating in certain businesses. The promulgators of these rules may be industry-based organizations that band together to address a concern that is common to industry members. For example, the credit card companies (Visa, MasterCard, American Express, etc.) have banded together to create the Payment Card Industry Security Standard. They may also be self-appointed watchdog organizations that have gained sufficient acceptance, prominence and/or moral authority over time that people turn to them as authorities in the field. For example, the ability to display the BBBOnline and TRUSTe seals in online commerce has achieved this type of prominence that makes it worthwhile to comply with those standards. Certain membership based organizations promote similar types of rules as a condition of membership. The unifying principle is that they all have something you want and you're willing to *contractually* commit to play by their rules to get it.

We'll get to the definition of a standard in a moment, but just because this one is *called* a standard (it can't be called a law, Act, or regulation because it does not come from the government), doesn't mean that it can be ignored without consequences. Compliance with these types of contractual standards are, legally speaking, optional. If a company is not interested in accepting credit cards as a form of payment, it is not obligated to comply with the PCI standards. However, anyone wanting to accept credit cards is required to *contractually* agree to comply with the PCI standard. Similarly, anyone wanting to display the BBBOnline seal must contractually agree to follow certain guidelines and processes. Failure to comply with these obligations creates a breach of contract and, depending on the contract terms, may result in a variety of fines and, potentially, the loss of valuable contractual rights – losing the ability to accept credit cards in the case of the PCI standards could have grave consequences to just about any merchant. Losing the right to use the BBBOnline or TRUSTe seals may not have as severe an effect on a merchant as being unable to accept credit cards, but it could drive customers away to competitor sites – particularly if the contractual breach is widely publicized. The payment card industry has already fined a great many organizations and affected the closure of at least one organization that we know of for not properly following their standard. Because the payment card industry *can* exercise *authority* over its user body, and that user body is so large, in this instance they can be compared to regulators even though they haven't been given the statutory mandate of a regulator. However, there is one big difference between the payment card industry and true regulators – while the payment card industry may be able put you out of business, they can't put you in jail.

Contractual standards promulgated by self-regulatory bodies are enforceable under contract. Failure to comply carries with it the remedies established by the contract which may include fines and/or loss of valuable contract rights and such consequences are enforceable under contract law.

Principles

A principle is a widely accepted rule, norm, doctrine, or assumed truth. A set of principles form the basic foundation for a specific set of guidelines. A good example of general principles are the seven principles of the OECD Guidelines for the Security of Information Systems and Networks (awareness, responsibility, response, risk assessment, security design and implementation, security management, and reassessment principles). Principles, then, are fundamental beliefs that set the course for the rest of the thinking on the subject at hand. Principles can be combined with a semi-detailed set of controls which flow from them, such as the Generally Accepted Internet Security Principles.

Many principles will find their way into standards and guidelines and even regulations as they serve as general behavior directives that drive standards discussions in the first place. One example of a principle directly creating standards are the Generally Accepted Accounting Principles found within the world of finance which have spawned the SAS 91 accounting standard.

Principles are not enforceable by law. Failure to follow principles may result in actions that are not within keeping of the rule of law or proper conduct.

International standards and control models

We love the origination of the term standard. Originally a standard was a conspicuous object (a tall pole with a banner, flag, or symbol on top) that was used to mark a rallying point in battle. Today, a standard is a criterion, a means of determining what rules, principles, and measures established by an authority should apply to a given situation in order to improve efficiency and compatibility. Control models are very much the same thing but tend to focus more specifically on certain aspects of implementation. In contrast to the original definition, a standard today comes into existence *because* people rally around it rather than the other way around. International standards and control models are consensus models that are generally accepted by the user community (or at least by the community creating the standard), such as the Control Objectives for Information Technology created by Information Systems Audit and Control Association (a control model) or the International Organization for Standardization's (ISO) various standards such as their ISO 27001:2005 Information Security Management System.

Formal international standards begin as draft documents which are then published as a Request for Comments (RFC) document. As these RFCs mature through the editing process, they become proposed standards, draft standards, and ultimately the final published standard.

Does your organization *have* to follow any given standard? Not if the standard's author isn't a regulator or a body with contractual authority over you – meaning that they can't *force* your organization to use their standard under threat of legal action or penalty. Some might think defacto standards must be followed, but that isn't true.

In the world of regulatory compliance for information services, the CobiT audit standard comes pretty close to being *the* defacto standard. We've seen presentations in which the speaker mistakenly told the audience that this or that regulation *called for* the use of CobiT as the measuring stick against which they must judge whether they were following the regulation. That just isn't so (though see our section "A note about Safe Harbors" that follows). There isn't one regulation that mandates the use of CobiT. However, the Sarbanes-Oxley Act did create the Public Company Accounting Oversight Board which created and mandates the use of its own auditing standards. The Payment Card Industry Association also mandates the use of its <u>PCI-DSS</u> standard as the audit standard that must be followed when proving that you've met their guidelines. Of course regulators are certainly free to require the use of a particular standard, but that hasn't happened yet and we think it unlikely to happen any time soon – the government tends to avoid ceding its authority to non-government groups and will, instead, plagiarize the standard and incorporate it directly into the text of the regulation.

Standards are not enforceable by law. However, failure to follow standards may result in actions contrary to regulations which **are** *enforceable by law.*

Guidelines

A great example of a guideline is The Business Continuity Institute's <u>Business Continuity Management Good Practice Guidelines</u>. This guideline doesn't attempt to provide every answer for business continuity planning. However, it prioritizes the steps that should be followed when creating, developing, and testing the plan.

The hallmark of a guideline is that it will have a set of general principles followed by a set of procedures which direct the user through the necessary steps that should be followed with respect to the given topic under consideration.

*Guidelines are even less enforceable than standards. However, failure to follow guidelines may lead to certain aspects of a standard or regulation being skipped or missing the mark, which in turn may result in actions contrary to regulations which **are** enforceable by law.*

Best practices

Best practices are leading edge models of methods or actions for others to follow. These are combinations of activities, processes, policies, or procedures that document the *best possible* way of doing something.

Are they enforceable? Nope. As a matter of fact, many times they aren't even *desirable* – in their fullest sense, the "best" way to do something is often also the costliest. Too many times we've seen people spending $1,000 to fix a $100 problem by using an industry "best practice." Best practices must always be viewed in context, weighing the cost vs. the benefit, and then adapted to the particular situation in which they may be applied.

Controls

Organizational controls (especially compliance controls) are the activities that comprise and are carried out by policies, standards, procedures, and practices designed to provide reasonable assurance that certain business objectives will be achieved and undesired events will be prevented or detected. These control activities help ensure that management directives are carried out by providing a description of what physical, software, procedural, or people related conditions must be met or be in existence in order to satisfy a core requirement.

*Following properly structured and validated organizational controls is **the** essential prerequisite to compliance, and failure to follow controls will directly lead to whatever fines or penalties the regulatory body can mete out.*

Organizational policies

A policy is a definitive plan or method of action to guide decisions and actions. Policies should be selected from the various possible alternatives in the light of organizational conditions and the impact that they will have. Policies are meant to limit individual discretion to make decisions about which choices and actions (or behaviors) can be taken regarding the topic in question. Because of this, a policy's intended purpose is to influence and guide both present and future decision making to be in line with the philosophy, objectives, and strategic plans established by the organization's management teams. In addition to policy content, well structured policies describe the consequences of failing to comply with the policy, the means for handling exceptions, and the manner in which compliance with the policy will be checked and measured.

In practice, an organizational policy is a formal document describing the organization's position on a particular aspect of compliance with regulations, standards, and guidelines. Therefore, it acts as an official statement of a position, plan, or course of action established by an identified sponsoring authority, which is designed to influence, to provide direction, and to determine decisions and actions with regard to a specific topic. Organizational standards, procedures, and guidelines flow from policies. Policies come in two basic forms; high-level policy statements and detailed policies.

Many times the high-level policy statements will have direct links to organizational standards and procedures, such as an organizational policy for the destruction of electronic media (tapes, drives, etc.) that would then point to the organizational degaussing standard and associated step-by-step procedures for more explicit information.

Detailed policies provide more in-depth information such as purpose, authority, and detailed definitions of sub-topics. Detailed policies often have direct links to individual procedures for follow-through methods. A good example of a policy-procedure pairing is an organizational records retention policy that details various definitions of record types and then links each type to the procedures that need to be followed to carry out that specific portion of the policy.

Policies, because they are mandatory within the organization, are enforced by the organization under the auspices of the Human Resources and/or Legal departments and failure to comply with a policy is generally punishable by disciplinary action that could include suspension or even termination to the extent permitted by law.

Organizational standards

Standards are definitional and clarifying in nature and established either to further understanding and interaction or to acknowledge observed (or desired norms) of exhibited characteristics or behavior. Organizational standards are used to define the commonality of parts and processes. A standard can be:

1. An object or measure of comparison that defines or represents the magnitude of a unit.

2. A characterization that establishes allowable tolerances or constraints for categories of items and parameter settings.

3. A degree or level of required excellence or attainment.

Thus, organizational standards may specify minimum performance levels, describe best practices within the company, or serve as the list of controls (or their parameters) that the organization must follow in order to attain compliance within a given area. In general computing terms, a standard is a set of detailed technical guidelines used as a means of establishing uniformity in an area of hardware or software development.

Standards can be put in place to support a policy, a process, or as a response to an operational need. Like policies, well structured standards will include a description of the manner in which noncompliance will be detected.

Because standards directly support organizational policies, they should be enforced with the same level of authority as the organizational policy they clarify.

Organizational procedures

A procedure is a step-by-step description of tasks required to support and carry out organizational policies. Therefore, a procedure can be thought of as an extension of a policy that articulates the process that is to be used to accomplish a control.

More formally, procedures are the step-by-step documentation of the course of action to be taken to perform a given task as a series of steps, followed in a definite regular order, ensuring the consistent and repetitive approach to accomplish control activities.

Because procedures directly support organizational policies, they should be enforced with the same level of authority as the organizational policy they support.

A note about "Safe Harbors"

Nothing muddies the waters better than a good "safe harbor." While a safe harbor is intended to make laws and regulations easier to follow, oftentimes the safe harbor is co-opted by consultants, speakers, and other well-meaning (or not so well-meaning) folks to support their position that a particular standard, guideline, procedure, or control is required under the law and that failure to adopt that particular standard, guideline, procedure, or control will subject the organization to legal action. Nothing could be further from the truth.

A safe harbor in a law or regulation is a shortcut used by the regulators to make it easier for people to determine whether they are in compliance with the law without requiring an in-depth analysis of each particular case. Thus, the safe harbor provides that *if* you take the steps required to be within the safe harbor, *then* you will (more or less) automatically be considered to be in compliance with that particular aspect of the law or regulation. However, the converse is not true – if you do *not* fall within the safe harbor, that does not necessarily mean that you are not in compliance with the law. What it *does* mean is that you will have to show that the steps you chose to take are *also* in compliance with the law.

Let's use our previously mentioned CobiT standard as an illustration. Supposed some regulator enacted a regulation requiring that certain types of organizations conduct annual audits of their information services systems that adhere to auditing standards that are reasonable and customary in the industry. Suppose further that our helpful regulator adds a statement along the lines of "The CobiT audit standards are reasonable and customary standards in the industry." This safe harbor offers organizations the opportunity to reduce compliance risk by adopting the CobiT audit standards. However, there could be many reasons why the CobiT standards are inappropriate for the particular organization – cost, complexity, etc., may simply not warrant the use of that standard. Is the organization bound to use CobiT anyway? (If you've read this far, you probably already know the answer.) The answer, of course, is **no** – the organization is free to use whatever auditing standard it chooses *provided* it meets the two-prong test of "reasonable" and "customary in the industry." However, if the organization chooses to use a standard other than CobiT and the regulator doesn't like it, the organization may have an uphill battle to convince the regulator (and, perhaps ultimately, the court) that the chosen standard is, in fact, reasonable and customary in the industry.

Safe harbors tend to be very conservative and avoid gray areas. If a safe harbor is available, it's always good to know – even if you choose not to follow it, it can provide valuable guidance and insight into the regulator's mindset. However, the needs of the organization may dictate that it leave the safe harbor and enter riskier waters.

The authority documents tracked by the UCF

To give you a scope of the authority documents that we've used to form this material, and all of the other material within the Unified Compliance Framework, here is a listing of all of the authority documents that we are currently tracking and referencing. Please know that this is an ever growing list and is subject to change as the documents themselves change. For the most up-to-date listing, along with URL links to each of the documents we track, see the Unified Compliance Framework website[2].

Sarbanes Oxley

- Sarbanes-Oxley Act (SOX)
- PCAOB Auditing Standard No. 2
- AICPA SAS 94
- AICPA/CICA Privacy Framework

---

[2] http://www.unifiedcompliance.com/about_the_ucf/the_list_of_authority_document.html

- AICPA Suitable Trust Services Criteria
- Retention of Audit and Review Records, SEC 17 CFR 210.2-06
- Controls and Procedures, SEC 17 CFR 240.15d-15
- Reporting Transactions and Holdings, SEC 17 CFR 240.16a-3
- COSO Enterprise Risk Management (ERM) Framework

Banking and Finance

- Basel II: International Convergence of Capital Measurement and Capital Standards - A Revised Framework
- BIS Sound Practices for the Management and Supervision of Operational Risk
- Gramm-Leach-Bliley Act (GLB)
- Standards for Safeguarding Customer Information, FTC 16 CFR 314
- Privacy of Consumer Financial Information, FTC 16 CFR 313
- Safety and Soundness Standards, Appendix of OCC 12 CFR 30
- FFIEC Information Security
- FFIEC Development and Acquisition
- FFIEC Business Continuity Planning
- FFIEC Audit
- FFIEC Management
- FFIEC Operations

NASD NYSE

- NASD Manual
- NYSE Rules
- Recordkeeping rule for securities exchanges, SEC 17 CFR 240.17a-1
- Records to be made by certain exchange members SEC 17 CFR 240.17a-3
- Records to be preserved by certain exchange members SEC 17 CFR 240.17a-4
- Recordkeeping SEC 17 CFR 240.17Ad-6
- Record retention SEC 17 CFR 240.17Ad-7

Healthcare and Life Science

- HIPAA (Health Insurance Portability and Accountability Act)

⚡ HIPAA HCFA Internet Security Policy

⚡ Introductory Resource Guide for HIPAA NIST (800-66)

⚡ CMS Core Security Requirements (CSR)

⚡ CMS Information Security Acceptable Risk Safeguards (ARS)

⚡ CMS Information Security Certification and Accreditation (C&A) Methodology

⚡ CMS Info Security Business Risk Assessment

⚡ CMS Business Partners Systems Security Manual

⚡ FDA Electronic Records; Electronic Signatures FDA 21 CFR Part 11+D1

Energy

⚡ FERC Security Program for Hydropower Projects

⚡ North American Electric Reliability Corporation Critical Infrastructure Protection Cyber Security Standards

Payment Card

⚡ PCI DSS (Payment Card Industry Data Security Standard)

⚡ PCI DSS Security Scanning Procedures

⚡ VISA CISP: What to Do If Compromised

⚡ American Express Data Security Standard (DSS)

⚡ MasterCard Wireless LANs - Security Risks and Guidelines

U.S. Federal Security

⚡ FTC Electronic Signatures in Global and National Commerce Act (ESIGN)

⚡ Uniform Electronic Transactions Act (UETA)

⚡ FISMA (Federal Information Security Management Act)

⚡ FISCAM (Federal Information System Controls Audit Manual)

⚡ FIPS 140-2, Security Requirements for Cryptographic Modules

⚡ FIPS 199, Standards for Security Categorization of Federal Information and Information Systems

⚡ FIPS 191, Guideline for the Analysis of LAN Security

⚡ Clinger-Cohen Act (Information Technology Management Reform Act)

⚡ The National Strategy to Secure Cyberspace

- GAO Financial Audit Manual
- Standard for Electronic Records Management Software, DOD 5015.2
- CISWG Report on the Best Practices Subgroup
- CISWG Information Security Program Elements
- Appendix III to OMB Circular No. A-130: Security of Federal Automated Information Resources
- NCUA Guidelines for Safeguarding Member Information, 12 CFR 748

U.S. Internal Revenue

- IRS Revenue Procedure: Retention of books and records, 97-22
- IRS Revenue Procedure: Record retention: automatic data processing, 98-25
- IRS Internal Revenue Code Section 501(c)(3)

Records Management

- Federal Rules of Civil Procedure
- Uniform Rules of Evidence
- ISO 15489-1, Information and Documentation: Records management: General
- ISO 15489-2, Information and Documentation: Records management: Guidelines
- The DIRKS Manual: A Strategic Approach to Managing Business Information
- The Sedona Principles Addressing Electronic Document Production

NIST Publications

- Generally Accepted Principles and Practices for Securing Information Technology Systems, NIST SP 800-14
- Developing Security Plans for Federal Information Systems, NIST SP 800-18
- Security Self-Assessment Guide, NIST SP 800-26
- Risk Management Guide, NIST SP 800- 30
- Underlying Technical Models for Information Technology Security
- Contingency Planning Guide for Information Technology Systems, NIST SP 800-34
- Creating a Patch and Vulnerability Management Program, NIST SP 800-40

⚡ Guidelines on Firewalls and Firewall Policy, NIST SP 800-41

⚡ Recommended Security Controls for Federal Information Systems, NIST SP 800-53

⚡ Guide for Mapping Types of Information and Information Systems to Security Categories, NIST SP 800-60

⚡ Computer Security Incident Handling Guide, NIST SP 800-61

⚡ Security Considerations in the Information System Development Life Cycle, NIST SP 800-64

International Standards Organization

⚡ ISO 73:2002, Risk Management - Vocabulary

⚡ ISO 13335, Information Technology - Guidelines for Management of IT Security

⚡ ISO 17799:2000, Code of Practice for Information Security Management

⚡ ISO 17799:2005, Code of Practice for Information Security Management

⚡ ISO 27001:2005, Information Security Management Systems - Requirements

⚡ ISO/IEC 20000-12:2005 Information technology — Service Management Part 1

⚡ ISO/IEC 20000-2:2005 Information technology — Service Management Part 2

⚡ ISO/IEC 15408-1:2005 Common Criteria for Information Technology Security Evaluation Part 1

⚡ ISO/IEC 15408-2:2005 Common Criteria for Information Technology Security Evaluation Part 2

⚡ ISO/IEC 15408-3:2005 Common Criteria for Information Technology Security Evaluation Part 3

⚡ ISO/IEC 18045:2005 Common Methodology for Information Technology Security Evaluation Part 3

IT Information Library

⚡ OGC ITIL: Planning to Implement Service Management

⚡ OGC ITIL: ICT Infrastructure Management

⚡ OGC ITIL: Service Delivery

- OGC ITIL: Service Support
- OGC ITIL: Application Management
- OGC ITIL: Security Management

General Guidance

- CobiT 3rd Edition
- CobiT 4.0
- ISACA IS Standards, Guidelines, and Procedures for Auditing and Control Professionals
- Disaster / Emergency Management and Business Continuity, NFPA 1600
- ISF Standard of Good Practice for Information Security
- ISF Security Audit of Networks
- A Risk Management Standard, jointly issued by AIRMIC, ALARM, and IRM
- Business Continuity Institute (BCI) Good Practice Guidelines
- ISSA Generally Accepted Information Security Principles (GAISP)
- CERT Operationally Critical Threat, Asset & Vulnerability Evaluation (OCTAVE)
- The GAIT Methodology
- IIA Global Technology Audit Guide (GTAG)

U.S. Federal Privacy

- Cable Communications Privacy Act Title 47 § 551
- Telemarketing Sales Rule (TSR), 16 CFR 310
- CAN SPAM Act
- Children's Online Privacy Protection Act (COPPA), 16 CFR 312
- Driver's Privacy Protection Act (DPPA), 18 USC 2721
- Family Education Rights Privacy Act (FERPA), 20 USC 1232
- Privacy Act of 1974, 5 USC 552a
- Video Privacy Protection Act (VPPA), 18 USC 2710
- Specter-Leahy Personal Data Privacy and Security Act
- Amendments to the FTC Telemarketing Sales Rule

- Children's Online Privacy Protection Act
- U.S. State Privacy
- Arkansas Personal Information Protection Act AR SB 1167
- Arizona Amendment to Arizona Revised Statutes 13-2001, AZ HB 2116
- California Information Practice Act, CA SB 1386
- California General Security Standard for Businesses CA AB 1950
- California Public Records Military Veteran Discharge Documents, CA AB 1798
- California OPP Recommended Practices on Notification of Security Breach
- Colorado Prohibition against Using Identity Information for Unlawful Purpose, CO HB 1134
- Colorado Consumer Credit Solicitation Protection, CO HB 1274
- Colorado Prohibiting Inclusion of Social Security Number, CO HB 1311
- Connecticut law Requiring Consumer Credit Bureaus to Offer Security Freezes, CT SB 650
- Connecticut law Concerning Nondisclosure of Private Tenant Information, CT HB 5184
- Delaware Computer Security Breaches DE HB 116
- Florida Personal Identification Information/Unlawful Use, FL HB 481
- Georgia Consumer Reporting Agencies, GA SB 230
- Georgia Public employees; Fraud, Waste, and Abuse, GA HB 656
- Hawaii Exempting disclosure of Social Security numbers HI HB 2674
- Illinois Personal Information Protection Act IL HB 1633
- Indiana Release of Social Security Number, Notice of Security Breach IN SB 503
- Louisiana Database Security Breach Notification Law, LA SB 205 Act 499
- Maine law To Protect Maine Citizens from Identity Theft, ME LD 1671
- Minnesota Data Warehouses; Notice Required for Certain Disclosures, MN HF 2121
- Missouri War on Terror Veteran Survivor Grants, MO HB 957
- Montana bill to Implement Individual Privacy and to Prevent Identity Theft, MT HB 732

- New Jersey Identity Theft Prevention Act, NJ A4001/S1914
- New York Information Security Breach and Notification Act
- Nevada Security Breach Notification Law, NV SB 347
- North Carolina Security Breach Notification Law (Identity Theft Protection Act) , NC SB 1048
- North Dakota Personal Information Protection Act, ND SB 2251
- Ohio Personal information - contact if unauthorized access, OH HB 104
- Rhode Island Security Breach Notification Law, RI HB 6191
- Tennessee Security Breach Notification, TN SB 2220
- Texas Identity Theft Enforcement and Protection Act, TX SB 122
- Vermont Relating to Identity Theft , VT HB 327
- Virginia Identity theft; penalty; restitution; victim assistance, VA HB 872
- Washington Notice of a breach of the security, WA SB 6043

EU Guidance

- EU Directive on Privacy and Electronic Communications, 2002/58/EC
- EU Directive on Data Protection, 95/46/EC
- US Department of Commerce EU Safe Harbor Privacy Principles
- Consumer Interests in the Telecommunications Market, Act No. 661
- OECD / World Bank Technology Risk Checklist
- OECD Guidelines on Privacy and Transborder Flows of Personal Data
- UN Guidelines for the Regulation of Computerized Personal Data Files (1990)
- ISACA Cross-Border Privacy Impact Assessment
- Information Technology Security Evaluation Manual (ITSEM)
- Information Technology Security Evaluation Criteria (ITSEC)
- Directive 2003/4/EC Of The European Parliament

UK and Canadian Guidance

- FSA Combined Code on Corporate Governance
- Turnbull Guidance on Internal Control, UK FRC
- Smith Guidance on Audit Committees, UK FRC

- UK Data Protection Act of 1998
- IT Service Management Standard , BS 15000-1
- IT Service Management Standard - Code of Practice, BS 15000-2
- British Standards Institute PAS 56, Guide to Business Continuity Management
- Canada Keeping the Promise for a Strong Economy Act, Bill 198
- Canada Personal Information Protection Electronic Documents Act (PIPEDA)
- Canada Privacy Policy and Principles

Latin American Guidance

- Argentina Personal Data Protection Act
- Mexico Federal Personal Data Protection Law

Other European and African Guidance

- Austria Data Protection Act
- Austria Telecommunications Act
- Bosnia Law on Protection of Personal Data
- Czech Republic Personal Data Protection Act
- Denmark Act on Competitive Conditions and Consumer Interests
- Finland Personal Data Protection Act
- Finland act on the amendment of the Personal Data Act (986/2000)
- France Data Protection Act
- German Federal Data Protection Act
- IT Baseline Protection Manual Germany
- Greece Law on the Protection of Individuals with Regard to the Processing of Personal Data
- Hungary Protection of Personal Data and Disclosure of Data of Public Interest
- Iceland Protection of Privacy as regards the Processing of Personal Data
- Ireland Data Protection Act of 1988
- Ireland Data Protection Amendment 2003
- Italy Personal Data Protection Code

- Italy Protection of Individuals Other Subject with regard to the Processing of Personal Data
- Lithuania Law on Legal Protection of Personal Data
- Luxembourg Data Protection Law
- Netherlands Personal Data Protection Act
- Poland Protection of Personal Data Act
- Slovak Republic Protection of Personal Data in Information Systems
- Personal Data Protection Act of the Republic of Slovenia of 2004
- South Africa Promotion of Access to Information Act
- ORGANIC LAW 15/1999 of 13 December on the Protection of Personal Data
- Sweden Personal Data Act
- Switzerland Federal Act on Data Protection

Asia and Pacific Rim Guidance

- Australia Better Practice Guide – Business Continuity Management
- Australia Spam Act
- Australia Spam Act 2003: A practical guide for business
- Australia Privacy Act
- Australia Telecommunications Act
- Hong Kong Personal Data (Privacy) Ordinance
- India Information Technology Act (ITA-2000)
- Japan ECOM Guidelines Concerning the Protection of Personal Data in Electronic Commerce in the Private Sector (version 1.0)
- Japan Handbook Concerning Protection Of Personal Data
- Japan Personal Information Protection Act (Law No. 57 of 2003)
- Korea Act on Promotion of Information & Communication Network Utilization and Information Protection, etc
- Korea Act on the Protection of Personal Information Maintained by Public Agencies 1994
- Korea Act Relating to Use and Protection of Credit Information
- New Zealand Privacy Act 1993

- Taiwan Computer-Processed Personal Data Protection Law 1995
- India's Information Technology Act, 2000

System job titles

Job titles, while useful when people want to quickly answer the question 'So what do you do?' don't help very much in terms of describing the specific activities a person may be expected to carry out. This isn't that big a deal until an organization attempts to make sense of the contents of documents such as ISO 17799 or something from the NIST 800 series. While the creators of each document might have a clear idea of what each job title represents, to a reader the casual way terms such as System Administrator and System Security Administrator are used may be confusing. Common questions, particularly if a reader starts reviewing multiple documents- include things like are these two terms defining the same job function? Different job functions? How much do certain terms overlap or differ across documentation? Fortunately, we can answer these questions.

By using a matrix, we were able to figure out what job functions are likely to overlap and what job functions aren't. All of this gets very interesting when you take into account that a lot of documentation insists on separation of duties. We'll start by displaying common overlaps, then talk about how to ensure appropriate separation of duties.

System Administrator, System Admin

It's fairly obvious that system administrator and system admin are the same job function with one simply being an abbreviation of the other. What might not be so obvious is what activities and duties this term is likely to represent when seen in a regulation, standard, guideline or best practice document. Here's what you can expect:

- Stay on top of new patches that are coming out
- Apply all new patches
- Test patches on specific target systems
- Assist in updating/maintaining organizational hardware and software inventory
- Monitor vulnerabilities
- Use vulnerability databases to help stay on top of necessary patches to add
- Configure automatic update of applications when necessary

- ⚡ (If using a management system) Analyze and interpret messages from the management system
- ⚡ Configure and manage remote access systems
- ⚡ Configure user access privileges
- ⚡ Manage user access privilege

Most of the time, system administrators have job descriptions that include thorough patch management. This includes staying on top of new patches and updating the organization's systems as appropriate, being aware of any vulnerabilities that aren't handled by patches and being personally involved with all patching activities. A system administrator also is responsible for designing the organization's computer systems, implementing technical security for them and for staying abreast of new technologies that may be used to enhance their systems.

System Maintainer, System Developer, System Programmer

We've grouped these three together because of their potential for overlap. Frequently, system maintainers are also system developers and system programmers, but not always. Generally speaking, when you see the term system maintainer, it describes someone who serves as a point of contact for the certification and accreditation process for the organization's system. The maintainer develops and maintains an information security risk assessment based on the organization's changing needs, and the condition of the existing system. So that others may make informed decisions about how to improve or repair the system, a system maintainer regularly monitors systems security and reports on its efficacy. To ensure certification and accreditation, this position also usually collaborates with the information system security officer (ISSO) to design and implement security controls and mechanisms that make it possible to meet CMS standards and requirements. System maintainers also collaborate with system owners to ensure availability of resources necessary to conduct components of the C&A process.

Another activity a system maintainer will carry out is the development and implementation of a system development lifecycle that aligns with the system requirements set out by system owners/managers.

Thus far we haven't mentioned the interchangeable terms system developer/system programmer. That's because sometimes these terms overlap with system maintainer job functions, and sometimes they don't. In essence, system developers/system programmers create system software and maintain it. They develop the security controls and special features a program may have. However some developers and programmers may move on to new projects once they create a system. People who do this have very little overlap with system maintainers. On the other hand, system developers/system programmers who create system software, then maintain it overlap directly with the system maintainer job function. That's because in order to maintain the systems and software they create, they will have to run risk assessments, conduct tests for accreditation and certification, monitor system efficiency, and work with others to ensure the system and system software meets the organization's needs.

When reading about system maintainers, system programmers or system developers, check to see what the documentation suggests for each job function, as it varies from document to document.

System Owner, System Manager

The terms system owner and system manager are interchangeable. System owners/system managers, like system maintainers/system developers conduct risk assessments and determine how long audit trail data is to be maintained for their system.

Effective system managers have a complete understanding of their portion of the system and what it supports in terms of security, managerial, technical and operational requirements. They select access controls for their systems and are responsible for cryptographic keys.

A quick, general definition of a system manager or system owner is found in the CMS version of SAS 70, which says a system manager is "the official who is responsible for the operation and use of an automated information system."

System Analyst, System Designer

System analysts and system designers are, in short, people who design systems. They are also involved in testing systems to ensure designs function appropriately.

System Security Administrator

While this term sounds very similar to system administrator, the difference is that this job title focuses solely on access privileges. A system administrator handles access privileges and other system issues as well. A system security administrator specifically keeps track of user access privileges, who needs them, who needs to have them reduced and ensuring the enforcement of any policies surrounding privileges. A system security administrator will also ensure that users have unique access IDs, appropriate passwords, and monitor access activity to ensure nothing unusual goes on.

System Security Coordinator

This term is used for a person who coordinates the varied efforts of different people to improve or implement security features. This position has complete oversight and responsibility for all aspects of security within an organization.

System Security Officer

The system security officer (who may also be referred to as the information system security officer – ISSO) is responsible for the organization's IT security plan. This person ensures that the plan is appropriately implemented, maintained and assessed. They oversee developing and updating of system security plans as well as coordinating with information system owners regarding any changes to the system. The system security officer will also assess the security impact of any changes that may be made.

ADDITIONAL INFORMATION

Say What You Do: building a framework of IT controls, policies, standards, and procedures

Our Say What You Do book (and accompanying website, templates, and sample documents) designed to help you with your information assurance communication projects. What are information assurance projects? The projects fall into the following categories:

- Documenting your information assurance framework
- Documenting your policies, standards, and procedures
- Measuring success
- Reporting your status of successes and failures
- Managing and documenting the change process

Why is all of this "stuff" important? Simple. With regulatory compliance hovering over our collective heads, policies, standards, and procedures are becoming more and more important and the impact more personal. Policies, standards, and procedures are profoundly important to our organizations because they are the only real way to convey to the auditors and others who care that we are dong our jobs properly.

Remember that it is the auditor's job to go through the remains of last night's dinner in order to figure out what was on the menu (go ahead, get graphic with that, we dare you). The only real way that auditors know whether or not we are *doing* our jobs and *being* compliant is to look at our policies, standards, and procedures to see if the direction has been set. And then to look for evidence to see if we've been following our own directions. Simple as that.

Find out more at http://www.saywhatyoudo.com

Make your life easier

If you are writing policies and procedures, you'll **have** to enter term definitions somewhere in those documents. You have a couple of choices: either create your own set of glossary terms, or use our pre-defined terms.

We've taken a lot of the word out of it and are making the entire glossary available in Word, Flare, and RTF format. Completely unlocked and editable, ready for you to import into your policies and procedures, intranet, whatever you want.

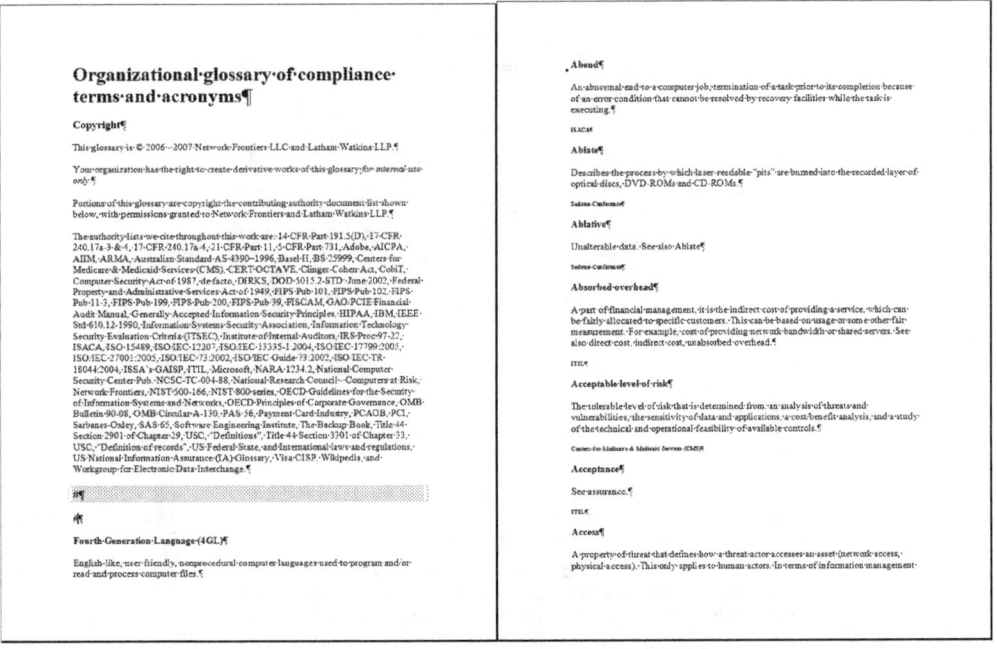

The entire glossary in editable Word/RTF format

The formatting is done in CSS style sheets and the documents are XML ready.

Find out more at http://www.glossarybook.com.

The IT Compliance Institute

1,376

IT Compliance Imperatives.

Standardize. Simplify. Unify.

The Unified Compliance Project.

Caught in the whirlwind of regulatory compliance? The Unified Compliance Project (UCP) can help you standardize and simplify your current compliance practice by showing overlaps in complex corporate regulations and standards.

Focusing on commonalities across regulatory requirements, standards-based development, and simplified architectures, the UCP supports a strategic approach to IT compliance that reduces cost, limits liability, and leverages the value of compliance-related investments across the enterprise.

Visit the Unified Compliance Project from the IT Compliance Institute, where you can download convenient IT Impact Zone guides that detail IT indications from nearly 230 key regulations and standards, view informative Web seminars, and explore critical technology solutions.

ITCi

IT Compliance Institute™

www.ITCinstitute.com/ucp

www.ingramcontent.com/pod-product-compliance
Lightning Source LLC
Chambersburg PA
CBHW080901170526
45158CB00008B/1954